An Introduction to Philosophical Logic

THIRD EDITION

A. C. GRAYLING

Birkbeck College, London and
St Anne's College, Oxford

Blackwell
Publishing

© 1982, 1990 and 1997 by A. C. Grayling

BLACKWELL PUBLISHING
350 Main Street, Malden, MA 02148-5020, USA
9600 Garsington Road, Oxford OX4 2DQ, UK
550 Swanston Street, Carlton, Victoria 3053, Australia

First edition published 1982 by Harvester Press
Second edition published 1990 by Gerald Duckworth & Co Ltd
Third edition published 1997

13   2011

Library of Congress Cataloging-in-Publication Data

Grayling, A. C.
    An introduction to philosophical logic/A. C. Grayling.–3rd ed.
        p.   cm.
    Rev. ed. of: An introduction to philosophical logic, c1982.
    Includes bibliographical references and index.
    ISBN 978-0-631-20655-2 (hbk. : alk. paper). – ISBN 978-0-631-19982-3 (pbk. : alk.
paper)
        1. Logic.   2. Language and languages–Philosophy.   I. Title.
    BC71.G7   1997
    160-dc21   97-3849
                                                                              CIP

A catalogue record for this title is available from the British Library.

Set in 10½ on 13 pt Galliard
by Ace Filmsetting Ltd, Frome, Somerset
Printed and bound in Singapore
by Markono Print Media Pte Ltd

The publisher's policy is to use permanent paper from mills that operate a sustainable
forestry policy, and which has been manufactured from pulp processed using
acid-free and elementary chlorine-free practices. Furthermore, the publisher ensures
that the text paper and cover board used have met acceptable environmental
accreditation standards.

For further information on
Blackwell Publishing, visit our website:
www.blackwellpublishing.com

Contents

Preface

Philosophers are fond of pointing out that there is no shallow-end in philosophy. This is true. Philosophy is a subject which is often complex and sometimes difficult. Books which purvey shallow-end philosophy are at risk of purveying shallow philosophy instead, and accordingly distort and falsify its problems. Because philosophy is, among other things, 'the dogged struggle to achieve clarity' as William James put it, shallow-end treatments of philosophy's problems are therefore not merely useless but counterproductive. So I have not tried, in this book, to pretend that the questions it deals with are simple. They are challenging, and demand careful study.

All this said, and philosophy's deep-endedness acknowledged, it remains that new swimmers must, somehow, be helped into the flood. There are various ways of introducing philosophy, but the best of them is the tutorial. In comparison with a tutorial's potential for heated dialogue, printed pages offer cold monologues merely. Still, books have important uses; one can mull over them, linger on this or that point, pencil insights and objurgations in the margins: *scriptae manent, verbae volant* after all.

My choice has been to adopt the primer method. Philosophical debates can be mastered only by reading the original literature which gives them their content; therefore I have conceived my task as one of providing prefaces to a number of important debates – that is, as providing some of the background to them, and an account of the arguments deployed in them, in order to orientate the beginner. But although what I say is decidedly not intended as a substitute for the literature, my procedure has been to discuss a good part of the literature, for to discuss the literature is to discuss the problems. This has the concomitant virtue of familiarizing the neomath with who said what, why, and where.

Despite the shortcomings that any introductory book in philosophy is likely to suffer, the attempt to introduce students to philosophical logic remains eminently worthwhile. The topics it comprehends are very important, and half the task in understanding them is achieved by locating them in their contexts. This book aims to do just that.

It is surprisingly difficult to write introductory books. One strives for clarity, simplicity, and economy, and at the same time – without attempting to be exhaustive – one strives to ensure that the student is properly equipped and launched. But the drive to clarity and simplicity has an impressive tendency to produce the opposite result, and the drive to economy is constantly bedevilled by the question, how little is too little? These difficulties notwithstanding, the aim here has been to say enough, clearly enough, to give a preliminary view of some main problems in philosophy, while whetting curiosity further – in regard to which, abundant references are supplied.

It is worth remarking that some sections of the following chapters might at first appear more difficult than others. Some contain technicalities, although these are kept to a minimum. But difficult sections are followed by easier ones, and it is often the case that topics treated in difficult sections are treated again, in different but related ways, in later chapters. A measure of patience, and a little faith, will carry the reader through. It is the relatedness of the topics that generates this dialectic of complexity and straightforwardness; but light, I hope, dawns as one proceeds. At the same time, each chapter is largely self-contained, for this is not a treatise but a textbook; anyone working on a particular topic can use the relevant chapter as a preface or supplement to a study of the original texts, without having to search too far into other chapters for illumination. The notes contain references in the standard way, but also occasional asides and amplifications.

It is assumed in places that the reader knows a modicum of basic logic. This assumption had to be made because it is not within the scope and objectives of what follows that it should serve as an introduction to logic as well as to philosophical logic. But the places where logical technicalities are invoked are few, and simplicity has been sought there as everywhere else.

The aim in this book, in sum, is to provide an introductory overview of the nature and background of some central problems in philosophy. Introductory books stand to their subject-matter as maps to actual terrain;

this one is no exception. It does not attempt to provide a comprehensive review of the debates on the problems introduced. Instead it tries to serve as the first few rungs of a ladder. The rest of the ladder is for the reader's fashioning.

Note to the Second Edition

This reissue provides an opportunity (the first, though there have been several reprints) to correct typographical errors, and to act upon the advice of several friendly reviewers who requested that as the book has acquired the status of a textbook, it should have an updated bibliography.

St Anne's College, Oxford, 1990

Note to the Third Edition

This third edition is, unlike the second, a substantial revision. I have taken the opportunity afforded by a change of publisher to correct, complete, expand, and update the text and bibliography extensively, especially in the later chapters. But the features that have made this book useful to students have been kept.

A careful consideration of recent introductory literature in allied fields of philosophy of language and the philosophy of logic, a number of them of outstanding quality, persuade me that the difficulty of our discipline is such that there remains a need for what this volume, in its earlier editions as in this one, aspires to be: a genuine first step. Some writers of introductory texts, with an eye over a shoulder at professional colleagues, write at too technical a level, and do not stop at the point where it would be better for readers to make progress on their own account. This book, in aiming to be genuinely introductory, aims to make an important central region of philosophy accessible even to those beginners who have few other helps to hand; and to interest them, thereafter, in going to the original sources of these debates for themselves.

In various ways directly and indirectly connected with this book, its evolution, and its appearance in other languages, I record my warm gratitude to Alex Orenstein, Mark Sainsbury, Pascal Engel, Laurence Goldstein, Mo Bo, and Masahiro Miura.

Birkbeck College, London, 1997

1

Philosophical Logic, the Philosophy of Logic, Philosophy and Logic

Philosophical Logic and the Philosophy of Logic

Philosophy's various branches closely interconnect. In thinking about metaphysics, for example, one must deal with epistemological and logical questions, and in the same way metaphysical issues arise in epistemology, and logical problems recur. This kind of interpenetration makes it wrong to draw sharp boundaries between the different philosophical pursuits. There are no such boundaries; one's ability to distinguish between a typically metaphysical problem (say, about what exists in some domain) and a typically epistemological problem (say, about what we do or can know about a given domain, and how we acquire such knowledge) rests mainly on having an appreciation of what set of problems is focal to each. Acquiring such an appreciation involves doing philosophy; there are no short cuts.

Nevertheless it is possible to give an advance sketch of the kind of topics dealt with in a particular region of philosophical enquiry. In this chapter I do so with respect to philosophical logic. I also, and therefore, look at the question, of how far philosophical logic is philosophical, and how far it is logical; and at the wider question this raises about the relation between philosophy and logic. Both are dealt with briefly.

The topics to be discussed are: the proposition, analyticity, necessity, existence, identity, truth, meaning and reference. These, at least, are the topics mentioned in chapter headings. In fact the list is more extensive, for in the course of these chapters there are also discussions of possible worlds, realisms of related sorts, anti-realism, and other questions. It is not possible to give an overview of philosophical logic without ranging widely in this way, but it will be clear that because each topic invites, and indeed commands, whole volumes to itself, the discussions I give do not pretend to be more than prefaces to the detailed treatments found in the original literature.

These topics are collected under the unifying label 'philosophical logic' for three principal reasons. It marks their interrelatedness, for a good understanding of any of them requires an understanding of the others. It marks their central importance in all serious philosophical discussion. And it reflects the influence of developments in logic since the late nineteenth century, which have afforded an access of power in dealing with many philosophical problems afresh, not only because we have become technically better equipped for the task, but also because developments in logical machinery have promoted and facilitated a certain methodological style which has proved extraordinarily fruitful in philosophy. That methodological style is analysis.

The invention of symbolic calculi would not have impelled philosophical developments by itself had it not been for the fact, quickly spotted by Frege and Russell, that they immediately prompt a range of philosophical questions, centrally among them questions about the nature of meaning and truth – which is in short to say, language; and language vitally interests philosophers because it provides our route to a philosophical understanding of thought and the world. The greatest single impetus to current preoccupations with philosophical logic comes indeed from interest in language, to understand which we need progress in this area.

The role played by 'logic' in 'philosophical logic' could be misleading. Philosophical logic is not *about* logic; neither *is* it logic, in the sense in which logic is the study of formal representations and regimentations of inference. Matters might best be put this way: logicians devise calculi which are strict paraphrases of the forms (not the content) of reasoning. They seek to construct simple but powerful languages in which the forms of inference can be expressed and investigated. They test such languages for completeness and consistency, studying the tools required for this task by looking at arithmetic and set theory, and by undertaking a precise exploration of the concepts deployed – such as variable freedom and bondage, axiomatization, regular substitution in quantification theory, and the like.

There then comes a point – never too far away – when thinking about logic involves having to raise certain philosophical questions. The problem of entailment, the significance of the Löwenheim–Skolem theorem, quantification theory's scope and limits, the relationship between logic and set theory, and the nature of set theory itself; these are matters, among others, which are properly the domain of the philosopher of logic. Philosophy of logic is thus an enterprise in which philosophical questions about the nature and some of the implications of logic constitute the subject matter.

But such questions, in their turn again, rapidly and naturally spill over into, or draw attention to, substantial and important philosophical problems of more general concern. The moment the concern widens in this way, and logic as such is no longer the object of the enquiry, but becomes involved with questions about the nature of language and thought, and the structure and contents of the world, then the enterprise in hand is philosophical logic. Thus philosophical logic is *philosophy*, philosophy logic-informed and logic-sensitive albeit, but philosophy notwithstanding; and the contrast between philosophical logic and the philosophy of logic can accordingly be put like this: when one does philosophy of logic, one is philosophizing about logic; but when one does philosophical logic, one is philosophizing.

Some, like Haack, hold that 'philosophy of logic' and 'philosophical logic' mean the same thing, *viz.*, the former.[1] For the reasons just given this does not seem to me a useful view. There is an informative distinction to be drawn here, which helps one to be clear about what tasks are to be tackled under each label. Nevertheless, it would be fruitless to insist on making the distinction too sharp; it is useful, but so also is it useful to bear in mind the rich overlaps and interconnections between the two pursuits.

Philosophy and Logic

Distinguishing between the philosophy of logic and philosophical logic does nothing to explain what relation subsists between philosophy as such and logic as such. The point is not trivial, for at least one major figure in recent philosophy held that philosophy as such just *is* logic as such, and such a view complicates our understanding of the difference and relation between the two. The philosopher in question is Russell.

Russell took the position, during what is generally regarded as his most important philosophical period (before 1920), that if any philosophical problem is a genuine one, it reduces upon analysis to a problem of logic: 'every philosophical problem, when it is subjected to the necessary analysis and purification, is found either to be not really philosophical at all, or else to be . . . logical'.[2] This is a proposal which looks as though it sets the pattern for much of the philosophy done this century. It is superficially (but only superficially) similar to Wittgenstein's later view, expressed in the *Philosophical Investigations*, that all philosophical puzzles need only to be unravelled to be resolved, having arisen in the first place merely because we have made mistakes in our use of language.[3]

What prompted Russell to take the view he did is explained by noting two elements in the development of his earlier thought. The first is that the governing preoccupation of his principal work in philosophy and logic relates to mathematics; specifically, to the attempt to demonstrate that 'all pure mathematics follows from purely logical premisses and uses only concepts definable in logical terms'.[4] Attempts to reduce mathematics to logic are known as 'logicist' programmes, and the received view is now that, owing to the work of Gödel in the 1930s, such a programme for mathematics is unfeasible. Nevertheless, Russell's work had important philosophical consequences beyond the purely logicist ambition for mathematics. From the former arose those of Russell's views expressed in *Our Knowledge of the External World* and 'The Philosophy of Logical Atomism'.[5] His celebrated Theory of Descriptions (cf. chapter 4 below) is exemplary both of the nature and the results of his approach to philosophical problems in the light of these convictions about methodology.

More specifically – and this is the second element in the development of his thought – the use of logical analysis seemed to Russell to sweep away the sources of confusion which in his view had hitherto bedevilled philosophers, chiefly because, he believed, they had been misled by the surface forms of language. Russell made much of the notion that to think there can only be subject–predicate propositions results in 'bad metaphysics', for the reason that it seduces philosophers into constructing ontologies of, for example, the Scholastic sort, in which there are substances and their attributes, or of the Absolute Idealist sort, in which all propositions, even relational ones, are construed as disguised predications on 'reality taken as a whole'.

Moreover, Russell believed that if there is to be knowledge of anything beyond what we are immediately acquainted with in episodes of perception, it has to be inferential. Most of what we know, indeed, is not 'knowledge by acquaintance' but 'knowledge by description'. Logic, which is the science of inference, is what enables us to demonstrate how we have such descriptive knowledge; for, to show what truths can be known about the world beyond the immediate deliverances of the senses, we have to be able to understand the structure of molecular or complex propositions, all of which are truth-functionally compounded out of atomic or simple propositions by the logical glue of the constants *not*, *if-then*, *or*, and others. Inference depends on molecular propositions; we have to be able to connect propositions together if we are to transcend the limits of mere acquaintance; and the science of connecting propositions is logic. Russell sometimes used the expression 'general knowledge' in place of 'descriptive knowledge', and thus his dictum, 'general knowledge belongs to logic'.

It is clear, and I earlier acknowledged, that developments in logic have provided much help in the treatment of traditional philosophical problems, and in revealing the existence of new ones. Nevertheless, Russell's view is not wholly convincing; few would agree that philosophical problems are all of them reducible to – or, more strongly, just are, although in woolly and preliminary form – logical problems. To state one obvious and not too question-begging objection, one is inclined to say that it is very much clearer that problems in ethics are genuinely philosophical problems than that they are reducible to, or covertly just are, disguised logical problems in the sense intended by Russell.

An alternative, and more colourful, characterization of the relation between logic and philosophy is given by Ryle, whose view provides a contrast to Russell's outlook.[6]

Ryle both drew a distinction between logic and philosophy (or, as he put it, between 'formal logic' and 'informal logic'; nothing much turns on the choice of terminology), and specified a relation between them. For Ryle, 'formal logic' consists in the study and manipulation of formal symbolized calculi and their elements, whereas 'informal logic' consists in the quite different enterprise of plotting the 'logical geography' of concepts, an enterprise often if not always conducted – to employ Ryle's picturesque metaphors – in the jungles and on the wild frontiers of thought, where the neat, straight railway tracks of formal logic have not yet reached, or where they cannot reach. In another metaphor Ryle said that formal is to informal logic as geometry is to cartography. In the latter, the irregular features of a landscape have to be plotted to scale, and the success of the enterprise depends upon the cartographer's being able to employ, or be guided by, the idealized regularities of Euclidean plane geometry. In the same way as the cartographer is the 'client' of the geometer, so the philosopher or 'informal logician' is the client of the formal logician. But the stock-in-trade of the formal logician does not and cannot solve philosophical problems, any more than a greengrocer's owning a pocket calculator can tell him what price to charge for his lettuces.

Ryle's conception of the differences and relation between formal and informal logic is, on the face of it, a convincing one. If his characterization is correct, then an unbridgeable gulf lies between the methods respectively involved, a gulf best characterized by remarking the difference between the methods we employ in solving the problem of, say, free will, and those involved in solving a differential equation. Depending upon one's point of view, that there is a marked difference of method between these two enterprises may seem an unfortunate state of affairs; but if Ryle is right, things are ineluctably so.

What Ryle's views remind us is that more goes on in philosophy than is amenable to the straightforward application of logic, still less to direct translation into logic. The point is well made by Passmore: philosophy is not solely concerned with proving something or disproving it 'at every step', as, for example McTaggart thought,[7] but consists just as often in attempts to classify, define, analyse, disambiguate, and assemble reminders, concerning concepts and the expressions by which we communicate and discuss them. Much philosophical work, far from exclusively consisting in strings of deductive transitions like those Spinoza set out to formulate *more geometrico* in his *Ethics,* are more like catalogues, collections, or display-cabinets, where notions are sorted and their connections shewn, in an effort to get us to grasp how our conceptual scheme works. Wittgenstein's *Philosophical Investigations* is a classic of this genre, and so is Alexander's *Space, Time, and Deity.* (Alexander indeed claimed to have an aversion to argument, and described his method as wholly descriptive.[8])

Taken too far, these thoughts can distort the picture; they make philosophy seem like a retired gentleman's preoccupation with his butterfly collection. In fact the drive to precision and rigour in philosophy is paramount, and if proof is not at issue at every step, then it is so at every second or third step. Indeed, none of the above says that logic has no place in activities of thought outside proof. The rules of consistency and demonstration apply as demandingly to the processes of disambiguating and classifying as they do in argument. What these comments about method say is that philosophy does not exclusively consist in establishing formal relationships between elements of an argument; but that, in addition, it involves clearly grasping the content of the argument, where much explication or analysis might be required before it is clear what relationship of logic obtains between the argument's parts.

It is interesting, by way of aside, to note that one of the motivations for the briefly flourishing school of 'ordinary language philosophy' in the decade or so after 1945 was a rejection of the over-logical approach to philosophy adopted by some philosophers beforehand. Formal efforts in philosophy, like Carnap's *Der Logische Aufbau Der Welt* (*The Logical Structure of the World*[9]) and the work of Goodman and Lesniewski and his followers[10] had been prosecuted with some vigour chiefly before the Second World War, and the impulse to their kind of programme remains in the work of Quine, with his view, characteristic of his outlook, that there is a lot to be gained in the direction of clarity and rigour by making a 'canonical ascent' over the vagaries of common parlance.[11]

A characterization of contemporary philosophical method would reflect a certain balance between these poles. However, philosophy is governed at every step by the need for precision, clarity and consistency, and though almost everyone would agree with Kripke's observation that 'there is no mathematical substitute for philosophy',[12] logic is, consequently, of the greatest importance to philosophy.

Consider how direct applications of logical analysis can be fruitful in philosophical enquiry. When arguments are at issue, one can, by the clean expedient of inspecting their logical credentials, determine their formal validity or otherwise; and in those cases where the form is evidently invalid, one has settled that the conclusion is unacceptable – a major gain. Note, for example, the simple logical insight underlying the main tenet of Popper's views in the philosophy of science.[13] Popper noted that a traditionally received view of the structure of scientific reasoning involves a logical fallacy – specifically, the fallacy of affirming the consequent. Suppose I say: I hypothesize that molecules in a gas move randomly. If this is right, then I should be able to observe motes of smoke in a glass phial being randomly displaced by the molecules constituting the gas in the phial. I conduct the experiment; indeed note that the smoke motes are randomly displaced; and conclude that my hypothesis is established. The logical form of this piece of reasoning is:

$$p \rightarrow q; q; p$$

Here p stands for: 'molecules in a gas move randomly', and q stands for: 'it is observable that motes of smoke in a glass phial are randomly displaced'. But a different pair of substituends will demonstrate the invalidity of this reasoning. Let p stand for: 'it is raining' and q stand for: 'the streets are wet'. Then on this form of argument we get: 'If it is raining, the streets are wet; the streets are indeed wet; therefore it is raining', which is a *non sequitur*. Accordingly, Popper argued that no scientific hypothesis can ever be proved; at best such hypotheses can be corroborated by the failure of the most rigorous efforts to falsify them. From the point of view of attaining to conclusiveness in science, outright refutations alone are possible. Conclusive refutations are possible along the lines of the above fallacy's valid cousin, modus tollens:

$$p \rightarrow q; -q; -p$$

If the experimental results turn out otherwise (*viz.* that q), the most this means is that the hypothesis has received some support; it is still liable to overthrow in the light of new evidence.

In at least this respect, then, formal procedures can be utilized in philosophy to effect. There are plenty of other cases. Even if Ryle might allow this, on the grounds that this constitutes a case (to use yet another of his metaphors) of parade-ground discipline holding the line on the battlefield, then we can point to other kinds of applications in which logic is philosophically informative. Consider the point made by Russell: to some philosophers in the past, owing to their underdeveloped or impoverished logical resources, it seemed self-evident that the proposition has one basic form, from which they took substantial metaphysical consequences to flow. Russell was somewhat ungenerous in his assessment of the logical skills of the Schoolmen, among others, but the point has force. It suggests a wider use of logical techniques in philosophy: formalization can show how tracts of language could, or even do, work in the light of some formal description; and postulating certain structures for our conceptual scheme, even idealized ones, can clarify it. Yet again, we learn about our thought and language by looking at how certain entrenched doctrines of logic arise from them. These are all issues of profound philosophical importance, and logic is a crucial tool for investigating them.

In viewing the question of the relation between philosophy and logic, then, a balance is required. On the whole Ryle's view invites agreement, so long as one adds the riders in the remarks above concerning the enormous utility of logical techniques and applications in philosophical research. It would of course be more than merely pleasant if Leibniz's dream of a universal calculus – by the mechanical application of which we could solve philosophical problems – were true;[14] but so much is a pipe-dream. Yet saying this does not belittle the importance of logic to philosophy. In much the same way as Ryle's cartographer would be nigh helpless without geometry, so the insights and the rigour which logic furnishes to philosophy are indispensable to it. How this works, particularly in connection with the chief concerns of philosophical logic, becomes apparent as the sequel unfolds.

Contents of this Book

The rest of the book proceeds as follows. In chapter 2 I consider the question whether there are propositions, and, if so, what they are. It is important to have a clear idea of the distinction between sentences, statements and propositions, and in the course of discussing this distinction I am able to introduce and explain several concepts which are fundamental to philosophical logic. These are: sense and reference; referential opacity; the principle of intersubstitutivity *salva veritate*, which is defining of extensional contexts; and nominalism and realism concerning abstract entities. There is nothing especially alarming about these concepts despite their long names, and I introduce them with a proper nonchalance, because they recur frequently during the following chapters, and familiarity with them ultimately breeds comprehension.

In chapter 3 I consider a set of three extremely important distinctions which serve to classify truths, the propositions in which truths are expressed, and the ways we can come to know truths. These distinctions are respectively the necessary–contingent distinction, the analytic–synthetic distinction, and the a priori–a posteriori distinction. In the course of discussing necessity I take a long and interesting detour through ideas about possible worlds and essentialism, which lie at the heart of much recent philosophy.

Questions of existence are the concern of chapter 4. I look at the two related matters of our talk about existence and the existential presuppositions of the way we talk. Quine's views on ontological commitment and Russell's Theory of Descriptions, together with Strawson's and Donnellan's responses, figure here.

In chapters 5 and 6 I discuss theories of truth. Chapter 5 contains discussions of the Pragmatic, Coherence, and Correspondence theories of truth, and I try to do the first two especially more justice than is customary in recent philosophical literature, partly because they are important theories in their own right, and partly because they are enjoying renewed interest as a result of work in the philosophy of language. Thus the Pragmatic theory has features which are interesting in connection with forms of anti–realism (see chapters 8 and 9), and the Coherence theory has features which are interesting to those attracted by, for example, Davidson's holistic truth-theoretic view of language (again, see chapter 8 and 9).

Chapter 6 continues the discussion of truth, and consists in examinations of the Semantic, Redundancy and Minimalist theories. The first of these, which owes itself to Tarski, has had much direct and indirect influence in contemporary philosophy, and after explaining it I discuss some of its wider philosophical consequences. Some technicalities are involved in understanding Tarski, but I go over that part of the ground twice, the first time informally and the second time technically. I conclude with a discussion of Davidson's claim that truth is indefinable, and a sketch of an evaluatory view of truth.

The question of meaning now moves to centre-stage, having obtruded throughout earlier chapters. In chapter 7, partly as a preparation for chapters 8 and 9, and partly because of their intrinsic importance and interest, I provide sketches of some 'traditional' theories of meaning, together with certain contemporary extensions of them. Among other things, the discussion touches upon Positivist verificationism, Wittgenstein's later views, Quine's behavioural theory, and the 'causal theory of reference' originated by Kripke and Putnam.

In chapter 8 I discuss first Grice's communication-intention theory of meaning, then truth-conditional theories of meaning, particularly Davidson's version, and Dummett's anti-realist criticism of the crucial idea that a realist conception of truth is central to the theory of meaning. This much-debated matter repays close study, and I have sought especially to make Dummett's thought accessible.

The consequences for metaphysics and epistemology of the views discussed in chapter 8 are so important that, in chapter 9, I explore some of them, and suggest lines of thought which follow from perspectives afforded by those other debates. In this chapter the impartiality preserved throughout chapters 2–8 is laid aside.

This book discusses some main problems in philosophy. However, it is possible to use the discussions provided here to get a picture of a particular philosopher's overall view, by consulting the index and looking at what he or she says about the various topics canvassed here. If, for example, one collects all the discussions throughout the book of the contributions of, say, Quine, or Strawson, or Russell, and reads them together, one will get a picture of that thinker's views in the relevant respects. This is a function of the large contribution to twentieth-century philosophy made by these and other thinkers whose names occur in any two or more of the chapters in this book.

Notes

1   S. Haack, *Philosophy of Logics*, p. 2.
2   B. Russell, *Our Knowledge of the External World*, p. 42. Pages 42–69 are reprinted in I. M. Copi and J. A. Gould, *Readings in Logic*, under the title 'Logic as the Essence of Philosophy'.)
3   L. Wittgenstein, *Philosophical Investigations*, cf. §§ 123, 133, 255, 309.
4   B. Russell, *My Philosophical Development*, p. 74.
5   B. Russell, 'The Philosophy of Logical Atomism', in R. C. Marsh (ed.), *Logic and Knowledge*, passim. Cf. also A. C. Grayling, *Russell*, chs 2 and 3.
6   G. Ryle, 'Formal and Informal Logic', in *Dilemmas*, passim; reprinted in Copi and Gould, *Readings in Logic*.
7   J. Passmore, *Philosophical Reasoning*, p. 7.
8   Cf. ibid.
9   R. Carnap, *The Logical Structure of the World*.
10   Cf. Kung's review and bibliography in G. Kung, *Ontology and the Logistic Analysis of Language*.
11   W. V. Quine, *Word and Object*, esp. ch. 5 passim; pp. 157 *et seq.*
12   S. Kripke, 'Is There a problem About Substitutional Quantification?' in G. Evans and J. McDowell, *Truth and Meaning*, p. 416.
13   K. Popper, *The Logic of Scientific Discovery*.
14   Cf. e.g., G. Leibniz, 'Of Universal Synthesis and Analysis', in Leibniz, *Philosophical Writings* (trans. and ed. G. H. A. Parkinson), p. 10.

2

The Proposition

Introduction

Truth is one of the most important concepts in philosophy, and one of the most problematic. Among the reasons for this latter fact is that, at the outset of discussion, there is no consensus about what sorts of things are truth-bearers. The usual candidates include propositions, sentences, statements and beliefs. The entity traditionally given the truth-bearing role is the proposition, which philosophers have distinguished from statements and sentences in various ways and for various reasons. But propositions are themselves problematic items, and the business of giving a satisfactory account of them – or alternatively, of giving an account which satisfactorily dispenses with them in favour of statements, or sentences, or some other candidate – raises a number of important questions in metaphysics and elsewhere.

Propositions are regarded as problematic because they are *abstract* entities. Such entities are supposed to be existing things which neverthe-less occupy neither space nor time, have no causal powers, and are graspable only in thought. The opposite of an abstract entity is a concrete entity, which is spatio-temporal, causal, and often perceptible. Universals such as roundness and redness, numbers, and propositions are paradig-matic abstract entities. The tendency is for abstract entities to be viewed with suspicion; the question, 'what are their criteria of identity?' goes to the heart of the problem. These matters are explored below.

Yet the notion of a proposition has a number of extremely important uses, which makes one hesitate to give it up. In addition to their role as truth-bearers, propositions can serve as the *meanings* of sentences, as the *contents* of what is conveyed by acts of language-use such as asserting, giving commands, or expressing desires, and as the *objects* of psychological attitudes such as believing, hoping, and desiring. These are different although related things. Given the utility of the notion it is worth examining it in some detail. The questions to be discussed are: what are propositions? Can we replace the proposition with a truth-bearer more to nominalist taste, or is it indispensable?

Sentences and What They Say

To be clear about the nature of propositions one has first to be clear about sentences. A sentence is a word or set of words in some language. The language in question might be a natural language like English or Swahili, or an artificial language like logic. In intuitive senses of 'grammatical' and 'meaningful', it can be said that sentences have to be grammatically well-formed, but do not have to be meaningful, to be sentences; one can talk of 'nonsense sentences' without paradox. Examples of such sentences are Carroll's 'Twas brillig, and the slithy toves/ Did gyre and gimble in the wabe', or the sentence beloved of grammarians, 'Green ideas sleep furiously'.

Moreover, a sentence may have different meanings: 'I gave a hand' may mean that I helped someone, or literally donated a human or ape-hand (to some museum), or that my opponent in an equestrian competition had a horse taller by one hand than my own.

Again, the same sentence may be used in a variety of ways: 'You hold the reins' may be a statement of fact, or a command. In some cases, according to Austin's view of performative utterances, a particular use of a sentence might constitute an action, for example when one says 'I do thee wed' or 'I promise'.[1] It has been argued that utterance of the sentence 'It hurts' constitutes a sophisticated piece of behaviour replacing wincing and groaning; this is a view taken by Wittgenstein.[2]

In general, philosophers have been concerned with declarative sentences, those which are used to make assertions. It is this class of sentences which are said to *express propositions*, to state that some predicate holds of some subject or that certain items are related in a certain way.[3]

The distinction between propositions and declarative sentences is drawn for a variety of reasons.[4] First, sentences may be, as noted, meaningless or nonsensical, and so express nothing. Secondly, the same sentence can be used by different people, or by the same person on different occasions, to state what is true on certain of those occasions but false on others; 'I have a headache' is true or false depending upon who utters it, or true for a given person at one time, but false for the same person at another time.[5] Thirdly, something is common to the sentences 'It's raining' in English, 'Il pleut' in French, 'Es regnet' in German, 'Xia yu' in Mandarin Chinese; a way of characterizing their common content is required. This common content is said to be the *proposition*.

These thoughts accordingly have it that propositions, not sentences, are either true or false, and that only 'significant' or 'meaningful' sentences can express propositions. Propositions are what get asserted by the utterance of sentences; and they are what enter into logical relations with each other – sentences do not entail one another, or contradict one another; it is what is proposed by a particular declarative use of a sentence which entails or contradicts some other particular declarative proposal. Talk of propositions avoids problems of ambiguity and nonsense. And as noted above, propositions, as the 'what is said' by assertions of sentences, can be usefully regarded as the content, or object, of the so-called 'propositional attitudes', such as believing, wishing, hoping, judging – that is (where p is any proposition) as the object in such propositional attitude ascriptions as 'I believe that p' and 'he wishes that p'.

So much for some of the general reasons for distinguishing propositions from sentences. I shall shortly canvass in more detail other, more fundamental, reasons for holding onto propositions; which it is important to do, for on the basis of this sketch a problem, already hinted at, can be seen to threaten: the problem of their ontological status.

A long-standing metaphysical dispute lurks behind this issue. For most of the history of philosophy there have been at least two schools of thought about abstract entities, proponents of which have been (since medieval times) respectively called 'realists' and 'nominalists'. Broadly speaking, realism in this context is the view that abstract entities, such as propositions, numbers and universals, *really* exist, just as do mountains and trees. Plato's doctrine of Forms constitutes the paradigmatic realist theory in this sense. In Plato's view, Forms in the 'realm of being' exist much more fully and really than do mountains and trees, which are merely imperfect and ephemeral instances (or copies) of their Forms.[6] Nominalists, on the other hand, take the view that abstract entities exist in name only – hence *nominally* – so that they do not exist in at all the same sense as mountains and trees, but merely as concepts attaching to a name. The nominalist tendency is to reduce abstract entities, to get rid of them by analysis; and it is precisely nominalist scepticism over abstract entities which lends force to the debate about propositions, giving rise to the questions: Do propositions exist? If they do, what are they? How does one individuate them? If there are no satisfactory answers to these questions, what is the best way to dispense with talk of them?

It naturally runs closer to common-sense notions of the world to dispute the existence of propositions *qua* abstract entities, and to say there is nothing, over and above the sentences we utter or write down, which is the 'content' or the 'what is said' of those sentences, than to say that there are propositions. But as I shall now endeavour to show, the motives one might have for entertaining realism about propositions – or, more weakly, retaining appeal to them under a suitable account – are compelling even if debatable ones; and, as a further complication, it is difficult to see how the notion can be dispensed with in practice, because alternatives more to a nominalist taste are equally, if differently, problematic.

In setting out more fundamental reasons for holding onto propositions it will be useful to follow a suggestion made by Ryle, namely that the motives for such commitment arise from two connected assumptions in the thought of philosophers with broadly realist sympathies. The first of these is a view about the intentionality of consciousness; the second is the denotative theory of meaning.[7]

The idea that consciousness is intentional is the idea that all acts of consciousness are directed towards an object. So, whenever I think, I think about something; when I hope, wish, believe, wonder, fear, then I hope that something, wish that something – and so for the others. This *directedness* of my acts of consciousness is the 'intentional relation' obtaining between these acts and the objects they 'intend' (are directed towards). The objects of my intendings are often called the 'accusatives' or 'intentions' of these acts. Such verbs as 'think', 'hope', 'wish', 'believe', 'judge', 'guess', 'consider' are called propositional verbs, and the mental activities they signify are called propositional attitudes or acts.

Propositional attitudes consist in a two-place relation between a mind, on the one hand, and on the other a complex entity named by the 'that' clause in such sentences as 'I believe that he has arrived', which constitutes the intention of the mind's propositional act.

That propositional attitudes, and their intentions or objects, appear to be distinct from one another, may be seen from the fact that what can be said of one, namely the acts, cannot always be said of the other, namely the intentions or objects of those acts. For example, my propositional act of believing that the Norman Conquest took place in the eleventh century AD, is something that occurs long after the eleventh century AD, whereas what it is I believe, namely that the Norman Conquest took place when it did, has nothing to do with my act of believing anything whatever about it.

What it is I believe or hope when I believe that something or hope that something, is – a proposition; *viz.* the proposition expressed by the sentence embedded in the 'that' clause of the whole. There is something of a circle here; the fact that *propositions* constitute the intentions of *propositional* attitudes is something already contained in the idea of a *propositional* attitude itself. Nevertheless, the circle is informative, for the reason propositions have to be invoked as the objects of intentional acts becomes manifest upon examination of the details relating to the independence from such acts of their intentions, as follows.

Suppose that you and I concur in believing that the Norman Conquest took place in 1066 AD. Then we both believe the same thing; we have the same belief. It is impossible that you and I should have numerically the same (act of) belief in this respect, for your believings are yours, and mine are mine. What is the same is *what* we believe; and what we believe is the proposition that 'the Norman Conquest took place in 1066 AD'. Therefore propositions must be independent of any acts of consciousness intending them.

Moreover, since I can believe that 'the Norman Conquest took place in 1066 AD' at different times of my life, that proposition must be temporally neutral with respect to my temporally several and various propositional attitudes towards it. So, indeed, does the consideration that I might have different propositional attitudes to the same proposition at different times; as when at one period of my life I believe in the existence of Santa Claus, and at another disbelieve in it. Here I am taking different propositional attitudes, at different times, to the same proposition that 'Santa Claus exists'. The same holds for cases where you and I disagree over the question of Santa Claus's existence: we take different attitudes to the same proposition, therefore the proposition is independent of our attitudes towards it.

Another, related, argument to the objectivity and independence of propositions derives from the timeless nature of many truths and falsehoods. That $5 + 7 = 12$, that lambda particle decay produces a proton and a pion, and that a great and terrible war ended in 1918, are truths which do not become true when I start thinking about them, and cease to be true when I stop thinking about them. They are eternally true, if true; I do not create them merely by assuming a propositional attitude towards them. My believing that George Eliot wrote *Middlemarch* is a feature of my own intellectual history, and so is a datable episode or series of episodes in that history; whereas George Eliot's authorship of *Middlemarch* is not part of my or anyone else's intellectual history (except, of course, her own), but is independent of anyone's having any propositional attitude towards the matter. Once again, the conclusion is that propositions are independent of the acts of consciousness intending them.

Propositions as the intentions of propositional attitudes must be distinguished from 'images' and 'facts'. What it is I believe when I believe that the Norman Conquest took place in 1066 AD is not a picture in my mind. Nor is it a 'fact', for however one understands the notion of facts, at very least they must be what is the case, and unfortunately it often happens that the intentions of those propositional attitudes which are described as 'wishful thinking', 'false hopes' and so on, are nowhere near being the case. But even wishful thinking and vain hopes are wishes that p, hopes that p; and in each case p is a proposition. Accordingly, propositions are not to be identified with facts. Facts, however, may be true propositions; or perhaps they are those states of affairs which true propositions somehow signify, 'name', or describe. This is a matter of ontology.

Propositions as Intentions Criticized

It will be evident to anyone who has read some philosophy of mind that the intentionality thesis invites objections on more grounds than just that it hypostasizes the objects of mental acts. I shall however restrict comment to this issue alone.

A distinction can be drawn between the propositional verbs listed earlier – 'believe', 'judge', 'hope' and the rest – and another class of verbs, often called 'cognitive' verbs, namely 'know', 'see', 'smell', 'taste', 'feel', and 'hear'. These share an important feature with propositional verbs, in that both classes of verbs demand a grammatical accusative. In just the same way as a cognitive verb like 'see' demands an accusative, as in 'I see x', so does a propositional verb like 'hope', as in 'I hope that p'. But, arguably, this shared feature at the level of grammar is misleading, for whereas something in reality must answer to the grammatical accusative of a cognitive verb, the same does not hold true of propositional verbs. This can be verified readily enough by a comparison of the following:

(1) Tom tastes the sweet, but there is no sweet there.
(2) Tom hopes that Santa Claus exists, but Santa Claus does not exist.

Leaving aside hallucinatory experience, in which case it would be more appropriate to recast the cognitive verb case (1) into a 'believes that' idiom, it is evident that one is involved in contradiction if one seriously asserts (1); to say that Tom tasted, felt, or saw something which was not there to be tasted, seen or felt, cannot do. By contrast, no contradiction infects Tom's hoping something which is false, non-existent, or impossible, as in (2). The contrast most forcefully displays itself when the cognitive verb 'knows' is set alongside the propositional verb 'believes'. A's knowing that p entails that p is the case; but if A believes that p, nothing follows as to whether p is or is not the case, and A's believing that p is quite consistent with p's not being the case. Other contrasts are equally illuminating: leaving aside hallucinatory cases again, if A sees x then there must be an x, whereas if A fears x, it is open whether there is x or not, and, as psychiatrists know only too well, A's fearing x is quite consistent with either or both of the physical and logical impossibilities of x.

The difference between propositional and cognitive verbs can be made out more clearly still if one considers cases of mistake. Suppose (the cognitive verb case) I say 'I see a dog', and then on closer inspection discover that it was a fox. Here I am bound to retract my claim to have seen a dog, by saying something like 'I thought I saw a dog, but what in fact I saw was a fox'. But (the propositional verb case) if I judge or believe that it is a dog, and then discover that it is a fox, I cannot retract my claim to have judged or believed that it was a dog. I cannot say: 'I only thought I judged it was a dog'. To put it another way: my cognitive attitudes are defeasible – that is, they may be mistaken, and if so can be withdrawn subsequently; but my propositional attitudes are not defeasible, and I cannot withdraw the fact that I judged or believed what it was that

I judged or believed, or the fact that I did so, even when I was mistaken.

Upholders of the claim that propositions are the objects of mental acts might therefore be understood as having committed themselves to the thesis on the misleading grounds of their noting a feature shared by cognitive and propositional verbs, namely the demand made by both kinds of verbs for an accusative. Because cognitive verbs require that something in fact answer to their accusatives, realists took it that the accusatives of propositional verbs must behave likewise. This is not the case. One moral of the story is that grammatical considerations are no sure guide to ontological ones (see Russell's application of this moral in chapter 4 below).

However, it is worth noting that the most this criticism does is to throw doubt on the idea, implicit in the construal which the intentionality thesis demands for propositions, that propositions are objective entities having a real (in the realist sense of 'real') existence independently of the sentences which express them and the propositional attitudes which intend them. This criticism shows that it is a mistake to say that when I hope or believe something, there is something – namely, a proposition – which I hope or believe, and that *therefore*, on analogy with the things which exist if I truly say I see or feel them, propositions exist.

This is by no means the only criticism that can be levelled at the intentionality construal of propositions. If the suspect philosophical psychology underlying the thesis is rejected, it of course follows that the thesis ceases to be an argument for using the notion of the proposition. More to the present point, the thesis is unintuitive, for it leaves it open that there are myriads of as yet unentertained or unintended propositions waiting to be discovered – indeed, every problem invited by the notion of an abstract entity is invited by this view of propositions, and the thesis itself does nothing to provide an account of their nature which secures them from those difficulties.

Some of the more fundamental difficulties raised by abstract objects also underlie criticisms of the second motive to be discussed. I shall come to them in due course, turning first to the motive in question.

Propositions as Meanings

An initially attractive idea about meaning is that the meaning of a word is the object it denotes. This is known as the denotative or referential theory of meaning. I shall have cause to mention it more than once in later chapters, and so shall be brief here. The theory constitutes the second motive for invoking propositions, for just as it holds that the meaning of a word is the object denoted by it, so the meaning of a sentence is the proposition it expresses. This seems a useful view, for it permits ready characterization of certain semantic features. Consider, for example, synonymity. The theory has it that a relation of synonymity obtains between two sentences when they both express the same proposition. Thus, suppose Jane has a husband, one brother, and no other siblings. If Jane says 'my husband is having a migraine attack' and her brother says 'my brother-in-law has a severe prolonged headache', then they are saying the same thing; which is to say, the sentences are synonymous because they both express the same proposition.[8]

Earlier I stated some of the general reasons why sentences and propositions have been distinguished from one another, which reasons render unattractive any simple identification of propositions with sentence tokens.[9] A further important reason is this. Many of the things which can be predicated of sentences cannot be predicated of propositions, for a sentence is an uttered or inscribed string of words having particular spatial and temporal properties – as, for example, being said in Oxford or printed in a Boston newspaper; taking so many seconds to say, or being so many centimetres long; being high-pitched or low-pitched; consisting of ink marks or chalk marks; and so on. It is the very point of saying that propositions are abstract that they are none of these things; they are non-physical and atemporal. Moreover, their objectivity is demanded by the fact that they must be available to more than one user of the language, and so cannot be dependent for their existence on this or that particular utterer or circumstance of utterance. They are thus both abstract and objective, precisely what nominalists least like about them.

To treat propositions as the meanings of sentences is to provide a forceful way of illustrating their abstractness and objectivity, particularly if one considers cases of translation of belief sentences. When I render the sentence (a) 'I believe he is here' into German, I translate it as 'Ich glaube er ist hier'. Now, if I take it that the object of my belief is the sentence 'he is here', then I am in effect saying (b) 'I believe the sentence "he is here",' which would have to be translated 'Ich glaube den Satz "he is here".' But of course we do not do this; even if we talked naturally, and we do not, of 'believing sentences', we should translate (b) into 'Ich glaube den Satz "er ist hier".' This gives the game away; it is not the sentence which is the object of my belief, but what the sentence means, that is, the proposition.[10]

This example is drawn from Church. In arguing like this for abstract propositions as the meanings of sentences, Church was defending the views of Frege, who carefully distinguished between (a) a written or uttered sentence, (b) the accompanying mental idea or ideas, and (c) the proposition (or 'thought', *Gedanke*) expressed by the sentence.[11] Whereas (b) is wholly subjective to the hearer, reader, utterer, or inscriber of the sentence, (c) is an objective abstract entity enjoying the same Platonic reality as numbers, classes, and Plato's own Forms. For Frege, propositions inhabit a 'Third Realm' with other abstract objects; the 'Third Realm' is atemporal, non-physical, and non-mental. To understand a sentence is to grasp the proposition it expresses; propositions are truth-bearers, and sentences have truth-value only in the derivative sense that they are true or false according to the truth or falsity of the propositions they express.[12]

Sense, Reference, and Opacity

Explaining Frege's point requires a detour. In connection with his views on the proposition, Frege drew a distinction which has come to enjoy considerable importance in philosophy: the distinction between sense and reference.[13] Here one needs to introduce and explain three pairs of terms: 'sense'–'reference', 'connotation'–'denotation', and 'intension'–'extension'. As these terms are standardly employed, 'sense', 'connotation' and 'intension' form a related family on one hand, and their respective pairings 'reference', 'denotation' and 'extension' form a related family on the other hand.[14] Speaking informally, the first family of terms concerns what we would ordinarily call the 'meaning' of a term, and the second concerns the range of items to which it applies.

The standard characterization of these distinctions is given in terms of the intension–extension pair, thus: The extension of the term, say, 'prime number' is the class of all prime numbers. What qualifies a number for membership of this class is its being a *prime* number (i.e. a number having no integral factors other than itself and 1); so the intension of the term 'prime number' is that property, primeness, in virtue of possessing which a number is a member of the class. Or consider the expression 'green plant'. The extension of the expression is all the plants in the world that are green. The intension of the expression is the set of properties, being a plant and being green, possession of which makes an item a member of the class.

The sense-reference distinction is a version of this. Consider the planet Venus; the Greeks thought it was not one planet but two stars, namely the evening star Hesperus and the morning star Phosphorus. Because the evening and morning stars are the same entity, it is evident that both expressions refer to the same entity, *viz*. Venus. But clearly the expressions 'morning star' and 'evening star' differ in *sense* despite having the same reference, which follows from the fact that if one says 'the morning star is identical with the morning star', the truth of what one says is a simple matter of logic and can be determined by inspecting the sentence itself; but if one says 'the morning star is identical with the evening star', the truth of what one says is a matter of astronomy, not logic. No one could discover that the morning and evening stars are in fact one and the same entity merely by inspecting the expressions 'the morning star' and 'the evening star' alone. It follows that although these two expressions are coreferential (refer to the same thing), they differ in sense.

It is noteworthy in passing that words or expressions which have the same meaning, that is are synonymous, are called 'intensionally equivalent'; and likewise, words or expressions which have the same reference or extension are called 'extensionally equivalent'. The foregoing remarks show that words or expressions may be extensionally equivalent without being intensionally equivalent; but if two terms are intensionally equivalent, they are extensionally equivalent as well.

Frege applied his sense-reference distinction in the following way. In his view the sense of a sentence is the proposition ('thought') it expresses; but sentences can be treated as complex names, and therefore as having references also. The reference of the name 'Joe Bloggs' is, unproblematically, the human individual – Joe Bloggs – who goes by and answers to that name. The references of sentences are not concrete objects but *truth-values*. All true sentences have the same reference, namely The True; and all false sentences, similarly, have as their references The False.

Frege's point in treating sentences as complex names is to allow sentences, like names, to be substituted for one another without change of truth-value in the larger context in which the substitution occurs. The notion in play is one first articulated by Leibniz: that of intersubstitutivity of coreferential terms *salva veritate* ('saving the truth', that is, 'preserving the truth-value'). If two terms A and B have the same reference, then term A can be substituted for term B in any sentence in which B occurs, without changing the truth-value of the sentence. Thus in the sentence 'Hesperus is the planet Venus' one can substitute, *salva veritate*, the name 'Phosphorus' for the name 'Hesperus' because they are coreferential terms. Frege was concerned to develop an extensional – that is, a truth-functional – logic, and it is defining of extensional contexts that intersubstitution of coreferential terms occurs *salva veritate*. Accordingly, just as with names, atomic co-referring sentences (co-referring in the sense of having the same truth-value) can be substituted for one another in molecular sentences truth-functionally compounded out of them, without change in the molecular sentences' truth-values, even when the substituted atomic sentence differs in sense from the atomic sentence it replaces.

However, in the case of sentences in which an embedded 'that' clause follows a propositional verb, as in 'Ptolemy believed that the earth is flat' or 'Philip is unaware that Tully is Cicero', the context is intensional (non-extensional), for the reason that the truth-value of the whole sentence is not a function of the sentence in the subordinate clause. Frege dealt with problem sentences of this kind by saying that the reference of the embedded sentence following 'that' is the proposition it expresses; which is to say, its reference is what its sense would be if it appeared in an extensional context. Because a sentence has a reference only if it has a sense, Frege identified the sense of sentences used non-extensionally with the sense of the words 'the proposition that . . .'. Church's view, that the reference of non-extensionally occurring sentences is its meaning or sense, is Fregean in just this way.

Quine's discussion of the difficulties that arise with non-extensional contexts, in particular where reference is 'opaque', has important results, as the following shows.[15]

Intersubstitutivity does not always occur *salva veritate*, and such failure is characteristic of intensional contexts. Consider the statements (using Quine's original numbering):

(3) Cicero = Tully
(4) 'Cicero' contains six letters.

If 'Tully' is substituted for 'Cicero' in (4), the resulting statement is false, because (4) does not contain a referential use of 'Cicero' but merely mentions that name.[16] Now evidently the principle of intersubstitutivity must not be used in contexts such as this, where the name one might misguidedly wish to replace occurs without referring straightforwardly to the object; which happens not only when the name is mentioned, as above, but whenever it occurs in a non-referential, or non-directly referential, context. Consider

(9)   Philip is unaware that Tully denounced Catiline.
(11) Philip is unaware that Cicero denounced Catiline.

If (9) is true, then, substituting on the basis of (3), one gets (11), but, granting that Philip both knows that Cicero denounced Catiline yet does not know that Tully is Cicero, (11) will be false although (9) and (3) are true.[17] It follows that 'a name may occur referentially in a statement S and yet not occur referentially in a longer statement which is formed by embedding S in the context "is unaware that . . ." or "believes that . . ." To sum up the situation in a word, we may speak of (such) contexts . . . as *referentially opaque*'.[18] It is then the case, on Quine's view, that one cannot quantify into referentially opaque contexts unless the values of the variables bound by quantification are intensional objects – which in Frege's cases would be the senses of names. For the further reason (to be discussed in more detail and in a wider connection later in this chapter and the next chapter) that individuating intensional entities rests upon a notion of analyticity, which Quine rejects outright, he concludes that the Fregean model will not do.

Propositions as Meanings Criticized Further

A more general criticism of the wisdom of identifying propositions with meanings of sentences is that to say this is to explain the obscure, *viz.* propositions, by something equally obscure, *viz.* meanings. The question of meaning is taken up in more detail in later chapters (chapters 7 and 8), so it will suffice at this juncture to put the matter in general and preliminary terms.

What is a 'meaning'? Consider the simpler cases of the putative meanings of names, which on the denotative theory are the objects they denote. In an intuitive sense, one understands very well what it is for the name 'Tom' to pick out some individual person who goes by and answers to that name; but it is by no means clear, other than intuitively, what the denoting relation is or how it works. Consider the simplest case of establishing a denotative word-world link – the ostensive (e.g. pointing with a finger) definition of a term like 'table'. Suppose I am teaching a foreign friend English, a language of which he is wholly ignorant; and suppose I point to a table and utter the word 'table'. What settles it for him that I intend him to understand the object taken as whole? Why should he not take me as pointing out to him its colour, or texture, or the stuff of which it is made? Imagine my pointing at the table-top and saying 'glossy'. Why should he not understand me as naming the object as a whole, rather than the style of its finish? At what is apparently the simplest level of demonstratively linking a name with the object it is supposed to 'mean', then, there are serious difficulties.

The more complex matter of sentence meaning presents added difficulties. Suppose one leaves aside the idea, for the present, that sentences are complex names which denote 'states of affairs' or 'facts' or 'possible facts', and holds to the idea of propositions as 'contents' of sentences. Once again, there is a clear intuitive sense in which one knows what is meant by sentence meaning. Suppose A shows B the sentence

(1) Νους ὁρᾷ και νοῦς ακούει᾽ τ᾽αλλα κωφά και τυφλά.

and B asks him what it means; to which A replies that it means

(2) Mens videt, mens audit, cetera surda et coeca.

If B's linguistic resources also fall short of Latin he would still not know what is being said. If A at last tells him that (1) and (2) both say

(3) The mind sees, the mind hears, all else is deaf and blind,

then B could at last be described as having grasped the meaning which all of (1)–(3) express, and to which, owing to mere nuisance of linguistic limitations, he could only gain access by means of (3). *What* he grasps is what all of (1)–(3) express in common – namely, the proposition that 'the mind sees and hears and all else is deaf and blind.'

But has anything informative been said by substituting talk of the proposition which (1)–(3) express for talk of the meaning which (1)–(3)

express, or *vice versa*? All that one can infer from the example is that meanings and propositions are somethings which attach to different sentence-tokens and, whether or not they are language-dependent in some sense left open, are none the less not dependent on *particular* languages.

In fact the problem sets in earlier, for it is not clear what is meant by 'expresses' in 'the proposition which the sentence expresses', or 'the meaning which the sentence expresses', for it is to go in a circle to explain 'expresses' by saying 'the proposition which the sentence expresses is that sentence's meaning', or 'the proposition is the "what-is-said" expressed by the sentence', or '. . . is the "content" of the sentence'; for now we are back with heuristics of the sort appealed to at the beginning of the discussion, when an intuitive grasp of the notion of propositions was being sought.

This criticism comes down to saying that to identify propositions with the meanings of sentences fails on two related counts; first, that the notion of 'meaning' is itself in need of clarification, and so can explain nothing about propositions while yet unclarified; and secondly, that in so far as there is any hint as to what meaning is – namely, denotation – it is as full of difficulty as the notion it offers to explain.

Much of the confusion here arises from taking meanings and/or propositions as 'meant entities'. Consider – again to pre-empt, briefly, later discussion – an alternative way of characterizing meaning. The later work of Wittgenstein brought into prominence a notion of meaning as *use*. The idea is that expressions do not (or that the great majority of them do not) simply name or label some extralinguistic item, but have a role or function in the language, such that to learn the meaning of an expression is to learn how to use it in those roles. Accordingly, to know a term's meaning is to know the rules governing its employment in the various linguistic enterprises of stating, asking, commanding, and so on, in which that term appears or can appear. On this view, it is misguided to think that 'meanings' are some sort of timeless entities called 'propositions' (or even just 'meanings' for that matter) occupying a Third Realm; for if the meaning of an expression consists in the rules governing its use in the language, then meaning is unmysterious. I do not wish to suggest, in advance of discussing it, that this theory is wholly satisfactory; the point, for present purposes, is that seeing how meaning might be handled otherwise than as denotation, shows, or goes some way to showing, that acceptance of propositions is not forced by considerations of meaning.

If propositions are not to be explained as the meanings of sentences on a denotative theory, which is what the foregoing criticism disallows, then other options need investigation. One is to take propositions as the meanings of sentences on a 'possible worlds' theory for intensional items; I allude to this in the next chapter. Another option is to avoid talk of denotation by appealing to the idea that propositions are logical constructions out of sets of synonymous sentences. Appeal is still being made to certain semantical properties of sentences – in this case synonymy – but the proposal has the virtue that it manageably restricts the abstract objects being invoked. On a strict presentation of such a theory, a proposition can be defined as a class of sentences all having the same meaning as some given sentence, leaving it open that 'meaning' might be independently specified in such a way as to avoid reification. Then the only abstract entity present is the class, and certain nominalists accept classes into their ontologies because they are required by mathematics and science. Nevertheless the problem here will be the notion of synonymity, which would require defending against Quine's attack upon it (see chapter 3); and further, synonymity itself, if successfully defended, would then have to be characterized in a way that did not make prior appeal to propositions (cf. above), for the account would otherwise be circular.

Chief among Quine's reasons for rejecting the notion of meaning is, he argues, that nothing can count as *the* meaning of a given expression; meaning is indeterminate. He takes this to be shown by considerations about translation from one language to another. In summary, his argument is that if one tried to compile a translation manual for an alien language by observing the behaviour, both vocal and general, of the speakers of that language, it will always be possible to compile a second such manual equally faithful to their behaviour, and the two manuals will give different translations of their expressions. There can be, in short, no scheme of translation uniquely determined by the behavioural data provided by the language's speakers.[19]

This view is called the thesis of the *indeterminacy of translation*, and Quine gives two arguments for it. The first is that someone trying to make a 'radical translation' – that is, a translation from scratch – of an entirely unknown language, and using only the observable behaviour of its speakers, would never be able to decide between competing renderings of a given sentence of their language. If the native speakers cry 'gavagai!' in the presence of rabbits (Quine's example), the data provided by their behaviour will not help him choose whether to translate the term as 'rabbit' or as 'slice of rabbithood' or even as 'favourite white meat' – and other possibilities abound.

The second argument results from combining two principles: an empiricist principle stating that a sentence's meaning consists of the difference its truth makes to experience, and a principle of 'holism' stating that the meanings of sentences are never determined individually, but only by their place in the language. The conjunction of these two principles entails that meaning is never determinate, because nothing can count as *the* difference that a single sentence's truth makes to experience; the *whole language* faces the *whole of experience* (or the *whole world*) as a single unit, and not sentence by sentence. (The view that sentences stand or fall by corresponding individually to bits of experience – or to bits of the world – is called 'atomism' and is the opposite of holism.)

If meaning is an indeterminate notion, then to define propositions as the meanings of sentences is unsatisfactory. So too therefore, of course, is using the notion to explain synonymity or 'sameness of meaning' by saying that two sentences are synonymous if they express the same proposition.

These of Quine's views have been very influential for reasons additional to their attack on the idea of meanings; they recur on the following pages, especially chapters 3 and 9, in which latter there is a more detailed account of the indeterminacy thesis's implications.

Nominalism and Realism

As the foregoing sections show, to give a full account of the questions raised by theories of the proposition requires discussion of matters not raised until later chapters, and so takes us further afield than the limits of this chapter allow. Nevertheless there is a minimal line to be taken on propositions which allows use of them without the attendant baggage of intensional realism. The desideratum is to reduce appeal to abstract items to the minimum, and it is worth noting why.

The realism-nominalism dispute is a dispute about ontological commitments. It is by no means an idle dispute, particularly in view of the role it plays in contemporary discussions of possible worlds theory (chapter 3, below) and in certain problems arising, as already noted, in the theory of meaning, for example in connection with the motives Russell had for devising his Theory of Descriptions (chapter 4, below). It also arises, in somewhat oblique form but crucially none the less, in the current argument between realists and anti-realists in the theory of meaning and elsewhere (chapters 8 and 9, below); 'realism' in this context has added complexities and perhaps some differences.

The problem can be illustrated by briefly inspecting Meinong's realist theory of 'Objects'.[20] Meinong took it that metaphysics deals with everything that both exists and subsists, the distinction being that the totality of existent things is 'infinitely small' in comparison to the totality of the 'Objects' of knowledge, which, when they are non-existent, are at least subsistent in the sense of being things about which we can think and talk. Meinong's Objects are thus construable as the accusatives, in general, of thought. Even impossible Objects like the round square subsist, as do the infinities of negative facts such as that 'Aristotle did not have thirty brothers', 'Aristotle did not have thirty-one brothers', 'Aristotle did not have thirty-two brothers' . . . , and so on.[21]

Russell and Quine were chief among those to reject this lavish violation of the principle of Ockham's Razor, which states that one should not posit the existence of more entities than necessary. This drive to ontological parsimony is the guiding principle of nominalism. In Russell's view, Meinong's postulation of a universe glutted with subsistent entities offends against a 'vivid sense of reality',[22] and Quine apostrophized Meinong's universe as 'overpopulated', 'rank', a 'slum,' and 'a breeding ground for disorderly elements'.[23] In another memorable tag Quine bracketed unnecessary entities as *entia non grata*, marking a resolution to exclude them from the ontological commitments we make.

There are good theoretical and methodological reasons for applying the principle of Ockham's Razor. In selecting one from among a number of competing and otherwise adequate hypotheses in any field of enquiry, certain metatheoretical criteria come into play; the hypothesis which is simplest and at the same time most powerful is the obvious one to choose. In the same way, limiting the number of entities invoked by a philosophical theory limits the hostages yielded to fortune from the point of view of the theory's efficacy: for the more hostages, the weaker the theory. It is for this reason that Quine's views on ontological commitment have as one of their motives the thought that if two theories give the same conceptual mileage, but one of them involves commitment to the existence of fewer entities, *that* is the one to choose.[24] Indeed one should, on both his view and Russell's, actively seek out the most parsimonious theory adequate to the phenomena requiring explanation, and not rest content with overpopulation, however much it smoothes the difficulties in hand; for it is all too easy to misguide oneself by invoking *ad hoc* entities, such as entelechies, or subsistent beings, or Forms, as 'explanatory' devices.[25]

One of the chief reasons for Quine's hostility towards abstract entities, including propositions, is – as we have just seen – that they lack clear *criteria of identity*. A criterion of identity for something is that criterion by means of which we can individuate it, specify which one it is, tell where it begins and another leaves off; in short, by means of which we can pick something out or tell that it is the same one again. The nub of the position taken by Quine is that there is 'no entity without identity'. In Quine's view, criteria of identity for propositions can only be afforded by relations of synonymy between sentences, for example by saying that proposition p is the proposition expressed by the distinct but synonymous sentences x and y. Then, on the grounds that synonymity is an empty notion (see above and chapter 3), Quine takes this to be grounds for rejecting propositions, at least in any but the most reducible nominalist sense – as a *façon de parler* in effect.

Innocuous Propositions and Statements

Because many of the issues touched on in this chapter recur in later chapters, we can leave the question of propositions in this undecided state by asking, in conclusion, whether there is indeed a satisfactory *façon de parler* sense of 'proposition', as just suggested.

Thomson suggests that there is.[26] In his view, there would only be a genuinely interesting theory of the proposition if it was claimed that there is only *one* proposition that snow is white, or that Santa Claus exists: for otherwise to say that a proposition is what gets asserted by use of a sentence is to say nothing unobvious, or wrong, or even interesting.

On this view a proposition comes to much the same thing as a 'statement', by which is meant: what a sentence can be used to say or express on a given occasion by a given utterer. Mackie has it that 'the words "statement" and "proposition" are just terms that enable us to speak generally about what is said, what is believed, what is assertable or believable, and so on'.[27] The point in being able to speak of statements or nominalistically-conceived propositions (to avoid confusion with propositions *qua* abstract entities, the term 'statement' is now often used as the chief term of preference) is to preserve the sense in which *sentences* cannot be truth-bearers, because sentences can be used by different speakers on different occasions to say what is true on some of those occasions and false on others. As we shall see, however, there are theories of truth which offer good reason to treat sentences as truth-bearers; so even this plausible and uncontentious proposal is not without question. But for the most part, in what follows, I shall use 'statement' and 'proposition' nominalistically as interchangeable with 'statement'.

Notes

1   J. L. Austin, 'Performative-Constantive', in C. E. Caton (ed.), *Philosophy and Ordinary Language*, p. 22 *et seq.*
2   L. Wittgenstein, *Philosophical Investigations*, cf. §§ 243–315, 348–412.
3   Often philosophers make a three-way distinction, between sentences, statements and propositions. A statement, on the received interpretation, is an actual use of an uttered or inscribed sentence on a particular occasion. Often, however, 'statement' is used as a synonym of 'proposition', and to keep clear of possible confusions I shall restrict attention to the sentence-proposition distinction alone. Cf. B. Aune, 'Statements and Propositions', *Nous*, 1967.
4   Henceforth I use 'sentence' for 'declarative sentence', unless otherwise specified.
5   The relativization of an utterance to a speaker and a time is known as 'indexicality'; thus, a sentence is said to be indexed to speakers and times.
6   Cf. Plato, *Republic*, 596a 6–7; cf. 507ab.
7   G. Ryle, 'The Theory of Meaning', in Caton, *op. cit.*, p. 128 *et seq.*, cf. esp. pp. 131–45, 148–53. See also J. F. Thomson, 'Truth-Bearers and the Trouble About Propositions', *Journal of Philosophy*, 66, 1969, p. 739.
8   This second motive is related to the first in that the propositions here said to be the meanings of sentences, also do duty as the intentions of propositional attitudes. However the two motives are separable in that commitment to one does not entail commitment to the other.
9   I use here a distinction between sentence 'types' and sentence 'tokens'. The sentence 'John likes Rover' is a particular instance, hence token, of that type. 'Type' is to 'token' what 'species' is to 'individual'.
10 A. Church, 'Propositions', *Encyclopaedia Britannica*.
11 G. Frege, 'The Thought', in P. F. Strawson (ed.), *Philosophical Logic*, p. 17 *et seq.*

12   Ibid., pp. 20–1. The expression 'Third Realm' is quoted by Ryle, ibid., p. 149.

13   G. Frege, 'Sense and Reference', in Frege, *Translations*, pp. 56–78.

14   'Intension' with an 's', note: not to be confused with the 'intention' with a 't' recently discussed.

15   Cf., W. V. Quine, 'Reference and Modality', in Quine *From a Logical Point of View* p. 139 *et seq.*

16   *Use* of a word and *mention* of it are standardly distinguished by enclosing *mentioned* words in single quotes. The sign of equality, '=', stands for 'is identical with'.

17   Quine, 'Reference and Modality', pp. 141–2.

18   Ibid., p. 142.

19   Quine, 'On the Reasons for the Indeterminacy of Translation', *Journal of Philosophy*, lxvii.

20   A. Meinong, 'The Theory of Objects', in R. Chisholm (ed.), *Realism and the Background of Phenomenology*.

21   Ibid., p. 79.

22   Cf. B. Russell, 'The Philosophy of Logical Atomism', in R. C. Marsh (ed.), *Logic and Knowledge*, p. 269 *et seq.*

23   Cf., W. V. Quine, 'On What There Is', in Quine, *From a Logical Point of View*. Meinong here appears as 'Wyman'.

24   Ibid. I discuss Quine's views on this in chapter 4 below.

25   Closely related issues appear in chapter 3 below. Cf. W. Lycan, 'The Trouble With Possible Worlds', in M. J. Loux (ed.), *The Possible and the Actual*, for a discussion of Meinong's and Quine's views.

26   J. F. Thomson in P. F. Strawson, *Philosophical Logic*, pp. 103 *et seq.*

27   J. L. Mackie, *Truth, Probability and Paradox*, pp. 20–1.

3

Necessity, Analyticity, and the A Priori

Introduction

Some propositions are said to be such that one can determine their truth-value merely by grasping the meanings of the terms that occur in them, while in order to determine the truth-value of others one needs to know how things stand in relevant portions of the world. The first kind are called *analytic* propositions, the second *synthetic*.

Some propositions, again, are said to be such that if they are true they *have* to be true, and if they are false they *have* to be false, and cannot be otherwise; whereas other propositions are said to be such that their truth-values are, so to speak, uncoerced – that is, they are a function of how things happen to stand in relevant portions of the world. The first kind are called *necessary* propositions, the second *contingent*.

And yet again, the truth-values of some propositions are said to be knowable without recourse to investigation, while the truth-values of others can only be known as a result of investigation. The first kind are called *a priori* propositions, the second *a posteriori*.

These three pairs of concepts seem to be closely related. All three have a central importance to philosophy. This chapter examines their nature and connections. I begin by showing why these concepts are important and how some early attempts to define them fared; and then I look in somewhat more detail at the first two.[1]

Three Distinctions

Leibniz held that all reasoning is underwritten by two principles, the principle of contradiction and the principle of sufficient reason. It is in virtue of the principle of contradiction that 'we judge *false* that which involves a contradiction, and *true* that which is opposed or contradictory to the false'; and it is in virtue of the principle of sufficient reason that 'we hold that there can be no fact real or existing, no statement true, unless there be a sufficient reason why it should be so and not otherwise, although these reasons cannot usually be known by us'.[2] These two principles are allied to a distinction between two kinds of truths, 'truths of reason' and 'truths of fact'. The former are *necessary* (true, as Leibniz put it, in all possible worlds) and their opposites impossible; the latter are *contingent, and their opposites possible*.[3] In his correspondence with Clark, Leibniz said that the connection between the two principles and the two kinds of truth is shown by the fact that the principle of contradiction is sufficient on its own for a demonstration of the whole of mathematics, but that the principle of sufficient reason is needed in addition in order to pass from mathematics to physics, which deals with a realm of contingent things.[4]

In Leibniz's view, truths of reason can be established by analysis, by resolving them into the simple ideas and primary principles out of which they are constituted and which themselves require no proof.[5] The distinction between this kind of truths and the second kind – the contingent truths or truths of fact – foreshadows Hume's division in the *Enquiry*, between 'relations of ideas' and 'matters of fact'.[6] (In the *Treatise* Hume had characterized the difference as one holding between 'knowledge' and 'probability', but the terminological variance is insignificant.[7]) Hume claimed that this distinction exhausts all the truths that can be known. Some truths depend only on relations between ideas in the sense that to deny a statement which is true in virtue of this relation is to fall into contradiction.[8] According to Hume, relations of ideas are discovered either by intuition, as when one simply sees that $5 + 7 = 12$, or by demonstration, as when one goes through a deductive argument that validly yields its conclusion. 'Matter of fact' truths, by contrast, are such that to conceive of them as false does not involve contradiction. Their discovery is effected by observation – which for Hume is something we have to assume to be trustworthy – and inference – which for

Hume is, in this case, non-demonstrative inference, proceeding by means of the relation of cause and effect.

The distinction both Leibniz and Hume were drawing is the distinction between *necessary* and *contingent* truths. The two other distinctions – the distinction between the a priori and the a posteriori, and between the *analytic* and the *synthetic* – appear to be closely allied to it.

The members of the latter pair may be contrasted by saying that analytic statements are those in which the concept of the predicate is already contained in the concept of the subject, so that to see whether it is true one need only inspect the terms occurring in the statement (one might say 'analyse' the statement – hence 'analytic'); whereas synthetic statements are those in which two different concepts are joined together or 'synthesized', and their truth-value is to be tested by going and looking at the world, to see whether things are as the statement claims them to be.[9] A tautology is an obvious example of an analytic statement: 'all married men are married'. But not all analytic statements are tautologies: 'all bodies are spatially extended' is non-tautologous but analytic, for its truth-value depends only on the concepts involved, not, as with a synthetic statement such as 'snow is white', on the way things are in the world.

The members of the former pair – a priori–a posteriori – are usually distinguished by saying that a truth is known a priori if it is known independently of experience of how things are in the world; whereas a truth known a posteriori is one which is known, and can only be known, on the basis of empirical investigation. It is accordingly held that such truths of arithmetic as $5 + 7 = 12$ are known a priori, whereas the empirical facts that grass is green and snow is white are knowable only a posteriori.

It is easy to see why these three pairs of concepts have been closely linked. If a truth is necessary, if it consists in a 'relation of ideas' and is a 'truth of reason', such as 'all bodies are extended', then it seems both to be the case that the statement expressing that truth is analytic – that is, can be judged true merely by inspecting the meaning of the terms involved – and that it is knowable a priori – that is, can be judged true without recourse to empirical investigation. If, on the other hand, a truth is contingent, if it is a 'matter of fact' or 'truth of fact', such as 'some bodies are speckled green', then it seems to be both the case that the statement expressing that truth is synthetic – that is, its truth-value depends on the way things are in the world – and it is only knowable a posteriori – that is, its truth-value can be ascertained only by empirical investigation. Such thoughts suggest that the relations between the three pairs of notions are straightforward and symmetrical.

Kant, however, had other ideas. He took the view that there can be synthetic a priori truths, and wrote *The Critique of Pure Reason* to prove it. His view cuts across the apparently ready grouping of the pairs of concepts just given; but this is not as surprising as it seems, for although the three pairs are indeed related, important differences block a simple characterization of that relationship. The differences, summarily put, are that 'necessity' and 'contingency' are metaphysical notions, 'analytic' and 'synthetic' are semantic notions, and 'a priori' and 'a posteriori' are epistemological notions. So much is suggested by the way they have just been characterized. Accordingly, the most that could be claimed is that the expressions 'analytic', 'necessary' and 'a priori' have the same extension, that is, apply to all and only the same statements. But that, as we have already seen, is questioned by Kant; and others, as we shall see below, join him. And in any event, none of the three sets of notions is unproblematic in its own right.

At first glance the notions of necessity and analyticity appear more opaque than that of the a priori, which since Leibniz, and particularly Kant has had a largely agreed epistemological rendering. The problem with the a priori is an example of a general problem here, namely, that coming to a clear grasp of the notion might depend on invocation of at least one of the others. Leibniz, for example, defined the a priori in terms of necessity, as the mode in which necessary truths are apprehended; in his view, to know reality a priori is to know it 'by exposing the cause or the possible generation of things, which contrasts with knowing reality a posteriori, which is to know, by means of sense-experience, what states of affairs in fact obtain in the world.[10] By 'exposing' Leibniz meant *proving*; therefore, because truths of reason are based on 'identical propositions',[11] a priori truths can be demonstrated on the grounds of the principle of contradiction, and so Leibniz could talk of 'truths a priori or of reason' as opposed to 'truths a posteriori, or of fact'.[12] Accordingly, for Leibniz the a priori–a posteriori distinction is one between, respectively, knowledge of necessary truths acquired by reason, and knowledge of contingent truths acquired by sense-experience.

This characterization will not quite do for Kant's employment of the terms, because unlike Leibniz he did not employ an exclusive distinction between sense-experience and reason, but invoked in addition a faculty of 'understanding'. Nevertheless, his view is essentially similar – the a priori is just the 'non-empirical' and the a posteriori 'the empirical' analogously to Leibniz's usage.[13] For Kant, likewise, a priori truths are necessary, and a posteriori truths contingent.

What is important, however, is to understand these notions in their own right. A great deal turns in particular on the notions of analyticity and necessity in contemporary philosophy; I take each in turn.

Analyticity

Analytic judgements were conceived by Kant as those in which the predicate-concept adds nothing informative to the subject–concept, but merely elucidates, analyses, or 'unpacks' it.[14] In synthetic judgements the reverse happens. An alternative way of characterizing analyticity is to say that a statement is analytic if its truth-value can be determined merely by inspecting the meanings of the terms involved; this way of putting things owes itself to the Logical Positivists. Ayer, for example, wrote of the contrast thus: 'A proposition is analytic when its validity depends solely on the definitions of the symbols it contains, and synthetic when its validity is determined by the facts of experience'.[15]

Analyticity, particularly when employed as the Positivists employed it, is an important notion. Consider for example what is at stake in the Positivists' view. They wished to demarcate a class of genuinely significant propositions in order to exclude those that lack cognitive content, for they took the task of philosophy to be the clarification of the language of science. Metaphysics and theology, together with ethics and aesthetics, seemed to the Positivists *cognitively* vacuous enterprises whose propositions are, at best, distinguishable from jumbles of nonsense syllables only in virtue of having meanings of an emotional, subjective, exhortatory, or prescriptive sort, none of which is germane to science. The principle they adopted to discriminate between meaningful and meaningless propositions was the celebrated 'verifiability principle', which states, roughly, that the meaning of a statement is the method of its verification, and that all and only those (synthetic) statements which are, at very least in principle, verifiable are cognitively significant.[16] The parenthetical 'synthetic' is important; for there is a way of accounting for certain propositions which are not synthetic but which play a vital role in the sciences – specifically, the propositions of logic and mathematics.

This is to view such propositions as analytic, and to say that their truth-values depend only on the meanings of the terms occurring in them. Wittgenstein in the *Tractatus Logico-Philosophicus* characterized these propositions as tautologies, and therefore empty of content, which accounted for their being propositions whose truth-value can be settled independently of experience.[17] Thus for the Positivists the class of cognitively significant propositions is made up of two kinds, synthetic and analytic; the rest go by the board from the viewpoint of science.

Quine is not persuaded by the Positivist view. He challenges the analytic–synthetic distinction – together with an allied 'dogma', reductionism – in a classic paper called 'Two Dogmas of Empiricism'.[18] His arguments are as follows.

In the Positivists' characterization of analyticity, which in Quine's view captures Kant's intentions also, a presupposed notion of 'meaning' plays a central role, analytic statements being those, in the way noted, whose truth-value is supposed to depend only on the meanings of their constituent terms. Quine's strategy is first to rid the discussion of appeal to meaning, for the following reasons (some familiar from the discussion in chapter 2 above). First, as Frege's distinction between sense and reference shows, meaning is not the same as naming.[19] That distinction is made out for singular terms like 'Hesperus' and 'Phosphorus', which, although co-referring, differ in sense. Singular terms purport to name entities, whether concrete or abstract, whereas general terms, like 'creature with a heart', do not name entities, but are said instead to be 'true of' some or other entity or entities, that is, to apply to or be predicable of some entity or entities. The class of entities a general term is true of, or to which it applies, is called that term's 'extension'. On analogy with the sense-reference distinction as applied to singular terms, two general terms can have the same extension while differing in meaning or 'intension', as in the case of 'creature with a heart' and 'creature with kidneys'. Indeed, the meaning of a general term is explicity to be contrasted with its extension, a point noted in chapter 1 above where the distinction was illustrated by its closeness to the related grammatical distinction between connotation and denotation respectively.

Quine takes the view that once one has the distinction between a theory of meaning and a theory of reference which the above considerations yield, what constitutes a theory of meaning changes character; for a 'conspicuous' question about any (pre-distinction) theory of meaning must be, in Quine's view, 'what sort of things are meanings?'[20] If one dispenses with the notion that there are 'meant entities', a theory of meaning comes down to a concern with no more than the synonymy of linguistic forms and the analyticity of statements; and 'meanings themselves, as obscure intermediary entities, may well be abandoned'.[21] Getting a grasp of the notion of analyticity has accordingly to be done without appeal to meanings *qua* 'meant entities'.

Two kinds of statements are generally reckoned to be analytic, one kind being what Quine calls 'logically true' statements such as 'no unmarried man is married', and the other kind being non-tautologous statements like 'no bachelor is married'. In Quine's view, a statement of the former kind is true solely in virtue of the logical particles occurring in it – these being 'no', 'un-', 'if', 'then', 'and' and so on – and remains true under any reinterpretation of its components other than the logical particles. Statements of the latter kind are not logical truths, but can be turned into them by replacing their terms (or one or some of them) by synonyms; thus, the example above can be turned into a logical truth by substituting 'unmarried man' for 'bachelor'. So it turns out that understanding analytic statements of the latter kind depends upon understanding synonymy. The next question, then, is whether we have a clear grasp of synonymy.[22]

Perhaps synonymy can be explained in terms of definition; the thought would be that 'bachelor' and 'unmarried man' *mean the same* because one can be defined in terms of the other. But the question arises, on what are definitions based? One cannot appeal to a dictionary to settle questions of definition, for lexicographers are empirical scientists who find, implicit in standard usage before they write their dictionaries, that speakers take a relation of synonymy to hold between certain terms, upon which the lexicographers therefore report. In consequence, the ground of the synonymy cannot be the fact that lexicographers observe it in linguistic behaviour. Definition rests on synonymy rather than explaining it – with the single exception, allowed by Quine, of the case of explicitly conventional introductions of new notations, where a definiendum has been expressly created as a synonym of its definiens. Otherwise definition is not the basis of synonymy.[23]

If analyticity is to be explained in terms of synonymy, and if appeal to definition will not explain synonymy, another approach is required. A suggestion might be that the synonymy of two linguistic forms is to be explained by their intersubstitutivity in all contexts *salva veritate*.[24]

Leaving aside cases of the failure of intersubstitutivity *salva veritate* of 'unmarried man' for 'bachelor' in ' "bachelor" has eight letters', and concentrating only on 'cognitive' synonymy, the question is whether intersubstitutivity is a strong enough condition for it. Evidently, it will not be strong enough if it turns out that heteronyms (that is, non-synonymous expressions) can be substituted for one another *salva veritate*.

Perhaps one way of trying to make the notion of intersubstitutivity do the trick is to say that because the statement 'necessarily all and only bachelors are bachelors' is true (construing 'necessarily' as applicable only to analytic statements), then if 'bachelor' and 'unmarried man' are intersubstitutable *salva veritate*, the statement 'necessarily, all and only bachelors are unmarried men' is also true. To say this is true, in turn, is to say that 'all and only bachelors are unmarried men is analytic' is true; and this, in turn again, says that 'bachelor' and 'unmarried man' are cognitively synonymous. Therefore it looks as though intersubstitutivity is indeed a sufficient condition for cognitive synonymy.[25]

Quine, however, rejects this manoeuvre as 'hocus-pocus'. The problem lies with the modal adverb 'necessarily'. Intersubstitutivity *salva veritate* varies in force according to the richness of the language in hand, and the above argument depends upon possession of a language rich enough to contain 'necessarily', construed as yielding truth only when applied to analytic statements. But 'can we condone a language which contains such an adverb? Does the adverb really make sense? To suppose that it does,' says Quine, 'is to suppose that we have already made satisfactory sense of "analytic".'[26] The reasons are as follows.

On Quine's view, intersubstitutivity *salva veritate* is meaningful only if relativized to a specified language. Consider a language containing the ordinary trappings of first-order predicate logic, with variables x, y and z . . . and with a stock of one- and many-place predicates, for example F where Fx is 'x is a man' and G where Gxy is 'x loves y'. The atomic wffs of this language truth-functionally concatenate into molecular sentences upon application of the operators 'and', 'if' and so on. There are also the quantifiers. Such a language contains descriptions and standard contexually-defined singular terms, even those naming classes, assuming a two-place predicate of class-membership; and it is a language adequate to classical mathematics and science, except in the case where this latter involves what Quine regards as debatable, if not downright suspicious, devices like counterfactual conditionals and the modal adverbs 'necessarily' and its kind.

Such a language is extensional, in the sense that any two of its predicates which agree in extension can be substituted for one another *salva veritate*. But such intersubstitutivity does not provide the cognitive synonymy needed to ground analyticity. To say that 'bachelor' and 'unmarried man' are intersubstitutable *salva veritate* in an extensional language says no more than that 'all and only bachelors are unmarried men is analytic' is true, which is not to say that the extensional agreement of the terms turns on their meanings rather than on contingent facts, which latter is the case with the contingent extensional agreement of heteronyms like 'creature with a heart' and 'creature with kidneys'. To get the required specification of analyticity in terms of cognitive synonymy, this latter would have to be something more than extensional intersubstitutivity; it would have to be such as to equate the synonymy of 'bachelor' and 'unmarried man' with the *analyticity*, not just the *truth*, of 'all and only bachelors are unmarried men is analytic'.[27]

It was noted that if the intensional adverb 'necessarily' is available, then intersubstitutivity succeeds in yielding cognitive synonymy; but Quine's point is that this can only be so if the notion of analyticity is understood in advance. Quine's opposition to talk of necessity will be canvassed more closely below.

Quine's attack, as it has been reported to this point, is summarized by him thus: 'Analyticity at first seemed most naturally definable by appeal to a realm of meanings. On refinement, the appeal to meanings gave way to an appeal to synonymy or definition. But definition turned out to be a will-o'-the-wisp, and synonymy turned out to be best understood only by dint of prior appeal to analyticity itself. So we are back at the problem of analyticity.'[28] He considers a last attempt to make sense of the notion, one this time turning on the alleged vagueness of ordinary language. Here it is claimed that in a more precise artificial language, call it L_0, the notion of analyticity can be perspicuously set out by reference to 'semantical rules'. Carnap, for example, had suggested how such a move might be made, by offering this sketch: a sentence S is analytic (strictly, L_0-true) in L_0 if and only if S's truth is to be established on the basis of the semantic rules alone, without reference to non-linguistic facts.[29]

Quine is not impressed by this idea. If there is an artificial language L_0 whose rules contain a specification of all its own analytic statements, then we are not helped, for the rules contain the very word – 'analytic' – which we are trying to understand. At best we could construe the rules as conventionally defining a new term, 'analytic-for-L_0; but this is still unhelpful, for it is not 'analytic-for-L_0' we wish to understand, but 'analytic'. 'Analytic-for-L_0' might less controversially be designated K, and indeed any class of statements K, M, N, etc., could be specified for any purpose whatever; but what does it mean to say that K is, as against M or N, the class of 'analytic' statements in L_0? If a semantical rule were invoked which did not contain 'analytic' but turned solely on what was to count as the truths of L_0 ('L_0-truths'), then perhaps an analytic statement could be derivatively defined as a statement not only true but true just in virtue of the semantical rules of L_0 as Carnap suggested. But even this fails to help, for now appeal is being made, not to the unexplained word 'analytic', but to the unexplained notion of a 'semantical rule'. Quine likens the process to trying to pull oneself up by one's own bootstraps.[30] On this note, and therefore, Quine gives up as hopeless the task of trying to define analyticity.

Part of the interest in Quine's attack on analyticity lies in what he claims to be the philosophical motivation for employing the notion: 'It is obvious that truth in general depends on both language and extralinguistic fact . . . Thus one is tempted to suppose in general that the truth of a statement is somehow analysable into a linguistic component and a factual component. Given this suggestion, it next seems reasonable that in some statements the factual component should be null; and these are the analytic statements. But, for all its a priori reasonableness, a boundary between analytic and synthetic statements has not been drawn. That there is such a distinction to be drawn at all is an unempirical dogma of the empiricists, a metaphysical article of faith.[31]

Defending a Dogma

From the fact that no *boundary* has been drawn between analytic and synthetic statements, Quine takes it to follow that no *distinction* has been drawn, and therefore that *no satisfactory sense* has been made of 'analytic', talk of which should therefore be eschewed. This conclusion is resisted by Grice and Strawson.[32] Their argument is twofold; it is, first, that difficulties with drawing boundaries do not entail that there is no genuine distinction in the case; and secondly, that 'satisfactory sense' can indeed be made of members of the family of notions to which 'analytic' belongs, contrary to Quine's claims. Their case is made in the following way.

A distinction can be criticized for not being sharp enough, for being confused or ambiguous; but such criticisms do not amount to a rejection of that distinction, rather they are a prelude to its clarification. Quine's criticism is not of this sort. Again, a distinction might be criticized for not being useful; but then it is not its existence but its value which is being questioned, and what Quine's criticism comes down to is that the distinction simply does not exist, that to think it exists is to be the victim of a philosophical illusion. Accordingly one is justified in asking whether there is no presumption to the effect that such a distinction exists. Surely, it does; for, apart from the mere fact of its use by Leibniz, Kant, and the Positivists among others, it is clear that its use is something on which philosophers generally agree, in the sense that the terms 'analytic' and 'synthetic' have a largely uniform application in philosophical usage which conformably extends to new cases – which is to say that it is not confined to a closed list of cases philosophers could have learned outright, but can be creatively and uniformly applied across fresh ranges of statements.[33] ' "Analytic" and "synthetic" have a more or less established philosophical *use*,' Grice and Strawson write, 'and this seems to suggest that it is absurd, even senseless, to say that there is no such distinction.'[34]

But Quine's complaints run deeper. In the cluster of concepts to which analyticity belongs there is the concept of cognitive synonymy, in terms of which analyticity could be defined if it were itself clear. Quine's view is that it is not clear. Now, to say x and y are cognitively synonymous is to say that they 'mean the same'. If Quine's attack on analyticity goes through, it will follow that no sense can attach to the distinction 'means the same' and 'does not mean the same', in so far as the concept of 'meaning the same' is something different, as applied to predicate expressions, from 'being true of the same objects'. Unlike 'analytic', 'means the same' is not a philosophical term of art; it is the property of common speech. If therefore Quine's views oblige us to say there is no distinction between 'means the same' and 'does not mean the same', which distinction is needed to make sense of the *difference* between ' "Bachelor" means the same as "unmarried man" but "creature with a heart" does not mean the same as "creature with kidneys",' then we are in a paradoxical situation. Not only would we have to give up the notion of predicate synonymy, but of sentence-synonymy too, one of the consequences of which would be that we could not translate between languages.[35]

Worse, if talk of synonymy is meaningless, talk of sentence-meaning is also meaningless, for if it makes sense to talk of sentence-meaning we can ask of any sentence 'what does it mean?', which would allow a characterization of sentence-synonymy of this sort: two sentences are synonymous if and only if any true answer to the question 'what does it mean?', when asked in connection with one of the sentences, is a true answer to the same question asked of the other sentence. Grice and Strawson therefore remark: 'If we are to give up the notion of sentence-synonymy as senseless, we must give up the notion of sentence-significance (of a sentence having meaning) as senseless too. But then perhaps we might as well give up the notion of sense.'[36]

What they pinpoint as going wrong in Quine's argument is that, instead of explaining the use made of the notion of 'meaning the same', he has measured it according to certain standards and found it wanting. Grice and Strawson regard this as a 'typical example' of how philosophers fall into paradox.[37] Quine appears to be seeking some standard of clarifiability which, if we attained it, would entitle us to claim that we have made 'satisfactory sense' of the notion under inspection; and he argues that analyticity is not clarified to standard. Grice's and Strawson's response is to say that the standard Quine seeks is inappropriate.

The clarifiability requirements Quine lays down are that, first, an explanation of analyticity must be provided which must not trade upon any concept in the cluster to which the concepts of analyticity and synonymy belong – some of the other concepts being that of definition and of what counts as logically impossible, self-contradictory, and necessary. And secondly, it must specify some common feature in all cases in which 'analytic' is applied so that we can give an account of the form 'a statement is analytic if and only if . . .'[38] It would seem, in short, that Quine desires a strict definition. And what makes matters more difficult is that, in addition to requiring a strict definition, Quine takes failure in providing one to entail that the notion has no satisfactory sense.

It is pertinent to remark in reply that, first, it is unreasonable to assume that a necessary condition of some notion's *having* sense is that we must *make* sense of it along Quine's lines; and secondly, that sense, employing other and less formal means, can indeed be made of a notion from the analyticity cluster. Consider, for example, the notion of logical impossibility. Suppose we are explaining this notion to someone, and choose to do so by displaying the contrast between natural impossibility and logical impossibility, using in particular the notions of the logical impossibility of a three-year-old child's being an adult, and the natural impossibility of a three-year-old child's understanding Russell's Theory of Types. Imagine that Y says, 'my three-year-old child is an adult', and that X says, 'my three-year-old understands the Theory of Types'. Now, one might construe X's remark as inspired by parental fondness and partiality; one answers, 'You mean your child is very bright'. If X insists that the child understands Russell's theory, one might then say, 'That's impossible; I don't believe you'. The child is brought in, expounds the theory, and criticizes it; what X said has turned out to be true. Natural impossibilities admit of counter-instances against the odds, however hard to credit; natural impossibilities are not logical impossibilities. In the parallel case of Y's claim, however, nothing whatever could *make* it turn out that Y was right; unless he is using 'adult' in a figurative or jocular sense, what he says *has* no sense – he is not using the word correctly. The matter can be summarized by saying that the appropriate responses to X's and Y's claims are, respectively, disbelief and literal incomprehension.[39]

This is one kind of informal explanation by means of which someone could be given a grasp of 'logically impossible'. It is *one* kind of explanation because other kinds of explanation might be needed for other concepts in the cluster; and it is an *informal* explanation in the obvious sense that it does not amount to a formal specification of necessary and sufficient conditions for the concept's application, of the sort 'a statement is—if and only if . . .', where in this case the first blank is filled by 'analytic'.

This species of explanation does however satisfy Quine's other requirement, in that it breaks out of the cluster of concepts and makes appeal to none of them.[40] That it does so is not to concede, except irenically, that this requirement is one which must invariably be met; Grice and Strawson point out that for many significant concepts, such as those in the cluster 'morally wrong', 'blameworthy', 'breach of moral rules', or in the cluster 'true', 'false', 'statement', 'fact', 'denial', 'assertion', it is not only that these are all intelligible and usable concepts despite not being formally defined, but that grasping any of them is something we standardly do just in terms of the other concepts in their cluster, which means that such a means of grasping a concept is acceptable and sufficient. The point is often enough made that not all circular explanations are vicious, and that some can be highly informative.[41]

Quine's response to Carnap's effort at a formal solution invites comment. One of Quine's most characteristic doctrines is that 'canonical paraphrase' – which is to say, translation of ordinary discourse into the clearer idioms of logic – makes for a better way of dealing with the philosophical questions posed by various ontological considerations and the nature of reference (see chapter 4 below).[42] Accordingly, it is odd that he should have little sympathy with formal attempts to clarify analyticity, dismissing them as he does by means of the bootstrap analogy.[43] One might challenge him on this, on the ground that treatment of analyticity in formal languages is not designed to explain the concept for natural languages, but to improve what pre-canonical understanding we have of it. Given an intuitive grasp of the notion in ordinary usage, of the kind pointed out by Grice and Strawson, consideration of borderline cases gives rise to interest in a sharper characterization of the notion in a context where rules can be provided explicitly to reduce vague areas of application. Quine argued that 'analytic-for-L_0' tells us nothing about 'analytic'; but this is mistaken, for on these lines 'analytic-for-L_0' is telling us *something* about 'analytic', or is showing in what way an analogy holds between analyticity-in-L_0 and L_0, on the one hand, and analyticity and natural language on the other hand. Moreover, the more closely L_0 models natural language, the more useful will be its specified feature of analyticity in throwing light on the analogous feature in natural language.[44]

'Analytic' Again

Where these reports of Quine's views and Grice's and Strawson's reply leave us is with the original problem of what analyticity is, which has not yet been explained but only defended against charges of being spurious or illusory. Grice and Strawson were concerned to show in a general way, against Quine, that the notion has content and that there are more ways of giving an account of it than he allows. They do not go much beyond gesturing at what a satisfactory account of it would be like.

From the sketches of analyticity given earlier, and from the targets Quine attacks, it is evident that among the options for an account of analyticity are these: that in some broad sense, an analytic statement is one which, if true, is true in virtue of meaning alone, or – if this is different – that it is in effect a tautology whose predicate does no more than iterate the subject or part of what is implicated in the subject, so that denying an analytically true statement is contradictory; or – if this is different from both or either of the foregoing – that it is a matter of linguistic conventions that certain statements are true if true, which statements are to be characterized as 'analytic'; or finally – and yet again leaving it open whether this is different from any or all of the foregoing – that a statement counts as analytic if it is, or can be reduced to, a logical truth.[45] Quine dismissed the first of these possibilities outright because it trades upon meanings; Grice and Strawson reassert it by saying that where there is established use there is meaning. The second possibility is to be found in Leibniz and Kant, and it immediately suggests an intimate connection between analyticity and necessity. The third, a conventionalist view, is one also often associated with talk of necessity, and it is at least as old as Hobbes. The last is Frege's view and the view of most logicians since. It is also the one which prompts most immediate interest, owing at very least to the fact that Quine himself allows that it yields a sense of 'analytic' impeachable only on the grounds of otiosity.

Grice and Strawson reassert the first option by saying that established use is a sufficient basis for meaning. This suggests a rebuttal of Quine constructed from a consideration he himself offers. One of his reasons for denying that we can make sense of synonymy, as the notion on which analyticity turns, is that efforts to explain it in terms of the *definition* of putatively synonymous expressions turn merely on how speakers view the relation of meaning between those expressions. Recall his remark about lexicographers as empirical scientists who find, implicit in standard usage before they compile their dictionaries, that speakers take a relation of synonymy to hold between certain terms, upon which they therefore report; and that definition is no more than this. Quine seems to regard this as reason for thinking that we have no good notion of synonymity. But on any theory which recognizes that the meaning of expressions in a language is determined by its speakers' uses and agreements, the fact that speakers standardly regard two expressions as meaning the same *ipso facto* makes them mean the same; that, indeed, can be the only ground on which, in the end, relations of synonymy – or of heteronymy – can rest. If the key concept of synonymity is thus available, so is analyticity.[46]

The last option mentioned above, described as Frege's view and the view of most logicians since, prompts interest because, as remarked, Quine himself allows that it constitutes a form of analyticity. Recall that Quine worked from a characterization of analytic statements that has them falling into two classes, one consisting of logically true statements such as 'no unmarried man is married', the other of non-tautologous statements such as 'all bodies are extended'. His attack is reserved for the second class; of the first class he says that, because its members are true or false just in virtue of the logical particles that occur in them, it is unexceptionable. His point then was that none of definition, synonymy, or rules could do the trick of transforming statements of the second class into statements of the first class, so that it is illusory to think that they possess the property, analyticity, whose possession distinguishes them from some other kind of statements (*viz.*, synthetic ones). The only cavil Quine has is that to call statements of the first class analytic is redundant, because uninformative; for we already have a perfectly good label for them – *viz.*, 'logically true'.

If, however, Grice and Strawson are right about the acceptability of talk of 'sameness of meaning', and therefore of talk of meaning, then *contra* Quine we have the prospect of rescuing analyticity by being able to transform what we customarily take to be such statements into logical truths via synonyms, which, if right, will settle the issue once for all.[47] We would in this case have a means of testing for analyticity in cases of non-tautologous analytic statements (more strictly, non-*obviously*-tautologous, where the tautologicality of logical truths is thought of in Wittgenstein's sense), by applying the transformation apparatus derived, thus eliminating the 'non-obvious' qualification. The chief requirement here is that the notion of meaning – granting that meanings are not entities – can be made sufficiently precise to be of use here;[48] but it is not obvious in advance that meaning, or more narrowly circumscribed talk of definitions, or of the conventions governing the use of expressions in a language, will always be too imprecise to allow for a characterization of analyticity in these terms. If anything, this tack has certain advantages, for it leads directly to a link with another in the crucial family of notions, *viz.*, necessity. For, to deny a logical truth, into which we may find all analytic truths turning, is to contradict oneself; and on at least one good construal of necessity, statements are necessary just in case denying them has this consequence. On such a view the classes of necessary and analytic truths may turn out to be coextensive.

Optimism at this juncture is however premature; for the idea that analyticity could be shown to reduce to logical truth depends upon whether there is a well-understood notion of 'logical truth' available. Unhappily, there is not. Quine defined logical truth in terms of the logical particles, understood as those words which have application in any context whatever – 'topic-neutral' words as Ryle called them. But what determines which words are the logical particles? The notion of topic-neutrality is unsatisfactory, for no word is utterly free of dependence on context; even 'if' and 'all' are so, given that the former is applicable only when possibilities are at issue, and the latter only when we are talking of a class of items taken in sum. If 'if' and 'all' are taken to be logical particles nevertheless, there appears to be no reason why 'when', 'above', 'thought', 'body', or any other term, should not likewise be a logical particle.[49]

One way out might be to explain topic-neutrality in terms of 'implicit definition'; whereas 'when' or 'above' require some kind of ostensive definition, 'if' and 'all' can be introduced by showing how they are used.[50] But it is not clear whether this helps, for any word could be implicitly defined by showing how it is used, given a rich enough vocabulary; and given a poor enough one, not even 'if' and 'all' could be so defined.[51]

Making connections between analyticity and necessity is itself far from uncontroversial. Saying this repeats a point made earlier about this family of notions; whereas certain *differences* between its members are reasonably perspicuous – we recognize that analyticity is a semantic notion, necessity a metaphysical notion, and a prioricity an epistemological one – the *connections* are much harder to clarify, because what connections we recognize as holding between them is precisely relative to what philosophical theory we accept in advance. The significance of this observation becomes clearer in due course.

It might be supposed, on the evidence of some of the foregoing, that talk of analyticity will yield little progress in isolation from talk of necessity. But there are no guarantees in advance that necessary truths will be thought of either as logical truths or (if these are different) analytic truths merely; indeed, turning now to the question of necessity, it appears that there may be reasons for holding apart the notions of necessity, analyticity, and logical truth.

The Notion of Necessity

In Leibniz's distinction between necessary and contingent truths the former are said to be such that denials of them are contradictions, whereas denials of the latter are not contradictions. Another way of putting this – and one that illustrates the interdefinability of necessity and possibility – is to say that the denial of a necessary truth yields an impossibility, whereas the denial of a contingent truth is as possible as its affirmation. But these remarks are too general; we need to add to them to get a more precise understanding of necessity.

A sketch of the sort we so far have aids recognition of the following as necessary truths:

(1) $7 + 5 = 12$
and
(2) If all humans are featherless and Aristotle is human, then Aristotle is featherless,

and of the following as contingent truths –

(3) There are nine planets in the solar system, and
(4) Aristotle was born in Macedonia.

Still, all we have succeeded in doing is to show, by means of an intuitive grasp of the difference in character between denials of (1) and (2) as against denials of (3) and (4), that we have prima facie reasons for distinguishing between them. What the distinction turns on is still imprecise. The reason for this is that to say '(1) and (2) are necessary because their denials are impossible or contradictory' is to appeal to notions – the notions of impossibility and contradiction – which are as complex as that of necessity itself.

A hint about how to proceed is afforded by the Grice–Strawson considerations in the preceding sections. Without trying to give an independent specification of one of this group of concepts in terms of which the others can be defined, we can draw a line around the area of application of these concepts by showing what work they do, and with what concepts they are not to be confounded.[52] More examples will help fix the first of these desiderata. Thus, it appears to be evident that such truths of arithmetic and logic as (1) and (2) are necessary, but that necessity is a wider notion than this, for 'Aristotle is not shorter than himself', 'no number is a mammal' and 'everything coloured is extended' are examples of necessary truths which are neither mathematical truths nor, as they stand, logical truths, in at very least the sense in which truths of first-order logic are logical truths. Perhaps therefore one should keep 'necessary truth' and 'logical truth' distinct to show that there are truths of the required stamp outside formal calculi.

Necessity, further, is narrower than merely 'natural necessity' (or 'causal necessity'). A donkey cannot run faster than a jet can fly; and a goldfish cannot swim the Atlantic in less than an hour; we say it is 'impossible' for donkeys and goldfish to perform feats of such athleticism, but we do not mean that it is logically impossible that these facts of nature should be other than they are, or that it is contradictory to deny them.

This prompts the thought that what distinguishes necessity from merely natural necessity is that whereas we might be obliged, on being confronted with, say, prodigious donkeys, to give up our belief that it is impossible for donkeys to gallop at speeds of Mach 2, we cannot give up necessary truths proper. Thus unrevisibility might be a focal characteristic of necessary truths, or even defining of them.

The thought that there might be wholly unrevisable truths has been resisted by Quine among others.[53] On Quine's view, our beliefs form a web or system impinging only at its periphery on the world of experience, rather like an inverted bowl resting on its lip. Generally speaking, recalcitrant experiences at the periphery do not make us give up or change the beliefs deeper in the system, but this is not to say that any one such belief is wholly immune to revision; we may, if there are compelling reasons to do so, go so far as to give up logical laws. 'Revision', Quine once pointed out, 'even of the logical law of excluded middle has been proposed as a means of simplifying quantum mechanics';[54] so there is in principle no reason why any belief or law of logic should not be revised if required. Accordingly, if unrevisability is a focal characteristic of necessary truths, then there are no necessary truths, a result which Quine regards with imperturbability.

Quine's views, in turn, have been resisted by champions of the notion of necessity like Plantinga, in whose view it is not the case that to say a truth is necessary is to say it will never be given up, for the reverse reason that there can be propositions which one might never give up (such as, say, the proposition that 'Willard is an exceedingly fine fellow') no matter how strong the countervailing evidence, which none the less does not mean 'Willard is an exceedingly fine fellow' is necessarily true.[55] Accordingly, on Plantinga's view, necessity is neither to be defined in terms of unrevisability nor conflated with it. It may still be that necessary truths generally display the characteristics of unrevisability, without unrevisability being defining of necessity; thus the rider, that if for some reason a necessary truth does have to be dropped it is no less necessary for all that, blocks any attempt to identify necessity with unrevisability.[56]

The idea of unrevisability carries with it certain tangentially allied notions which might seem to be characteristic of necessary truths, this time concerning the question of how they are known. These are the epistemological notions of self-evidence and a prioricity. If one asked, concerning some such necessary truth as (2) or of any instance of *modus ponens* $[(p \rightarrow q) \cdot p] \rightarrow q$, how one knew it to be true, the answer might be that it is just self-evident, we just *see* that it is true. But this will not do, for in order to see, for example that $z = (a \times 10^3) + (b \times 10^2) + (c \times 10) + d$ is necessarily true, one has to know some mathematics; specifically, that this is an example of the general way of representing integers using a positional notation in a decimal system, which relatively few people know and therefore relatively few people find self-evident. An easier example would be that the arithmetical proposition '1233 + 4041 = 5274' is necessarily true, but not self-evident; one has to work the calculation to see that it is true. Neither is it uncontroversial to say that these truths may be arrived at by a chain of self-evident steps from immediately self-evident propositions, for, say, if Goldbach's Conjecture is true it is necessarily true despite the fact that it is not self-evidently true (it is not known whether it is true or false). In fact there are quite a number of necessary truths which are not self-evident – an example might be 'Kant could not have been a canary' – so that defining necessary truths as self-evident, or self-evidently derivable from self-evident truths, will not on the face of it do.

If necessary truths are not the same thing as self-evident truths, are they a priori truths? What this must at least mean is that if they are a priori then they are knowable independently of empirical investigation. Both Leibniz and Kant, as remarked, held that necessary truths are so known. Perhaps the question ought only to arise in connection with *known* necessary truths, for in the case of, say, Goldbach's Conjecture, we have a necessary truth or falsehood without its being known which, and so a fortiori without its being known a priori.[57] Restricting attention to known necessary truths, then, the question whether they are known a priori becomes either: is every necessary truth known a priori to everyone who knows it; or, is every necessary truth a truth knowable a priori to at least someone? The answer to the first of these alternatives is that anyone might come to know a necessary truth a posteriori, by the simple expedient of learning it second-hand from some source or other. Thus someone might come to learn that twelve is a composite number by being told or by looking it up in a book, having never given the matter any thought beforehand. Experience, of a sort, has played a role here.

The second question is not so easy to answer. It asks whether necessary truths are truths which are in principle knowable a priori. This is not the same thing as saying that a truth is necessary if and only if someone or other knows it a priori; it is by contrast to say that any known necessary truth would not be necessary unless it *could* be known a priori – the distinction here arising from the fact, already noted, that there might be unknown necessary truths. One way of finding out if necessary truths must be knowable a priori is to ask the reverse question, whether any necessary truths are discoverable only a posteriori, that is, *only* on the basis of empirical investigation. (This is not the same as the case in the preceding paragraph where a necessary truth was discovered on the basis of investigation; here the question is whether there are necessary truths which could *only* have been so discovered.) It would appear difficult to think offhand of a necessary truth that could fit this bill, but there are indeed some candidates, offered by Kripke, which will be discussed in due course.

For the present it suffices to take yet another tack, and to ask whether any *contingent* truths can be known a priori, for to say that necessary truths are to be identified with truths knowable only a priori would fail if it could be shown that certain contingent truths could be so known. According to Plantinga, there are indeed contingent truths knowable a priori. He argues that some such statement as 'I believe that $7 + 5 = 12$' is a contingent fact about one of my beliefs, which however I do not have to conduct an empirical investigation to find out I hold; therefore I know a contingent fact a priori, and because this is so, the a priori cannot be defining of necessity.[58]

De dicto and *De re*

So far necessary truths have been characterized by a few examples and by some thoughts suggesting that they are not the same thing as logical truths, being wider than these, nor natural necessities, being narrower than these; nor yet that they are unrevisable or self-evident propositions, or propositions known a priori.

The conception of necessity being picked out in these largely negative ways is a conception of necessity as a property attaching to propositions. Necessity in this sense has been called necessity *de dicto* (*dictum* = 'proposition' and *de dicto* = 'about a proposition'), and what this means is that there is a property – called a *modal* property – in this case the property of *being necessarily true* (or *false*) – which we are predicating of propositions. The proposition 'Necessarily Aristotle is not shorter than himself' is an assertion of modality *de dicto*, which is to say is a proposition predicating upon the proposition 'Aristotle is not shorter than himself' the property of being necessarily true.

The notion of *de dicto* necessity is invoked to allow a distinction, important in much traditional philosophy, and once again important in contemporary philosophy, between *de dicto* necessity and *de re* necessity. This latter is a notion of the essential or necessary possession of a property by an object; accordingly, a proposition in which it is predicated of an object that it possesses some or other property essentially or necessarily, is a proposition expressing *de re* modality. The example often used to make the *de dicto–de re* distinction clear is taken from Aquinas, where in the *Summa Contra Gentiles* he considers the problem whether freedom of will is consistent with the foreknowledge of God. Suppose at a time t_1 God sees Aristotle sitting at a later time t_2. Then, given the truth of the proposition 'what is seen to be sitting is necessarily sitting', it would appear that Aristotle could not do anything other than sit at t_2. Here the *de dicto–de re* distinction becomes of use, as Aquinas saw; for if 'what is seen to be sitting is necessarily sitting' is taken *de dicto*, that is as saying 'it is necessarily true that whatever is seen to be sitting is sitting', then it is true; but if it is taken *de re*, that is as saying 'whatever is seen to be sitting has the property of sitting necessarily or essentially', then it is false. An argument to the truth of determinism requires that this latter *de re* reading be true; accordingly, the thesis that determinism follows from God's foreknowledge is false.[59] The distinction between modality *de dicto* and modality *de re* can therefore be summarized as follows: A proposition expressing modality *de dicto* is one in which a modality is predicated of some other proposition, whereas a proposition expressing modality *de re* says that a property belongs necessarily or essentially to an object.

Needless to say, the notion of modality *de re* is controversial. It played an important role in Aristotle, whose view was that the properties possessed by an object fall into two classes: those that make it *what* it is, and those that tell us *how* it is but which do not make it what it is. The first kind of properties constitute the essence; 'the essence of each thing is that which it is said to be *per se*'.[60] The second are the accidental properties, those that are predicated of the thing *per accidens*. Thus it is essential to a man that he be a rational animal, but not that he be this or that particular height or have this or that hair colour.[61] If you 'remove' an essential property from something x, it ceases to be x and becomes either nothing or something y instead. On the other hand, any of x's accidental properties – since x has them contingently, non-essentially – can be removed or changed without x ceasing to be x.

The Aristotelian notion and its variants played a central role for philosophers up to and including Leibniz, who called the essence of an individual entity its 'complete individual concept' from which all of the entity's properties flow, making it possible for an omniscient mind to know everything about it by inference from its individual concept. The effect of this view is to make all of an entity's properties essential; indeed Leibniz held that it is only from the viewpoint of finite minds that a distinction between essential and accidental properties is apparent. Locke distinguished between *real* and *nominal* essences, the latter being the property or set of properties by means of which we recognize an item and which justifies, on any given occasion, our application of its conventional name. For example, gold is a malleable, heavy, yellow metal (these properties constituting its nominal essence), and it is in virtue of its having these properties that we recognize it as such and call it 'gold'.[62] Locke took the most plausible view of 'real essence' to be 'the real but unknown constitution of the insensible parts' of things, 'from which flow those sensible qualities which serve to distinguish them one from another', which latter qualities constitute the nominal essence.[63] This way of putting things seemed to make talk of essences, *qua* 'real' essences, superfluous in the end, for, in line with the increasingly phenomenalist character of empiricism after Berkeley, it was unnecessary (and indeed for many, like Berkeley himself, unjustified) to postulate the existence of occult entities lurking behind or beneath the sensible world, such as 'matter' or 'substance' or 'essence'. Accordingly, the notion of essence fell into disuse, and it is only in the context of the issues presently under discussion that it has revived.

Formalization and Essence

The renewed appeal to essence, together with the equally rich notions of possible worlds, possible objects, transworld individuals, and unactualized individuals – all of which are commented on shortly – arises from the contemporary effort to give an account of the modalities in rigorous terms. Briefly, formalizations of modal interference were constructed in the earlier part of this century,[64] using standard logical apparatus together with the operators $\Box$ and $\Diamond$ (sometimes written L and M), respectively standing for 'necessarily' or 'it is necessary that . . .' and 'possibly' or 'it is possible that . . .'. The operators are interdefinable: if $\Box$ is taken as primitive then $\Diamond$ is definable thus: $\Diamond p = df. \sim \Box \sim p$. Depending upon choice of axioms, one can get stronger and weaker systems of modal logic. The root system is M, which adds to the truth-functional tautologies the rules of *modus ponens* and necessitation, which latter is a rule to the effect that $\Box p$ is a thesis of M if p is; and it has as additional axioms the formulae $\Box(p \rightarrow q) \rightarrow (\Box p \rightarrow \Box q)$ and $\Box p \rightarrow p$. Adding axioms adds strength; but it also adds diversity, and for this reason a pressing need was felt for a semantic interpretation of modal calculi to settle the issues which the diversity of uninterpreted mechanisms raise.[65]

Early efforts in this direction, such as Carnap's,[66] made use of the obvious and suggestive idea owing to Leibniz, to the effect that the necessity of a necessary truth resides in the fact that it is not contingent upon how things happen to be, but upon its being and remaining true in this world and in any possible rearrangement of how things might have been in this or any world. More succinctly, a necessary truth is one which is true in all possible worlds. Carnap's move was to make use of a notion of maximally consistent sets of atomic sentences (such that if S is such a sentence then either it or its negation is a member of the set), which sets he called 'state descriptions'. Then what is meant by saying S is necessarily true is that S is true under every state description.

Similar notions were taken up and prosecuted vigorously in the following decades, notably by Kripke and Hintikka among others;[67] and a semantics for quantified modal logic was worked out using Leibniz's notion – and terminology – of possible worlds and possible objects.[68] The technical details are such as to provide fruitful extensions to the formalizations of other non-extensional logics such as epistemic, deontic, and tense logic. In its wake it brings the metaphysical baggage presently under discussion. With characteristic acuity, Quine early recognized the metaphysical implications of modal formalism, and contested it.[69]

Quine's objections focus precisely on the fact that quantified modal logic forces a commitment to what he calls 'Aristotelian essentialism' (the intention is pejorative), for these reasons. Modal contexts are, in Quine's terminology, 'referentially opaque'.[70] The statements (using Quine's original numbering)

(15) 9 is necessarily greater than 7
(24) the number of planets = 9

are both true, but it would be a mistaken use of substitutivity to exchange 'the number of planets' for '9' in (15) because the resulting statement

(18) the number of planets is necessarily greater than 7

is false; there could have been more or fewer planets – their actual number is a contingent matter. It is because modal contexts are referentially opaque that Quine finds them at best obscure and at worst wrongheaded, particularly as he thought it generally undesirable to quantify into opaque contexts; the move from (15) to

(30) (x) (x is necessarily greater than 7)

simply does not have a clear sense, unless it is thought that objects have necessary and contingent properties independently of our ways of specifying them – which is to say, have their properties essentially. For Quine such a commitment is unthinkable, because in his view something's being 'necessarily' this or that way is not a trait it possesses in itself, but depends on the manner in which we refer to it,[71] a nominalist view similar to the one mentiond in Chapter 1 above. Consider the thing x purports to refer to in (30); by consulting (15) from which (30) was inferred, x would appear to refer to 9, which is the number of the planets – but this conflicts with the fact that (18) is false. The only way out seems to be essentialism; 'evidently,' says Quine, 'this reversion to Aristotelian essentialism is required if quantification into modal contexts is to be

insisted on',[72] from which he concludes 'so much the worse for quantified modal logic'.[73]

Despite the debate generated by these of Quine's objections, which
antedated the provision of possible-worlds semantics for modal logic by
a decade, the latter proceeded with success, establishing the possible-
worlds idiom – and on some views its concomitant essentialism – as the
chief way to understand the modalities and much besides.[74] Essentialism,
together with certain other metaphysical commitments prompted by
interest in the modalities, provides one way of evaluating the notion of
possible worlds; for talk of possible worlds might be objectionable if
these metaphysical offerings are so.[75]

It is at this point that a detour through talk of possible worlds, and its
implications, needs to be taken, if we are to see whether (and if so, how)
the notion of possible worlds helps us to understand necessity.

Possible Worlds

A well-known possibilist *credo*, owing to Lewis, runs like this: 'I believe
that there are possible worlds other than the one we happen to inhabit.
If an argument is wanted, it is this. It is uncontroversially true that things
might be otherwise than they are. I believe, and so do you, that things
could have been different in countless ways. But what does this mean?
Ordinary language permits the paraphrase: there are many ways things
could have been besides the way they are. On the face of it this is an
existential quantification. It says that there exist many entities of a certain
description, to wit "ways things could have been". I believe that things
could have been different in countless ways; I believe permissible
paraphrases of what I believe; taking the paraphrase at face value, I
therefore believe in the existence of entities that might be called "ways
things could have been". I prefer to call them "possible worlds".'[76]

The doubts implicitly raised at the end of the last section about the
acceptability of talk about possible worlds might be expressed as two
objections. One is that in giving an interpretation of a formal system one
is free to choose the interpretative domains and their constituent objects
in different ways, consonant with informativeness and consistency; and
therefore a logic with the operators $\square$ and $\lozenge$ need not turn on the notion
of 'possible worlds' at all. The other thing is that the very idea of possible
worlds, together with their attendant baggage of (on some views)

possible objects, essences, and the rest, conflicts with our common-sense ontology. There is a more or less cavalier rejoinder to this second objection; namely, that our everyday ontology is altogether too rude to be of service in working out a thorough account of the notions in play. For all that it is cavalier, this rejoinder is forceful.[77] The first objection requires a more studied reply.

The formalization of modal inferences starts from the fact that in our ordinary discourse we employ the concepts of necessity and possibility, and much of our reasoning involves them. Any interpretation of calculi employing the notions represented by $\Box$ and $\Diamond$ must somehow, if they are indeed to be formalizations of *modal* inference, preserve the senses in which $\Box$ says something about what is the case no matter what else, and $\Diamond$ says something about what can be the case depending on these or those circumstances. By using the notion of possible worlds we succinctly capture these ideas; we can give tight definitions of necessity and possibility without destroying their pre-theoretical flavour, and in terms of the resulting calculus can map the logical relationships obtaining between modalized propositions. The test then is to see whether in addition to these virtues, the appeal to possible worlds is fruitful and suggestive in application to further problems. And, indeed, so it is claimed to be.

For example, it is notorious that standard extensional logic cannot adequately deal with counterfactual conditionals, conditionals of the form 'if such and such *were* or *had been* the case, this and that (respectively) *would be* or *would have been* the case'. The antecedent suggests a 'contrary to fact', hence 'counterfactual', state of affairs, and the consequent says or claims how things would have been accordingly different. The problem is that conditional sentences, those of 'if . . . then . . .' form, express propositions which are functions of their constituent propositions, but which – when the main verb of the conditional sentence is in the subjunctive mood ('if . . . *were* or *had been* . . . then . . .') – are not *truth-functions* of their constituent propositions. How is one to deal with them? The problem has more than one aspect; there is the matter of giving an account of the formal properties of conditionals in general, and there is the matter of solving the difficulty which arises from the fact that even when we have a formal specification of conditionality together with all the facts relevant to a given counterfactual conditional, we might still not be in a position to determine its truth-value. The idiom of possible-worlds is proposed as a solution.[78] The idea is to construe a counterfactual as stating that in some possible state of affairs in which things are *that* way – understood as other than the way they actually are or have actually turned out – some other thing or things are *this* way.[79] A possible state of affairs is just a possible world.

This approach is inviting because it captures the sense in which we commonly think how things might be or might have gone if . . . or will be if . . . In particular connection with problems in the philosophy of science, such as the nature of scientific laws and the need to secure an adequate account of causation, possible-worlds analysis of counterfactuals is richly suggestive.[80]

Another problem, or collection of problems, for which talk of possible worlds holds promise concerns giving of an adequate account of such intensional items as meanings, properties, relations and propositions. (The question of one component of theory of meaning – *viz.*, theory of reference – in which talk of possible worlds offers advances will be canvassed in chapter 7 below.) The idea in general is that meaning can be understood by way of an enriched grasp of the extensions of singular and predicate expressions, enriched in the sense that they are taken to range not only over actual objects or n-tuples of them, but also objects in worlds other than the actual world. Employing this technique, a set-theoretical account of the meaning of a language's constituents can be given by saying that the meaning of a singular term is a function from possible worlds to objects, the meaning of a predicate is a function from worlds to ordered n-tuples of objects, and the meaning of (declarative) sentences is a function from worlds to truth-values.

Something of the same technique can be applied to *properties* and *relations*. A property can be defined as a function from worlds to sets of objects, and a relation likewise as a function from worlds to ordered n-tuples of objects. A neat circle is completed by construing *propositions* as functions from worlds to truth-values; for on this account it turns out that a proposition is the meaning of a declarative sentence, *vide* the discussion in chapter 2 above; and because, like the other two classes of abstract objects, propositions are identified with set-theoretical entities, no difficulty arises over their identity conditions.

These last thoughts make it notable that the concept of possible worlds offers to solve some of the problems that appear most intractable from an extensionalist point of view. Quine's early hostility to such intensional notions as meaning and necessity sprang precisely from a desire to operate strictly extensionally; the result was difficulty over this family of notions. The idiom of possible worlds offers progress with respect to them.

Objections to Possible Worlds: Identity and Transworld Identity

But talk of possible worlds invites a number of difficulties. There is the problem about essentialism; there is a problem about possible but nonactual entities; and there is a problem related to these concerning the identity of individuals across worlds. Each is potentially vitiating with respect to the possible-worlds enterprise – or at any rate, compromises its usefulness. I consider them in reverse order.

The problem of *transworld identity* can be stated as follows. The possible-worlds theorist wishes to say that a tractable and fruitful way of dealing with the thought that, say, Aristotle might not have tutored Alexander the Great is to say 'there is some possible world in which Aristotle is not Alexander's tutor'. This introduces the idea of Aristotle's existing in more than one world; not only in the actual world, in which he was tutor to Alexander and a pupil of Plato and the son of a Court physician, but in a plurality of possible worlds in which he is variously only some, or only one, or perhaps none of these things, or in which he was all these and more. In the parlance of possible-worlds theory, Aristotle's existence in all these worlds makes him a 'transworld individual'. According to the theory, all individuals are transworld individuals, as it happens, because any individual might well have been what it, she, or he is or was *ceteris non paribus*.

The objection to this is that the idea of a transworld individual violates the principle of the indiscernibility of identicals.[81] This principle states that for any objects x and y, if they are identicial then all the properties belonging to one belong to the other and *vice versa*. If some object x is supposed to exist in more than one world, say in the two worlds W_n and W_m, then because W_n and W_m will be *different* worlds only if there is at least one respect in which matters are different in W_n from the way are in W_m – perhaps, let us say, that in W_n Aristotle has a beauty-spot on his cheek, but in W_m he is beauty-spotless – then at very least x-in-W_n will have a property (the conjunctive property of 'being x and Aristotle has a beauty-spot') which x-in-W_m fails to have (the cognate property for x-in-W_m is 'being x and Aristotle has no beauty-spot'). But if this is so, x-in-W_n and x-in-W_m are discernible, and hence not identical. There is, therefore, no way one can identify individuals across worlds: in consequence, either one rests content with a notion of 'worldbound individuals', which is to say individuals existing in only one world at a time, which threatens to reduce the interest of possible-worlds talk to vacuity, or, better, one gives up such talk altogether.[82]

Matters are in fact worse for possible-worlds theory than this argument at first suggests. For suppose, in the interests of argument, one concedes the notion of transworld identity; then one can show that it collapses into dilemma. Take two distinct objects x and y, which we grant retain their identities across worlds though suffering changes from one to the next, and a series of worlds $W_1 \ldots W_4$. Imagine that in W_1 x is a thing large, round, green and soft, and that y is a thing small, square, red and hard, and that these properties are determinate and exhaustive of the identifying properties x and y respectively possess. Further imagine that in moving from W_1 to W_2 x and y exchange their colours; that in moving from W_2 to W_3 they exchange their shapes . . . and so on, such that in W_4 x is both x and small, square, red and hard, which is what y was in W_1; and that y is both y and large, round, green and soft, which is what x was in W_1. Thus x-in-W_4 is indescernible from y-in-W_1, and therefore, according to the principle of indiscernibility, identical with it; yet *ex hypothesi* and adhering to the principle of the transitivity of identity, x-in-W_4 is not identical with y-in-W_1 but with x-in-W_1, which is now indescernible from y-in-W_4 . . . and so on. Thus dilemma.[83]

The only way out of this difficulty would seem to be to appeal to essences, and say that all entities have contingent properties C and essential properties E such that an entity x has C in some worlds but not in others, yet has E in every world in which it exists; and further, that if there is an entity z which has E in at least one possible world, z and x are identical. Then in the case of x and y just given, the properties they exchange while passing from one world to the next are C and not E properties, and it is in virtue of the preservation of their E properties that they preserve their identities across worlds.

But will this manoeuvre do? For presumably E properties are not universal properties, but are unique to their bearers because they constitute their bearers' essences, and the problem of how to specify them accordingly arises. What properties are essential to, say, Aristotle? Evidently 'being Plato's pupil' is not essential, for in other worlds he might have been Socrates' pupil, or pupil to no one. How about 'being the greatest philosopher of antiquity to hail from Macedonia'? But then in some worlds he might have hailed from Athens or Miletus, or not been a philosopher at all. And so on for all Aristotle's properties. In short, it appears no easy matter to settle which subset of Aristotle's properties are his E properties. If Aristotle's E properties cannot be picked out, how do we know that in moving from W_n to W_m we have not left one or more of the E properties behind, and with them Aristotle?[84]

The upshot of such considerations would seem to be that talk of possible worlds is either incoherent because the concept of transworld identity is incoherent, or at best is of limited value because we can only employ a notion of worldbound individuals. In view of the fact that such a notion leads to the seemingly counter-intuitive result that Aristotle can only be Aristotle if things could not have gone otherwise with him – that is, that all the properties he in fact possessed are essential to him – this entire way of talking would seem to be misguided.

Possible-worlds theorists counter these objections with some ingenuity. Lewis, for a salient example, has a theory designed specifically to steer a middle course between the problematic notions of transworld identity and worldbound individuals. It is called 'counterpart theory'.[85] The idea is that individuals are indeed worldbound; are, indeed, bound to the actual world; but have counterparts in other worlds, which resemble their actual-world counterparts 'more closely than do other things in their worlds', and in such a way that for anything x in the actual world W, its counterpart x-in-W_n just is what x-in-W would have been, had things been different in the way things are different as between W and W_n.[86] Using these notions, we can express the idea that Aristotle might not have tutored Alexander by saying that Aristotle has a counterpart in some world W_n which resembles him in all respects save that counterpart-Aristotle did not tutor counterpart-Alexander.

The most damaging criticisms of counterpart theory are offered by other possible-worlds theorists, notably Kripke and Plantinga.[87] Consider the case of counterfactuals: 'if Alexander had paid attention to Aristotle's tutoring, he might not have died from drink'. Aristotle might, we say, have felt personal regret (or, for that matter, relief) at not having been a more vigorous tutor in view of Alexander's early death due to excessive potation. On Kripke's view, we can make no sense of Aristotle's regret or relief; for the persons referred to in the counterfactual are not Aristotle and Alexander, but their counterparts. Plantinga's complaint is a variant of this; it is that counterpart theory does nothing to avoid the worldboundedness problem, for to make sense of the idea of something's being different or going otherwise for a given individual or entity x, we must be able to say that x's being F in one dispensation of things W_n, and being G in some other dispensation W_m, is such that in W_n the properties F and x's-being-self-identical are co-exemplified, and in W_m the properties G and x's-being-self-identical are co-exemplified. If however we say that x-in-W_n and x-in-W_m are counterparts, then we have failed to account for our intuitions to the effect that x might have been G rather than F. To say, in other words, that Aristotle might not have tutored Alexander is to say that Aristotle might have been Aristotle yet not have tutored Alexander, which is surely what we want to say; but if Alexander's-tutor-Aristotle and not-Alexander's-tutor-Aristotle are mere counterparts of one another and not the self-same Aristotle, then we have lost the sense in which things might have gone differently for that one and the self-same man Aristotle.

The line preferred by possible-worlds theorists who reject counterpart theory is to tackle the question of identity directly, chiefly by providing an enriched characterization of the notion of identity itself. The key lies in the fact that the arguments sketched above threaten damage to identity across time as well as across worlds; for evidently the infant Aristotle and the aged Aristotle will have very few identifyingly manifest properties in common – infant Aristotle might, so to say, be small, pink, round and soft, and adult Aristotle large, brown, square and hard – while yet being the self-same Aristotle. In changing over time, an item loses some and gains other properties; and our insistence on regarding the item as self-identical throughout shows that the principle of identity we are working with is more complex than the objections suggest. Thus, the possession by an item of a property ought perhaps to be temporally indexed – x has F at a time t – and accordingly a statement of the principle of identity ought to carry a temporal quantifier, thus: for any objects x and y, if they are identical then for any property F and time t, x has F at t if and only if y has F at t. Then a statement of identity in worlds parlance would carry quantification over both worlds and times to yield: for any x and y, if x = y then for any W, F, and t, x has F and W at t iff y likewise.[88]

A summary solution to the difficulties posed by transworld identity is offered by Kripke. In his view it is a pseudo-problem, which arises from taking 'the metaphor of possible worlds much too seriously in some way. It is as if a "possible world" were like a foreign country, or distant planet way out there. It is as if we see dimly through a telescope various actors on this distant planet.'[89] Kripke rejects the metaphor. In doing so he thereby takes a position directly opposed to Lewis's style of possibilist realism.

Unactualized Possibilia

The foregoing discussion of identity marks a point in the debate on the matter, not a resolution of it. It is evident that possible-worlds theorists have, however, a reasonably robust account to give of themselves in that arena. Considerably more vexed an issue is the question of what further and more focal ontological commitments are demanded by the appeal to possible worlds; specifically, the question is: what sense can be made of talk about 'possibilia', that is, possible but non-actual worlds and the objects they contain?

There are, broadly speaking, two strategies which have been adopted by proponents of possible-worlds theories in this connection. One is an extreme possibilism of the kind favoured by Lewis; the other consists in a set of variant theories taking it that there is only one actual world, namely this world, and defining possible worlds and their contents in terms of one or more such intensional items as properties, propositions, or states of affairs, together with certain modal notions like 'instantiability' (a *de re* notion) or 'possible truth' (a *de dicto* notion) employed as primitives.

The problem is, simply, that the idea that *there are* such *non-existent* items as possible worlds and possible objects looks like a paradigm case of contradiction. The reply offered by Lewis is that there is only an appearance of contradiction here owing to the fact that assertions of existence are being taken univocally; to paraphrase 'there is something x which is nonactual' by means of the starkly contradictory formula $(\exists x) \sim (\exists y) (x = y)$ is to fail to capture the possibilist's intentions. One has to distinguish between an unrestricted form of the existential quantifier and a restricted form which indexes the existence-assertion to a particular world. Then to say that x is an unactualized possibilium is to say $(\exists x) (\exists^{\omega} y) (x = y)$, where $(\exists^{\omega}. . .)$ is a restricted quantifier asserting actuality in the world in which the utterance is made. The formula reads, 'there is something x which does not exist in W_n', W_n being understood as *this* world, the actual world, from which the legitimacy of saying x is existent but not actual follows.[90] The analogy is to time; present time is only one time among others, which we call 'present' because we inhabit it; inhabitants of other times use that same indexical expression to refer to their own presents.[91] The term 'actual' functions indexically as does 'present', such that use of it does not confer special ontological status on any world in which it is indexically used, but merely picks out which world it is in which the relevant utterance is issued.

Lewis is in earnest when asserting that possible worlds other than the actual world exist just as the actual world does. 'When I profess realism about possible worlds, I mean to be taken literally . . . Our actual world is only one among others. We call it alone actual not because it differs in kind from all the rest but because it is the world we inhabit.'[92] This, one notes in passing, explains why Lewis is committed to counterpart theory; for if all possible worlds are equally real, an individual can exist in one of them only, rather as a thing can only be in one place at a time.

Some of Lewis' critics claim to find these views unintelligible,[93] though in view of the fact that they have precedents – for example, in part in Meinong – and are consistent, they must at least be discussable.[94] Nevertheless most other possible worlds theorists are fastidious enough to shy away from what Haack, taking her cue from Quine, calls 'Lewis's ontological slum',[95] for the reason that there are, at least potentially, strategies available for handling these difficulties without resort to an overpopulated universe.

Briefly, the strategies in question turn, as noted, on admitting only one actual world – our own – and giving an account of possible worlds in terms of modal constructions from it. Any view of this general kind is called 'actualism'. One variant turns upon a distinction between existence and instantiation applied to such intensional items as states of affairs, relations and properties. Stalnaker, for example, argues that a possible world is to be identified with existent but uninstantiated properties, and that the actual world is the world whose properties are in fact instantiated.[96] Plantinga's views resemble this; possible worlds are obtainable states of affairs, the actual world is the world in which the constituent states of affairs actually obtain.[97] The notions of 'instantiability' and 'obtainability' are *de re* notions. There are important differences of detail between the two views, affecting among other things what account is to be given of properties, propositions, and states of affairs, all of which are closely related – for example, having the concept of some state of affairs, like that of Aristotle's being Alexander's tutor, is to know the corresponding proposition 'that Aristotle is Alexander's tutor'.[98]

The closeness of this connection gives rise to a third alternative view, owing to Adams who originated the label 'actualism'. In his view a possible world is a set S (a 'world-story') of propositions such that, both, for every proposition either it or its contradictory is a member of S, and it is possible for there to be a true conjunction of all members of S. The first condition is a 'maximalization' condition; the actual world is that maximal set of propositions the conjunction of whose members is in fact true. Adams' theory is a *de dicto* actualism because the modality invoked is a property of propositions; from which it is evident that the existence of propositions is not dependent upon their truth.[99] This view resembles Carnap's use of the notion of state descriptions.

Adams' theory faces two difficulties. Unless it contains a mechanism for resolving semantic paradoxes, such as the case of a proposition asserting of itself that it is false,[100] then because a possible world is a maximally consistent set of propositions, there can be no possible worlds.[101] The second difficulty arises from set-theoretical considerations and suggests that the notion of a maximal set of propositions is incoherent. The reason is that for any putatively maximal set S of propositions, its power set will have a greater cardinality than S. Each member of the power set will be a proposition and the set itself consistent, and the new set will have a greater cardinality than the old; the power set of their union, again, will have a greater cardinality . . . and so on.[102]

Existence and Actuality: Some Problems

There are yet further strategies for making out a difference between existence and actuality to allow for the coherence of possible-worlds discourse.[103] Diversity of opinion is frequently a good measure of the difficulty which giving a satisfactory account faces, and this case is exemplary. Apart from the problems that beset the detail of the various proposals, there are certain *general* cavils emphasized by opponents of the programme. Among them is the problem whether 'exists' is a predicate, that is, whether existence is a property, a question that arises prior to the question whether there can in some sense be some things having and other things lacking that property. (See chapter 4 below). On the face of it, common parlance suggests we do indeed employ the notion of existence in this way; but at the cost, as it turns out, of commitment to a Meinongian or at any rate quasi-Meinongian universe. Now, the reasons offered by possible-worlds theorists for dispensing with Ockham's Razor have to be very good ones; it may be that what is promised and delivered by possible-worlds discourse, in the way of dealing with a broad range of philosophical problems, itself constitutes such reasons; but on the whole one is inclined to think that the detail of specific proposals will have to carry the weight of persuasion to the effect that existence and actuality are properties, and moreover properties distinct from one another. Such a view seems at least highly questionable. Among the difficulties of the enterprise is that, as the foregoing sketches show, the concept of properties itself acquires content on the basis of possible-worlds talk, defined as functions from worlds to objects; accordingly it would be circular to explain possible worlds in terms of them (or, say, in terms of propositions) unless they are taken to be primitives or are given some independent specification.

The root difficulty with possibilia is that they are unintuitive in a quite serious way. Intuitively, there seem to be good reasons for understanding the concepts of existence and actuality univocally, as having the force of qualifying what there is, of stating what can be encountered in the universe. The idea of a possible item, one which might be encountered if things were this or that way different, certainly occurs in our discourse; but the question is whether it occurs as an idea of something that exists, so that we can comfortably grasp the idea that there is x, but that x is not actual, is not to be encountered in this world. Alternatively put, the question is whether the fact that we can grasp the idea that things might be otherwise or might have developed otherwise, commits us to believing that these alternatives, in order to be thinkable, must *be*. Put thus baldly, the claim that they must or do exist seems misguided. It might be argued this is appropriate as a response only to possibilist realism of less modest kinds, such as Lewis' theory. It is not so clear that the views of Plantinga, Stalnaker, and Adams are as unacceptable. Here, it could be argued, the ontological bullet one is asked to bite is not nearly so tooth-shattering; there is no quantification over nonactual objects, at least, and given a soundly drawn distinction between existence on the one hand and instantiation or obtainability on the other, possible worlds can be constructed out of actually existing items – or, alternatively, sense can be made of them by using the notions, surely not too exotic, of propositions and possible truth, as in Adams' view. Any plausibility will lie in these or cognate directions.

Whether this appearance of plausibility is more than appearance will depend, again, largely on details; but there are some thoughts about the general notion of nonactual items of which, to be adequate, detailed theories will need to give an account. These thoughts are not those offered by Quine, whose attack on possibilia is, predictably, that they lack identity criteria.[104] (He savages them by saying. 'Take the possible fat man in that doorway; and again, the possible bald man in that doorway. Are they the same possible man, or two possible men? How do we decide? . . . What sense can be found in talking of entities which cannot meaningfully be said to be identical with themselves and distinct from one another?'[105] Possibilists might reply that two possible objects are identical when their defining descriptions are equivalent; which is one way of saying, when they have all and only the same essential properties in common.) Rather, the thoughts are that, outside extreme realism, it might be correct to say that possibilia are essentially dependent on conception. Whereas we can talk meaningfully of the existence of thoughts of possibilia, we cannot (without being extreme realists) talk in the same way at least of the existence of the possibilities we think of;[106] and then difficulties arise, because in order for possibilia to be useful items, their dependence on thought must not be such that they have in fact to be conceived of by someone in order to exist, but that they be, generically, conceivable; for there are infinities of them, and they have to be objective in the sense that they are available to any conceptualizer, rather than being subjective to some particular conceptualizer at some particular time.[107] Thus a concept of objectivity is required which either satisfactorily denies, or accords with, the mind-dependence of possibilia, a concept which will form one of a perspicuously understood family of concepts including 'real', 'exists', and 'actual',[108] So far, thinking in this region is anarchic.

Essentialism

Throughout these discussions there has been talk of essences. Minimally, any thesis having it that there are such things is one that recognizes a twofold distinction between the properties possessed by some x, namely, a distinction between its essential properties and its accidental properties. The former are those properties x possesses necessarily, that is, which x could not lack; the latter are those properties x possesses contingently, that is, which x might equally well have or not, either way still being x. Some of the motives for commitment to essentialism of some form have been displayed in preceding sections. The question now is: is such commitment plausible?

Critics of essentialism aim to show that the notion of essence is either trivial (and therefore uninteresting), or unintelligible. On the first count, it is pointed out that, in giving examples, essentialists cite as paradigms such cases as that everything is essentially self-identical, and that everything is essentially not what it is not; but these cases, critics say, are philosophically uninteresting.[109] Other candidates for essential properties lose their triviality only at the expense of controversy. One way of sorting through these issues is as follows.

There are various formulations of essentialism, but most standardly have it that some subset of the properties of a thing x are essential to it, the rest being accidental. The essential properties might not be sufficient to pick out x from other individuals, but they are severally necessary for the task. It is this that gives rise to the appearance, at least, of difficulties over transworld identity; if an individual A exists in more than one possible world and differs only accidentally from world to world, how does one pick out A in any given world? The readiest solution is offered by Kripke; we stipulate that some world contains A with these and those accidental differences as against A in the actual world.[110] This manoeuvre explicitly presupposes a clear distinction between essence and accident, for what is not stipulative on this view are A's essential properties. This view in turn invites the rejoinder, discussed shortly, that what properties count as essential and accidental to A are in fact always stipulative; Quine's 'paradox of the mathematical cyclist' (see below) is intended to show that essence is always relative to interest, and does not lie out there in the world – which is to argue, in other words, that there are no *de re* necessities.

On the view that essential properties are a subset of x's properties, one way of discriminating between them and x's accidental properties is to say that x's essential properties in some sense 'make x the particular individual it is'. This is not at all a clear formulation as it stands, but it has similarities to Locke's suggestion, that essence is the underlay – perhaps, the structure or internal constitution – of x, which is such as to give rise to x's manifest nature. What do 'makes' and 'give rise to' mean in these formulations? An obvious suggestion is that they mean 'cause'. This creates difficulties; on certain plausible views, causal nexuses obtain between events, not between properties of objects and their being the objects they are. Nevertheless, it is intuitively clear that there is a determinate relation between x's having the essential properties it does and its being the thing it is; whether the relation is causal is open to argument.[111]

However such a notion is made out, it will evidently not do unless it admits of a restriction on what effects follow from or are given rise to by x having the essence it does. If there were no such restriction it would turn out that, say, Averroes' authorship of a commentary on Aristotle is a function in some sense of Aristotle's essence, and it is surely counterintuitive to claim that what Averroes wrote is a part of Aristotle's being who he was – which would be to say that Averroes having written this or that is a property of Aristotle. But what sort of restriction would do the trick? If appeal were made to just those features of x which engage our interest in x, then our specification of x's essential properties will be open to attack on conventionalist lines of Quine's kind (see below). If, alternatively, x's essential properties are taken to be those that are somehow crucial to x's being that individual x, then we are moving in an unexplanatory circle.

Such considerations make a roughly Aristotelian notion of essence a more attractive alternative.[112] Here one moves away from trying to explain what makes x the individual it is to what makes x the *kind* of thing it is. Thus, talk of essential properties is talk of those properties which make x a member of a kind K; if x is a man, then x's essential properties are those which make him a member of the kind *man*. Not only does this strategy avoid the difficulties encountered, it has certain apparent virtues in addition. For one thing, there is a short way of proving an important essentialist claim to the effect that if x is a K then x is necessarily a K. Provided one allows that 'x has all the properties of a K' entails 'x is a K', then if x is a K, the properties which make it a K are, by the Aristotelian notion stated, essential properties of x; therefore, it is necessary that x is a K.[113]

The Paradox of the Mathematical Cyclist

A problem arises at this juncture, however, concerning what are to count as the essential and what the accidental properties of some x. According to Quine, our decisions on this are always relative to our interests, a view known as 'conventionalism'. It is forcefully displayed in this passage: 'Mathematicians may conceivably be said to be necessarily rational and not necessarily two-legged, and cyclists necessarily two-legged and not necessarily rational. But what of an individual who counts among his eccentricities both mathematics and cycling? Is this concrete individual necessarily rational and contingently two-legged, or vice versa? Just in so far as we are talking referentially of the object, with no special bias towards a background grouping of mathematicians as against cyclists or vice versa, there is no semblance of sense in rating some of his attributes as necessary and others as contingent.'[114]

Commitment to essentialism, in other words, appears to result in paradox, for the reason that, relative to certain interests, certain properties will be essential, while, relative to others, they will be accidental; and so a given individual will be both essentially and accidentally so-and-so.

It has been pointed out that Quine's observations will not do as a refutation of essentialism, for the reason that ambiguity infects the sentences 'mathematicians are necessarily rational and not necessarily two-legged' and 'cyclists are necessarily two-legged and not necessarily rational'.[115] On a *de dicto* reading they assert that 'mathematicians are rational' and 'cyclists are two-legged' are necessary truths, whereas 'mathematicians are two-legged' and 'cyclists are rational' are not necessary truths. On a *de re* reading they assert that every mathematician is necessarily rational and not necessarily bipedal, and conversely for the cyclist. But there is no reason to suppose that the essentialist is committed to both propositions.[116]

Quine's concern is to prove the unintelligibility of the *de re* reading by presenting the dilemma we face if we take our classifications of things to be governed by anything other than our interests. Presented with a mathematical cyclist, how would we decide that he is necessarily or not necessarily rational? An essentialist reply appears to be available if one adheres to the idiom of kinds. On this view the relevant question is: 'what kind of thing is x'? Thus suppose x is a dog; then it is legitimate to ask 'what kind of thing is x?' to get the answer 'an animal', and 'what kind of animal?' to get the answer 'a dog'; but hereafter, for such questions as 'what kind of dog?' inviting answers like 'a vicious dog' or 'a large dog', the point is being missed: 'large dogs' and 'vicious dogs' do not denote kinds.[117] This restriction turns on a thesis about kinds having it that any x is of at least some one K, and if it is a K_1 as well, it is such only if K_1 comprehends or is comprehended by K.

There are, however, some uncomfortable cases for the Aristotelian notion as thus understood to avoid Quine's criticism. A good example is provided by the histories of bacteria. Bacteriologists use the immuno-logical properties of bacterial strains as criteria of identity for them; but bacteria undergo mutations, often very far-reaching, in response to antisera, and so belong to different groups of strains at different times. Essentialists are apt to deny either that the groups in question are kinds, or, if they are, that bacteria preserve their identity across groups; but neither strategy is of help to empirical scientists, who in this connection prefer to be conventionalists in order to make sense of the task in hand. Here essence is relative to interest, because kinds are relative to interest and essence depends on kinds.[118] In this case, further, the kinds to which bacteria belong at different times do not comprehend one another as the essentialist modification, in response to Quine, demands. The result appears to be that the essentialist claim, or at any rate this version of it, is of doubtful value.

Critics of essentialism arrive at this conclusion by insisting that impediments to understanding modalities *de re* arise from the fact that, as Quine's observations show, the modal status of a statement about a given object depends upon the choice of designation for the object in question. Thus '9 is greater than 7' is necessarily true, but 'the number of the planets is greater than 7' is not. A reply might be that the impediments are illusory. Consider cases where we can effect 'transparent' readings of opaque constructions, as when Philip believes that Cicero denounced Catiline but, because he does not know that Cicero is Tully, does not believe that Tully denounced Catiline. In such a case we perfectly well understand that there is a person, namely Cicero, of whom Philip believes it to be true that he denounced Catiline. Why then can we not understand the notion of 9's being essentially greater than 7? The necessary truth of '9 is greater than 7' says something about a property 9 necessarily possesses; and the fact that 'the number of planets is greater than 7' is contingent does nothing to alter our grasp of the independent fact about 9. Alternatively put, if the contingency attaching to the number of the planets somehow casts doubt on 9's being necessarily greater than 7, then how it does so is not clear. There is, after all, a perspicuous remedy at hand for the difficulty: the truths (and the relations between them) 'the number of planets is in fact 9; 9 is necessarily greater than 7; the number in fact of the planets is necessarily greater than 7' are all consistent with its being contingent that there are nine planets.

Essence, Origin and Structure

It is still unclear, however, how to specify which properties of a thing are essential and which accidental. Two suggestions for solving this difficulty are found in Kripke.[119] One is that the origin of an individual, or the material of which it is made, are essential to it; another is that the essence of a kind of individuals consists in the internal structure of individuals of that kind, such that membership of that kind essentially depends upon having the appropriate internal structure. Neither suggestion is uncontroversial.

Kripke's origin argument has it that if a given table is made of wood, then that table essentially originates from wood, even if it later turned into some other substance – say, silver.[120] Slote has offered a counter-argument to this.[121] Suppose that a table *t* came from a block of wood *w* which, before being made into t, had changed into a block of silver and then back again into wood 'steadily and lawfully' both ways. Then surely it is possible that *t* might have been made from *w* during its silver stage, and later, as *t*, have changed into wood. If so, then *t* only accidentally originates from wood, and in general it follows that at least some things might accidentally be of the material out of which they are in fact originally composed.

It seems more intuitive to argue the Kripkean point about origin for the case of persons. McGinn has offered an initially compelling argument on this head, which is that the necessity of personal origin arises from the fact that a person is necessarily identical with the zygote from which he grew, and that there is a necessary link between the zygote and the pair of gametes supplied by his parents.[122] On the first point, it is taken by McGinn to be evident that adults are identical with the children they used to be, children with infants, infants with foetuses, and these with zygotes. On the second point, the zygote cannot be identical with the pair of gametes since they are two and the zygote one, so McGinn appeals to intuition: consider a world in which McGinn comes from Napoleon's gametes, with its being the case that the actual gametes from which McGinn came are also present in that world. Which individual has the stronger title to be McGinn? He suggests the latter.[123]

The plausibility of this argument has been contested.[124] It happens that one's intuitions do not invariably run the way McGinn suggests they do;[125] and because this is so, it can further be shown – contrary to

McGinn's first point – that biological (or, more generally, scientifically-grounded) continuity does not always settle identity. The argument is as follows. Imagine, using Johnson's example, a world in which gametes develop into a person whose every stage of life is indistinguishable from the corresponding stages in Hitler's actual life; and suppose Hitler's gametes in that same world to develop indistinguishably from Napoleon's actual development.[126] Which has the greater title to be Hitler? Our intuitions suggest the former; which runs counter to McGinn's example despite having the same form.

These thoughts suggest that if there were two possible people, A and B, whose life histories were such that from birth to a time t A's history is indistinguishable from that of some third person C but differs thereafter, and B's history is different from C's history until t but indistinguishable thereafter, then it is not clear that only A, who has the right origin, has a title to be identical with C; for B can also plausibly be identified with C. Often used in this connection is Sprigge's example of Queen Elizabeth; suppose that C is Queen Elizabeth, and that A and B are two women. Then A and Queen Elizabeth have indistinguishable histories of birth and childhood to t, and B and Queen Elizabeth have indistinguishable histories thereafter. What makes it plausible to say that B has as much title as A to be Queen Elizabeth would be some such occurrence as constitutes the subject of Mark Twain's story *The Prince and the Pauper*.[127]

What is at issue here is whether a biological or scientifically-grounded claim is sufficient to uphold a claim about the necessity of origin; and the argument is that it is not.[128] Consider a related case: if A and B are in different worlds, they are both easily identified with Queen Elizabeth. This is because the worlds in question may reflect in their constitution quite different emphases on contextual features, a familiar way of (and reason for) discriminating between worlds. In such a case, Queen Elizabeth might quite well not develop from Queen Elizabeth's actual zygote, and if so would, literally, not be identical with it.[129]

The other suggestion made by Kripke concerns kinds. His view is that it is necessary that a thing has a certain internal structure if it does indeed have that structure; if cats are animals (have a certain internal structure which makes them animals) then any cat-like creature which fails to have the appropriate internal structure is not a cat.[130] Varying his choice of example, he says 'tigers . . . cannot be defined simply in terms of their appearance; it is possible that there should have been a different species with all the external appearances of tigers but which had a different internal structure and therefore was not the species of tigers'.[131]

Does the notion of internal structure as essence make sense? There are various difficulties. Suppose that internal structures are nested. Tigers are composed of a certain arrangement of internal organs and other physiological structures, which in turn have an internal structure of cells, which in turn have an internal structure of molecules . . . atoms . . . subatomic particles . . . and so on perhaps, to quanta of energy and beyond. Which level of internal structure is the level constituting the essence? Suppose two tigers have the same internal structure at all levels IS . . . IS_n (where IS = internal structure) but differ thereafter. Which is the tiger? It might be replied that any level of internal structure entails that all other levels are uniformly correspondent, so that specifying similarities at one level is sufficient; but if levels of structure are uniformly correspondent, then there is every reason to suppose that the correspondence runs up to and includes external structure, such that – a point Kripke denies – external structure (which is to say, appearance) is enough to settle that something is a thing of a certain kind. Moreover, if differences of internal structure mark differences of kind, then a counterintuitive result appears to follow, to the effect that each individual is its own kind. For, every individual is unique – this tiger has longer hairs on its left ear than that one – and such differences result from differences in internal structure. This unpalatable result can be blocked by saying that it is a logical sum of the internal properties which count, namely the sum of inclusive disjunction. However, this notion is one which Kripke contests for external appearance; yet here the appeal to a logical sum of properties arises in connection with internal structure, which is, epistemologically, a far less appetizing situation than relying upon a logical sum of appearances for kind differentiation.

Internal structure is invoked principally because it seems precise and unequivocal to give the essence of, say, gold or water by saying that all and only the stuff of atomic number 79 in any world is gold, and water is all and only the stuff of molecular structure H_2O in any world. At first blush elements and compounds like these may seem to require an alternative analysis, given their simplicity as against the complexity of biological kinds like tigers; but the same arguments – and criticisms – go through. H_2O is a molecular structure with an 'internal' structure of atoms which in turn have an internal structure . . . and so on. It is logically possible that internal structures be infinitely nested; because this is so, essentialists cannot say that *whatever* the internal structure something x may have (that is, even if we do not know what it is), it is a K in virtue of it – for if we could not in principle know what made x a K, we could not recognize some further thing y as a K owing to its having the same internal structure as x.[132] At one point Kripke indeed relies on this 'whatever it is' strategy for internal structures, which on this argument will not do.

These sketches show that the notion of essence is by no means perspicuous. If it is not clear what essences are, it cannot be clear how they are to be recognized. Like that other crucial ingredient of possible worlds discourse, namely, the concept of unactualized possibles, the concept of essence plays an important role, and to the extent that it is itself problematic, it casts doubt on the value of appeal to possible-worlds notions wherever these latter rely upon commitments to essentialism. This does not refute essentialism or certain kinds of possible-worlds talk outright; ingenuity might provide us with formulations of the relevant notions yet.

Necessity Again, Analyticity, and the A Priori

The foregoing sections constitute an excursus into talk of possible worlds, together with a number of the attendant consequences and commitments of such talk; the idea being that if necessary truth is to be explained as truth in all possible worlds, necessary falsehood as truth in none, and contingency as truth in at least one, then the concept of possible worlds itself demands scrutiny. The discussion shows that it is at very least controversial. In defence it is often argued that in so far as possible worlds are stipulative devices, to be construed as sets of sentences having such features as maximal consistency, no particular dangers are invited. Nevertheless it seems worth remarking that it is too easy, as the foregoing sketches show, to indulge talk of possibilia and essence without having a precise way of containing these notions; to this extent it is well to be wary about worlds, which are metaphysically seductive creatures. Kripke himself commented: 'the apparatus of possible worlds has (I hope) been very useful as far as the set-theoretical model-theory of modal logic is concerned, but has encouraged pseudo-problems and misleading pictures'.[133]

If one employs the idea of necessary truth as truth in all possible worlds, however, one is equipped with a useful *point de prise* for the family of notions – necessity, analyticity, and the a priori – at issue in this chapter. Moreover, certain rather interesting consequences appear to follow for the relations between them.

Necessity on this construal becomes the limiting case for truth; it is truth in all possible states and arrangements of the ways things can be. Thus, no matter how things are, 2 + 2 = 4 is necessarily true, and so is Goldbach's Conjecture if it is true. In Kripke's view, our grasp of the notion of necessity arises from our understanding answers to the question whether something might have been true or false. If something might have been false, then it is not necessary; if it is true, and if it is not possible that the world might have been otherwise in relevant respects, then it is necessarily true.[134] In a way this makes necessity a rather simple notion, echoing Quinton's view, representative of a certain tradition in this matter, that the distinction between necessary and contingent statements is a 'commonplace' one: 'A necessary truth is one that is true in itself, true, in Lewis' phrase, "no matter what", must be true and cannot be false. A contingent truth, as etymology suggests, is one that is true dependently on or because of something else, something outside itself. As depending on this something else it does not have to be true. The necessary and the contingent make an exclusive and exhaustive division of the realm of truths.'[135] Quinton's characterization, like Kripke's, echoes Leibniz's, a characterization also accepted – and without discussion – by Kant. A possible-worlds treatment of necessity thus characterized fits well with the informal intuitions it embodies. The community of agreement evident here appears extensive, and tolerant of variation in emphasis, seeming able to accommodate for example Swinburne's account of necessity as turning either on the idea that denials of necessary propositions are incoherent, or on the idea that necessity is non-contingency, with the notion of contingency being taken as antecedently well established.[136]

However, the consensus is superficial, for disagreements arise directly more detail is called for. Quinton argues that all necessary a priori truths are analytic in all four at once of the senses of 'analytic' noted above. On this view, the identification of necessity with analyticity arises from an argument for necessity's being conventional: 'a statement is a necessary truth because of the meaning of the words of which it is composed. The meaning that worlds have is assigned to them by convention. Therefore it is linguistic convention that makes a form of words express a necessary truth,' which ill accords with the idea that there are *de re* necessities, necessities 'objectively discoverable in the nature of things'.[137] Kripke's views are in agreement to the extent at least that, if only by stipulation, analytic truths can be regarded as truths which are both a priori and necessary: 'Let's just make the stipulation that an analytic statement is, in some sense, true by virtue of its meaning, and true in all possible worlds by virtue of its meaning'.[138] But not all necessary truths are a priori for Kripke; and this is where the big difference lies.

It had been crucial to Kant that there should be a class of synthetic a priori truths, but, on the conventionalist view shared by Quinton, because all necessary truths are analytic and only these can be known a priori, there can be no such class. Kripke's novel departure against conventionalism lies in his introduction of the startling idea that there can be necessary a posteriori truths, and even contingent a priori truths. This results from the application of his views to the problem of reference.[139]

It is essential to recall Kripke's observation that the notions of necessity, apriority, and analyticity (and their converses) are respectively metaphysical, epistemological, and semantic notions.[140] Accordingly, one may *discover* certain necessities, for example that Hesperus and Phosphorus are the same entity; thus, the identity statement 'Hesperus = Phosphorus' is a posteriori necessary because the entity referred to by the names 'Hesperus' and 'Phosphorus' is necessarily self-identical; the names themselves, given that they refer to that entity, are 'rigid designators' (which means, by Kripke's definition, that they refer to the same object in every possible world in which that object exists); and it is an empirical, that is, an a posteriori, discovery that Hesperus and Phosphorus are the same object.

Again, in Kripke's view there may be a priori contingent truths, such as that there is a certain stick S in Paris which is the standard for the metre.[141] If 'S is one metre long (at a time t)' fixes the reference of 'one metre', and is not an abbreviative or synonymous definition of 'one metre', then one knows that S is one metre long a priori; yet its being the case that S is one metre long is not a necessary but a contingent matter, for the stick selected as the standard unit of length might have been any length – it might easily have been longer or shorter by much or little.

The result of inspecting Kripke's line on these issues and contrasting them with Kant's views is instructive. For Kant, propositions divide into two classes, the analytic and the synthetic. All the former are necessary and a priori, some of the latter are known a priori, the rest a posteriori. Those synthetic truths known a priori are fundamental to Kant's philosophical theory. In virtue of being a priori, they are necessary, for all truths known a priori are necessary for Kant. Kripke has nothing to say about the synthetic a priori, which is not surprising owing to the fact that his concern is with a nonintensional theory of naming, in which names are not synonymous with descriptions, but have reference only (see chapter 7 below). Because analyticity and syntheticity are intensional notions, the question whether 'Hesperus is Phosphorus' is either analytic or synthetic, as well as being necessary and a posteriori, does not arise.

It follows from Kant's view that all a priori truths are necessary, but only some are analytic. Kripke simply stipulates that any statement which is both necessary and a priori is analytic, but because not all necessary truths are a priori, the question whether some of them are either analytic or synthetic does not, as just noted, arise. Thus whereas some synthetic truths will be necessary for Kant, there will be no categories of synthetic necessary and synthetic a priori truths for Kripke. Instead he has categories of a posteriori necessary and a priori contingent truths, neither of which Kant contemplates.

Kant, perhaps Kripke, and most people who thought about it, would agree that all contingent truths are synthetic and not vice versa, except for Kripke's special case of the contingent a priori where this classification does not arise. Almost everyone would be inclined to agree that any proposition which is a posteriori is synthetic, but, again, not vice versa; except, yet again, for the Kripkean case where the classification does not arise.

For Kant, all necessary truths are a priori; for Kripke the two classes do not always coincide, for he admits a class of a posteriori necessities. Finally, Kripke thinks there can be contingent a priori truths, which is a novel idea and would be denied by Kant; and at least many (mindful of Kripke's contingent a priori) would hold that contingent truths will be discoverable a posteriori, although not all a posteriori discoveries are discoveries of contingent truths if Kripke is right about a posteriori necessary truths. Whatever else all this shows, it shows that the original natural-seeming pairings among these sets of concepts is highly misleading.

Concluding Remark

Despite disagreements in theoretical approach, and despite the complexities just illustrated, at a certain level there is, as Grice and Strawson point out, a core of agreement about what is meant by 'analytic', 'a priori', 'necessary' and their opposites. These concepts figure in philosophical discussion as among some of the most important, by and large exploiting that consensus. Much of what has been discussed in this chapter is relevant to the discussion in chapter 7 below, and I shall there assume the apparatus of possible worlds, and Kripke's views on necessity, as presented here.

Notes

1 The a priori–a posteriori distinction is best discussed in the context of epistemological theories, which is why it is not given separate attention here.

2 G. W. Leibniz, *The Monadology*, §§ 31–2.

3 Ibid., § 33.

4 Cf. Ibid., n. 54, pp. 236–7.

5 Ibid., §§ 33–5.

6 D. Hume, *Enquiry Concerning Human Understanding* § IV, pt. 1.

7 D. Hume, *Treatise of Human Nature*, bk. I, § pt. III.

8 Ibid.

9 This way of putting things owes itself to Kant. Cf. *Critique of Pure Reason*, A7/B10–11; cf. B4.

10 Leibniz, *New Essays Concerning Human Understanding*, III. 3.

11 Leibniz, *Monadology*, § 34.

12 Leibniz, *New Essays*, IV. 9.

13 Kant, *Critique of Pure Reason*.

14 Ibid.

15 A. J. Ayer, *Language, Truth and Logic*, p. 78. and cf. chapter 4 passim.

16 Cf. chapter 7 below, where the verification theory is discussed at more length.

17 L. Wittgenstein, *Tractatus Logico-Philosophicus*.

18 W. V. Quine, 'Two Dogmas of Empiricism' in Quine, *From a Logical Point of View*, 2nd edn, Harvard, 1961, and often reprinted – as in H. Feigl et al. (eds), *New Readings in Philosophical Analysis*, pp. 81–94.

19 Cf. chapter 2 above.

20   Quine, 'Two Dogmas', p. 82.
21   Ibid.
22   Ibid., pp. 82–3.
23   Ibid., pp. 83–5.
24   Cf. chapter 2 above.
25   Quine, 'Two Dogmas', p. 80.
26   Ibid.
27   Ibid., pp. 86–7.
28   Ibid., p. 87.
29   R. Carnap *Meaning and Necessity*, Chicago, 1947, pp. 3–4.
30   Quine, ibid., pp. 87–8.
31   Ibid., p. 89.
32   H. P. Grice and P. F. Strawson, 'In Defense of a Dogma', *Philosophical Review*, 1956 pp. 41–58; reprinted in Feigl et al., *New Readings in Philosophical Analysis*, pp. 26–36, to which the following references are made.
33   Ibid., pp. 26–7.
34   Ibid., p. 27.
35   In fact, Quine believes that translation will in any case be indeterminate; for his thesis regarding the indeterminacy of translation cf. chapter 9 below.
36   Grice and Strawson, 'In Defense of a Dogma', p. 29.
37   It has to be pointed out that in the 1950s, under the influence variously of Wittgenstein and Austin, and in a way characteristic of that decade's briefly-flourishing school of 'Ordinary Language Philosophy', the sharpest needle in the philosophical work-basket was the 'look at the use' one (cf. chapter 7 below). Philosophical misunderstanding was thought to arise chiefly from failure to do so. Still, this does not invalidate Grice's and Strawson's point here: they are remarking that where there is agreed use for a notion, it is appropriate to take it that the notion has content – a sometimes controvertible point, as reflection on the notion of, say, witchcraft will show. But this does not affect the substance of the argument to follow.
38   Grice and Strawson, 'In Defense of a Dogma', p. 30.
39   Ibid., p. 31.
40   Ibid., p. 32.
41   Cf. B. Mates, 'Analytic Sentences', *Philosophical Review*, 1951, pp. 525–34; reprinted in Feigl et al., *New Readings in Philosophical Analysis*, pp. 47–52, to which the following references are made.
42   Cf. Quine, 'Two Dogmas of Empinicism', p. 87, where in an aside he talks of reversing the attempt to define 'analytic' in terms of 'cognitive synonymy', defining the latter in terms of the former instead – 'cognitive synonymy' is thus to be defined in terms of intersubstitutivity *salva analyticitate*.

43 Mates, 'Analytic Sentences', p. 40.

44 Cf. Quine, *Word and Object*, esp. ch. 2, passim.

45 Cf. Mates, ibid.

46 Cf. ibid., p. 42. Also see the papers by Carnap, and Quine's response, in Feigl et al., *New Readings in Philosophical Analysis*, where the issue of the artificial treatment of analyticity is discussed. Also cf. chapter 1 above where this kind of point was made about the use of formalities in philosophy.

47 Cf. A. M. Quinton, 'The A Priori and the Analytic', *Proceedings of the Aristotelian Society*, 64, 1963–4, p. 31 *et seq*. Reprinted in Strawson, *Philosophical Logic*; see p 126.

48 Cf. chapters 7 and 8 below, which are devoted to discussion of meaning.

49 R. G. Swinburne, 'Analyticity, Necessity, and Apriority', *Mind* 84, 1975, p. 226.

50 Cf. Quinton, 'The A Priori and the Analytic', p. 49.

51 Swinburne, 'Analyticity, Necessity, and Apriority', p. 227.

52 A useful guide is to be found in A. Plantinga, *The Nature of Necessity*, chs 1 and 2, pp. 2–6.

53 Quine, 'Two Dogmas', p. 93.

54 Ibid.

55 Plantinga, *The Nature of Necessity*, pp. 3–4.

56 Ibid., p. 4.

57 Cf. P. Kitch, 'Apriority and Necessity', *Australasian Journal of Philosophy* (58 no 2), June 1980, p. 89 *et seq*.

58 Plantinga, *The Nature of Necessity*, p. 8.

59 Ibid., pp. 0–11.

60 Aristotle, *Metaphysics*, Z 1029 b 14; cf. 1028 a 10–1032 a 11.

61 Cf. ibid., 1031 a 15 ff.

62 This kind of view is hotly contested by some contemporary reference theorists; cf. chapter 7 below.

63 J. Locke, *Essay Concerning Human Understanding*, III. 37.

64 Cf. e.g., C. I. Lewis and C. Langford, *Symbolic Logic*

65 If one adds to M the axiom $p \rightarrow \Box\Diamond p$ one gets the Brouwer system; if instead of this one adds $\Box p \rightarrow \Box\Box p$ one gets the system S-4, in which are derivable the formulae $\Box p \equiv \Box\Box p$ and $\Diamond p \equiv \Diamond\Diamond p$, showing that a string of iterated operators can have substituted for it the last operator in the string alone. The system S-5 has M and the Brouwer and S-4 axioms; more briefly, one can add to M the axiom $\Diamond p \rightarrow \Box\Diamond p$, and show by the derivation $\Diamond p \equiv \Box\Diamond p$ and $\Box p \equiv \Diamond\Box p$ that the final operator in a mixed string can be substituted for the string. There are yet other modal systems. See Kripke, n. 67 below; and G. E. Hughes and M. J. Cresswell, *An Introduction to Modal Logic*.

66 Cf. Carnap, *Meaning and Necessity*.

67   Cf. S. Kripke, 'Semantical Considerations on Modal Logic', reprinted in L. Linsky (ed.), *Reference and Modality*, J. Hintikka, 'Models of Modality', reprinted in M. J. Loux (ed.), *The Possible and the Actual.*

68   Kripke's semantics for quantified modal logic may be illustrated briefly thus: We use a model structure <G,K,R> where K = {G,H}, G ≠ H, and R = K². The model is quantificational when we define ψ (G) = {a}, ψ (H) = {a,b}, a ≠ b. For a monadic predicate letter 'P' we define a model φ such that φ (P,G) = {a}, φ (P,H) = {a}. Now: □Px is true in G when x is assigned a. Since a is the only element of ψ (g), (x)□(Px) is also true in G. When x is assigned b, ψ (Px,H) = F, from which it follows that (x)(Px) is false in H and □(x)(Px) is false in G. The connection with possible worlds arises thus: we notice □Px is true in G when x is assigned a, because then Px is true in both G and H. Intuitively this is to say a falls under the extension of P in H and in G, that is, in all possible worlds. As Kripke puts the intuitive unpacking of the ordered triple G,K,R'K is the set of all possible worlds, G * kR is a reflexive relation on K, such that $H_1 R H_2$ means that H_2 is 'possible relative' to H_1, i.e., that every proposition *true* in H_2 is *possible* in H_1, and G is the 'real world', *op. cit.*, p. 64.

69   Quine, 'Reference and Modality', *From a Logical Point of View*, to which the following references are made. Reprinted in Linsky, *Reference and Modality.*

70   Cf., chapter 2 above, where identity is discussed.

71   Quine, 'Reference and Modality', p. 48.

72   Ibid., p. 55.

73   Ibid., p. 56.

74   The papers in the Linsky volume, particularly those by Marcus, Smullyan, Follesdal and Kaplan represent the core of the early debate over Quine's objections. The net burden of their replies to Quine is that his attitude to quantifying into modal contexts is over-anxious.

75   Kripke, 'Semantical Considerations on Modal Logic'.

76   D. Lewis, *Counterfactuals*, pp. 84–5.

77   A point often made against philosophers of G. E. Moore's persuasion. I shall revert to this and allied points in later chapters.

78   Cf. R. C. Stalnaker, 'A Theory of Conditionals', in N. Rescher, *Studies in Logical Theory*, pp. 65–79, reprinted in E. Sosa (ed.), *Causation and Conditionals.* Cf. also the contributions by Sellars, Chisholm, Rescher and Kim, in E. Sosa.

79   Cf. Lewis, *Counterfactuals.*

80   Cf. E. G. Lewis, 'Causation', in Sosa, *Causation and Conditionals*, pp. 80–91.

81   Which is the converse of Leibniz's principle of the identity of indiscernibles, which states that if x and y are indiscernible, in the sense of all x's

properties being the same as y's properties and vice versa, then x is identical with y.

82 Cf. Chisholm, 'Identity Through Possible Worlds', in Loux (ed.) *The Possible and the Actual*, pp. 80–2.

83 This is a modified version of Chisholm's Adam and Noah example, ibid., pp. 82–4.

84 Ibid., pp. 85–6.

85 D. Lewis, 'Counterpart Theory and Quantified Modal Logic,' in Loux (ed.), *The Possible and the Actual*, pp. 2–8.

86 Ibid., p. 12.

87 Cf. Kripke, 'Identity and Necessity', in M. Munitz, *Identity and Individuation*; and S. P. Schwartz, *Naming, Necessity, and Natural Kinds*, p. 66ff., to which the following references are made; and A. Plantinga, 'Transworld Identity or Worldbound Individuals?', in Loux, (ed.), *The Possible and the Actual*, pp. 46–65; and *The Nature of Necessity*, ch. vi, passim.

88 Cf. Plantinga, 'World and Essence', *Philosophical Review*, 79, 1970, pp. 461–92; and *The Nature of Necessity*, pp. 94–5.

89 Kripke, 'Identity and Necessity', p. 80.

90 Lewis, *Counterfactuals*, pp. 84–91; reprinted as excerpt in Loux (ed.), *The Possible and the Actual*, p. 82ff; cf. p. 85.

91 Ibid., p. 84.

92 Ibid., pp. 83–4.

93 Cf. in particular W. Lycan, 'The Trouble with Possible Worlds', in Loux p. 274ff.; S. Haack, 'Lewis's Ontological Slum', *Review of Metaphysics* 33, 1977, p. 415ff.; and T. Richards, 'The Worlds of David Lewis', *Australasian Journal of Philosophy*, 5–3, 1975, p. 25ff.

94 Cf. Lycan's discussion ibid., for the Meinongian dimension. At p. 297 Lycan says 'I do not believe that it is possible to refute Lewis' position', which suggests reasons for its discussability.

95 Haack, ibid.

96 Stalnaker 'Possible Worlds', in Loux (ed.), *The Possible and the Actual*, cf. p. 228.

97 Plantinga, 'Actualism and Possible Worlds', in Loux, *The Possible and the Actual*, pp. 237–52.

98 Cf. Plantinga's discussion of his differences with Stalnaker, ibid.

99 R. M. Adams, 'Theories of Actuality', in Loux, *The Possible and the Actual*, p. 90ff., esp. p. 204ff.

100 Cf. The discussion of Tarski in chapter 6 below.

101 Cf. Adams, ibid., pp. 207–8.

102 A power set is the set of all subsets of a given set including the null set.

103 Cf. Lycan, 'The Trouble with Possible Worlds', in Loux, *The Possible and*

the Actual, for a survey of these, esp. p. 302 *et seq.*; and Loux's own 'Introduction'.

104   Quine, 'On What There Is', p. 1 *et seq.*

105   Ibid., p. 4.

106   Rescher, 'The Ontology of the Possible', in Loux, *The Possible and the Actual*, p. 66 *et seq.*, surveys the options; cf. esp. p. 69.

107   Ibid., pp. 73–4.

108   Cf. F. Mondadori and A. Morton, 'Modal Realism; The Poisoned Pawn', in Loux (ed.), *The Possible and the Actual*, p. 235 *et seq.*

109   Cf. M. Slote, *Metaphysics and Essence*, pp. 6–7.

110   Kripke, *Naming and Necessity*, p. 42.

111   Cf. B. Enc, 'Necessary Properties and Linnaean Essentialism', *Canadian Journal of Philosophy*, vol. V, 1975. pp. 85–7, and refs. p. 86.

112   I say a 'roughly' Aristotelian notion because Aristotle's theory of essence is a matter of live scholarly discussion still, and I do no more than appeal to a concept of essence which is approximately central to the tradition, and which is shared by some contemporary essentialists.

113   Cf. Enc, 'Necessary Properties', p. 88.

114   Quine, *Word and Object*, p. 99.

115   Cf. R. L. Cartwright, 'Some Remarks on Essentialism', *Journal of Philosophy*, vol. lxv, 1968, pp. 61–9.

116   Ibid.

117   Cf. Enc, 'Necessary Properties', p. 89.

118   Ibid., p. 90.

119   Cf. Kripke, *Naming and Necessity*, and 'Identity and Necessity' in Schwartz, *Naming, Necessity and Natural Kinds*, particular page references are given in various footnotes following.

120   Kripke, *Naming and Necessity*, p. 13.

121   Slote, *Metaphysics and Essence*, p. 8.

122   C. McGinn, 'On the Necessity of Origin', *Journal of Philosophy*, 73, 1976.

123   Ibid., p. 32.

124   P. Johnson, 'Origin and Necessity', *Philosophical Studies*, 32, 1977, p. 413 *et seq.*

125   Dummett argues that just such appeals to intuition often fail at crucial points in setting up possible-worlds talk and its ramifications.

126   Johnson, 'Origin and Necessity', p. 414.

127   Sprigge, 'Internal and External Properties', *Mind*, 71, 1962, pp. 202–3.

128   Johnson, 'Origin and Necessity', p. 416.

129   Ibid.

130   Cf. Kripke, *Naming and Necessity*, p. 26 *et seq.*

131   Ibid., p. 56. For the argument against Kripke which follows, see my 'Internal Structure and Essence', *Analysis*, June 1982.

132   The theory of essence at issue is realist, and is therefore infected by a notion of logical possibility of this scepticism-inviting kind. Cf. chapter 8 below.

133   Kripke, *Naming and Necessity*, p. 48n.

134   Ibid., pp. 35–6.

135   Quinton, 'The A Priori and the Analytic', p. 19.

136   Swinburne, 'Analyticity, Necessity and Apriority', pp. 232–8.

137   Quinton, 'The A Priori and the Analytic', pp. 15–16.

138   Kripke, *Naming and Necessity*, p. 39.

139   Kripke's theory of reference is discussed in chapter 7 below.

140   Kripke, *Naming and Necessity*, p. 34 *et seq.*

141   Ibid., pp. 55–7.

4

Existence, Presuppositions and Descriptions

Introduction

A central concern in philosophy is the question of what exists, of what there is in the universe.[1] Some of the difficulties that present themselves have been mentioned in each of the preceding chapters. It seems clear that there are tables and trees, people and planets; but are there subsistent entities in Meinong's sense? Are there unactualized objects, propositions, numbers, classes, minds, God? And if there are any of these things, do they exist in the same way as tables and planets do, or in some other way? And if so, what way is that? Attempting answers demands a different approach to each of these disputed items or classes of items; showing that there are numbers, for example, does nothing (or very little) to show that there are, say, minds, or even how one might go about showing that there are minds. In general, any argument for the existence or nonexistence of some particular candidate for either state has to be geared specifically to that candidate.

Nevertheless there are general features of existence, or talk about existence, which enter into all ontological discussion; and it is with these more general issues that this chapter is concerned.

It was remarked in chapter 1 that, on one view of these matters, philosophical interest in language is prompted chiefly by the idea that investigating language gives access to thought and the world, in the sense that understanding the former goes a long way towards providing an understanding of the two latter. In the present case, the first step towards clarifying ontological questions is to investigate two related matters: the way we talk about existence, and the existential implications and assumptions of the way we talk.

The first matter concerns assertions of existence. How does one make sense of predications of existence and nonexistence as in 'Socrates exists' and 'Pegasus does not exist'? Is 'exists' a genuine predicate? The first half of the chapter deals with this and related questions.

The second matter concerns the underlying ontological assumptions of assertions, particularly in connection with the use, truth-conditions, and meaning of sentences. If there is no King of France, is the sentence 'the King of France is wise' a false sentence or a meaningless one? Or does the question of its truth-value not arise? The expression 'the King of France' is a definite description. Russell's Theory of Descriptions, discussed in the second half of the chapter, constitutes a proposed analysis of these, and in so doing draws together a number of the considerations prompted by questions of reference and existence.

Is 'Exists' a Predicate?

In the fifth *Meditation* Descartes gives a version of the Ontological Argument for the existence of God, commenting 'I clearly see that existence can no more be separated from the essence of God than can its having three angles equal to two right angles be separated from the essence of a triangle'.[2] The idea is that the notion of the nonexistence of God is a contradiction; for God is perfect and existence is a perfection, so God must exist. Kant objected to the Ontological Argument, with Descartes' formulation of it in mind, and one of his reasons for objecting to it was that, in his view, existence is not a property – that is, that 'exists' is not a genuine predicate. His view lays bare the essentials of the problem concerning 'exists'.[3]

Kant's reasons for denying that 'exists' is a predicate are that whereas *grammatically* 'exists' is indeed a predicate, *logically* it does not function as one. Consider genuine predicates such as '. . . is red', '. . . is square', '. . . is a tame tiger'. If I inform you that x is red, is round, or is a tame tiger, then I am furnishing you with facts about x. But if I say x exists, I am not giving you any information about x, or offering a further description of it. It would seem odd to say that all three of the following are important facts about x – that it is a tiger, that it is tame, and that it exists. As Kant put it: 'Being is obviously not a real predicate; that is, it is not a concept of something which could be added to the concept of a thing'.[4] This constitutes a rejection of Descartes' version of the

Ontological Argument because if existence is not a property, it cannot be a perfection; hence if (which is independently debatable) perfection is a necessary property of God – that is, is essential to God – it still does not follow that there is God.[5]

In short, Kant's analysis of the problem of 'exists' centres on the view that, since to say of some x that it exists adds nothing to the concept of x, 'exists' is not a predicate; for however we understand predicates, at least what happens in predication is that something is *said about* x, and on this view of 'exists', saying 'x exists' says nothing about – adds nothing to the concept of – x.

What has been said so far is not quite right as it stands. For, in a sense, to say of tigers that they exist *does* add something; it says that the concept of a tiger has instances in reality – that is, that *there are* tigers to be met with in the world. Clearly, although it might seem peculiar in normal circumstances to assert that tigers exist with this purpose in view, a difference can be made by doing so. Kant himself conceded that a hundred pounds which exist make a difference to my bank balance which a hundred nonexistent pounds cannot make. So indeed might an existent tiger make a difference; I can imagine circumstances in which someone might say, 'What would you do if there were a tiger in the room?' and (as a variation on 'Well, there *is* a tiger in the room') then add 'that tiger exists'. It would be a relief if the tiger were tame to boot.

Moreover, as Pears points out, it is not true that in saying 'tigers exist' one is saying nothing about tigers; for if anyone were to ask 'what are you talking about?', the appropriate answer is 'tigers'.[6] The same holds good if someone said 'tigers do not exist' or 'winged horses do not exist'; he is talking about tigers and winged horses. Consequently it is incorrect to hold that nothing is being *said about* whatever is asserted to exist or not exist. The view, therefore, that 'exists' is not a predicate because (a) it adds nothing to the concept, and (b) says nothing about the concept, needs refinement.

Part of the peculiarity which attaches to uses of 'exists' arises from the difference between saying 'tigers exist' and 'tigers are striped'. According to Pears, the peculiarity of the assertion 'tigers exist' arises from the fact that the expression is *referentially tautologous*. Consider the case of one's saying 'this room exists'. The expression 'this room' implies that there is a room, namely this one; and it implies this in virtue of having been used to make reference to this room. To add 'exists' is to assert the existence of the room all over again; it is as if one were saying 'this room (which exists) exists' – hence the tautology. If one says 'this room does not exist', the existence of the room is implied by reference having been made to it, after which the speaker implicitly contradicts himself by saying, in effect, 'this room (which exists) does not exist'. Pears calls this *referential contradiction*. These notions of referential tautology and contradiction constitute a refinement of the Kantian thesis in this way: they assert that 'exists' is not a genuine predicate because (a′) it adds nothing *new* to the concept, and (b′) it says nothing that has not been said *implicitly* already. Contrast (a′) and (b′) with (a) and (b) above.

Pears calls (a′) the 'minimal thesis'. It needs qualification in three ways. First, the subject term of a singular existential statement might refer to something or somebody in the world of fiction, for example David Copperfield, and thus imply existence in that world but not in the real world. If one says of David Copperfield that he existed in real life, the subject term of the statement, *viz.*, 'David Copperfield', would imply existence only in the fictional world created by Dickens, and so one's saying of David Copperfield that he existed in the real world would indeed be adding something new. Accordingly one would not be guilty of referential tautology. The reason is clear: the statement has application to two worlds, the fictional and the real. It *implies* existence in the fictional world but *asserts* it in the real world; and it is certainly novel to claim that Dickens's David Copperfield is a genuine historical figure. For the same reasons, if one denied that David Copperfield existed in real life, one would be guiltless of referential contradiction.

Secondly, someone might say 'the Euston Arch no longer exists', and accordingly appear to be guilty of referential contradiction because existence has been both implied and denied in the real world. But since the Euston Arch's existence has been implied for one time and denied for a later time, referential contradiction is avoided. And *mutatis mutandis* for affirmative cases.

Thirdly, suppose someone hallucinates, like Macbeth, a dagger before him, and says to himself 'that dagger does not exist'. Here matters are more complicated, but Pears offers a way round. Referential contradiction is escaped if it is held that there are two senses in which the dagger might be considered to exist: as a visually-experienced dagger, so that the expression 'that dagger' refers to it at least at that level; and as a dagger in space, that is, a real dagger whose occurrence in someone's visual experience is not a product of that experience. Then one's saying 'that dagger (*qua* visually-experienced dagger) does not exist (*qua* dagger in space)' does not involve a referential contradiction, for what is being implied at one is being denied at another level – rather on analogy with the time case.

So, with the following cases excepted, namely that implication and assertion are about different worlds, or different times, or different 'levels', we have Pears' thesis as follows: if the subject term of a singular existential statement implies existence, then, if the verb asserts existence, the resulting statement will be a referential tautology; and if the statement denies existence, it is referentially contradictory.

An idea being exploited by Pears in this account is that of a 'presuppositional implication', which owes itself to Strawson.[7] Presupposition, according to Strawson, is a relation between two statements p and q, such that p is said to presuppose q if and only if p is neither true nor false unless q is true. The statement 'the man in the garden is whistling' can only possess a truth-value if the presupposed statement 'there is a man in the garden' is true. The presupposition relation must be distinguished from the relation of entailment. In cases where p entails q, the conjunction of p with the denial of q is a contradiction; that is, it is contradictory to affirm p and at the same time to deny q, because the truth of q is a necessary condition for the truth of p. But where p presupposes q, the truth of q is a necessary condition for the truth *or* the falsity of p; which is to say, q's truth is a necessary condition for p's possessing a truth-value at all. As Strawson put it, it would constitute a 'different kind of absurdity' to conjoin the affirmation of p with the denial of q. Pears is appealing to just such a notion of presupposition in saying that subject terms, in referring, imply (that is, presuppositionally imply) the existence of that to which they refer.[8]

Pears himself specifies the major weakness of his thesis; which is that it turns upon, but leaves unanalysed, a notion of reference. This question arises again here and will be discussed in a later chapter, so I shall leave it aside for the present.

The suggestions in Pears' paper are developments of ideas mooted by Russell, who argued that 'to say that [things actually found in the world] do not exist is strictly nonsense, but to say that they do exist is also strictly nonsense'.[9] They also reflect ideas put forward earlier by Moore, whose thoughts were as follows. Consider the expressions

1. tame tigers growl
1'. some tame tigers growl

2. tame tigers exist

2′. some tame tigers exist.

Whereas 1 admits of the more explicit variant formulations 'all tame tigers growl', 'most tame tigers growl', and 'some tame tigers growl', 2 does not; one cannot say 'all tame tigers exist' or 'most tame tigers exist', although one can say 2′, that is 'some tame tigers exist'.[10] In 1 the truth of the 'all' and 'most' formulations depends on the truth of the 'some' formulation; in 2 this latter formulation is the only possible one. The sentences 'all tame tigers exist' and 'most tame tigers exist' are in Moore's view 'queer and puzzling expressions'; they have 'no clear meaning'.[11]

The difference between the two cases can be made out by contrasting

3. some tame tigers don't growl

and

4. some tame tigers don't exist.

Both 3 and its contrary 1′ have 'perfectly clear' meanings, but 4 does not, despite the fact that 2′ does; 2′ after all just means 'there are some tame tigers'.[12] In Moore's view 'exist' must have different meanings in 2′ and 4, because a sense can indeed be attached to the latter, as when someone says 'some tame tigers are not real tigers' or '. . . are imaginary'.[13] But if the sense of 'exist' were univocal and 'exist' means only what it does in 2, then 4 would be meaningless, and 2′ would be meaningless also, which is not the case.

On the basis of these thoughts Moore says that he can see why some philosophers have held that existence is not a property as redness or (so to say) growlingness are. Another reason is that 1′ and 2′ differ in the fact that whereas the former asserts that some values of the propositional function 'x is a tame tiger *and growls*' are true, the latter asserts only that some values of 'x is a tame tiger' are true; 2′ asserts only what it does because it is not used to say 'this is a tame tiger *and exists*'. As Moore puts it, 'by pointing and saying "this exists" we . . . express *no proposition at all*, whereas by pointing and saying 'this growls' we do express a proposition.[14]

Although these constitute reasons for saying that 'exists' does not function predicatively in the way that 'growls' does, and, accordingly, that existence is not a property, Moore was uncomfortable about the analysis because it is at odds with certain other considerations. One is that it can be said of something 'this might not have existed', which, if it is significant, permits one to say the converse, 'this exists', with propriety.[15] Moore suggested that perhaps it is the case that 'this exists' is part of what is meant by asserting, say, 'this is a book' or 'this is red'; and further, perhaps part of what it means to say that such predicates as 'is a book' or 'is red' stand for properties, 'is that *part but not the whole* of what is asserted by any value of "x is a book", "x is red" etc., is "this exists",' in which case 'exists' would not stand for a property 'solely because the whole of what it asserts, and not merely a part, is "this exists".'[16]

Pears' notion of referential tautology accords with the later points made here; the earlier idea, to the effect that the status of the predicate depends upon what quantifiers its subject takes, is echoed by Strawson in a more recent discussion, commented on below.

Logical Predicates and Ontological Commitment

The topic to which Moore specifically addressed himself was whether 'exists' functions as a *logical* predicate. What it means to distinguish logical from grammatical predicates, and why 'exists' may not count as the former, can be set out in the following way.[17]

It is obvious enough that the verb 'exists' serves as a grammatical predicate, for one would parse the sentence 'this room is warm' and 'this room exists' in exactly the same way. The argument against 'exists' does not consist in a denial of this, but, as noted, in a denial of its being a logical predicate; and in fact it is precisely because it is the former that one might feel a need to point out that it is not the latter. For its being the former can naturally lead to the assumption that it is the latter as well, which gives rise to confusions. The question therefore is: what is meant by saying that 'exists' is not a logical predicate?

By a 'logical predicate' is meant something that would count as a predicate in an interpretation of first-order predicate logic. In this logic, familiarly, there are the individual constants a, b and c . . ., variables x, y and z . . ., predicate letters F, G and H . . ., quantifiers $(\exists x)$, (x), and truth-functional operators $\rightarrow, v, \sim, \cdot$. Among the well-formed formulae constructed from these primitive materials there are, for example, Fa

(John is happy), Gab (John loves Catherine), ($\exists$ x)(Gxa) (someone loves John), and so on. The idea of a logical predicate is just the ordinary idea of a grammatical predicate, but in a special language. So when it is said that 'exists' is not a logical predicate what is meant is that it is not treated as one in first-order logic. Any statement one wished to make containing the word 'exists' has a translation in the language of logic which serves the same purpose but does not contain 'exists'; hence 'exists' is dispensable. Although people habitually utter sentences containing 'exists' as a (grammatical) predicate, there is no need to do so; for example, instead of saying 'the round square does not exist' one can say 'no square is round' or 'for any figure, that figure will not be both square and round': (x)(Sx $\rightarrow$ ~Rx) or ~($\exists$ x)(Sx·Rx). This interpretation draws on ideas advanced by Russell – a point which becomes clearer by the end of the chapter. It demonstrates that we may be misled as to the logical form of facts by the grammatical form of sentences stating them; Russell regarded this as an important insight.

Still, the apparent ease of dealing with 'exists' in this way might itself be misleading. One can translate existence statements into regimented form with impunity so long as one's interpretation of the quantifiers (x), ($\exists$ x) is *objectual* or *referential*, in the sense that the variables bound by the quantifiers are taken to refer to objects in a given domain of discourse. Some philosophers of logic are discontented with objectual readings of the quantifiers, and argue for alternatives – the chief of which is the proposed substitutional reading, in which the values of the variables are names, not objects.[18] Consider the case of:

1. Pegasus is a flying horse.

This would seem to entail directly

2. There is a flying horse.

Now, 1 is true; but if 2 is given a regimented translation as

3. ($\exists$ x) (x is a flying horse),

then 2 is false. How is this difficulty to be overcome? One solution is to interpret 2 as

4. There is a term x such that 'x is a flying horse' is true,

which makes 2 true and allows 3 to be inferred from 1. What has changed is the interpretation of the quantifiers and variables in 3; ($\exists$ x) no longer reads 'there is an object . . .' but 'there is a term . . .' with according changes throughout. The choice of a substitutional in preference to an objectual reading in consequence yields an apparently more intuitive result.

On second thoughts, however, it is not so clear that the result is intuitive.[19] Whatever the logical form of 1 may be, it is not a sentence composed of a denoting singular term and a monadic predicate. The difference between 1 and

1'. Arkle is a horse.

is that in 1' 'Arkle' is a denoting singular term whereas in 1 'Pegasus' is not. (Arkle was a famous racehorse, Pegasus a winged horse of myth.) This is a difference that makes a difference. What then is 'Pegasus'? In Russell's view as widely understood – it is discussed in full shortly – 'Pegasus' is to be thought of as a *description*, and analysed accordingly. The fact that 'Pegasus' is, like 'Arkle', syntactically a name, might in other words be misleading as to the analysis which one ought properly to give of sentences containing it. One thing that the substitutional reinterpretation of 1 does is to render 3, like 1, *not* an existential claim after all, whereas intuitively 3 seems to consist in the very paradigm of an existential claim, thus suggesting a treatment of 1 which makes clear that the syntactical role of 'Pegasus' in it cannot alone determine what treatment 1 as a whole should receive.

These issues, and their importance, become clear if we look at them in connection with an influential theory advanced by Quine.

Taking the view that talk about existence is properly to be effected in the idiom of quantificational logic has, on Quine's view, significant results for ontology. He argues that we are committed to counting into our ontology all and only the values of the bound variables of (objectually construed) quantification, a view summarized in the slogan 'to be is to be the value of a variable'.[20] Ontological commitments are, he says, relative to theory, including our 'immemorial' theory of the everyday world; and they are revealed by the use to which we put quantification. 'The ontology to which an (interpreted) theory is committed comprises all and only the objects over which the bound variables of the theory have to be construed as ranging in order that the statements affirmed in the theory be true'.[21] More explicitly as to the role of the quantifiers, Quine holds that recasting our talk into the canonical notation of quantificational logic reveals that

> the objects we are to be understood to admit are precisely the objects which we reckon to the universe of values over which the bound variables of quantification are to the considered to range. Such is simply the intended sense of the quantifiers '(x)' and (∃ x): 'every object x is such that' and 'there is an object x such that'. The quantifiers are encapsulations of these specially selected, unequivocally referential idioms of ordinary language. To paraphrase a sentence into the canonical notation of quantification is, first and foremost, to make its ontic content explicit, quantification being a device for talking in general of objects.[22]

Quine's theory has it that if we are prepared to infer from such sentences as 'Arkle is a horse' the existential generalization (∃ x)(x is a horse), then we are committed to horses in our ontology. But this view invites a difficulty for cases where the name or singular term is empty, such as the Pegasus case. For from the true sentence 'Pegasus is a flying horse' it ought to be inferable by existential generalization (∃ x) (x is a flying horse), but this as we saw is false. Quine's solution is to argue for the eliminability of singular terms – of which names are a subset – in two steps. The first is to paraphrase them into definite descriptions. Thus 'Pegasus' becomes 'the unique object which has the property of being Pegasus', or, more succinctly, 'the unique object which pegasises' where 'pegasises' is a predicate expression doing duty for the predicate 'has the property of being Pegasus'. The second step is then to eliminate the description by giving it a Russellian analysis, on which analysis quantifiers and variables do all the work. The sentence 'Pegasus is a flying horse' becomes:

$$(\exists \text{ x}) \text{ (x pegasises \& } [(\text{y}) \text{ (y pegasises} \rightarrow \text{y = x})] \cdot \text{x is a flying horse})$$

Because there is nothing in the domain of discourse which is a flying horse – which is to say, since no object in the domain satisfies the predicate 'is a flying horse' – the whole sentence is false.[23] Quine's expedient of turning a name into a description and then analysing the description Russell-fashion has been jocularly called 'Quinizing the name and Russelling away the description.'

Ascending from ordinary ways of talking, where we say 'Pegasus is a flying horse', to the regimented forms of first-order logic, where we say $(\exists x)(x \text{ pegasises} \ldots)$ as above, is not to indulge in translation, for the two expressions are not synonymous. In Quine's opinion, the ascent from ordinary to formal discourse constitutes a clarifying paraphrase of the former by the latter; all that is philosophically essential is preserved, and what is misleading is eliminated.[24]

It is now clear why the proposed substitutional reading of the quantifiers is important, for anyone who takes this alternative view is thereby contesting Quine's results, which, if right, are obviously significant for our treatment of ontological issues. Accordingly, let us look at the substitutional reading again.[25]

The power of the substitutional reading reveals itself in the handling of certain difficulties which affect the regimented forms of opaque sentences like

1. John believes that Helen = Helen.

The existential generalization of 1 is

2. $(\exists x)$ (John believes Helen = x)

which on an objectual reading yields

3. There is an x such that John believes Helen = x.

If there were no Helen, 3 would be false even though 1 is true. But if 2 is read substitutionally it yields:

4. For some instance x it is true that John believes Helen = x,

and the happy result is that 4 is true if 1 is, which is as it should be.[26]

A substitutional reading does not, then, offer an alternative analysis of the ontological features of language, but places the emphasis elsewhere; specifically, on the truth-conditions of particular substitutions. The main issue is which of the two readings is to be preferred. Part of the reasons dictating which reading should be chosen will involve more general ontological considerations; for one example, it seems odd to accept the objectual reading for $(\exists x)(Fx \lor \sim Fx)$ because on such a reading it appears that the fact that anything exists at all is a matter of logic.[27] The virtue of the substitutional reading is that in general it does not force ontological commitments every time we wish to clarify what we say by means of canonical paraphrase. This, together with the fact that we are able, without ontic absurdity, to retain names and singular expressions in analyses, and to quantify into opaque contexts as in the above example, constitutes a strong recommendation of the strategy. Nevertheless, the issue is an open one.

There are other criticisms of other aspects of Quine's views in this connection. Strawson, for example, raises doubts about whether singular terms can be dispensed with, as Quine's theory requires, owing to the fundamental role they play in identifying the topic of a particular assertion or discourse, a function which is to be distinguished from, and not assimilated to, that of asserting there is one and only one thing which is thus-and-so.[28] This point comes out strongly in Strawson's criticism of Russell, discussed below; Quine's views derive as noted, from those of Russell. In any case Quine himself set up the class of unfamiliar predicates like 'pegasises' – required for substantiating his views – by saying that they could be thought of as meaning '. . . is identical with a' where 'a' is a name like 'Pegasus'; so that '. . . pegasises' is to be explained as meaning '. . . is identical with Pegasus'. Although this manoeuvre was intended by Quine as no more than a heuristic comment on the new style of predicates, the question remains whether he really succeeds in dispensing with appeal to singular terms, or whether, at some point, essential reference would have to be made to them in a presentation of his account. And there is a problem in the opposite direction: whether or not singular terms can be treated as Quine desires, it turns out that quantifiers and variables are themselves eliminable, if use is made of the combinatory logic devised by Curry and Schönfinkel.[29] But these technicalities need not detain; it is enough for the present to note that Quine's proposals invite debate.

Existence and Presupposed Classes

Trying to analyse assertions and denials of existence by means of the quantificational apparatus of logic carries one away from the use of 'exists' in ordinary discourse. A more recent attempt to give an account of 'exists' as a logically unexceptionable predicate, without at the same time assimilating it to a quantificational apparatus, is offered by Strawson.[30]

The key idea in his suggestions derives in part from points made by Moore, and in part from Strawson's own notion of presupposition. The proposal is as follows.

'Exists' is a logical predicate when it satisfies the condition which, whenever satisfied, makes any grammatical predicate a logical predicate. (The force of 'logical' here is 'genuine'.) The condition is this: if the grammatical subject of a sentence admits of commencing with all of the quantifying adjectives 'all', 'most', 'many', 'some', 'a few', 'none', 'at least one', and so on, then it is a logical subject; and the predicate of a logical subject is a logical predicate. Accordingly, if 'exists' is the grammatical predicate of a subject which admits of commencing with all of the quantifying adjectives, then it is a logical, that is a genuine, predicate.[31] The subject of existence-asserting statements will still carry an existential presupposition; but an account of this can be given.

Strawson devises the notion of 'presupposed class' and explains it by means of the example of a classical dictionary. Consider the fact that of the characters listed in a classical dictionary, some are mythical and some are genuine historical figures. On Strawson's view, one can talk in this connection of a class of characters whose existence is presupposed in virtue of their being the topic of discourse in a given situation – as when someone says of the characters in the dictionary 'some of those listed are mythical but most of them existed'.[32] This class is however 'ontologically heterogeneous', since it contains a subclass of genuine historical characters and a subclass of mythical characters.

Consider now the sentences 'King Alfred existed' and 'King Arthur did not exist'. In Strawson's view, 'we have only to see the names as serving to identify, within the heterogeneous class of kingly characters being talked about – a class which comprises both actual and legendary kings – a particular member of that class in each case; and then see the predicate as serving to assign that particular member to the appropriate subclass. Thus "exists" appears as a predicate, and not as a predicate of a concept; but as a predicate of some, and not of other, members of the heterogeneous class'.[33]

An heuristic device employed by Strawson to clarify the point is the idea of a graphic representation of property-ascription. Suppose one draws a circle to represent a class of items. Then to say of some of these items that they have a certain property is to shade part of the circle; to say all of them have a certain property is to shade the whole circle; and so by shading parts of the circle more and less one can capture the sense of any of the quantifying adjectives we standardly use. There is no circle at all prior to asserting that something exists; saying 'at least one x exists' is to draw the smallest circle possible, saying 'some xs exist' is to draw a somewhat larger circle – and so on.[34] But in the case of the use of 'exists' to assign an item to a subclass as above, what one is doing is more akin to the former than the latter enterprise – that is, to shading some or all of a circle, rather than drawing a circle of some size. The use of 'exists' in such a case is predicative in character.

The first thing to be noted about this proposal is that the concept of presupposition has been widened in an unusual way, from one having to do with the presupposed existence of the referent of a subject expression, to one having to do with the classes whose existence is presupposed, not by the use of a singular expression, but by *contexts of discussion*. This creates a difficulty. In this widened sense of presupposition, what is presupposed, namely the class of things being talked about, requires a way of being demarcated. It is not easy to see for all, or even most, imaginable cases of presupposed classes how one would determine their extension. More importantly, it is left open how we are to know when to affix 'exists' to a subject term by way of assigning its referent to the appropriate subclass; for, if anything, it would seem that the question whether an item merits membership of one rather than another subclass has to be decided in advance of its election to such membership; and this would mean that we know when to predicate 'exists' legitimately already – that is, without prior appeal to a context and the class presupposed to it.

Much the same criticism can be arrived at from another angle. By asking how the use of 'exists' marks off the subclass of real or existent entities, the question can be raised whether this subclass is to be determined extensionally or intensionally. If the former, then the subclass would be composed of an indefinite collection of singular statements 'x exists', 'y exists', and so on; and this seems to resurrect, with a vengeance, the problem of how to understand the logic of statements of the form 'x exists' without getting involved in regress. If the latter, then the problem is even less tractable, since one would now be faced with pondering whether 'exists' is to be a primitive or undefined concept, or whether it is to be defined. Yet whichever is the case, what will come to be understood by 'exists' in application to subclasses will be the same as what is understood by 'exists' in application to their individual members; which would be wholly unenlightening as to the predicative use of the term.

On either an extensional or an intensional reading, then, what the appeal to a presupposed class seems in effect to do is to postpone rather than clarify the problems of determining how 'exists' is used as a logical predicate, of determining when it is so used, if ever, and determining what effect follows for the 'absurdity' problem which Strawson had himself identified in earlier writings. In these earlier writing Strawson argued that 'x exists' statements were not subject–predicate in form, for to say a subject expression x in 'x exists' presupposes the existence of x is patently absurd, because it carries as a presupposition what the statement, of which it is a part, as a whole asserts. Hence x can have no particular-referring role, and that is why 'x exists' is not subject–predicate in form. At this point Strawson had felt that the 'x exists' form is better dealt with in the quantificational idiom after the fashion of Quine's proposals. He put the same argument alternatively like this: if one attempted to assimilate 'x exists' to any of the four traditional types of categorical propositions, 'or to regard them as subject–predicate statements at all, we should be faced with the absurd result that the question of whether they were true or false could only arise if they were true; or that, if they were false, the question of whether they were true or false could not arise.'[35]

Strawson's solution in terms of presupposed classes rests on a premiss to the effect that every singular statement of subject–predicate form is such that its subject, if it has or looks to have a particular-referring role at least, carries a presupposition concerning the existence of its referent. One suggestion is that the entire debate could be undercut by refusing to accept this premiss for cases where a statement explicitly asserts the existence of its subject's referent. We could say that in cases where 'exists' occupies predicate position, it effects an estoppal of presupposition, so that we would have a rule to the effect that all subject–predicate statements, with the exception of those asserting existence, involve a presupposition concerning the existence of the subject's referent. Then one could proceed to attempt an account of existential claims unencumbered by anxieties of absurdity.[36]

So much is the merest sketch of a programme, but it suggests two virtues: it would avoid the cumbrous business of appealing to heterogeneous classes of entities presupposed by contexts of discourse, and it would run closer to pretheoretical intuitions to the effect that there is point and substance in saying of some things – like Arkle – that they exist, and of other things – like Pegasus – that they do not exist. This is not to deny the value of the notion of presupposition; it is just to say that we sometimes put up our ontological interests for debate, and need an account of the forms of talk used in doing so.

A suggestion in some respects similar to, but in detail different from, Strawson's view is offered by Gareth Evans. This is to treat negative existential sentences – those that deny existence of something, as in 'Pegasus does not exist' – as rather like utterances in a game of make-believe, except that one intends to show that it is indeed a game of make-believe one is engaged in. In saying 'Pegasus does not exist' one as it were pretends to use the name 'Pegasus' as if to refer some existing thing, only to reveal the pretence by the predicate '. . . does not exist'. As Evans puts it, 'I propose that we regard singular negative existential sentences as [a] serious exploitation of the game of make-believe. The general idea is that someone who utters such a sentence should be likened to someone who makes a move within a pretence in order to express the fact that it is a pretence'.[37] If you leaped onto the stage at the theatre, pointed at the actor playing Julius Caesar, and said, 'Julius Caesar is only an actor', this is what you would be doing. (You would not be doing this if you leaped on the stage, pointed, and said 'this is only an actor', because you would not be using the fiction to show that it is a fiction.)

This suggests that we treat such sentences as 'Pegasus exists' and 'Pegasus does not exist' as implicitly containing an operator 'really', so that assertions and denials of Pegasus's existence respectively have the form 'Pegasus really exists', 'Pegasus does not really exist'. To give an account of the truth-conditions of sentences containing this implicit operator, we must introduce a way of giving truth-conditions for fictional discourse – for sentences such as 'Emma married Mr Knightley', which, in the context of the novel *Emma*, is true, or as Evans puts it to show that it is *true in the given fiction*, *true*. So 'Emma married Mr Knightley' is *true* if the novel *Emma* tells us that she did, *false* otherwise. The novel, in other words, specifies the *truth-conditions* for that sentence. Now we can say of any sentence S containing 'really' that:

(1) S has *truth-conditions*
(2) S has truth-conditions
(3) S is true (and not merely *true*)

Few sentences have both *truth-conditions* and truth-conditions. One might find them in novelized versions of the lives of genuine historical figures, say, where properties are ascribed to them that they had in real life.[38] In *Vanity Fair* Thackeray implies that George IV of England had certain character traits which, in real life, he indeed had; so the sentences making these attributions have both *truth-conditions* and truth-conditions, and some of them are accordingly both *true* and true.

On Evans' suggestion we are therefore to treat a case such as 'Pegasus does not exist' as follows: 'Pegasus really exists' can be true only if 'Pegasus exists' has a truth-condition; but it does not, so it is false; and therefore 'Pegasus does not exist' is true.

The merit of the suggestion is that it allows 'exists' to be a genuine predicate of individuals. This is disallowed by analyses such as those of Pears, described earlier, in which to assert or deny existence of some individual is (with the exceptions noted) to involve oneself in tautology or contradiction respectively. But on such views it is difficult to give a satisfactory account of singular negative existentials. The problem is that such existentials seem to be in good order, having the frequent merit of truth, as with 'Pegasus does not exist'. Evans' treatment allows a good account to be given of them.

Two other comments might be made. One is that the suggestion needs adjustment to take account of cases where it is not fictional entities but, say, hypothesized entities which are in view. Suppose two quantum physicists are disputing whether 'strings' exist, where 'strings' are entities from which elementary particles are formed. Sainsbury suggests that we employ a notion of 'unwitting fiction' to allow for cases where what speakers say diverges from reality without their intending to produce fiction.[39] Then if there turn out not to be strings, what will have transpired is that the sentence 'there are strings' only has *truth-conditions* in the unwitting fiction, but lacks truth-conditions. In this case 'strings do not really exist' would be true.

The other comment is that Evans' suggestion has a certain similarity to Strawson's suggestion, not just in proposing something analogous to the latter's subclass assignments, but in relying on an especially introduced notion – Strawson offers presupposition, Evans *truth-conditions* – to do so. A virtue of Evans' case is that it accords with plausible efforts to understand the nature of fictional discourse. Both views allow 'exists' to be a predicate of individuals; it is interesting to speculate how integral this is to treating it as a 'genuine' predicate.

The Theory of Descriptions

I turn now to give an account of Russell's theory of definite descriptions. Its relevance to the foregoing has already been made apparent by the fact that recent discussions of 'exists' proceed with Russell's theory lying somewhere close in the background. The theory is best appreciated when seen in the context of certain more general philosophical issues, and these I sketch, together with the theory's epistemological corollaries.

Russell's distinction between two species of knowledge, 'knowledge by acquaintance' and 'knowledge by description', was mentioned in chapter 1. The distinction is drawn as follows. Knowledge by acquaintance is a dyadic relation between a knowing subject and an object of direct awareness. 'I say that I am *acquainted* with an object when I have a direct cognitive relation to that object, i.e., when I am directly aware of the object itself'.[40] By 'directly aware' Russell meant 'without the intermediary of any process of inference or any knowledge of truths'.[41] The kinds of thing we may be acquainted with – the objects of acquaintance – are particulars, such as sense-data, memories, and our own awareness of objects; and universals, such as redness and roundness, the awareness of which Russell calls 'conceiving', and which he calls 'concepts' for those cases in which anyone is in fact aware of them. Russell regarded relations as also being objects of acquaintance under this heading.[42] Particulars and universals exhaust the domain of our epistemological acquaintances.

Physical objects and other minds are not, as the foregoing makes apparent, among the objects of acquaintance. On the contrary, these are known by *description*. By a 'description' Russell meant any phrase of the forms 'a so-and-so' and 'the so-and-so'. The first, 'a so-and-so', Russell called an ambiguous description.[43] The second, 'the so-and-so', is the form of a definite description in the singular, and it attracts Russell's particular attention because 'the', the definite article, appears to make the description a referential device of an ontologically committal kind. 'We shall say that an object is "known by description" when we know that it is "the so-and-so", i.e. when we know there is one object, and no more, having a certain property; and it will be generally implied that we do not have knowledge by acquaintance of the same object'. For Russell 'common nouns, even proper names' are descriptions, owing to the fact that 'the thought in the mind of the person using a proper name correctly can generally only be expressed *explicitly* if we replace the proper name by a description'.[44] (This is one of the controversial aspects of the theory; on some readings of his views, Russell is not taken to have claimed that names are concealed descriptions, or that to every name there is annexed a uniquely identifying description, or even a set of them. These points recur in chapter 7 below in the discussion of reference.)

Underlying Russell's enterprise in formulating the theory of descriptions is a view of the nature of philosophy, which is that one of its principal concerns is the analysis of language. A correct analysis of language exposes what its sentences are really about – or alternatively put: what we are really saying when we use them. Analysis is necessary, in Russell's view, for the reason that ordinary language is ontologically misleading; not because we do not usually have good grounds for what they say, but because the grammatical and logical forms of language are too often incongruent. It is the logical rather than the grammatical structure of language which reveals what there is. If care is not taken over the points where logic and grammar diverge, Russell argued, there is a danger of assimilating grammatical to logical, and thence to ontological, categories – often with disastrous results, as for example finding that one has to postulate the existence of subsistent entities.

It was Russell's rejection of Meinong's position in this respect, which, together with his rejection of Idealism and his early work in logic, was the immediate source of the Theory of Descriptions.

Russell shared with Meinong and others a commitment to a denotative theory of meaning – the theory, crudely put, that the meaning of a word is the object it denotes. In terms of this theory it is a serious problem that sentences like 'the present King of France is wise' are palpably meaningful despite there being nothing for the grammatical subject–expression to denote. It was to solve this problem that Meinong accepted a notion of subsistence – a notion as venerable as Parmenides, who had argued (to paraphrase Quine's paraphrase) that 'what is not must in some sense be, otherwise what is it that is being said not to be?' Russell, who at one time accepted Meinong's view, soon came to find it intolerable because it offended his 'vivid sense of reality'. The Theory of Descriptions was devised to avoid Meinong's result while at the same time preserving the denotative theory of meaning, which seemed to Russell correct. His solution was, as noted with qualifications, to say that most common nouns and proper names are, or can be analysed as, concealed descriptions, and are not 'logically proper' names at all; which latter are alone suitable for occupying the subject place in genuine subject–predicate propositions. This in turn is because (and this is the crucial move) descriptions are not referring expressions either – and Russell gave an analysis of descriptions to show this, by making explicit the logical form of sentences containing them.

Russell thus argues that it is only logically proper names which directly and unambiguously denote something in the world. To hold that descriptions function as names would be to fall into the Parmenidean or Meinongian trap of having to accept that, since each constituent of a proposition is tied to something in the world, a proposition like 'the unicorn does not exist' obliges one to assert that there have in some sense to be unicorns in order for one meaningfully to deny that they exist. Russell's theory centres on the transmutation of descriptions into 'incomplete symbols', which acquire meaning only in context and have no significance on their own, and which can be seen on analysis to make nondescriptive claims about the existence and uniqueness of the entities the original description purported to describe – in this way securing the meaningfulness of the sentences in which they occur without blunting Ockham's Razor. 'In the true analysis of the proposition, the description is broken up and disappears'; thus descriptions cease to have the unpalatable ontological implications that a denotative theory entails.[45]

Russell gave the following as examples of sentences containing definite descriptions:

1. Scott is the author of *Waverley*.
2. The present King of France is wise.
3. The square root of –1 is half the square root of – 4.

The descriptive phrases here are respectively, 'the author of *Waverley*', 'the present King of France', 'the square root of –1' and 'the square root of – 4'. What is the correct analysis of sentences containing them? The most obvious (and naïve) response is to say that descriptive phrases are complex names and function as such; but for the reasons just given, this will not do. Russell offers a quick demonstration of why it will not do, as follows. Consider the identity statement 'Scott is the author of *Waverley*'. (I shall symbolize this for convenience as 'a is D' where 'D' stands for the description.) If D is another name for Scott then 'a is D' = 'Scott is Scott', which is a tautology. If, on the other hand, one tries to substitute a name other than 'Scott' for D, for example 'Keats', the resulting assertion is false. Therefore under any substitution of a name for D, the sentence 'a is D' is either tautologous or false. Since 'a is D' is neither, D is not a name.

Secondly, names are arbitrary, so if D is taken to be synonymous with 'Scott' then the identity of Scott with the author of *Waverley* is a nomenclatural decision; but you cannot, as Russell observed, settle by choice of nomenclature whether or not Scott is the author of *Waverley*.[46]

Descriptions therefore cannot be names. The correct analysis of sentences in which descriptive phrases occur, then, Russell set out as follows. Sentences containing descriptions are to be analysed into an equivalent set of statements in which no descriptive phrases occur and which make explicit the logical structure of what is being asserted. In the case of 2 above, the analysis yields:

2a. There is a King of France,
2b. there is not more than one King of France, and
2c. anything which is King of France is wise;

or, more accurately still:

$$(\exists x) [[Kx \cdot (y)(Ky \rightarrow y = x)] \cdot Wx].$$

Because 2a is false, 2 is false.

In the formalism, sentence 2a is captured by the existential generalization; 2b is the uniqueness condition embodied in 'the', the definite article; and 2c asserts that the unique existent x has a certain property, in this case wisdom. The formal symbolism into which sentences containing descriptions are to be cast is itself, rather than the set of English sentences 2a–c, alone totally unambiguous; it is the 'perfect language'.

This is what Russell meant by saying that the surface forms of language are misleading; for in 2 the description appears to have a denoting role, whereas in the formal paraphrase of the whole sentence there occur no singular terms, only quantifier-bound variables, predicate letters, and the identity sign. This eliminates the difficulty created by vacuous descriptions – descriptions to which nothing answers – by showing that they are not logically proper names, that is names which denote and are therefore entitled to serve as the logical subjects of predication.

It is worth stressing that the point is naturally an important one for Russell, because he was committed to the principle of bivalence, that is, the principle that every meaningful sentence determinately has one of the two truth-values 'true' or 'false'. Thus, if 'the present King of France' were a logical as well as a grammatical subject expression, either it would have to denote something – a Meinongian subsistent entity, say – or sentences in which it occurred would be meaningless. Neither option was attractive to Russell for the reasons given. Accordingly the Theory of Descriptions provides what is, given the terms in which Russell set the problem for himself, a masterly way out, by saying that sentences with descriptions in subject place are not logical subject–predicate sentences, and that descriptions, far from being representable as singular terms in a formal language, are in fact concealed existence and uniqueness assertions. When these latter are false, as shown above, the original sentence is as a whole false.

Quine, it is worth noting, derives his view of ontological commitment directly from Russell's strategy, but without espousing either of Russell's doctrines concerning logically proper names or the correlative epistemological notions of acquaintance and description. On this score, Russell held that the only logically proper names are expressions like 'this' and 'that' – that is, demonstratives picking out objects of direct acquaintance. Quine's epistemological outlook, which is holistic, is quite opposite in character to this thoroughgoing atomism, an outlook in large part forced by Russell's view of logical form.

The central point for Russell is that definite descriptions are not referring devices. The main criticism against the theory is that descriptions are indeed – or do indeed have uses as – referring devices.

Strawson on Descriptions

Strawson's criticism of the Theory of Descriptions consists in a rejection of the theory of meaning underlying it, so laying an axe to its root. The criticism is that no words or expressions have as their meaning some designated object. In Strawson's view, meaning resides in the activities of language users. If meaning is not denotation there cannot be 'logically proper names', nor descriptions in Russell's sense, for in Strawson's view no one uttering such a sentence as 'the present King of France is wise' is asserting that there is a King of France. Russell, as Strawson saw it, had failed to distinguish between the use of an expression to make a unique reference, and asserting that there is one and no more than one individual possessing certain characteristics.[47]

Russell's objective in devising the Theory of Descriptions is identified by Strawson as an attempt to escape the consequences of arguments like these: (1) the phrase 'the King of France' is the subject of the sentence S. If S is a significant or meaningful sentence, then S is *about* the King of France. But if the King of France does not exist, then S is not about anything, and hence not about the King of France. But it *is* about the King of France, and it *is* meaningful; therefore there must in some sense be (exist, or subsist) the King of France; or (2) if S is significant or meaningful, it is either true or false. It is true if the King of France is wise, and false if he is not wise. But 'the King of France is wise' and 'the King of France is not wise' have the truth-values they do only if there is, in some sense, something which is King of France; therefore in some sense there must be (exist, or subsist) the King of France.

Strawson commended Russell's desire to avoid the consequences of these arguments, which are bad ones; but he argued that Russell, in the process of doing so, mistakenly accepted the assumptions on which those arguments are based. These are that meaning is denotation, and that if the subject of a subject–predicate sentence is a logically proper subject – that is, not merely a grammatical subject – and the sentence is meaningful, then there is something to which its subject–term refers. Strawson pointed out that Russell recognized only two ways in which meaningfulness can attach to sentences that seem, in virtue of their grammatical form, to be about some particular person, object, or event. One is that if their grammatical and logical forms are incongruent, then they should be analysable as an existential sentence of a special sort. The other is that the meaning of the grammatical subject of such a sentence should be the individual thing it designates, that is, that it should be a logically proper name.

To make out his case Strawson draws a three-way distinction among a sentence, a use of a sentence, and an utterance of a sentence.[48] One can imagine the sentence 'the King of France is wise', call it K, being uttered in successive reigns of French kings, and it is natural to speak of K as being the same sentence each time. Evidently, however, there are differences between the *occasions of use* each time; users of K would be talking about different kings, and, depending on the nature of the kings in question, would sometimes be saying something true and sometimes something false. These are different *uses* of K. Similarly if two people used K during the same reign, then their use of K would be the same.

On Strawson's view, it follows from these distinctions that it is not the *sentence* which is true or false, but, instead, that what is true or false is the statement or proposition which the sentence is used to make.

Analogously, a three-way distinction can be drawn among an expression, a use of an expression, and an utterance of an expression. The expression at issue is the description 'the King of France', call it D. As for K, it cannot be said that D refers to or mentions the King of France, but that it can be *used* to mention or refer on a particular occasion of utterance. ' "Mentioning" or "referring" is not something an expression does; it is something one can use an expression to do ... [it] is a characteristic of *a use* of an expression, just as "being about something", and truth-or-falsity, are characteristic of *a use of* a sentence.'[49]

Strawson is not saying that there are sentences and descriptions *and* uses of them *and* utterances of them, as there are ships *and* shoes *and* sealing-wax; he is saying we cannot say *the same things* about these linguistic forms *and* their uses *and* utterances of them. But Russell thought we could do this; and this is where he went wrong, in Strawson's opinion, for 'to give the meaning of an expression ... is to give *general directions* for its use to refer ... [and] to give the meaning of a sentence is to give *general directions* for its use in making true or false assertions ... the meaning of an expression cannot be identified with the object it is used, on a particular occasion, to refer to. The meaning of a sentence cannot be identified with the assertion it is used, on a particular occasion, to make'. Russell, however, thought that referring, if it occurred at all, was meaning; he confused the description, on the one hand, with its *use in a particular context* on the other hand. 'The important point,' Strawson wrote, 'is that the question whether the sentence is significant or not is quite independent of the question that can be raised about a particular use of it, *viz.* the question whether it is a genuine or spurious use.'[50]

In Strawson's view, Russell has said two true things and two false things about K. The two true things are that K is significant, and that K would be true only if there exists one and no more than one King of France who is wise. The two false things are that anyone now uttering K would be making an assertion which is either true or false, and that part of what K would be asserting is that there is one and only one King of France.

The two false things are false for the following reasons. If someone uttered K seriously now, we would not reply, 'That's false'. We would point out that there is no King of France at present, so the question of whether K as a whole is true or false does not arise; K is truth-valueless. And secondly: there is an obvious difference between a uniquely existential sentence, of the form 'there is only one such-and-such', and a sentence containing an expression, like D, which on particular occasions can be used to mention or refer to a particular person or thing. When someone uses K he neither *asserts* that there is someone who is uniquely King of France, nor does his use of the expression *entail* that there is someone who is uniquely King of France (even though, if his use of K is serious, he *presupposes* that there is such a person). As Strawson puts it, 'When we begin a sentence with "the such-and-such" the use of "the" shows, but does not state that we are, or intend to be, referring to one particular. . . "such-and-such".'[51] Russell conflated sentences which can be used to make particular reference, on the one hand, with uniquely existential sentences on the other; and this mistake is induced by his denotative theory of meaning.

An important feature of Strawson's proposed alternative analysis is the distinction he insists upon between statements and sentences. The former are actual uses of the latter on some particular occasion, as noted. A sentence has meaning, but it is not a sentence, or a constituent of it, which refers; rather, reference happens when a given sentence is used on a given occasion to make a statement. The expression 'the King of France' is therefore meaningful, but when actually used, it fails to refer to anything. The statement in question is truth-valueless – that is, is neither true nor false. Thus Strawson admits 'truth-value gaps' for statements in those cases where reference fails.

There are certain points in this account which need clarification. It is not clear whether Strawson's view is that use of the kind of sentence in question does not make a statement, or whether it does make a statement but one which is truth-valueless. The solution to this is connected with the solution to a further doubt, concerning whether in Strawson's view the presupposition that there is a King of France is something entertained by the utterer of the sentence, or whether it is a relation obtaining between the statement and a further, suppressed, existential statement asserting that there is a King of France. Strawson's intention was that presupposition should not be construed as an epistemological relation of the first sort, but as a logical relation of the second sort, as his later papers show; accordingly, in line with the sketch given above, presupposition is a relation such that a given statement A has truth-value if and only if a presupposed statement B is true.[52] This then solves the first problem: the use of a sentence makes a statement, but in the case of uses of sentences like K, the statement made is truth-valueless.

But now a different problem arises. Truth-valuelessness is a controversial notion. Among the critics of Strawson's view are those who are anxious to preserve bivalence, the principle – as noted – that there are just two truth values, true and false, and that all statements are determinately one or the other. Truth-valuelessness violates the principle of bivalence because it constitutes a third truth-value. Moreover, bivalence is a semantic principle to which corresponds the syntactic principle known as the Law of Excluded Middle, which states 'everything is either A or not A'. This 'Law', one of Aristotle's three 'Laws of Thought' (the other two being the principles of Identity and Non-contradiction, respectively 'A is A' and 'not both A and not A'), appears self-evident. But in intuitionist logic and in anti-realist critiques of realist theories of meaning (see chapter 8 below) bivalence is rejected, and with it the Law of Excluded Middle.[53] From the abandonment of bivalence, in short, significant results follow for other central philosophical concerns.

Strawson's views echo those of Frege who, unlike Russell, did not recognize a class of logically proper names, but who was able, by means of the sense–reference distinction, to allow sense to sentences containing expressions which fail to refer. In Frege's theory, to say that a sentence has sense is to say that it expresses a 'thought' (proposition). References of sentences – namely, truth-values – depend upon the references of their parts, so it follows that if one constituent of a given sentence has no reference, the sentence as whole has none – that is, it is truth-valueless.[54] This makes his account somewhat like Strawson's presuppositional theory, in the sense that a sentence will have a truth-value only if there is something to which the constituent terms refer.

Owing to his view that vacuous singular terms (singular terms which fail to refer) constitute one of the nuisances of natural language, Frege suggested that in a perfect language – a fully specifiable formal language like logic – all singular terms should be guaranteed referents, even artificial ones if necessary. He suggested that the number O could be taken as the object referred to by expressions otherwise lacking referents, or whose referents are difficult to locate. A systematic effort to work out these ideas was offered by Carnap.[55]

A minor reservation about Strawson's position is worth noting at this juncture. The theory of meaning he prefers to Russell's has it that to give the meaning of an expression is to give 'general directions' for its use to refer or mention; and to give the meaning of a sentence is to give 'general directions' for its use in making true or false assertions. But as this sketch of a theory of meaning stands, it is by no means self-evident. What does 'giving directions' amount to? It may include giving information – perhaps even ostensive information – of a sort that makes the theory covertly very similar to the denotative theory it purports to displace; for if the directions are too general, and cover any mentioning or referring expression, they will apply equally to 'the pig in the sty' and 'the King of France'. But if they apply equally to both these expressions, they will not explain the differences between them. Directions for using words to refer might, then, actually include explanation of their meanings so like denotation that it is hardly worth arguing about.

Strawson points out that the use of descriptive phrases only implies uniqueness in context. A couple with a baby who live in an apartment block of many couples with babies might speak of 'the baby', but obviously not thereby mean to imply that there is one and only one such thing in the world. To this Russell had a reply: the context specifies which baby is uniquely of interest to the couple in question. All uses of 'the so-and-so' can be taken to be restricted to a domain in this way. The need then arises for a systematic way of circumscribing domains.

Referential and Attributive Uses of Descriptions

The preceding discussion concerns what form an analysis of descriptions should take, given that descriptions may sometimes be vacuous. According to Donnellan, the analyses offered by both Russell and Strawson are both unsatisfactory, because they fail to recognize that descriptions have two possible functions, and that a given description may have either function depending on the use made of the sentence in which it occurs.[56]

Donnellan calls the two uses to which descriptions can be put the 'referential' and the 'attributive' use respectively. When using a description attributively, a speaker is asserting something about whoever or whatever is 'the so-and-so'; the description occurs essentially, because the speaker is attributing something to whoever or whatever fits the description. The attribute of being the so-and-so is all-important in this case.

By contrast, when a speaker uses a description referentially, he is doing so to enable his audience to pick out or identify whoever or whatever he is talking about; the description here is merely a tool for effecting reference, and the job might equally well be done by any other referential device, such as a name or some other description.[57]

Illustrations clarify the distinction. Consider the sentence 'Smith's murderer is insane', which we might utter in the case of a man called Smith who has been vilely murdered. If I do not know who the murderer is, I can none the less attribute insanity to him. If however some particular person, say Jones, has been arraigned for the crime, then in my uttering this sentence I use the description referentially, to pick out Jones. The contrast is even clearer in the case where, say, Smith was not murdered but (unknown to us) had an accident. Then by using the description 'Smith's murderer' we presuppose or imply that there is a murderer, with different results according as to which use the description is being put.[58] If attributively, the predicate '. . . is insane' applies to nobody, for there is nobody to whom insanity could be correctly attributed. If referentially, however, we may still succeed in picking someone out (the wrongfully accused Jones – 'wrongfully accused' on this version of the story) even though the description 'Smith's murderer' does not fit him or anyone else. And even if someone in the audience knew or believed Jones to be innocent, he would still know who was being referred to by use of the description.[59]

To vary the example: using a description referentially, one can successfully pick out a man as 'the man drinking Champagne' even if the description does not fit, say because it is water and not Champagne in the glass. But if the chairman of the Teetotaller's Union has been told there is someone at the party drinking Champagne, and asks 'which is the man drinking Champagne?', thus using the description attributively, then if there is no one who fits the description, no one can be picked out as the person of whom the question has been asked.[60]

One of the important results flowing from Donnellan's distinction is the difference made to the issue of the existential presupposition or implication carried by descriptions. In general, there is a presupposition that a person using a description referentially believes that there is a whoever or whatever, and that the description fits it. Misdescriptions usually mislead an audience; nevertheless, even if nothing in fact fits a referentially-used description, it can still successfully serve to pick out whatever it was that the speaker intended to pick out for his audience.

By contrast, there is not the same possibility of misdescription in the attributive case. 'Smith's murderer' attributively used cannot misdescribe because it is not being used to pick out Jones or any particular person, but *anyone* who happens to fit the description, even if it is not known whom. Rather, the presupposition or implication is carried by the attributively-used description because, if nothing answered to the description, the purpose of the speech-act in which it figured would be thwarted. Thus the description might figure in a statement, or a command, or a question; if it failed to fit anyone or anything, then the speaker would have failed to make a statement, or to command anyone to do something, or to ask a question.[61]

This shows in what respect both Russell and Strawson have gone wrong in Donnellan's view. Russell held that 'the ϕ is' Y' entails 'there exists one and only one ϕ'; but whereas this might be so in the attributive case, it does not appear to be so in the referential case. Here there is a presumption based on what is normally true of the referential use of descriptions, namely that there is something which is the ϕ; but this does not amount to an *entailment* of an existence and uniqueness assertion by the sentence containing the description. Russell's analysis, in consequence, fits only the attributive case.

The definition of denoting given by Russell was that a term denotes if there is an entity which it picks out. This fits both uses of descriptions; and accordingly, on Donnellan's view, shows that denoting (which both kinds of descriptions do) and referring (which only one kind of description does) are different things. Russell recognizes only the former. Donnellan argues that a denoting–referring distinction is fruitful, for it provides a way of dealing with such cases as the following. One naturally does not know in advance who will be the prime minister in 3000 AD, but suppose one says 'the prime minister in 3000 AD will be a Labour politician'. Suppose it in fact turns out that a Labour politician is indeed prime minister in that year. The description denotes that person; but one used the description attributively and did not – because one could not – *refer* to that person. The denoting–referring distinction makes clear what is and what is not going on in uses of descriptions in this way.[62]

Donnellan's criticism of Strawson is that Strawson's theory goes too far in the direction of making descriptions referential, thus obscuring their attributive function. On Donnellan's view Strawson's theory consists in the following propositions:

1. If someone asserts that the ϕ is Y he has not made a true or false statement if there is no ϕ.
2. If there is no ϕ then the speaker has failed to refer to anything.
3. The reason he has said nothing true or false is that he has failed to refer.[63]

The first proposition may be true in the attributive case; for if Smith had no murderer then 'Smith's murderer is insane' says nothing true. However if the description was used referentially to pick out Jones, then even if Jones is innocent he may none the less be insane, and so something true has been said.[64] For this same reason, proposition 2 is simply false; there may be no ϕ, that is no 'Smith's murderer', yet Jones has been successfully referred to.[65]

Matters are more complicated with regard to proposition 3. Strawson took it that 3 ties together 1 and 2. But 3 does not work, for the attributive case at least, as an account of the truth-valuelessness of statements when their presuppositions are false. For the reason given is that reference has failed; and this does not explain why a speaker making an attributive use of a description fails to state anything true or false when nothing fits the description.[66] In the referential case, it would seem that a speaker fails to refer only in rather extreme cases of perceptual or, more generally, epistemic error, as when someone, deluded by a trick of the light, say, says 'is that man with the handkerchief the Emeritus Waynflete Professor of Metaphysics?' when there is in fact no one at all, so that it cannot be said to whom or what it was that the speaker intended to refer.

Donnellan concludes that 'neither Russell's nor Strawson's theory represents a correct account of the use of definite descriptions – Russell's because it ignores altogether the referential use, Strawson's because it ignores altogether the distinction between the referential and attributive and mixes together truths about each (together with some things that are false)'.[67]

There are difficulties in Donnellan's account, arising chiefly from independent problems about the notion of reference and a distinction which can be drawn between speaker's reference and semantic reference. Grice, for example, proposed that we should distinguish between what a speaker's *words* mean and what the *speaker* means by using those words on that occasion, as when someone says 'The cops have arrived' meaning 'Let's get out of here'. The speaker means the latter by using the former, and in this case the words constituting the former do not at all mean in their own right what the speaker used them to mean.[68] (See chapter 8 below.)

Kripke employs a similar notion to challenge Donnellan's account.[69] In Kripke's view, the *semantic* referent of a referring expression is given by the speaker's *general* intention to refer to a certain object on a specific occasion. If the speaker believes that an object he wishes to talk about satisfies the conditions for being the semantic referent of the term he uses, then he believes that there is no conflict between his general and specific intentions. Kripke thinks Donnellan's views should be considered in the light of this, because there are two ways in which the speaker's belief in the coincidence of his general and specific intentions arise. One – the 'simple' case – is when the speaker's specific intention just is his general semantic intention, as when he uses 'Jones' as a name of Jones; the other – the 'complex' case – is when he has a specific intention distinct from his general intention, both which he believes to be coincident in fact, as when he wishes to refer to 'the man over there' believing that that man *is* Jones.[70]

Kripke's argument is that Donnellan's attributive use of descriptions is nothing but the 'simple' case, and the referential use the 'complex' case; and that accordingly it was wrong for Donnellan to assimilate the referential use of descriptions to the referential use of proper names; for the simple–complex distinction applies just as much to proper names as descriptions.[71] The argument is made out by means of a test involving languages with more and less specific forms than the one (in this case English) for which Donnellan's case is made out, with a view to seeing whether the referential – attributive ambiguity postulated by Donnellan holds for English. Kripke concludes that it does not necessarily hold for English, since in more specific variants of English the ambiguity vanishes; and that therefore Russell's unitary account of descriptions is preferable.[72] The details of this argument turn on considerations specific to the nature of reference, and since I deal with these in a later chapter I shall leave the matter aside for the present.

One way for Russell's views to deal with Donnellan's concerns is to show that they turn on pragmatic considerations about the uses made of language, rather than semantic considerations where the interest is to specify the truth-conditions of utterances. The Theory of Descriptions is a semantic theory; but it is obvious that descriptions can be used pragmatically, a fact which Russell's theory can comfortably acknowledge.[73]

Notes

1 This enquiry is called *ontology*, 'theory of being'.
2 R. Descartes, *Meditations*, pp. 59–124.
3 Kant, *Critique of Pure Reason*, cf. A590/B618 *et seq.*
4 Ibid., A598/B626.
5 Aristotle concluded much the same: 'that there is such a thing is not what anything is . . . being is not a genus', *Analytica Posteriora*, II, 7, 92 b 13.
6 D. F. Pears, 'Is Existence a Predicate?', in Strawson (ed.), *Philosophical Logic*, pp. 79–102. For some reason it has become traditional to put the question this way; more accurately, one should ask whether 'exists' is a predicate or whether existence is a property. The word 'exists' cannot be a property of anything, and existence is not a linguistic entity.
7 Cf. Strawson, *Introduction to Logical Theory*, p. 175 *et seq.*
8 The notion of presuppositional implication is not without its problems. See below; and cf. G. Nerlich, 'Presupposition and Entailment', *American Philosophical Quarterly*, 2, 1969; and 'Presupposition and Classical Logical Relations', *Analysis*, XXVII, 1967. Cf. also M. K. Munitz (ed.), *Existence and Logic*, and M. A. E. Dummett, *Truth and Other Enigmas*.
9 G. E. Moore, 'Is Existence a Predicate?', *Proceedings of the Aristotelian Society*, 1936, pp. 175–88. Moore was replying to a paper on the same topic by W. M. Kneale.
10 Moore, 'Is Existence a Predicate?' pp. 177–8.
11 Ibid., pp. 178–9.
12 Ibid., p. 179.
13 Ibid., p. 180.
14 Ibid., p. 185, Moore's italics.
15 Ibid., p. 186.
16 Ibid., p. 187, Moore's italics.
17 See J. Thomson, 'Is Existence a Predicate?', in Strawson, *Philosophical Logic*, passim.
18 Cf. A. Orenstein, *Existence and the Particular Quantifier*, passim.
19 M. R. Lipton, Review of Orenstein, in *Philosophical Review*, July 1980, p. 487 *et seq.*
20 W. V. Quine, 'Designation and Existence,' *Journal of Philosophy*, xxxvi, 1939, pp. 707–8; reprinted in Feigl and Sellars, *Readings in Philosophical Analysis*.

21 Quine, 'Ontology and Ideology' *Philosophical Studies* II, 1951, p. 11, reprinted in Feigl et al., *New Readings in Philosophical Analysis*.
22 Quine, *Word and Object*, p. 242.
23 Cf. below, this chapter, for Russell's treatment of descriptions, and cf. chapter 6 below for a discussion of the notion of 'satisfaction' in the sections on Tarski.
24 Quine, *Word and Object*, pp. 258–9.
25 A. Orenstein, 'On Explicating Existence in Terms of Quantification' in M. K. Munitz (ed.), *Logic and Ontology*, p. 73.
26 Cf. ibid.; the example is drawn from Hintikka and shows that the substitutional reading has advantages over the objectual for quantification in opaque contexts.
27 S. Haack, *Philosophy of Logics*, p. 50; and pp. 50–5 for a discussion of which choice to make. Haack is fond of diagrams and provides some useful ones in her text.
28 Strawson, 'Singular Terms and Predication', in Strawson, *Introduction to Logical Theory*, pp. 69–88; cf. esp. p. 77.
29 Cf. Haack, *Philosophy of Logics*, p. 47 *et seq.*
30 Strawson, 'Is Existence Never a Predicate?', *Freedom and Resentment*.
31 Ibid., pp. 193–4.
32 Ibid., p. 196.
33 Ibid., pp. 196–7.
34 Ibid., p. 194.
35 Strawson, *Introduction to Logical Theory*, p. 191. (ed), *Logical and Ontology*, p. 85 *et seq.*
36 Cf. Munitz, 'Existence and Presupposition,' in Munitz (ed.), *Logic and Ontology*, p. 85 *et seq.*
37 Evans, *Varieties of Reference*, Oxford 1982 Ch. 10 passion, esp. pp. 369–72; and see Sainsbury, 'Philosophical Logic' in Grayling (ed.) *Philosophy*, pp. 89–91.
38 Sainsbury, 'Philosophical Logic', p. 90.
39 Ibid.
40 B. Russell, *Mysticism and Logic*, p. 209, and *The Problems of Philosophy*, p. 25.
41 Russell, *Mysticism and Logic*, pp. 212–13.
42 Russell discussed these in R. C. Marsh (ed.), 'Lectures on Logical Atomism 5', *Logic and Knowledge*, London, 1956.
43 Russell, *Problems of Philosophy*, p. 29.
44 Ibid.
45 Russell, *Logic and Knowledge*, pp. 247–8.
46 Ibid., p. 245.
47 Strawson, 'On Referring', *Mind*, 1950, pp. 320–44; reprinted in Feigl et al., *New Readings in Philosophical Analysis*, pp. 35–50.

48 Ibid., p. 38.
49 Ibid., p. 39.
50 Ibid., p. 41.
51 Ibid., p. 42.
52 Cf. Strawson, 'A Reply To Mr Sellars', *Philosophical Review*, 1954, reprinted in Feigl et al. *New Readings in Philosophical Analysis*, pp. 51–4; and 'Identifying Reference and Truth-Values', *Theoria*, 30, 1964; reprinted in *Logico-Linguistic Papers*.
53 Matters are more complex than I have just sketched them here; cf. chapter 8 below, where the discussion is more extended. Note that Dummett attacks the notion of presupposition and the principle of bivalence, cf. *Truth and Other Enigmas*.
54 Cf. chapter 2 above.
55 Cf. R. Carnap, *Introduction To Semantics and Formalisation of Logic*.
56 K. S. Donnellan, 'Reference and Definite Descriptions', *Philosophical Review*, LXXV, 1966, pp. 281–304; reprinted in S. P. Schwartz (ed.), *Naming, Necessity, and Natural Kinds*, pp. 42–65. References are to this edition. 'Description' means 'definite description' here as throughout this chapter.
57 Ibid., p. 46.
58 Use of this disjunction leaves open the issue between Russell and Strawson as to whether the description presupposes or implies that there is a murderer.
59 Ibid., pp. 47–8.
60 Ibid., p. 48.
61 Ibid., pp. 52–3.
62 Ibid., pp. 54–5.
63 Ibid., pp. 55–6.
64 Ibid., p. 56.
65 Ibid.
66 Ibid., pp. 56–7.
67 Ibid., p. 58.
68 H. P. Grice, 'Speaker's Meaning, Sentence-Meaning, and Word-Meaning', *Foundations of Language*, 4, 1968, pp. 225–42.
69 S. Kripke, 'Speaker's Reference and Semantic Reference', in French et al., *Contemporary Perspectives in the Philosophy of Language*.
70 Ibid., p. 15.
71 Ibid.
72 Ibid., pp. 16–18.
73 For other discussions see C. A. B. Peacocke, 'Proper Names, Reference and Rigid Designation' in S. Blackburn (ed.), *Meaning, Reference, Necessity: New Studies in Semantics*; M. Sainsbury, 'Philosophical Logic' in A. C. Grayling, *Philosophy*; and especially, S. Neale, *Descriptions*, which is the most significant current contribution to the debate.

5

Truth: The Pragmatic, Coherence and Correspondence Theories

Introduction

It is a philosophical commonplace that there can be no progress in understanding a concept unless one's enquiry begins with the right questions. The wrong question to ask about truth is 'what is truth?' for the following reasons.

Consider the difference between the questions 'what is kelp?' and 'what is rationality?' The first is relatively easy to answer; the appropriate reply is, 'it is a kind of seaweed'. The second poses more difficulties and demands a more studied reply. What is being requested is an account of a complex concept, and it would seem fruitful to begin by investigating what one's possession of the concept consists in, which is in part at least to ask how and when one uses it. So it is better to reply in this second case in a way which, although more circuitous, is in the end more informative, by recasting the question into 'what is it for someone to make a rational decision or choice?', the idea being that answers to this question provide the first step to understanding the concept of rationality in general.

Questions about truth are, for the same reasons, best approached in the same indirect way. 'What is truth?' has the character of a smooth sheer cliff, which one cannot see how to climb. As it stands, the question looks like a request to know what truth ('Truth') is in some ultimate, inclusive, perhaps mystical sense; but it is evident that even if there were Truth in this sense, it would be necessary to begin with more modest aims. The task, accordingly, is made easier by asking 'what is it for a proposition (statement, sentence, or belief) to be true?' The purpose of this chapter and the next is to investigate the major theories framed in reply.

There are a number of 'theories of truth' – or more accurately, families of views about truth. A preliminary characterization of the chief of them runs as follows. The *pragmatic* theory has it that true beliefs are those which work, which are fruitful, which have as it were 'cash-value' in terms of experience. The *coherence* theory has it that truth consists in a relation of coherence between beliefs or propositions in a set, such that a belief is false when it fails to fit with other mutually coherent members of a set. The *correspondence* theory has it that a proposition is true when it corresponds to the facts; the relation here is between propositions and the way things are in the world. *Deflationary* theories have it that there is nothing more to the concept of truth than (if anything) certain conveniences; they take several different forms, for example the *redundancy* theory which has it that because 'p is true' and 'p' mean the same, 'is true' is redundant; and the *minimalist* theory, which holds, more weakly than the redundancy theory, that 'p is true' and 'p' are equivalent. In the *semantic* theory truth is a property of *sentences*, defined in terms of a recursive notion of *satisfaction* construed as a relation between sentences of a given language and objects in a domain. There are variants and sophistications of each of these theories, and some overlaps between some of them; these features emerge in the following.

Chapter 2 above contained among other things discussion of the difference between propositions and sentences. The usefulness of that distinction now becomes manifest. It is crucial to traditional versions of the correspondence theory that the correspondence relation holds between propositions (not sentences) and states of affairs in the world; whereas in the semantic theory, truth is taken to be a property of sentences. Again, it involves difficulties to render the coherence and pragmatic theories as asserting, respectively, coherence between sentences, or the utility of accepting certain sentences – remembering that sentences are grammatically well-formed strings of uttered or inscribed (and therefore spatio-temporal) sounds or marks, and not *uses* of them on occasions by speakers, nor *what they (can be used to) convey.*

The problem of truth has been taken to turn on two principal points: the first concerns the meaning of the word 'true', while the second concerns the criterion or criteria by means of which truth-value can be recognized as attaching to truth-bearers.[1] It is important to take note of this distinction because whereas one of the truth theories might offer a definition of 'true', another might offer a test for ascertaining what truth-value some truth-bearer has. For example, it might be held that, in meaning, 'true' is an evaluative term, like 'good', whereas the criterion of truth is utility – such a view was held by the pragmatist Schiller. Bradley seemed to think that in meaning 'true' is a form of correspondence – 'truth to be truth must be true of something' – whereas coherence furnishes the criterion or test of truth.[2] Most pragmatists identify the definition and the criterion by saying that one gives the meaning of 'true' by supplying criteria for its application – a view with affinities to Wittgenstein's later thought and 'use' theories of meaning generally.[3] Some coherence theorists, like Blanshard, also held that the definition and the criterion run together, in this case because (in his view) that truth *is* coherence, and so the notion supplies at once a test for truth and a definition of 'true'.[4]

In this chapter I survey three theories of truth which have for long commanded attention in philosophical debate: the pragmatic, coherence, and correspondence theories.

The Pragmatic Theory of Truth

Articulation of the pragmatic theory's main original variants owes itself to three of the leading figures in American philosophy in the late nineteenth and early twentieth centuries – Peirce, James and Dewey. Owing to the presence of common ground in their philosophical views they are grouped as 'pragmatists'; hence the label for their theory – or, more accurately, variants on a theory – of truth. Their influence is apparent in the work of Quine, Davidson and a number of other recent thinkers.[5]

In the pragmatists' view, a concept's meaning is given by reference to the practical or experimental (hence 'pragmatic') consequences of its application. As James had it 'there can *be* no difference that *makes* no difference',[6] which directly echoes Peirce's less aphoristic dictum 'there is no distinction of meaning so fine as to consist in anything but a possible difference of practice'.[7] This comes down to saying that the right approach to truth is to enquire what *difference* is made by a belief's being true.

Peirce held that truth is that opinion upon which scientists (in the broad sense of 'those who use the scientific method') will, if they go on long enough, eventually agree; and he held this in consequence of a prior view about what is, in effect, the psychology of enquiry. For Peirce, beliefs consist in dispositions to action, and doubts are the negative effects on such dispositions which result from unruly experiences, experiences which subvert our theories or fail to fit some general pattern manifested by our views of the world. Such doubts, said Peirce, prompt enquiry because they induce an unpleasant state in us, which we try to overcome by acquiring stable beliefs. Scientific method enables us to acquire such beliefs, because alone among belief-acquiring methods it is constrained by the way things actually are – that is, by reality – and since the way things are is independent of anyone's beliefs, that constraint will bring about an eventual convergence of opinions among enquirers. This eventual consensus is truth. Not only will the truth be wholly satisfying to believe, since it is immune from the disturbances of doubt, but it will also consist in correspondence with reality. In this way Peirce's version of the pragmatist theory incorporates elements of the correspondence theory.

James' version in some ways elaborates upon, and in some ways differs from, Peirce's view. James argued that the value of having true beliefs consists in their immunity from unruly experiences; and true beliefs are those which are confirmed by experience in the long run, that is, which are verifiable. James believed that we accommodate awkward experiences by adjusting our system of beliefs in such a way as best to preserve its internal consistency, while finding a place for recalcitrant experiential results within it. This foreshadows the 'web of beliefs' view mooted by Quine, and incorporates elements of a coherence theory.[8]

Whereas Peirce was a realist, James had nominalist instincts, and was accordingly troubled by the fact that verifiability seemed to commit him to the existence of truths not yet verified – that is, to the existence of possible, but unrealized, verifications. This is embarrassing to nominalist scruples, and James sometimes therefore wrote as if implying that truths are *manufactured* by the process of verifying beliefs. This tack was adopted by Schiller, and more recently by, for example Feyerabend and (typically for the same relativist reasons) some 'postmodernist' thinkers.[9] But the idea that truths are created by enquiry is inconsistent with the view that beliefs converge to truth by verification processes; so there is tension in James' theory in this respect.

A feature of James' view that invited much criticism is his propensity to speak of truth as what is 'good', 'useful', or 'expedient' to believe. He wrote, for example, that 'the true is only the expedient in the way of our thinking, just as the right is only the expedient in our way of behaving'.[10] Russell and Moore took James to task for this on the grounds that he was making the crude, and also morally objectionable, point that truth is the same as congenial belief. But defenders of James argue that he was trying to show that the superiority of true over false beliefs consists in their immunity to falsification, and that since empirical evidence is by itself frequently unable to help us adjudicate between competing theories, considerations of utility can and should be invoked to aid decision.[11]

Dewey accepted Peirce's definition of truth as 'absolute fixity of belief'. Together with Peirce he believed that making sense of our ideas demands that we examine them at work, in their contexts of use.[12] When we recognize that these or those ideas work successfully and provide solutions to doubts or problems – that is, are confirmed in practice – then we are warranted in asserting those ideas – which is to say, warranted in committing ourselves to them as true. Thus Dewey preferred to speak of truth as a property attaching to ideas which we are warranted in asserting.

To say that truth is a property which beliefs come to possess by being verified in practice has, however, apparently counter-intuitive results. Suppose White murders Brown on Tuesday, and a detective verifies White's guilt on Thursday. Then it would seem that the proposition 'White murdered Brown' *became true* on Thursday, and was not true beforehand. But surely 'White murdered Brown' was true the instant of White's murdering Brown; if Dewey's views are correct, we might not be able to convict White at all, owing to the fact that for a period after Brown's murder it was *not* true 'that White murdered Brown'. This suggests that there is an important difference between the notions of confirmation and truth, for whereas confirmation appears to be a datable occurrence (the detective confirmed White's guilt on Thursday), truth is standardly taken to be such that a proposition does not become true upon being verified or grasped, but simply is or is not true – even, on some views, whether anyone knows it to be true or not. (Such a view is often described as 'realist'.

This last thought suggests a criticism an upholder of the principle of bivalence might make. This is that to define 'true' as 'confirmed' violates the principle; for if 'true' means 'confirmed' then, since the principle requires that for every proposition either it or its negation, but not both, be true, it would follow that every proposition or its negation is confirmed. But this is simply false; for although it is either true that 'it snowed in Oxfordshire in 10,000 BC', or true that 'it did not snow in Oxfordshire in 10,000 BC', as the principle demands, it is certainly not the case that either proposition is confirmed.

The attacks on pragmatism mounted by Russell, Moore and Carnap gave rise for a time to some crude misunderstanding of its associated theory of truth. This is that it defines 'true' simply as 'what works', and that this is wholly mistaken since it is quite obvious that many falsehoods 'work' (only consider Plato's view that the general population should be encouraged in religious beliefs, since although these beliefs are false, they will promote good conduct), whereas many truths, for example that 'Aristotle's father was a physician', do no real 'work' at all (as has been said, they 'bake no bread'). But it will be clear, even from the foregoing sketches, that the pragmatic theory is rather more subtle than the imputed equation 'true = what works' suggests.

James' Defence

Consider James' view in more detail. He did most among the pragmatists to contest misunderstanding of the pragmatic theory, and wrote about it often.[13] There is no better statement of his view than one provided by himself, worth quoting at length:

> Truth is a property of certain of our ideas. It means their agreement, as falsity means their disagreement, with reality . . . Pragmatism asks its usual question. 'Grant an idea or belief to be true,' it says, 'what concrete difference will its being true make in anyone's actual life? What experiences [might] be different from those which would obtain if the belief were false? What, in short, is the truth's cash-value in experiential terms?' The moment pragmatism asks this question, it sees the answer: *True ideas are those we can assimilate, validate, corroborate, and verify. False ideas are those that we cannot.* That is the practical difference it makes to us to have true ideas; that therefore is the meaning of truth, for it is all that truth is known as.
>
> The truth of an idea is not a stagnant property inherent in it. Truth *happens* to an idea. It *becomes* true, is *made* true by events. Its verity is in fact an event, a process, the process namely of its verifying itself, its *verification* . . . Any idea that helps us to deal, whether practically or intellectually, with reality, that doesn't entangle our progress in frustrations, that *fits*, in fact, and adapts our life to the reality's whole setting, will agree sufficiently to meet the requirement. It will be true of that reality. *The true*, to put it very briefly, *is only the expedient in our way of thinking, just as the right is only the expedient in the way of our behavior.* Expedient in almost any fashion, and expedient in the long run and on the whole, of

course; for what meets expediently all the experience in sight won't necessarily meet all further experience equally satisfactorily. Experience, as we know, has ways of *boiling over*, and making us correct our present formulas.'[14]

Moore and Russell, as noted, took this view to come down simply to an equation of truth with utility, and rejected it on the grounds that some falsehoods are useful, some truths inexpedient – 'Is it not clear', Moore asked, 'that we do actually sometimes have true ideas, at times when they are not useful, but positively in the way?'[15] But this objection misses the point, for James' claim that truth is satisfactory or useful belief identifies it with belief secure 'in the long run', safe – given a theory of how we assimilate subsequent experiences to our scheme of things – from overthrow.[16] If the Moore–Russell criticism touches a nerve at all, it does so in connection with James' opinion that religious beliefs are expedient (in the ordinary sense of this term) because they maximize the coherence of one's experience and one's values together.[17]

When the connection is grasped between, on the one hand, expediency or utility in James' main sense, and on the other hand the notion of maximizing coherence across the totality of experience, the relation between utility and verifiability becomes clear. Moore and Russell did not see this connection; but they objected as strongly to the assimilation of truth to verification as they did to the assimilation of truth to utility. Their grounds for doing so were similar; namely, that just as there may be inexpedient truths that are nevertheless truths, so there may be truths which have never been verified but which are nevertheless truths. If James had identified truth with verification there would be force to this objection, but in fact he made the subtler identification of truth with *verifiability*, so leaving it open that there can be as yet unverified truths which are none the less truths because they are verifiable.[18] This manoeuvre does however create the tension in James' views, noted above, between truths as an accreting corpus of individual beliefs each becoming a member upon verification, and truths as something which were always true before being verified owing to the fact at they were, antecedent to verification, verifiable. This tension James did not resolve.

The pragmatist theory of truth is an epistemological theory. A question that typically presses when *truth* and *having grounds for taking a belief to be true* are assimilated or at least closely linked, is: what metaphysical picture is associated with such a view? Peirce in the end adopted a fallibilist realism about the objects of perception, but James' anti-realism (these notions are discussed at length below in chapters 8 and 9) left him with certain difficulties. Having rejected the concept of 'trans-empirical' reality – that is, a realm of things independent of, and perhaps inaccessible to, experience – he found it difficult to resolve the tension just identified.[19]

Saying this does not substantiate another of the common criticisms of the pragmatist theory, however, the criticism this time that it is subjectivist in the sense that it makes truth depend on a knowing subject's perspective. Although the pragmatists were under an obligation to offer a workable notion of objectivity, and did not do so to satisfaction, they were nevertheless firm in holding, in their several ways, that part of what it is for a belief to be true is that it corresponds to reality. 'The only *real* guarantee we have against licentious thinking', James wrote, 'is the circumpressure of reality itself, which gets us sick of concrete error, whether there be a trans-empirical reality or not.'[20] The point is not that beliefs are true because they suit the believer in some epistemologically solipsistic way, but because they accord with experience and help the believer to deal with it; it is then a further, although related, matter to supply an account of the reality over which that experience ranges. But at any rate it cannot do to reject the pragmatic conception of truth outright on the grounds, as Moore and Russell did, of an assumption about the nature of reality, in particular where that assumption is 'realistic' in the sense to be discussed; for realism has an inbuilt slant on truth quite opposed, as the very labels suggest, to anti-realist theories such as James'.

The Coherence Theory of Truth

The coherence and correspondence theories are generally regarded as the two chief traditional doctrines of truth. In point of antiquity the correspondence theory takes all laurels; it is discussed by Plato in the *Sophist*. The coherence theory, as a recognizable theory, comes considerably later, dating in the main from Kant's critique of the notion of *adaequatio intellectus et rei* – the adequacy or correspondence of thought to things. In Kant's view, because noumenal reality (the *Ding an sich*, or what James called 'trans-empirical reality') is inaccessible to human intuition, it must follow that the idea of a correspondence between, on the one hand, the mind's apprehension of things, and on the other hand things themselves, is questionable.[21]

The domicile of the coherence theory of truth is, speaking generally, rationalist thought, such as that of Spinoza and Leibniz in the seventeenth and early eighteenth centuries, and Hegel and Bradley at the beginning and end of the nineteenth century respectively. But a coherence theory was also held by some of the twentieth century's logical positivists, in particular Neurath and Hempel, and from oddly similar motives as will be seen. More recently the theory has been discussed by Rescher and Walker.[22]

The basic idea of the coherence theory is a simple one. It is that a proposition is true if it coheres with other propositions in a system, and false otherwise. This is sometimes alternatively put as: truth consists in a relation of coherence among the members of a set of beliefs.

The theory is best explained in context of the metaphysical or epistemological views it has been invoked to serve. Bradley, for example, was concerned to argue that reality is a unified and coherent whole, which he called the Absolute, and nothing short of the whole taken as such is fully real, from which it follows that anything said of parts of the whole can be at best only partly true. If we consider just a part of the whole we may attain to a degree of truth; but since in any case we apprehend parts of the whole by means of *appearances*, which unlike reality (the Absolute) are riddled with contradiction, this partial grasp of the truth is unsatisfactory. It is important to note that if Bradley is right in holding that appearances are at least somewhat deceiving because contradictory, then knowledge (and hence truth) has no incorrigible basis in the judgements of perception. This is what makes Bradley a rationalist as to method; if one denies that sense-experience furnishes the basis for knowledge, and holds instead that excogitation – rational inference – alone carries us to the truth (a view taken, in their fashion, by all of Plato, Leibniz, Spinoza, Hegel, and Bradley himself), then a coherence theory of truth is essential to one's epistemology. For the only test available for the truth of a belief in the context of a rationally-deduced system of beliefs, is whether it coheres with that system of beliefs. No reference to discrete parcels of fact standing over against thought is acceptable in rationalist epistemology, and hence no relation of correspondence can be invoked to explain truth for beliefs on a blow-by-blow basis.

The theoretical basis of the coherence theory lies in the notion of a system. Bradley epitomized the connection between coherence and system by saying 'truth is an ideal expression of the Universe, at once coherent and comprehensive. It must not conflict with itself and there must be no suggestion which fails to fall inside it. Perfect truth, in short, must realise the idea of a systematic whole'.[23] The suggestion is that for a set of beliefs to be coherent, its constituent beliefs must be consistent with each other and, in some way to be specified, dependent upon other beliefs in the set.

Coherence as Dependence

Consistency is a minimum and unproblematic requirement. The major difficulty is to specify what relation of dependence holds between the set's member beliefs or the judgements expressing them. One suggestion is that any judgement must entail and be entailed by every other judgement; this was held by Blanshard, who cited geometry as the nearest to a paradigm of a system in which this is the case.[24] '[In] a completely satisfactory system,' he wrote, '. . . no proposition would be arbitrary, every proposition would be entailed by the others jointly and even singly, no proposition would stand outside the system'.[25] But this will not do; the proposed relation is far too strong, and makes the coherence theory a theory of assertive redundancy, with the effect that in such a system of judgements each says the same as the rest.[26] This seems to imply not only that the true statement 'Alexander was King of Macedon' entails and is entailed by, say, 'my next-door neighbour is wearing a white shirt today', but, worse, that the two statements are intensionally equivalent. In the preferred idiom of the Absolute idealists, in which all statements are diguised predications on the Absolute, 'the Absolute is Alexander-King-of-Macedonly' and 'the Absolute is neighbour-white-shirtly' would thus be repetitions of one another, a view by any standards hard to swallow.

A more promising line is taken by Ewing, who suggests that coherence should be understood as a more diffuse relationship of logic between propositions in a set; specifically, that 'any one proposition in the set follows with logical necessity if all the other propositions in the set are true' and 'no set of propositions within the whole set is logically independent of all propositions in the remainder of the set.'[27] This preserves the idea of interrelatedness of the set's members without collapse into assertive redundancy. As it stands, however, the characterization is vague, and seems to require that the set be complete. But then any proposition added to the set will make it incoherent; and these include the logical consequences of the set's members themselves, an unsatisfactory consequence. Moreover, there is the equally important fact that it is unclear how we could know when a set of propositions is complete – this is in particular so regarding the set, if the idea of a 'set' makes sense here, of propositions about the universe; matters might be different in a formal system.

Positivism and Coherence

The coherence theory has it that truth is determined by a test, somehow specified, of a proposition's value in relation to other propositions in a set, and accordingly the notion of a context or system plays a crucial role in the account. The notion of a system, in turn, might be made out in terms of consistency, connectedness, and completeness. One view that offers a promising basis for such a conception is holism. Holism in the theory of knowledge is the view that the whole system of our beliefs stands or falls together, and that smaller units of belief – individual theories, particular judgements – are confirmed or infirmed only according as they fit or fail to fit the background system. Quine's views, as other chapters show, exemplify just such a commitment. In this he has been anticipated by some of the Logical Positivists and followed by Davidson.

The debate over truth that split the Positivists is instructive. They began by adopting a form of correspondence theory in which statements reporting immediate perceptual experience (called 'basic' or 'protocol' statements) are incorrigible and certain because they directly correspond to the facts; whereas the truth of other (non-protocol) statements is determined by their logical relations to the basic statements. Carnap, in an influential paper, argued that scientific knowledge rests upon protocol statements, which by their nature stand in no further need of verification.[28] Schlick likewise had it that protocol sentences constitute 'the unshakable point of contact between knowledge and reality', and that 'we come to know these absolutely fixed points of contact, the confirmations, in their individuality; they are the only synthetic statements that are not hypotheses.'[29]

This view marks a departure from classical correspondence theories, for it states that only a certain class of statements earns truth by corresponding to facts, while the remainder do so in virtue of relations with other statements – a coherence-flavoured doctrine. It was, accordingly, a fairly short step for some of the positivists, notably Neurath, to go from this view to a full-blown coherence theory. Neurath decided that protocol statements could not be incorrigible, chiefly because, at best, it can only be a conventional matter which propositions are regarded as basic; and accordingly a direct verifying check on correspondence between protocol statements and 'the facts' is impossible.[30] He therefore settled for a test of truth as consisting in the relations between statements themselves, and in so doing departed from the orthodox fold of the positivists under Schlick, with whom he engaged in controversy over the question.

Neurath's view was that no statement is immune to revision because all statements are 'subject to verification, that is to say . . . may be discarded'.[31] 'There is no way,' he wrote, 'of taking conclusively established pure protocol sentences as the starting point of the sciences. No *tabula rasa* exists. We are like sailors who must rebuild their ship on the open sea',[32] meaning by this that we do not begin our investigations with a clean slate, but have an apparatus of theories and assumptions which condition our enquiries, so that we have to refine or change them bit by bit as we proceed. Because the object is to construct a consistent system of observational and theoretical – that is, protocol and nonprotocol – statements, the only test available for new statements offered as candidates for membership of the system is to 'compare it with the system . . . and determine whether or not it conflicts with that system. If the sentence does conflict with the system, we may discard it as useless (or false) . . . One may, on the other hand, accept the sentence and so change the system that it remains consistent . . . the sentence would then be called "true"'.[33] This is a full-blown coherence theory.

For Neurath as for the rationalist metaphysicians mentioned earlier, the primary motive for adopting a coherence theory is the apparent impossibility of getting outside thought or language to reality, in some way that is not conditioned by thought or language itself. The view is that we cannot step aside to some point of privilege which allows comparison between judgements and the reality they apply to; and since there is no word-world relation which can serve as the foundation for truth, truth must consist in a relation of coherence between statements themselves, viewed as constituting a system or belief set, as a whole satisfying the criteria – identified above – of consistency, connectedness and completeness.

Criteria for Coherence

The question of criteria for a coherent system, as already noted, is important, because only by clarifying them can one dispel the vagueness of the theory. An effort to address the question is found in Rescher.[34]

We need a way of choosing, from among the array of data available to us, the set of beliefs we are warranted in holding true. Since there is more than one consistent subset of beliefs in the data available, and since no external criteria can be invoked to help choose between them, Rescher suggests that we employ a 'plausibility filter' to reduce the number of eligible subsets – by which is meant a procedure for discriminating which data are *prima facie* plausible. Since even this proceeding might be insufficient to pick out a unique subset of maximally consistent beliefs, Rescher suggests that we constitute our belief system from the disjunction of all those subsets let through by the filter.

The need for something like a filter arises from a ready criticism available to opponents of the coherence theory. This is that since it is logically possible for there to be any number of internally coherent systems of beliefs, and since there are no external criteria for choosing among them, it cannot be known which is the 'right' one. Russell had put this criticism by saying that the coherence theory cannot distinguish the truth from a consistent fairy-tale.[35] Positivist coherentists had replied that 'the belief-system system accepted by the scientists of our culture circle' is the right one; but this answer is obviously unsatisfactory, for in appealing to an external criterion (to a fact *about* the belief system which can only be determined true from without), it breaches contract with the coherence theory itself.

Difficulties and Objections

It is by no means fortuitous that some who have adopted a coherence theory have been among those whose philosophical outlook is shaped by admiration for mathematics. Seventeenth-century rationalists, and Plato long before them, were sceptical of the power of sense-experience to deliver truths about the world, and correspondingly impressed by the power of formal deduction, as in mathematics and geometry, to generate knowledge from a limited base of self-evident assumptions. Spinoza's major work, the *Ethics*, has as its full Latin title *Ethica Ordine Geometrico Demonstrata*, which makes explicit the rationale of his own and this general attitude.

It is plausible to think that coherence is the criterion of truth in formal systems of mathematics and logic. To say of some statement that it is 'true within a system' is just to say that it is a theorem of that system, that is, that it is provable on the system's axioms and rules. But this way of speaking is apt to be misleading, especially if generalized to truth *tout court*. For, as noted earlier, in the wider case 'coherence' would have to be explained either negatively as the absence of inconsistency between statements in a set, or positively as the presence of supporting relations between statements in a set. If 'coherence' is understood negatively it is unhelpful to the point of vacuity; if positively, it is still insufficient for truth, owing at very least to the fact that however consistent a set of statements may be, it is possible that it fails to describe the world correctly. To deal with this latter problem the theory needs to be supplemented by views to the effect that there is no world existing independently of the set of statements, or that if there is such a world it is inaccessible, or some such; just as the coherentist Positivists and certain kinds of Idealists variously claim.

Again, it can be denied that comprehensiveness is ever claimable for any set of statements; what grounds can there be for saying that any current stock of available statements expresses all that can be said about the world, or even some portion of it? It could be argued that comprehensiveness is in principle an impossible characteristic to claim for any set; and if this is so, consistency alone furnishes no guarantees.

Moreover, it is worth nothing that whereas a negative construal of coherence states a necessary (but not sufficient) condition for truth, the positive construal does not do so much on any count. Apart from difficulties about the notion of 'support' between statements which the positive account demands – entailment is too strong; what are the other candidates? – it remains natural to talk of the truth of a statement whose logical, or even merely aesthetic, relations to some (still less all) members of a relevant set are opaque to us; how this can be so is left worse than unexplained by the coherence theory.

Some critics put this objection to the coherence theory as follows: they see the fault of the theory as lying in the fact that whereas coherence furnishes a test for truth in respect of a priori propositions, only the (incorrect) view that all propositions about the world are a priori could motivate one to see coherence as the test for truth in general. Since some rationalists thought that all propositions are, like mathematical ones, a priori, they naturally adopted this view of truth. (An assumption of this version of the criticism is that there are a posteriori propositions which are not only individually about bits of the world, or episodes of experience, but are individually testable against those bits or experiences – that, in other words, correspondence determines truth. Such an assumption falls foul, in its own turn, of Neurath's criticism: thus the dialectic.)

Among other criticisms of the coherence theory is the thought that coherence cannot serve as a characterization of truth because any understanding of its constituent notions of consistency and the interdependence of statements or judgements rests on logic, and therefore, circularly, on an antecedent grasp of truth.[36] One reply available to coherentists is to say that logic is regulative, that it consists not in theses construed as truths but in rules or principles of inference; and that these in turn are to be judged on the basis of considerations not involving appeal to truth but, say, to pragmatics.[37]

More plausibly, perhaps, a coherentist might say that coherence provides a test of truth for matters of fact and value outside logic, for which truth is otherwise determined, and which forms part of the foundation of the coherence theory itself. This has the virtue of providing a more substantial basis for the coherence theory, but it does so at the cost of rendering the theory less than global, and no longer fundamental; and leaves open the problem of what is to be said about truth in the new fundamental sense now required.

In any case, one thing these considerations do is to contradict the idea expressed two paragraphs ago, that coherence naturally attaches to sets of a priori statements; for it now appears that coherence is to be regarded primarily as a test of empirical truth. If this is so, then the objection sketched earlier, to the effect that there might be a plurality of equally coherent but distinct and perhaps mutually contradictory sets of beliefs or propositions, becomes especially embarrassing to the coherentist.

A final criticism worth mentioning also concerns the vagueness of the notion of coherence, but this time in another direction. The question can be asked, 'coherence *with what?*'[38] It would be absurd to hold that a proposition is true only if it coheres with *all* other statements, because the class of all meaningful statements necessarily contains inconsistency, owing to the fact that at least most of these have equally meaningful denials. Thus the class of all meaningful statements contains both 'it is rational to believe that there is a deity' and 'it is irrational to believe that there is a deity'. On the other hand, to say that a statement must cohere with *some* other propositions to be true is to say too little. Any statement whatever coheres with some others; on this view, astrology is a body of truths, and so is *Lord of the Rings*. And of course it would not do to say that a statement is true if it coheres with other truths, for this is to beg the question.

A coherentist reply might be to specify a 'target domain' of statements, as Rescher calls it, in the context of which coherence applies as a test of truth.[39] One candidate for such a domain is the set of statements describing or reporting experience. But again, the difficulty arises that there can be more than one coherent set of statements describing experience, a point on which Quine (for example) insists in his thesis of the indeterminacy of translation. It is anyway unclear how from the perspective of the coherence theory itself one is to select the 'right' one – which, if there is to be *truth* in anything more than a relative sense, has to be possible.

One reason for the vagueness of coherence might be that it is not a logical notion at all, but an epistemic one – and even then, one that asks to be understood in a certain strategic sense. Thus perhaps the vagueness of 'coherence' does not stem from its indeterminate place between entailment (too strong) and absence of inconsistency (too weak), but from the view that what counts as a coherent system is just what counts as a *rational* system (to adapt the slogan of Hegelianism, 'the true is the rational'). If so, since what counts as a rational system of beliefs depends entirely on the assumptions and objectives any such system is concerned to connect, it will indeed follow that coherence is the required test. This is not implausible; to see the coherence test, in particular in the context of rationalism and its typically attendant forms of metaphysics, as constituting this strategy, has explanatory possibilities; but then the content of the notion of truth is settled by the theories, not by the test they license for applying the term to those statements it identifies as admissible.

The Correspondence Theory of Truth

It has already been noted how venerable, and therefore how enduring, the correspondence theory is: after Plato's discussion of it in the *Sophist* one finds Aristotle defining truth as the saying 'of what is that it is, or of what is not that it is not'.[40] How close his view of truth stands to modern versions of the correspondence theory is evident from a passage in the *Categories*: 'The fact of the being of a man carries with it the truth of the proposition that he is . . . for if a man is, the proposition wherein we allege that he is, is true . . . the fact of the man's being does seem somehow to be the cause of the truth of the proposition, for the truth or falsity of the proposition depend on the fact of the man's being or not being'.[41] This captures what is basic to the correspondence theory, namely that truth consists in a relation between propositions and the way things are in the world. A proposition that says the facts are thus-and-so when they are indeed so, is true; and a proposition successfully says the facts are thus-and-so when it corresponds to those facts.

The theory is intuitively compelling. It seems obvious that a proposition is true if, simply, it states what is the case, 'tells it like it is' in the once popular phrase. But initial plausibility diminishes as soon as one considers the three crucial terms in which the theory is articulated. They are 'proposition', 'correspondence', and 'facts' (or their cognates). Chapter 1 canvassed some of the difficulties with propositions. 'Correspondence' and 'facts' are no less controversial. What is the relation of 'correspondence' that marries propositions to facts? What are 'facts'?

Correspondence and Atomism

The empirical character of the correspondence theory in its traditional forms is significant; it is natural to see truth as a relation of correspondence between what we say and what we are talking about if either or both the source and test of contingent knowledge is experience. This is illustrated by Locke's dictum that 'truth seems to me, in the proper import of the word, to signify but the joining or separating of the signs, as the things signified by them do agree or disagree with one another'.[42] In Locke's theory, words 'signify' ideas and ideas in turn signify 'things'; ideas are combined in 'mental propositions' (words are combined in 'verbal propositions' which – with a number of complications that need not detain us here – in effect express the former) which if true correspond to the way the things signified are combined in the world. On all counts there are problems with Locke's statement of his view. Do words 'mean' by being 'signs of ideas'? What is it for signs to be 'joined' together into propositions such that, if true, they are 'as' the 'agreeing' of the things their constituent words signify?

A more systematic account is given by Russell and, indirectly and with differences, Wittgenstein in the period during which their views over-lapped as forms of Logical Atomism.

In the *Tractatus* Wittgenstein held that propositions are complexes truth-functionally compounded out of elementary propositions, which in turn are constituted by arrangements of names. This structure mirrors the way the world is arranged; there are facts built out of states-of-affairs, which in turn are constituted out of objects in certain arrangements. Names directly refer to objects; and because elementary propositions are constituted by names arranged in the way that objects are arranged in states-of-affairs, elementary propositions 'picture' those states-of-affairs. Thus the propositions compounded out of elementary propositions correspond to the facts built out of the states-of-affairs. Graphically, the situation is this, in order of logical decomposition:

Wittgenstein's aims in the *Tractatus* were to elucidate the structure of language (as just sketched) and its function, which he said is to describe the world. Epistemological concerns did not come into it, so he offered no examples of names and objects, or of elementary propositions and states-of-affairs. Wittgenstein and Russell developed their atomist views independently after a short period of contact between them prior to the First World War, and the latter gave more prominence to epistemologi-cal considerations. His version of correspondence is accordingly more informative.

For Russell, the logical atoms or simples (his version of the 'objects' of the *Tractatus*) are sense-data – for example, colour patches in the visual field. These are the objects of direct acquaintance. The names out of which propositions are built refer to the simple objects of acquaintance: propositions accrue meaningfulness from the relation of their constituents to the atomic simples with which we are directly acquainted in perception. Descriptive knowledge is inferred from, or can be justifyingly referred back to, episodes of acquaintance, where a simple proposition – 'this green' for example, or 'this green now' – directly links to the state-of-affairs presented in the episode.

What is central to both these views is that correspondence is a relation of *structural isomorphism* between propositions and facts. The related structures are said to carry information about the other relatum, rather as information about the appearance of one half of a torn sheet of paper can be reconstructed from the other half.

It is questionable, though, whether the notion of correspondence is clarified by interpreting it as a structural isomorphism, since neither the idea of structure in propositions and facts, nor the idea of a putative isomorphism between them, is clear, as we shortly see. In any case, isomorphism itself seems to require explanation in terms of structure and correspondence; for one would naturally define it, as dictionaries do, as 'an information-preserving similarity or correspondence of structure holding for and relating two or more items', and this raises the spectre of circularity.

Consider the familiar example of the proposition expressed by 'the cat is on the mat'. This proposition seems to have at least three elements – the cat, the mat, and the relation between them; but out there in the world there are two things – the cat and the mat, and if the spatial relation that obtains between them is a third thing, then it is not the same kind of thing as the first two. Are we confident that the proposition's structure is isomorphic with the fact's structure? Actually, it is difficult to say how many constituents a proposition has, since it is possible that in some language other than English there is a proposition expressible in a single word which says the same as 'the cat is on the mat'. How would we count the 'constituents' of such a proposition in order to match them to the putative constituents of that state-of-affairs in which the cat is on the mat?

This is a simple case, yet the difficulty it illustrates is puzzling enough. Worse is the difficulty of specifying a structural isomorphism between such propositions as 'the weather is bad' or 'the political situation is complicated' and their relevant states-of-affairs.

Austin and Conventions

The view that correspondence is an isomorphism between the structures of propositions and facts is conditioned by the atomistic metaphysics, and the thrust towards an ideally perspicuous language, that characterizes Logical Atomism. An attempt to state a correspondence theory independently of such commitments was made by Austin.[43] He sought to explain correspondence in terms of conventional relations between words and the world, which he held to be correlated in two ways: (a) by means of 'descriptive' conventions correlating words (= sentences) with *types* of situations to be found in the world, and (b) 'demonstrative conventions' correlating words (= statements; that is, actually issued sentences) with situations in fact found in the world on particular occasions.

Suppose someone *s* says at a time *t* 'I am eating'. The descriptive conventions correlate the words with situations in which people eat, and the demonstrative conventions correlate the words with the actual activity of *s* at *t*. What *s* says at *t* will be *true* if the actual situation, correlated with the words *s* utters by the demonstrative conventions, is of the type correlated with those words by the descriptive conventions. Austin's use of 'conventions' was seriously intended; any arbitrary words could be correlated with any situation as long as the correlations are sufficiently consistent for communication to take place successfully; and this shows that the correlations in no way covertly substitute for, or in any way resemble, something like a relation of isomorphism.

One immediate problem with Austin's view is that, as it stands, it appears to work only for indexical statements, that is, statements tied to a particular utterer and time of utterance. For they are statements which, in virtue of not being explicitly referential as general or indefinite statements are, cannot be employed in different situations; so the demonstrative conventions would have no part to play in the determination of their truth – and Austin's account essentially depends on both species of correlation. Austin might reply that the truth of these statements, although not determined by the two conventions in the way described, nonetheless might depend on the truth of other, more basic, statements whose truth *is* so determined.

Another, more serious, objection is that Austin's account implies that in pronouncing a statement true one is (as Ayer put it) 'engaging in a semantic disquisition about the conditions of its being meaningful'.[44]

Certainly for a statement to be true in the way Austin describes, it is necessary that it should possess the meaning it does; but this does not come to the same as our 'profiting by the occasion to give semantic rules' – Strawson's words[45] – when we say a certain statement is true; nor does it amount to saying that the utterer of the statement has used his words correctly in making that statement. So whereas we do 'use the word "true" when the semantic conditions described by Austin are fulfilled . . . we do not, using the word, *state* that they are fulfilled'.[46] And if what Ayer called the 'semantic accretions' of Austin's theory are removed, what is left – namely the bare point that a statement is true if what it states is the case – hardly constitutes a defence, still less a challenging reformulation, of the correspondence theory.

This criticism, proffered chiefly by Strawson, has it that Austin was guilty of a fundamental confusion between the semantic conditions that must be satisfied for the truth of a statement S_1 which states of some other statement S_2 that S_2 is true, and what is asserted when S_2 is stated to be true. For, if Austin is right in holding that to say a statement is true is to say that the relevant demonstrative and descriptive conditions are satisfied, it follows that in predicating truth of some statement we are either talking about the meanings of the words used by the speaker, or we are saying that the speaker used the words properly. Yet, in Strawson's view, 'it is patently *false* that we are doing either of these things', for we are not talking about the words used at all, but confirming or agreeing with what was said.[47] The damage is done,' Strawson wrote, 'by asking the question: *When* do we use the word "true"? instead of the question: *How* do we use the word "true"?'[48]

Correlation and Congruity

What of the crucial notion of 'correspondence' itself? In his introduction to *Truth* Pitcher usefully sets out and discusses two possible interpretations of the notion of correspondence, and I borrow aspects of his approach here.

The competing interpretations are of correspondence as *correlation*, which is a 'weak' relation, and *congruity*, which is a 'richer' one. Correlation may be exemplified by the pairing-off of items on a one-to-one basis. Suppose we put the series of integers into one-to-one correspondence with the series of even integers thus:

Integers:	1	2	3	4	5	....	n
Even integers:	2	4	6	8	10	....	2n.

In the series of integers 1 corresponds to 2 in the series of even integers, 4 in the series of integers corresponds to 8 in the series of even integers, and so on. Clearly we have to specify a rule or principle for the correspondences, since in the absence of a context and rules, saying '5 corresponds to 10' would be meaningless.

Congruity, on the other hand, might best be understood in terms of 'fit' or 'match', as when we say that the rejoined edges of a torn piece of paper fit together or match. That 'correlation' and 'congruity' pick out different conceptions of correspondence is evidenced by the fact that whereas we can say of the halves of a torn sheet of paper that they fit together (correspond) *exactly* or *perfectly* on being rejoined, we cannot say of 3 in the series of integers that it exactly or perfectly corresponds to 6, nor indeed that it *im*perfectly corresponds to 6; such qualifications are wholly misplaced.

White puts the contrast as one obtaining between 'correspondence *with*' and 'correspondence *to*'; the former is correspondence as congruity, and the latter correspondence as correlation.[49] Thus 'a key may correspond *with* its key-hole and one half of a stamp *with* the other half, while an entry in a ledger may correspond *to* a sale, and one rank in the army *to* another in the navy'.[50]

The question then arises as to which of these best interprets the relation required in the theory. Traditionally it has always been 'correspondence *with*', that is, *congruity*. In the views of Wittgenstein and Russell, for example, the correspondence between the constituents of facts and propositions is a correspondence of 'fit', demonstrated by Wittgenstein's talk of the 'picturing' relation which holds between elementary propositions and states-of-affairs. But the difficulties on this construal of the correspondence relation are formidable.

To begin with, as already noted, there is the difficulty of determining how many constituents a proposition has; and even if there were rules for doing so, it is by no means clear that every proposition has the same number of constituents as the fact to which it corresponds. In talking of constituents, a parallel difficulty infects 'facts'. Suppose someone argues that in the cat case there are indeed three constituents; the cat, the mat, and in addition the spatial arrangement in which they stand. This reifies relations – that is, makes them actual constituents of the world as cats and mats are – and this is a metaphysical thesis in need of defence. Whether correspondence makes sense, then, turns not just on the question of how we count the constituents of thoughts and count the constituents of facts, but of how we carve up thoughts and facts into those countables in the first place.

Another aspect of the difficulty is illustrated by examples of monadic predications, as in 'the car is blue'. On the congruity interpretation, for there to be constituents of the fact to 'fit' both 'car' and 'blue' we should have to commit ourselves to the view that properties such as blueness are separable from the things that instatiate it. Some respectable views offer us properties as ontologically so separable – as existing in the Platonic sense. One need not go so far; one can 'separate' the car from its colour in thought, and think of the fact's structure nominalistically. But what governs this act of slicing, if not offered by the world but effected by us? A relation between facts and propositions where the former are articulated at the latter's convenience is not interesting.

These objections are directed at the least complex case, that of the relation in which fairly straightforward propositions such as 'the cat is on the mat' and 'the car is blue' are supposed to stand with respect to the facts that the cat is on the mat and the car is blue. Difficulties multiply rapidly and decisively if one asks how there can be a correspondence as congruity between true negative, conditional, or disjunctive statements, and whatever it is that makes them true. In other words: to what does 'if the cat is on the mat, then he is warm' correspond? Or to what does 'the cat is not on the mat' correspond?[51]

Meaning and Truth

The problems, in sum, that bedevil a congruity interpretation of correspondence chiefly concern the 'constitualization' of propositions and the problematic nature of 'facts'. Its failure might lead one to reconsider the weaker 'correlation' interpretation, a strategy favourably regarded by some.[52] One apparently persuasive suggestion arises from what has already been noted in the example of correlating integers and even integers: that expressions of a language are paired with situations in the world according to a rule. Austin's view is thus a view of correspondence as correlation. A virtue of it is that it respects the fact that word-world relations are arbitrary in at least the sense that any sign or mark can be agreed upon to stand for something in the world, and it exploits the fact that those correlations, and the conventions governing them, can be read off for appropriateness on their occasions of application. But the objection – to repeat – is that when we talk of truth we are not talking of meaning or of whether a speaker used words properly. Max Black observed that it will not do to explain one difficult concept, that of truth, by means of others, here meaning; one is appealing from obscurity to obscurity, without advance.[53] The foregoing does not exhaust the possibilities for a correspondence theory; one more is considered among the views about truth discussed in the next chapter.

Notes

1   Cf. B. Russell, 'James' Conception of Truth', *Philosophical Essays*, J. L. and Mackie, *Truth, Probability and Paradox.*
2   F. H. Bradley, *Essays on Truth and Reality*, p. 325.
3   Cf. chapter 7 below.
4   B. Blanshard, *The Nature of Thought*, p. 268.
5   Cf. the diagram and accompanying text in Haack, *Philosophy of Logics*, p. 87.
6   W. James, *Pragmatism*, esp. Lect. vi, p. 197f *et seq.*
7   C. S. Peirce, 'How to Make Our Ideas Clear', *Collected Papers*, Hartshorne et al. (eds).
8   Cf. Quine, 'Two Dogmas of Empiricism', in Feigl, et al., *New Readings in Philosophical Analysis.*
9   Cf. P. Feyerabend, *Against Method.*
10 James, *Pragmatism*, p. 222.
11 Cf. Haack, 'The Pragmatist Theory of Truth', *British Journal for the Philosophy of Science*, 27, 1976, pp. 234–5.
12 Cf. Dewey, 'A Short Catechism Concerning Truth', in *The Influence of Darwin on Philosophy*; and also *Experience and Nature.*
13 Cf. James, *Pragmatism*, which collects his papers on truth.
14 Ibid., pp. v–vii.
15 G. E. Moore, 'Professor James' Pragmatism', *Proceedings of the Aristotelian Society*, 1908, p. 110.
16 Haack, 'The Pragmatist Theory of Truth', p. 234.
17 Cf. James, 'The Will To Believe', in *Selected Papers in Philosophy*, passim.
18 James, 'Pragmatism's Conception of Truth', in *Pragmatism*, p. 197 *et seq.*
19 Cf. Haack, 'The Pragmatist Theory of Truth', pp. 242–4.
20 James, 'Humanism and Truth'. *The Meaning of Truth*; and *Pragmatism*, Lect. vii. p. 239 *et seq.*

21   Cf. G. E. Moore, 'Truth', in Baldwin's Dictionary.
22   N. Rescher, *The Coherence Theory of Truth*, R. C. S. Walker *The Coherence Theory of Truth: Realism, Anti-Realism, Idealism.*
23   Bradley, *Essays on Truth and Reality*, p. 223.
24   Blanshard, *The Nature of Thought*, p. 264. Cf. also H. H. Joachim, *Logical Studies*, as another coherentist of this strong type.
25   Blanshard, *The Nature of Thought*, pp. 265–6.
26   Rescher, *The Coherence Theory of Truth*, p. 35.
27   A. C. Ewing, *Idealism: A Critical Survey*, pp. 229–30.
28   Cf. R. Carnap, *The Unity of Science*, p. 47ff.
29   M. Schlick, 'The Foundations of Knowledge', in Ayer, *Logical Positivism*, pp. 209–27.
30   O. Neurath, 'Protocol Sentences', in Ayer, *Logical Positivism*; pp. 201–4.
31   Ibid.
32   Ibid.
33   Ibid. Carnap was eventually won over to Neurath's view, and Quine is an obvious adherent of this line. There are echoes of pragmatism here too. For a discussion of the positivists' debate on these issues see G. C. Hempel, 'On the Logical Positivists' Theory of Truth', *Analysis*, 2, 1935, pp. 49–59; and I. Scheffler, *Science and Subjectivity*. esp. ch 5, passim.
34   Rescher, *The Coherence Theory of Truth*, esp. ch. iv S3, p. 78ff.
35   Russell, *The Problems of Philosophy*, p. 190.
36   Cf. Ewing, *Idealism*, pp. 237, 241.
37   Cf. Rescher, *The Coherence Theory of Truth*, p. 45.
38   Cf. ibid., p. 49.
39   Ibid., p. 50.
40   Aristotle, *Metaphysics*, 1011b 26.
41   Aristotle, *Categories*, 14b 14–21.
42   Locke, *Essay Concerning Human Understanding*, iv, v., § 2.
43   J. L. Austin, 'Truth', in G. Pitcher, *Truth*, p. 18 *et seq.*
44   A. J. Ayer, *The Concept of a Person*, p. 184.
45   P. F. Strawson, 'Truth', in Pitcher, *Truth*, p. 44.
46   Ibid.
47   Ibid., pp. 43–4.
48   Ibid., pp. 47–8; and cf. G. J. Warnock, 'A Problem About Truth', in Pitcher, *Truth*, p. 55 *et seq.*
49   A. R. White, *Truth*, p. 105.
50   Ibid.
51   Ibid., pp. 106–7.
52   Cf. e.g., G. E. Moore, *Some Main Problems of Philosophy*, ch. 14 passim; and White *Truth*, pp. 108–9.
53   M. Black, 'The Semantic Definition of Truth', *Analysis*, 8, 1948, p. 52.

6

Truth: Semantics, Deflation, Indefinability and Evaluation

Introduction

Theories of truth fall into two classes. One consists in those theories stating that truth is a *substantive property* of whatever the truth-bearers are. The property might be a relational one, where the relation is some form of correspondence or coherence; or a functional one, for example, epistemic utility, as in the pragmatic theory. A further member of this class asserts that truth is a substantial but *indefinable* property; Davidson takes such a view.

The other class comprises theories stating that truth is not a substantive notion; *there is nothing more* to truth, these theories say, than use of the predicate '. . . is true' as a convenience for certain logical and rhetorical purposes. Such views are called, for obvious reasons, 'deflationary' theories.

This chapter considers deflationism and certain substantive views of truth other than those canvassed in the preceding chapter. But I begin with discussion of a theory which, although not a theory of truth in the same sense as the others (for strictly speaking it offers a definition of the predicate '. . . is true' for a formal language only), has been especially influential in its wider philosophical applications. This is the Semantic Theory of Truth, devised by Alfred Tarski.[1]

The Semantic Theory of Truth

Tarski set himself the task of giving a satisfactory definition of truth, meaning by 'satisfactory' a definition which is both *materially adequate* and *formally correct*,[2] and which does justice to the intuition expressed in what he calls the 'classical Aristotelian conception of truth',[3] namely 'to say of what is that it is not, or of what is not that it is, is false, while to say of what is that it is, or of what is not that it is not, is true', which, as noted in the preceding chapter, would find expression in contemporary terminology as a correspondence theory.[4] In Tarski's view both Aristotle's formulation and contemporary correspondence theories are, however, imprecise and a source of misunderstanding. Accordingly he sought to provide a more precise expression of these intuitions by meeting a specific set of demands: 'we must determine on what the formal correctness of the definition depends. Thus, we must specify the words or concepts which we wish to use in defining the notion of truth; and we must also give the formal rules to which the definition should conform. Speaking more generally, we must describe the formal structure of the language in which the definition will be given.'[5]

One way into an exposition of Tarski's proposals is to note a proffered solution to the Antinomy of the Liar (the Liar Paradox).[6] The solution turns on a distinction between what is said in a sentence of a language, and what it is said about this sentence in a 'metalanguage', that is, a language of higher order than the language which it takes as its 'object language' and in which this latter is discussed. Consider this version of the Liar:

<u>The underlined sentence on this page is false.</u>

The paradox is that if what is written in the box is false, then it is true; and if it is true, then it is false. Tarski diagnosed the source of the paradox as the *self-reference* of the sentence, that is, the fact that it talks about itself. Strictly, the fault lies in the fact that the sentence belongs to a 'semantically closed' language, that is, one containing not only its normal stock of expressions, but also the names of these expressions, and semantic terms such as 'true' referring to its sentences; and moreover, the tacit assumption is that all sentences which determine the use of 'true' can be asserted in that language itself.[7] Tarski drew the object language–metalanguage distinction to prohibit self-reference of this sort, and held that ascriptions of truth or falsity to sentences are metalinguistic: thus ' "New York is a large city" is true' is a metalinguistic assertion about the sentence 'New York is a large city'. Truth is construed as a predicate of a metalanguage applicable to sentences of its object language; it is a semantic property of sentences of the latter, predicated whenever the metalanguage states that an object language sentence designates what is in fact the case.

Sentences can only be true or false as components of a given language. There might be a language, say Anglish, in which 'snow is black' means the same as is meant by the English expression 'snow is white', for the reason that in Anglish 'black' designates what 'white' standardly designates in English. Then 'snow is black' is true in Anglish, because the extension of 'black' is identical to that of 'white' in English, and because snow is white. So to say a sentence S is true is to say it is true in some language L. But then to say 'S is true in L' cannot be a sentence of L itself (at risk of paradox), but is a sentence of a metalanguage that takes L as its object language, and in which the sentences of L are not *used* but only *mentioned* and discussed. This affords one of the clearest illustrations of the importance of the distinction between *use* and *mention*.

Tarski sought to provide a definition of the expression 'true sentence' for a given language L in the metalanguage M of L, such that it will entail all sentences of M of the form 'S is a true sentence of L if and only if p', where 'S' is the name, or a structural description, of a sentence in L, and 'p' is the translation of that sentence into M.[8] Since M may include L as part of itself, such sentences of L are their own translation into M. The requirement that the definition entails sentences of this form constitutes a criterion of material adequacy for any satisfactory definition of truth, and is called 'Convention(T)'.

To say that Convention (T) furnishes a criterion of adequacy for truth definitions is to say that any acceptable definition of truth should have as a consequence all instances of the schema:

(T) S is true in L if and only if p.

An example of an instance of this schema is:

'Snow is white' is true in English if and only if snow is white.

Here 'snow is white' on the left-hand-side of 'if and only if' is the 'name' of the sentence on the right-hand-side. Note again that Convention (T) is not a definition of truth but a *material adequacy condition*, requiring that all its instances must be entailed by any definition of truth if that definition is to be minimally satisfactory. Thus the (T) schema determines not the *intension* of the concept of truth (the meaning of the word 'true'), but its *extension* – its range.

In order to provide a *definition* of truth something has to be added to the adequacy condition – namely, proof of formal correctness in respect both of the structure of the language in which truth is defined, and of the concepts employed in the definition. Definitions of truth are given in L's metalanguage M, and this is why L must be included in or translated into M. Because all equivalences of the form (T) must be implied by a definition of truth as required by the adequacy condition, not only must M contain L or translations into itself of all L-sentences, but also the equipment to refer to L-sentences; for (T) instances have L-sentences and expressions referring to them on the right- and left-hand-sides respectively. Moreover, Tarski required that both M and L should be 'formally specifiable'; we must be able to specify the well-formed formulae (the 'wffs') of L in order to define truth-in-L, since these are the items which the predicate 'true-in-L' qualifies. Since no natural language (for example English, Swahili, Japanese) is formally specifiable, Tarski regarded this requirement as ruling out the possibility of defining 'true' for natural languages. This prompts controversy, for some believe that Tarski's theory can indeed be extended to natural language, or at least part of it. I return to this point below.

Tarski's definition of truth turns on the concept of 'satisfaction', which is a relation between objects, on the one hand, and on the other hand expressions called 'sentential functions', such as 'x is white' or 'x is greater than y'. These expressions are sentential *functions* rather than sentences because they contain free variables marking gaps into which, to form a sentence proper, suitable terms must be inserted. The definition of a sentential function involves the notion of a 'recursive procedure'. First the simplest sentential functions are described, and then it is shown what operations can be performed to construct compound functions out of them. Examples of such an operation are the formation of the logical disjunction or conjunction of any two functions, by 'or' and 'and' respectively.

A sentence, accordingly, can be defined as a sentential function containing no free variables. To explain satisfaction heuristically, one could say: a given object satisfies a given function if the function can be turned into a true sentence by replacing the free variable occurring in it by the name of the given object. Thus, for example, snow (not the name 'snow' but the actual stuff) satisfies 'x is white' because the sentence 'snow is white' is true. However this is a merely heuristic way of explaining satisfaction, for 'true' is being *used* here; because we wish to define 'true' we must seek for an account not involving 'true'.

This is done, again recursively, by first indicating which objects satisfy the simplest sentential functions, and then by stating under what conditions given objects satisfy compound functions constructed out of those simple functions. For example, we say of certain numbers that they satisfy the disjunction 'x is greater than y or x is equal to y' if they satisfy either the function 'x is greater than y' or the function 'x is equal to y'.

The notion of satisfaction thus defined applies automatically to sentential functions containing no free variables – that is, to sentences. On investigation of the formal details it turns out that only two cases are possible for a sentence: it is either satisfied by all objects, or by no objects. The sentence is true in the first case and false in the second.[9]

This is an informal presentation of the key concepts used by Tarski to define truth. I now give a condensed formal account of the same points, which those who have no taste for technicality may ignore.[10]

A Formal Sketch

Open sentences such as Fx do not have truth-values, but are satisfied (or not satisfied) by sequences of objects – which is to say, by pairs of objects, or triples of objects – in general, by any ordered n-tuple of objects. Thus 'x is a man' is satisfied by Socrates; 'x is the teacher of y' is satisfied by <Socrates, Plato> (though not the other way round; hence the importance of the *ordering* of n-tuples); and 'x taught y who taught z' is satisfied by <Socrates, Plato, Aristotle>. Thus satisfaction is a *relation* between open sentences and ordered n-tuples of objects.

Since n could be any number whatever, Tarski defined satisfaction as the relation between open sentences and *infinite* sequences under a certain convention, *viz.*, that $F(x_1, x_2 \ldots x_n)$ is to be satisfied by the sequence '$<O_1 \ldots O_2 \ldots O_n + \ldots >$' (where 'O' is any object) in those cases where it is satisfied by the first n numbers of the sequence; the rest of the sequence is ignored. The negation of an open sentence S_1 will be satisfied by all sequences which do not satisfy S_1; the conjunction of S_1 and S_2 will be satisfied by those sequences which satisfy both S_1 and S_2; and the existential quantification of an open sentence will be satisfied by a sequence of objects in those cases where there is another sequence, differing from the first sequence in at most the ith place, where the ith is the variable bound by the quantifier, which satisfies the sentence obtained by dropping the quantifier. For example, $(\exists x)(x$ is a country between y and z) is satisfied by the sequence (a) <London, Holland, Spain> because for example the sentence (b) <France Holland, Spain> satisfies 'x is a country between y and z'. Here the difference in the sequences ('London' in (a) and 'France' in (b)) occurs at no more than the place of the bound variable x; and sequence (b) satisfies the open sentence which results from dropping the existential quantifier in front of 'x is a country between y and z'.

Sentences with no free variables, that is, sentences in which all the variables are bound by quantifiers, are 'closed' sentences, and closed sentences are in effect special cases of open sentences – they are open sentences with no places (they are o-place open sentences). Now, the first and all subsequent members of a sequence are irrelevant to whether or not that sequence satisfies a o-place open sentence. Accordingly Tarski defined a sentence as true in those cases where it is satisfied by all sequences whatever, and false when it is satisfied by none. For example, the open sentence with two places 'x is the teacher of y' is satisfied by all sequences, for example <Socrates, Plato, . . .>, no matter what their third, fourth, and subsequent members. The one-place open sentence 'x is a teacher' is satisfied by all sequences, for example <Socrates, . . .>, irrespective of their second and subsequent members. And the o-place open sentence – that is, closed sentence – $(\exists x)$ (x is a teacher) is satisfied by all sequences <.. ., . . ., . . .> no matter what their first and subsequent members – for there is a sequence, for example <Socrates, . . .>, which is different from any other sequence you like in at most the first place, and which satisfies the sentence (formed by dropping the quantifier) 'x is a teacher'. Closed sentences cannot be satisfied by just these and not some other sequences; they are satisfied by all sequences or by none.

So Tarski's definition is that 'true = $_{df}$ satisfied by all sequences' and 'false = $_{df}$ satisfied by no sequences'. To see why, consider the closed sentence $(\exists x)$ (x is a teacher) again, and let there be a sequence of objects A. As stated, this sentence is satisfied by any sequence of objects if and only if there is some other sequence B, different from A in at most the first place, which satisfies the sentence 'x is a teacher' formed by dropping the quantifier. This sentence will be satisfied by an object O where O is a teacher; so there is such a sequence if there is some object which is a teacher. Accordingly (∃ x) (x is a teacher) is satisfied by all sequences if something is a teacher.

One can give the formal definition as follows. Tarski defined truth for a class calculus using a formalized metalanguage. Following Quine and Haack, however, it is simpler to demonstrate the procedure for a sparse version of standard first-order predicate calculus.[11] We have the usual variables and predicate letters; just two sentence-forming operators, ~ and · ; the existential quantifier; and brackets. That completes the syntax. The atomic sentences are strings consisting of n-place predicates followed by n variables. Nothing is a wff other than atomic sentences A,B . . ., and whatever can be well-formed from them by applying ~, ·, and (∃ . . .); thus ~ A is a wff, (A · B) is a wff, (∃ x)A is a wff.

The recursive definition is then as follows. Let A and B range over sentences of our sparse first-order language, and let the expressions X and Y range over sequences of objects, with the expression 'Xi' denoting the ith member of any sequence X. Satisfaction is then defined for atomic sentences thus:

1.i. For all i and X:
X satisfies 'Fxi' if and only if Xi is F.

This provides a clause for one-place predicates.

1.ii. For all i and X:
X satisfies 'Gxi ix$j$' if and only if Xi and Xj stand in the relation G.

This provides a clause for two-place predicates. And so on for all predicates. We then turn to negation, conjunction and quantification in similar fashion.

2. For all X and A:
X satisfies '~ A' if and only if X does not satisfy 'A'.
3. For all X, A, and B:
X satisfies 'A and B' if and only if X satisfies A and X satisfies B.
4. For all X, A, and i:
X satisfies (∃ xi) A if and only if there is a sequence Y such that Xi = Yj for all $j \neq i$, and Y satisfies A.

A closed sentence, that is a wff with no free variables, will be satisfied by all sequences or none. 'True' accordingly is defined thus for this sparse first-order language L: a closed sentence of L is true if and only if it is satisfied by all sequences. That, in essentials, is the manner of Tarski's definition of 'true'.

Tarski, Neutrality and Physicalism

As noted above, Tarski held that his formal correctness conditions rule out the possibility of an adequate definition of truth for any language which is semantically closed, that is, which itself contains such semantic terms as 'true' and 'refers,' and which is not formally specifiable; hence there can be no adequate definition of truth for natural languages, because it is only formal languages which have the required characteristics of semantic openness and formal specifiability.

Natural languages, in short, contain their own metalanguages, and this in Tarski's view is the source of paradox in them. Moreover they are living things, constantly in a state of change and development, and infested with such features as vagueness, indexicality, and ambiguity. These considerations persuaded Tarski that natural languages are not amenable to a truth-definition.[12] He also believed that because his theory applies only in a formal context, it is neutral with respect to traditional epistemological and metaphysical controversies; we could, in his view, accept the semantic theory of truth and retain whatever philosophical convictions we had antecedently nourished.[13]

However, Tarski's own assessment of the implications and applications of his theory has not been accepted; it is claimed that philosophical consequences of moment follow from it, and that it rests on philosophically significant assumptions. Consider first the facts that (a) Tarski's account makes use of an objectual reading of the quantifiers – $(\exists x) Fx$ is true if there is an object which is F; (b) that the objects over which the variables range are located in the world, and not in a model domain or possible world – 'x is white', in his own example, is satisfied by snow (the stuff, not the name 'snow'); and (c) that the material adequacy condition rules out all non-bivalent truth theories, as is demonstrated by the fact that if 'p' in ' "p" is true if and only if p' is truth-valueless, then ' "p" is true' is false, with the result that ' "p" is true if and only if p' as a whole must be, if not false, then at least not true. The net result of (a)–(c) is that

Tarski's theory appears both to assume and to promote a particular metaphysical view, namely 'physicalism'.[14]

This point is made by Field.[15] Tarski's intentions are revealed by his saying that truth must be defined without appeal to semantic primitives, because such an appeal produces unclarity and makes it 'difficult to bring this method into harmony with the postulates of the unity of science and of physicalism'.[16] Tarski wished to make semantics a respectable enquiry from the viewpoint of science,[17] and since it is an assumption of the notion of unified science – that is, of 'physicalism' in Tarski's sense – that all phenomena can be so reduced that they admit of subsumption by physical laws, it follows that Tarski took himself to be providing a characterization of truth of an appropriately physicalist kind.

Having identified Tarski's non-neutral objectives in this way, Field argues that Tarski failed to realize them. He did not succeed in providing an account of semantic primitives in acceptable physicalist terms, Field says, for his definition turns out to rest on them. Tarski demonstrates how to reduce truth to the relation of satisfaction, and satisfaction to the relation of primitive denotation; but this is to reduce semantic notions to other semantic notions, and does not amount to definition in physicalistic terms. To achieve a reduction that defines the target notions in non-semantic terms, one has to appeal to facts about the circumstances of their employment. Field accordingly offers a reworking of Tarski's theory, turning chiefly on the claim that extensional equivalence is not enough for a successful semantic-term to physical-term reduction, but that something stronger is required; his suggestion is that one gets true reduction by defining reference as a causal relation obtaining between the physical facts and the semantic facts they sustain. (Causal accounts of reference are discussed in chapter 7 below.)[18]

Is Tarski's Theory a Correspondence Theory?

In what respect, if any, does the semantic theory support, or preserve the essential intuitions of, or even perhaps constitute, a correspondence theory of truth? Popper's grateful reception of Tarski's theory as at last providing what had hitherto been lacking in correspondence theories, namely a proper characterization of the correspondence relation, suggests the third possibility;[19] but Tarski's own comments at very most suggest the first two.[20] Popper's claim is a strong one; it is that Tarski has 'rehabilitated the correspondence theory of absolute or objective truth' and 'vindicated the free use of the intuitive idea of truth as correspondence to the facts'.[21] The claim merits investigation.

One way of looking at such instances of the (T) schema as ' "snow is white" is true if and only if snow is white' is to take it that the left-hand-side refers to a linguistic item – a sentence – and that the right-hand-side refers to an extralinguistic item – a fact or state-of-affairs. It then looks as if the (T) schema itself – that is, ' "p" is true if and only if p' – states a recipe for correspondence between linguistic and extralinguistic items. But this, by Tarski's own account, will not in fact do; for the (T) schema, constituting as it does no more than a condition of adequacy for any truth theory, does not specify the correspondence theory as uniquely correct, but is consonant with other truth theories too. For example, it shows that a redundancy theory – in the form '(p) (p is true if and only if p)' – is materially adequate; and, as Haack observes, it is even compatible with fanciful theories of the sort we would get if ' "p" is true' were defined as, say, ' "p" is asserted by a philosopher', for ' "snow is white" is asserted by a philosopher if and only if snow is white' is an instance of the (T) schema in just the required sense that anyone who accepted this definition of ' "p" is true' would accept or reject the left-hand-side just in case he accepted or rejected, respectively, the right-hand-side.[22]

Matters are slightly more promising if, instead, one looks at Tarski's definition of truth itself. The definition seems to contain material for supporting a correspondence construal in this sense, that it proceeds in terms of a definition of satisfaction, and satisfaction is a relation between sentences and sequences of objects. But the difficulty is that Tarski's definition states that true and false sentences are respectively satisfied by all sequences and none, with no appeal being made to *specific* sequences.[23] Moreover, as Haack points out, 'it is symptomatic that analytic as well as synthetic truth is embraced by Tarski's theory; yet it is surely less plausible to suppose that analytic truth consists in "correspondence to the facts" than that synthetic truth does so'.[24]

Part of the problem here is that because there are no satisfactory correspondence theories, it is hard to see what features Tarski's theory must display in order to count as one. There are, for instance, considerable differences between Austin's account of correspondence and Tarski's theory, yet Austin's account was offered as an alternative to such 'congruity' views as Russell's, improving on all those respects in which such views fail. Thus in Austin's account, indexical statements (not sentences) occupy centre-stage, whereas Tarski ignores indexicality altogether and takes sentences (not statements) as truth-bearers. Tarski selects sentences as truth-bearers because crucial use is made of their syntactic structure in order to define truth by means of satisfaction. Austin on the other hand held that the descriptive conventions – that is, the conventions correlating expressions to types of situations in the world – are *purely* conventional; any words would do, let structure fall where it may.[25]

If therefore Austin's theory is at least a good example of an attempt at a correspondence theory, Tarski's theory is after all unlike a correspondence theory. If Tarski's theory is considered a correspondence theory because it is analogous to, say, Russell's theory in relying on structure, then for one thing the analogy is to an unsuccessful version of a correspondence theory, and for another the analogy, turning as it does on the notion of 'structure', is weak, because in the one case the appeal is to an isomorphic relation, in the other to syntactic features of object–language sentences.

The question asked about Tarski's theory is 'does it support, or at least preserve the intuitions of, a correspondence theory?', and one is tempted to reply that if it does either, it is because it is also compatible with other truth-theories (which must be at least to say that it does not impugn the intuitions they embody), and therefore it does not do so in any specially significant way. Thus far, one element of Tarski's own claim that his definition is neutral is vindicated, at the cost of contradicting his other claim that the theory makes precise the intuitions of the correspondence notion.

This result makes claims about the *objectivity* of Tarski's theory problematic. On the face of it, it would seem inappropriate to characterize Tarski's view of truth as 'absolute and objective' because it views truth as essentially language-relative; the definition is not of 'true' *simpliciter* but 'true-in-L'. 'The extension of the concept to be defined,' Tarski wrote, 'depends in an essential way on the particular language under consideration. The same expression can, in one language, be a true statement, in another a false or meaningless expression. There will be no question at all here of giving a single general definition of the term'.[26] There are two very good reasons from Tarski's point of view why this must be so; the definition relies essentially on syntactic structure, and language-relativity is required for avoidance of the paradoxes.

One of the critics answered by Tarski had complained that the semantic theory involves itself in an 'uncritical realism', because a sentence like 'snow is white' is true if and only 'if snow is *in fact white*'.[27] Tarski objected to the 'in fact', replying that the definition of 'true' implies nothing whatever as to the conditions under which 'snow is white' can be asserted; instead it only implies that whenever we do assert or reject 'snow is white' we must be ready to assert or reject the correlated sentence 'the sentence "snow is white" is true'.[28] And Tarski goes on immediately to remark, 'Thus, we may accept the semantic conception of truth without giving up any epistemological attitude we may have had; we may remain naïve realists, critical realists or idealists, empiricists or metaphysicians – whatever we were before. The semantic conception is completely neutral towards all these issues.'[29]

Because Tarski's definition is compatible with rival views of truth – rival in both senses of supplying different definitions of truth and different criteria or tests for ascription of truth – what Tarski says about the semantic theory's independence from particular philosophical commitments appears unexceptionable. But this claim conflicts with what was identified earlier as the physicalist character of Tarski's views. Could it be that the charge of assumed realism has some basis after all, despite Tarski's own pronouncements?

Two suggestions seem to support this possibility. One is to deny that, in the end, there are different languages. If this is so, then Tarski's theory ceases to be genuinely relative, but applies across the board. Davidson has argued, for example, that no sense attaches to the idea of genuinely different – in the sense of mutually unintelligible or inaccessible – languages, for the very criterion of languagehood is 'translatability into a familiar idiom' (see the discussion of relativism in chapter 9 below).[30] A related idea underlies Popper's view that if p is a true sentence of L and there is a translation p_1 of p in another language L_1, then p and p_1 have the same truth-value.[31]

However, even if this is right, it only goes as far as supporting the contention that Tarski's theory is 'absolute' – that is, universally applicable – for it is a further matter to show how, or even perhaps that, this entails its also being objective. For the most that one seems entitled to claim is that a notion's being absolute is a necessary condition for its being objective; something more is required for sufficiency.

The other suggestion arises from the fact that Tarski's view countenances only bivalent theories of truth. It is a tenet of Dummett's arguments that bivalence is closely linked to realism, on the grounds that if sentences are determinately true or false something independent of us and our knowledge must make them so. (This is discussed in chapter 8 below.) To be a realist about truth is indeed to regard truth as in some strong sense objective. If these thoughts are right, they lend support to Field's account of Tarski as described above.

Formal *versus* Natural

But Tarski's own strictures, as noted, rule out adaptation of the semantic theory to understanding 'true' in natural language contexts. This is not a difficulty to be solved by so rationalizing natural language as to make it apt for Tarski-style theory; in ordinary speech the truth-value of what is said is heavily indexed to speaker, time and context of utterance, so the mere *sentence* uttered appears too thin a plank to bear truth's load, and the whole indexed complex *too* complex to be explained just in terms of entailment via Convention (T). In this respect Tarski's pessimism seems justified. And this consideration touches only on indexicality; matters are in fact more complex owing to the presence in natural language of ambiguity, vagueness, ellipsis, irony, and other complicated features.

To say that a Tarski-style definition of truth cannot be given for natural languages does not of course amount to saying that truth cannot be explained for natural languages – still less that there are no truths expressed or expressible in natural languages. What it might rather mean is that Tarskian truth, because it is specific to formal contexts, is not truth but truth-in-a-formal-context, a quite different matter and therefore irrelevant to truth *simpliciter* if there is such a thing (Tarski contemplates the possibility that a number of *different* things get misleadingly lumped under the label 'truth'). Tarski was prepared to acknowledge as much, offering if necessary to call his account of truth an account instead of 'fruth', where 'frue' means, roughly, 'true-in-a-formally-specifiable-language'. But this should not be permitted to mislead, as it would if it suggested that truth is to natural languages what fruth is to formal; that, in other words, points of analogy might appear on inspection. For we do not have a theory of truth of which a theory of fruth can be the formal analogue.

Moreover, as Strawson argued, it might be that even if a Tarski-style theory could be extended to natural language, it would not really explain the meaning of 'true', but, at best, of 'true if and only if; because such equivalences as ' "New York is a large city" is true if New York is a large city' could be construed as degenerate cases of equivalences in which we could read 'means that' for 'true if, as for example in ' "New York est une grande cité" is true if New York is a large city'. Davidson, as we shall see, takes this to be no criticism at all, but the specification of a virtue (again, see chapter 8).

Evidently, then, the general (as opposed to strictly formal) relevance and, if relevant, importance of Tarski's theory of truth is something that can only be determined by looking at an attempt like Davidson's to make it work in the context of natural language. It is plain that Tarski's work has great merit in its formal setting; truth-conditional semantic theory, if successful, extends that merit to philosophy in general.

The Redundancy Theory of Truth

In his criticism of Austin as described in the preceding chapter, Strawson put forward an alternative view of truth, which is that to say a statement is true is in effect to support or endorse it, as if to say 'yes' or to nod in agreement – a view sometimes therefore called the 'performative' theory of truth. Strawson claimed that the right question to ask about truth is, '*how* is "true" used?', the answer implying that there is no more to truth than the performance of agreement, endorsement or emphasis just sketched. This view has affinities with the 'Redundancy Theory' put forward by Ramsey.[32]

In the course of discussing judgement Ramsey offered some remarks about truth 'to show that there is really no separate problem of truth but merely a linguistic muddle'[33] His argument is as follows. Truth and falsity are primarily ascribed to propositions, and propositions can either be explicitly given or described. In the case of an explicitly given proposition such as 'Caesar was murdered', it is evident, in Ramsey's view, that 'it is true that Caesar was murdered' means precisely the same as 'Caesar was murdered', and 'it is false that Caesar was murdered' means precisely the same as 'Caesar was not murdered'. Accordingly, the ascriptions of truth and falsity in these cases are redundant; at best they add emphasis, or mark the place the proposition has in the argument, or are placed there for stylistic reasons.[34] One could equally well say 'it is a fact that Caesar was murdered' or 'that Caesar was murdered is contrary to fact'. Yet appeal to 'facts' is as redundant as appeal to truth and falsity.

Similarly, 'is true' and 'is false' are redundant in the case of described propositions, although matters are somewhat more complex here. If I say 'he is always right', I mean that 'the propositions he asserts are always true', and on the face of it there seems no way to dispense with the word 'true' in expressing the point. However Ramsey suggests an analysis to eliminate 'true'; the first step is to recast 'the propositions he asserts are always true' as 'for all p, if he asserts p, p is true', and then we see that the propositional function 'p is true' is simply the same as p, just as in the Caesar case above; 'for all p, if he asserts p, then p'.[35]

Ramsey suggested that we add 'is true' in English to give the sentence a verb, forgetting that 'p' already contains one. The point is clearer if one considers, say, the relational form of the proposition, aRb; then 'he is always right' can be put as 'for all a,R,b, if he asserts aRb, then aRb'. Adding 'is true' is obviously superfluous.

In general, Ramsey took it that our real interest in this connection does not concern the nature of truth and falsity, but the nature of judgement or assertion; for the problem in the foregoing example is how to analyse 'He asserts aRb'.

The redundancy view comes down, then, to saying that 'true' and 'false' are predicates which can be dropped without semantic loss, having only a stylistic or otherwise pragmatic role. There are certain virtues attaching to this view; for one thing, it avoids all the difficulties of a correspondence theory, for no question arises about any of the three correspondence terms – the relata of facts and propositions and the relation of correspondence itself. 'It is a fact that' is as redundant as 'it is true that', which does away with facts; and because 'is true' is an eliminable predicate, it does not introduce a genuine property to be attached to whatever is asserted, and so there is no need to invoke propositions as truth-bearers – for where there is no truth to be borne, no bearers of truth are required. And then, if neither facts nor propositions occur in the picture essentially, there is no need to specify a relation between them. Thus every difficulty encountered by the correspondence theory is avoided.

Nevertheless there are problems beneath the surface simplicity of Ramsey's proposal. His account demands a suitable handling of second-order quantification for the case where propositions are described – that is, where what is asserted is not explicitly given but introduced obliquely. Ramsey's offering was 'for all p, if he asserts p, p' as an analysis of such cases, containing no use of 'true'. But now the question arises: is the universal quantifier 'for all . . .' to be understood objectually or substitutionally?[36]

If objectually, then for one thing it looks as though propositions might after all have to be retained as the objects quantified over, and if the bound variables, 'p's, are to have the syntactic function of singular terms, as on this interpretation is required, then the final 'p' in 'for all p, if he asserts p, then p' will have to be regarded as an ellipsis of 'p is true' for it to be sufficiently sentence-like to serve as the conditional's consequent. And if so, 'is true' is not redundant after all.

If on the other hand the quantifier is interpreted substitutionally, then 'for all p, if he asserts p, then p' turns into 'all substitution instances of "if he asserts p, then p" *are true*'; and again 'true' remains firmly entrenched in the analysis.

Proforms and Redundancy

Because 'true' refuses to be redundant on either of these standard interpretations of the quantifiers, another tack is required. An ingenious idea to this end is proposed by Grover.[37] It has often been remarked that there are words and expressions which behave, in respect of other grammatical categories, in the same useful portmanteau fashion as pronouns ('he', 'it') which stand in for nouns and descriptions. Thus the verb 'do' can serve in place of most active verbs, and 'nice' is a portmanteau adjective of positive purport. On analogy with pronouns, such words can be called proverbs and pro-adjectives respectively. Grover specifies a general category of *proforms* to collect pronouns, pro-verbs, pro-adjectives, and the like, and this category has the feature that all of its members must be capable of anaphoric use – that is, can be cross-referentially used in the way pronouns are as in '*Tom* wished to buy it, but *he* hadn't enough money', or 'if a *bomb* falls, get out of *its* way'.

The proform Grover is chiefly concerned to introduce is a *prosentence*, 'thatt', which can be used anaphorically for any sentence. The proposal is that 'for all p, if he asserts that p, then p' is to be recast as 'for all propositions, if he asserts that thatt, then thatt'. The idea is that the difficulty encountered by Ramsey's view arises only because there are no words or phrases which can stand for sentences as pronouns stand for nouns, thus blocking the required richer reading of the quantifiers. Supplying prosentences removes the difficulty. One virtue of the suggestion is that, from the purely formal point of view, this reading is compatible with both the objectual and substitutional interpretations of the quantifiers.

Two difficulties infect Grover's manoeuvre. One is that there have to be strong reasons for supplementing English in this way, or, at least, it must be the case that there is room, made available by the analogical similarity of prosentences to other anaphoric devices already available in the language, which as it were invites just this kind of proform to fill it. The room does not naturally exist (English gets along without prosentences), and so the question becomes: does anything oblige us to make that room? Now, the chief motive for inventing the prosentence is to free us from having to make essential use of 'is true' and 'is false'. But is it clear we have to be free in this way? Ramsey's argument itself does not, at least as it stands, show that the notions of truth and falsity are genuinely redundant, still less (as he claimed) misleading. Why then accept the neologism 'thatt' in the first place, if its purpose is merely to force a reading of the quantifiers which will conform to Ramsey's view?

The answer lies in the fact, as Grover and before her Prior noted, that without suitable expressions for second-order quantifiers, we appear to be bound to use noun-like idioms such as 'every*thing*' and '*something*' with all the objectual implications of so doing.[38] Prior himself suggested using '–whether' as the appropriate reading, so that ($\exists$p) would be 'somewhether' and (p) 'anywhether', and thus such a string as '(p)(p $\rightarrow$ p)' would be read 'if anywhether, then thether'.[39] Grover's proposal is a refinement along the same lines. The thought is, in other words, that Ramsey had groped for a way of saying that if one could only make out a proper account of propositional quantification, predications of 'true' and 'false' would be recognized as otiose, just as it appears when we see that 'it is true that Caesar was murdered' says no more than 'Caesar was murdered'. The innovations provided by Prior and Grover supply materials for such an account.

Still, there is the second difficulty, and it is more of a difficulty. Grover and others applied the prosentence idea to the redundancy theory by proposing that 'that is true' is itself to be regarded as a prosentence.[40] Use of 'it is true' as an atomic prosentence eliminates the need for ascriptions of truth; 'true' itself remain only residually as a non-separable part of the prosentence. But will this do? Haack, for one, thinks not: ' "True", one is told, is eliminable; not from English, to be sure, but from English [plus] "*thatt*". But how are we to understand "thatt"? Well, there's nothing *exactly* like it in English, but it works like "that's true", except for being atomic rather than compound' – and so 'true' remains.[41]

Deflation and Minimalism

But what is the truth that thus remains? Not all deflationary theories are redundancy theories; they reserve a role for the concept of truth, but claim that it is a minimal one. What they deny is that truth is a *substantive* property. Ramsey's theory (and Strawson's performative version of it) are in a sense too deflationary, because they deprive the notion of truth of an important role in inference. On the redundancy theory, 'it is true that p' and 'p' mean the same. But this blocks an understanding of how we can conclude 'p is true' from 'S said p' and 'what S said is true'; the inference turns on applying Leibniz's Law – if x and y are identical, they have all and only the same properties – which one cannot do unless truth is a property. But according to Horwich's version of a deflationary theory, which he calls 'Minimalism', truth *is* a property (and a property of propositions) but not a substantive one. There is however no more to truth than its use in the logical role just illustrated. For the reason offered by that illustration, it is, he says, therefore better to limit the deflationary view to a weaker claim, namely, that 'p is true' and 'p' are equivalent.[42]

Horwich claims that the truth predicate's only *raison d'être* is to satisfy the logical need felt in the above example. The claim is more fully made out as follows. We have the need on occasion to adopt an attitude to a proposition, for example, to believe or assume it; but we do not exactly know what the proposition is (maybe we did not hear clearly what someone said when expressing it). Perhaps we just know that it is 'What Oscar thinks', say. 'In such situations,' Horwich writes, 'the concept of truth is invaluable. For it enables the construction of another proposition, intimately related to the one we can't identify, which is perfectly appropriate as the alternative object of our attitude. Consider, for example,

(1) What Oscar said was true.

Here we have something of the form

(2) x is F

whose meaning is such that, given further information about the identity of x – given a further premise of the form

(3) x = the proposition that p

– we are entitled to infer

(4) p.

And it is precisely from this inferential property that propositions involving truth derive their utility.'[43]

The concept of truth is able to play this role because for any declarative sentence p we can give an equivalent sentence 'the proposition *that p* is true' where the sentence 'p' has been replaced by the noun phrase 'the proposition *that p*' and the truth predicate 'is true' has simply been employed to keep a sentence structure ('it acts simply as a *de-nominalizer*', Horwich says).[44] Nothing more about truth need be assumed; this exhausts the notion. Nevertheless Horwich claims, and sets out to show, that the minimalist view is neither too obvious nor too weak to have significant philosophical implications. Both in respect of general principles involving truth – for example, that verification indicates truth and that true beliefs conduce to successful action – and with regard to solutions of problems about, for example, vagueness and scientific realism, the minimalist view is, he argues, sufficient.[45] It is summed up in the claim that the notion of truth contains nothing more than is expressed by uncontroversial instances of the equivalence schema:

(∃) It is true *that p* if and only if p.

The theory to this effect is the 'minimalist theory'; the account of the motivations, consequences and defences of the theory Horwich calls 'the minimalist conception', and it is from this latter, rather than the theory as such, that some of the material for discussion of problems about vagueness and scientific realism come.

There are a number of objections to deflationism thus conceived. One is that there are some clearly false instances of the equivalence schema (∃). Horwich gives as an example, 'THE PROPOSITION EXPRESSED BY THE SENTENCE IN CAPITAL LETTERS IS NOT TRUE'. Substitution of this into (∃) generates a Liar-type paradox: 'The proposition that *the proposition expressed by the sentence in capital letters is not true* is true if and only if the proposition expressed by the sentence in capital letters is not true' easily yields a contradiction. So not all instances of (∃) can be included in the theory of truth; but it is hard to specify which they are. Horwich remarks, in defence, that deflationism is not alone in this dilemma.[46]

Another objection is that although the theory can be described it cannot be formulated explicitly, for it has an infinite number of axioms. Horwich argues that the response to this, in the form of the construction of theories showing how the truth of propositions derives from their constituents' referential properties, faces two difficulties: that we cannot be sure that all propositions get their truth in this way, and that anyway there is no satisfactory finite theory of reference in the offing.[47]

A number of Horwich's critics object to his choice of propositions as truth-bearers, on the familiar grounds of their alleged unsatisfactory character. They apply the deflationary account to *sentences* instead: a schema might be, ' "s" is true if and only if s'. In this guise the redundancy theory is called the 'disquotational theory', for, as Quine puts it, 'Attribution of truth to "Snow is white" just cancels the quotation marks and says snow is white. Truth is disquotation.'[48] In Horwich's view the disquotational theory fails to cope with terms that change their reference according to occasions of use, as with indexicals ('now', 'here') and demonstratives ('that'). It is not true, for example, that every instance of 'I am weary' is true if and only if *I* am weary. To adapt the disquotation schema to accommodate these cases is difficult; Horwich recommends defending propositions instead – among the virtues of doing which, he says, is fidelity to ordinary language and a plausible concomitant account of belief.[49]

The chief difficulty, or set of difficulties, with the Minimal Theory, or indeed any deflationary theory, is the *stubbornness* of the idea that truth is a substantive notion that plays an explanatory role in thought. Ramsey, like Strawson after him, cited examples in which 'is true' is used merely corroboratively, and pointed out that there are more ways of agreeing or endorsing than by saying 'that's true' or affixing 'is true' to a repetition of what is said; and took this as among the reasons for thinking appeals to truth are redundant. But 'is true' might have such uses, yet in other typical uses might also introduce a substantive property. It might function in some of its uses in the way Horwich describes, and yet also introduce a substantive property. It might disquotationally capture the triviality that 's' is true if and only if s, and in other typical uses introduce a substantive property. In short, everything deflationists say about truth could be true *except* that *there is no more to truth than these uses*. This is the essence of the deflationary claim, and it is what that stubborn thought about truth resists.

The stubborn thought arises whenever something important hangs on whether or not some proposition is true. Suppose Tom tells Dick something of central importance to Dick's life, liberty or estate. Dick may urgently wish to know whether what Tom said is as Tom said, and accordingly checks with Harry. If Harry says 'what Tom said is true', what is of crucial interest to Dick is that Harry means 'things are actually as Tom says they are', for it would be much less interesting to Tom if what Harry meant was, say, 'I agree with or endorse what Tom said'. It is the fact that there is a difference between saying 'that *is* the case' and 'hear, hear' that makes for the interest – and puzzle – in truth; and in any case one suspects that the notions of corroboration and agreement in part turn on an account of 'taking to be true' and hence again of 'true'. It might be that there is 'no *separate* problem of truth', as Ramsey argued, in the sense that truth might turn out to be inextricably linked to epistemological or semantic considerations; but it is not immediately clear that this entails some form of deflation.

For this reason the test of deflationism is whether it can satisfy us on a range of questions where truth seems to play a substantive role – as the goal of enquiry; as explanatorily powerful; as the reason for the empirical success of theories; as required to sustain realist conceptions turning on a distinction between truth and verification; as figuring in an explanation of valid inference; and much more. These points are considered by Horwich, who as noted takes his view to be adequate to them. If right, he shows that it is indeed a misconception, as he claims, to think truth has a hidden structure which, if we could discover it, would explain fundamental philosophical principles and solve many problems.[50] He diagnoses the cause of this misconception to be a misleading linguistic analogy: 'Just as the predicate, "is magnetic", designates a feature of the world, *magnetism*, whose structure is revealed by quantum physics, and "is diabetic" describes a group of phenomena, *diabetes*, characterizable in biology, so it seems that "is true" attributes a complex property, *truth* – an ingredient of reality whose underlying essence will, it is hoped, one day be revealed by philosophical or scientific analysis.' This characterization of what truth is not suggests a different misconception, about what is meant in saying that truth is a substantive property of its bearers; I discuss this below, after first turning to the idea that it is a *primitive* substantive property which cannot therefore be defined.

Truth and Indefinability

The idea that truth is an indefinable substantive property is put forward by Davidson. Truth plays a crucial role in his views about meaning and other matters (see chapters 8 and 9 below), and therefore the idea that a concept so fundamental and consequential can just, so to speak, be *available* without requiring definition or analysis, is a seductive one. In this view the burden lies not on the concept of truth itself but on the indefinability claim. What follows discusses this claim.

'Truth is beautifully transparent compared to belief and coherence,' Davidson claims, 'and I shall take it as primitive.'[51] The comparison is drawn because whereas belief and coherence might be thought necessary for a definition of truth as coherence among beliefs, Davidson has no intention of so defining it. To take truth as primitive is to say that it is indefinable. This strategy turns out to recommend itself generally to Davidson as a way of dealing with most major concepts in philosophy.

In the introduction to his paper 'The Folly of Trying to Define Truth'[52] Davidson tells us how to address the concept of truth and by extension these other major concepts, such as belief, memory, perception and causality. The proposal amounts in effect to a suggestion about philosophical method. His suggestion is that we are to eschew the strategy of seeking *definitions* of a certain sort, and to practise instead what might be called a Strawsonian strategy (not Davidson's term) of tracing connections among concepts.

Davidson begins with a cautionary tale, concerning the failure of Socrates ever to arrive at what he seeks in Plato's earlier dialogues, namely, definitions of beauty, courage, justice and other important notions. His quest seems bound to fail because he seeks a *sharp* answer to the questions (where X is justice or beauty or some such) 'what is Xness?', 'what makes X things X?' And Socrates does not accept definition by extensional paradigms, that is, proffered examples of, say, beautiful people or just actions.

Davidson appears to identify the kind of definition Socrates mistakenly seeks as *reduction* of a target concept to 'other concepts that are simpler, clearer and more basic'.[53] He also describes this style of definition as the 'formulation in a clearer, more basic vocabulary' of the elements that must figure in the analysis of some concept.[54] In Davidson's view, Plato failed to notice that some philosophically important concepts are not amenable to such definition. When you add the fact that in discussing one concept – say, knowledge – philosophers typically pretend they understand the other concepts required – in this case, at least truth and belief – you see a moral: in Davidson's words: 'however feeble or faulty our attempts to relate these various basic concepts to each other, these attempts fare better, and teach us more, than our efforts to produce correct and revealing definitions of basic concepts in terms of clearer or more fundamental concepts.[55]

And he goes on to say that this is only to be expected, because the concepts that attract philosophical attention – truth, action, knowledge, belief, cause, the good and the right – are 'the most elementary concepts we have' without which we might not have any others. So why do we presume that they can be definitionally reduced to simpler, more basic concepts? 'We should', he concludes, 'accept the fact that what makes these concepts so important must also foreclose on the possibility of finding a foundation for them which reaches deeper into bedrock'.[56]

And this insight is to be applied to the concept of truth: we cannot hope 'to underpin it with something more transparent or easier to grasp'; it is indefinable.[57] Nevertheless, to say that truth – along with the important concepts – is indefinable is not to say that nothing revealing can be said about it, or that it is 'mysterious, ambiguous, or untrustworthy', for the strategy of tracing its connections with other concepts (such as belief, desire and action) shows otherwise.[58]

There is much to say about these points. Davidson's preferred strategy, that of tracing connections among concepts, is reminiscent of Strawson's 'descriptive metaphysics' in *Individuals*. Davidson contrasts it with the strategy of trying to understand what is problematic in terms of something clearer, simpler, or more fundamental, a strategy which perhaps should be called Russellian rather than Socratic; it does not merit the label Socratic, for Davidson has chosen to treat definition in effect as analysis, which Russell distinguished sharply from definition. Socratic definition, so far as it can be separated from Platonic definition associated with the Theory of Forms, is *exact specification of the essence* of something – typically, an abstract reality such as piety or goodness. Plato took it that the Theory of Forms offers an account of this which is lacking in Socrates, although his procedure can also sometimes be construed as definition *of concepts* rather than things, however conceived, as when in the *Theaetetus* he discusses knowledge.

The point of remarking the historical prefigurings of the opposition Davidson sets up is that they help us to understand his argument. He identifies definition with the Russell-like strategy of analysing concepts into clearer and simpler ones, cites examples of how this fails, and urges in its place a Strawson-like strategy of tracing conceptual connections. I shall give reason for saying that the two strategies are not exclusive, that the Russellian strategy has much going for it, but is not one of stating definitions (Russell *expressly* conceived analysing as distinct from defining), and that the Strawsonian strategy is not entirely satisfactory for Davidson's purposes, and anyway suffers a severe limitation. All this shortly.

Davidson's remark that most philosophically significant concepts 'are the most elementary concepts we have' invites comment.[59] The examples, recall, are truth, action, knowledge, belief, cause, the good and the right. There would be near consensus that these are among the most important in philosophy. The quite different claim that they are the most basic – even in the weaker sense that they are the most basic in some respect or for some discourse – precisely constitutes the substance of much philosophical debate, against which it begs the question simply to *claim* that they are. For one example, consider a view of truth which has it that truth is a portmanteau concept for a range of more specific evaluatory concepts individuated by discourse.[60] Such a view denies that the concept of truth is basic, but affirms its importance against deflationary views; it says that truth is not one insubstantial thing but several substantial ones, each in its different way more fundamental than the generic concept. It is the possibility rather than the merits of such a theory that illustrates the present point: that the question whether a given concept is basic is frequently moot, and in every such case the claim that it is indeed so needs an argument.

It might be the result of a Strawsonian enquiry into the order of dependence among concepts that we can specify which are more and which are less basic, but to begin such an enquiry with the ordering already assumed renders such enquiry pointless.

But here is the respect in which a Strawsonian strategy – and more specifically, Strawson's own strategy – seems not to fit Davidson's bill in any case. As the foregoing remarks imply, for Strawson a major part of the tracing task is to identify the order of dependence among concepts, with the target, or at least the guiding ideal, being the discovery of which occupants of the logical space under scrutiny are fundamental to others. This strategy naturally fits one that finds transcendental arguments a useful device for identifying fundamental concepts, for their purpose is to show which concepts must be in one's possession as a condition for the possession of given others. This strategy, when successful, offers an anchorage in certain concepts which, although they might not turn out to be simpler than the concepts whose possession they make possible, would by the argument be more fundamental, and might therefore constitute a resource for analysis or even definition of non-fundamental concepts. It seems implicit in the Strawsonian strategy, in other words, that tracing connections yields an ordering of the more and the less fundamental; and analysis (or what Davidson calls definition) is thereby made possible.

The question whether a concept is basic is quite different again from the question whether it is elementary or simple. Basic concepts can be complex, and arguably many are. That is why we think them in need of analysis, or explication, or perhaps even definition. Elementary or simple concepts are those which are by definition *incapable of further analysis*. But this by itself – and I return to the point later – does not mean that they are *incapable of definition*. It again begs questions to label a concept 'elementary' if the point is thereby to warrant its indefinability, for the two are not the same thing.

To call a concept 'elementary' is to accord it a distinctive structural role in some conceptual edifice – in effect, a foundational one. When the foundation in question is that of our thought we require the elements to be more exact and perspicuous than less elementary parts of the structure – that is, than the dependent concepts in the scheme. But this is obviously, in fact notoriously, not so with the concepts Davidson describes as elementary.

Davidson says that 'we should accept the fact that what makes these concepts so important must also foreclose on the possibility of finding a foundation for them which reaches deeper into bedrock.' One has to guard against versions of what might be called the 'argument from impotence', employed by Descartes in saying that the mind–body problem is best solved by being ignored because it defeats human understanding, a view repeated by McGinn in claiming that humans are constitutionally barred from knowing how consciousness arises from brain-function. Arguments from impotence are an objectionable resource for philosophers to employ: such arguments release one from thinking about the allegedly unsolvable problems, which is the opposite of what one *should* be doing. For present purposes, the remark suggests that Davidson's version of the Strawsonian strategy sees it as tracing conceptual connections on the same epistemic and logical level; it is an anti-foundational version of the strategy; and this arguably compounds what is anyway the most serious limitation of the strategy: its invitation to a form of relativism not envisaged in Davidson's other well-known anti-relativistic arguments (see chapter 9 below).[61] Of this, more in a moment.

The worst problem with allegedly elementary concepts as with allegedly indefinable ones is that they can be over-permissive. Specifying a concept as elementary or indefinable without also specifying constraints on its use, carries a risk. It is that such concepts permit too much in the way of inferences. Consider this comparison: suppose you count into your scheme the concept of an omnipotent deity. Then almost anything goes; because, for example, the laws of nature can be suspended at any time, in any way, and therefore practically nothing is ruled out as to what can and might happen. I say 'almost anything goes' because one does not know whether an omnipotent deity can do logically impossible things, or eat himself for breakfast, and so forth. But almost everything else goes. So we approximate to the acceptance of a contradiction as a premiss: here absolutely anything goes. Simple or indefinable concepts, if unconstrained, or not subjected to the government of conditions of application, are over-permissive in this way, allowing anything or at least too much to be thought or inferred. But the danger is that if anything or too much is licensed by employment of some concept, nothing or too little of any use is. This is a cousin of the thought that if a theory explains everything and accommodates all cases, it explains nothing.

To deal with this problem Davidson says that although truth is indefinable, this does not mean that there is nothing revealing to be said about truth. The revealing things consist in tracing conceptual connections.

This is, however, as stated, a strategy with serious limitations. Consider as an example the sentence, 'He has Jupiter on the midheaven, with Sagittarius rising, and Mars in the seventh house'. This introduces a spate of concepts whose interrelations, once grasped, clarify one other. But the question is not whether astrological concepts clarify each other by their interrelations, but whether any sort of reality answers to them; or more weakly, even whether they stand up to scrutiny, however well they hang together from an internal perspective.

Now, Davidson might say that this misses a point, namely, that these clusters of concepts must themselves relate to yet others in the larger discourse, and our adjudications of their value flow from understanding those larger relations. For example, theological claims compete for the truth with scientific ones over such matters as the origin of the universe, or whether water can turn into wine without the help of grapes; and when we see how the concepts domiciled in each more largely relate to others, we see which are the more acceptable.

But this reply only enlarges the scope of the difficulty. Contrast the Strawsonian strategy with what looks like a legitimate ambition to understand individual concepts (no insignificant matter even for the task of ascertaining how the nature of each influences the relations it can have with others) and to find some maximally stable basis for doing so in the light of how things are in the world, or in the limits of experience, or in the constraints of logic or at least of rationality – all in the hope of securing objectivity, or its closest approximation, for them. This is not something a Strawsonian strategy even tries to offer. That strategy offers an account only of *relations among concepts*, and therefore what applies to theological or astrological concepts as a family – namely, that the Strawsonian strategy offers no guide to their legitimacy or justification beyond what that family of concepts internally claims for itself – applies to the whole family of all our concepts.[62] We do not escape what is wrong with parochiality and relativism by claiming that the whole scheme is the parish. (Rorty finds Davidson's views agreeable for this very reason, which suggests some familiar forms of criticism.) It might be questioned how far anything has been clarified if the terminus of enquiry is just: an internal mapping of connections.

Definition

One might remark that Socrates' refusal to accept definition by extensional paradigms is a serious mistake. This form of definition operates by the giving of focal examples, grasping which as such enables normally intelligent persons to apply the concept thereafter in usual conformity with their fellow-conceptualizers. Many general concepts, such as those of colours, are not amenable to definition by, say, the statement of necessary and sufficient conditions for their application; rather, they are learned and used on the basis of agreements about focal cases, focal non-cases, and shared hesitancies at the margins. The ability to display the right skills in application, and to behave in closely similar ways to other conceptualizers in cases of vagueness, constitutes our test of whether someone has mastery of given concepts. *Mutatis mutandis*, the same applies for mastery of the general terms that denote them.

This prompts one to remember that there are many kinds of definition. This is not the place for a detailed taxonomy, but it is helpful to recall the following, doubtless incomplete, assortment: there is 'analytic definition' in Moore's sense, where 'analytic' has its chemical connotation (analysis into constituents or components), and his preferred view of philosophically proper definition, which is analytic in the semantic sense. There are lexical definitions, of the kind familiar in dictionaries, where approximating paraphrases do as well as the provision of synonyms. There is ostensive definition, which is actually a family of procedures of defining by showing, manifesting, displaying or demonstrating the definiendum, of which denotative definition – pointing a finger, perhaps while uttering the name of the thing picked out – is a focal case. There is definition in use, there is definition by paradigms (these differ technically from ostensive definitions because in order to grasp them the beneficiary of such definition must be able to extend application to relevantly like cases – the complexity of the procedure is considerable on the take-up side). There are stipulative and abbreviating definitions, the latter in Russell's and Whitehead's *Principia Mathematica* sense. And all these are to be distinguished from – though they stand in close relation to – explication, description, analysis in the standard Russellian sense, and the tracing of connections between concepts as in the Strawsonian strategy.

Of these many kinds of definition Davidson considers only two: the extensional paradigms kind just mentioned, and what he describes as the 'definitional reduction' to simpler, clearer, and more basic concepts of the target concept. As already noted, this definition of definition is problematic. Russell insisted that definition and analysis are different, and that where a definition cannot be given, an analysis often can and should be.[63] But, again as noted earlier, Russell meant by 'analysis' exactly what Davidson means by 'definition'. Russell contrasted analysis both with definition as he and Whitehead defined it in *Principia*[64] and

– for the cases he recognized as more germane to the treatment of problems outside the formal context – with definition as Moore understood it. The first kind is stipulative; it records a decision to use symbols in a certain way. Moore's famous account focuses upon concepts; he rejects what, for present purposes, he confusingly calls 'analytic definitions', namely, definitions of *things* in terms of their parts and arrangements, as philosophically irrelevant. As to concepts, he requires that definitions should be analytic; definiens and definiendum must be synonymous if the former is to provide us with what we want in respect of the latter.

But for Russell an analysis breaks up and typically dissipates its target in the analysandum, so that it does not figure in the analysans. The lump of rock vanishes into a cloud of charged particles; the sentence with a definite description in grammatical subject place becomes a tripartite conjunction with, in the perfect language, bound variables in logically proper place: the definite description has vanished.[65] So there is a sharp contrast between Russellian analysis and Moorean definition. Might it be that Davidson tacitly assumes Moore-leaning constraints in the reduction he has in mind as defining of definition? The fact that one has to ask suggests that we need a fuller account of what he takes definition to be; we cannot properly evaluate claims that important concepts resist such definition until we have it.

Definition and analysis are, however, closely related, in a family whose other members include explication, description, classification, and what philosophers loosely call 'making sense' and 'giving an account'. It might be that these last two convey the inclusive notion, with the others as different members. In carrying on what James described as 'the dogged struggle to achieve clarity' we are accordingly not without resource, even if restricted to these. We should therefore be untroubled to find that *strict* and *precise* definitions, of the kind respectively possible in formal contexts and the natural sciences, are not generally available in contexts outside these. Certainly, few if any of the concepts important to philosophy admit of that kind of definition; irrespective of the exact nature of Davidson's understanding of definition, he is surely right about that.

But to say that such concepts cannot be *strictly* or *precisely* defined is not to say that they cannot be defined. The mistake arises from thinking that definitions must be definite. Think of the etymology of the term: to seek to define is to seek to find or – just as importantly – to draw limits, to mark boundaries, to feel the edges of application. Often we have to negotiate and renegotiate these. A fuzzy boundary does not fail to be a boundary because it is fuzzy; as we have seen, we would have a very impoverished stock of general concepts if that were so.

A surely unintended implication of Davidson's remarks is that stating definitions (however conceived) and tracing conceptual connections exhaust the alternatives for philosophical method. But as suggested already, these are not mutually exclusive procedures. And apart from these – together with analysis and explication – there are a number of other characteristic vehicles of philosophy: for example, proof and argument, construction of theory, assembling reminders, persuasion, taxonomizing, criticism. It does not do to circumscribe, even by implication. So it seems that our ambition to get to grips with the important concepts of philosophy, not least among them truth – even to arrive at definitions of them in one of the many ways of definition – does not involve so much folly after all.

Truth and Objectivity

What of the matter left hanging earlier, the question of *objectivity*, which the strategy of tracing conceptual connections seems not to provide? A feature of Davidson's views – his 'externalism' – might be supposed to help here.

Davidson holds that language-users understand one another by being interpreters of one another's utterances. Interpretation at its simplest is a mutual activity of two speakers who share experience of a portion of the world, and who hold each other's beliefs about that portion of the world to be true (the interpretative principle that another's beliefs are largely true is called the 'Principle of Charity'). The two speakers, and the portion of the world available to both, form a triangle. The three-way relation underwriting mutual interpretation is called 'triangulation'. It is this that might secure the objectivity that the Strawsonian strategy fails to provide.

We learn from Davidson's views about triangulation that this essen-tially relational condition of interpretation is tied to the causal role of the world in giving beliefs their content. Events in the world cause beliefs, Davidson says, in a 'fairly direct' way by sensory stimulation; we have to connect beliefs with what they are about as regards their empirical content – truth-value and empirical content come from perception, or more precisely, the circumstances of perception.

So far, these remarks have a reassuringly familiar ring. But their tendency is not, it turns out, to give our beliefs extra-mental anchorage of the kind offered in traditional theories. Davidson's talk of the 'environment, the shared distal stimulation' that plays a part in causing our beliefs is, first, not talk of what provides justification for them. Only beliefs can be evidence for beliefs; what gives rise to beliefs cannot. A dualism between our concepts and what they are of – their content – is rejected because there cannot be content by itself, and because it is not propositionally articulated, and therefore cannot do what empiricists want it to do, namely, provide warrant for the scheme (see chapter 8 below).[66] This rejects the empiricist claim that sensory awareness is the uniquely authoritative source of contingent knowledge.

Nor is the relation between the apex of the triangle in triangulation and its base angles to be understood as connected to a familiar set of various relations: perception and its objects, thought about things, truth and its makers, reference and singled-out bits of the world. Davidson rejects all these, or at least – in the case of reference – accepts only a severely deflated version, as conceptually toxic versions or by-products of the scheme-content dualism.[67]

So we know what is *not* meant by talk of 'the world' in Davidson, and we note that it consorts well with a particular choice of emphasis. The objectivity of our concepts on what Davidson calls 'the social or externalist view' is a function of the mutuality of interpretation. In setting out this view Davidson gives the environment an error-or-divergence-adjusting role, but 'nature does not speak to us', it is not on its own a contributor to meaning. For meaning we must look to mutual interpretation, and interpretation is *essentially* social. Objectivity for Davidson is therefore intersubjectivity. And this is consistent both with the coherence flavour of much that Davidson says – 'no point in looking outside sentences' – and his advocacy of a Strawsonian-like strategy.

Despite having entitled a paper 'A Coherence Theory of Truth and Knowledge', Davidson dislikes the coherence label, and for the very reason identified above as a flaw in the Strawsonian strategy, namely, that it provides only internal justification for beliefs. The point can be put by saying that in addition to seeing connections between beliefs, we need a reason to think that most of them are true. And familiarly, instead of seeking an external anchorage to provide this assurance, Davidson thinks that we have one in the Principle of Charity. To get our interpretations of others going, we must take it that most of their beliefs are true. So let us just do ourselves the same good turn, and take it that most of the beliefs in our own scheme are true. The principle is: 'belief is in its nature veridical'. Here then is a further feature of the interpretational considerations that yield objectivity.

Two large objections suggest themselves. First, one is left feeling multiply dissatisfied with the claim that one can invoke 'the world' as playing a causal role in determining the content of beliefs, and that one can invoke 'bits of the world' to serve in a lean account of reference, while at the same time being told that these relations have nothing to do with questions of meaning and epistemic justification. Dissatisfaction is prompted when a notion of 'the distal', or 'the environment of communication', or just 'the world', is invoked to tidy the edges of a theory which has no substantive role for them, when one wishes to know – in relation to 'the world' or 'the environment of communication' – something about how the concepts of knowledge, truth and meaning engage with our interest in 'the world', by no means an intuitively misplaced concern. After all, we take language to range over an independently existing realm of spatio-temporal items, including events, and we wish to know – that is, to have a way of recognizing – which sentences about this realm are true, so that we can know what we can know: for we have severely practical interests at stake.

The dissatisfaction here is with Davidson's seeming to have and eat several cakes at once. It is prompted, for example, by the opening paragraphs of 'A Coherence Theory of Truth and Knowledge', where he speaks of 'meaning being given by *objective truth conditions*' which can be satisfied (that is, by a thought-independent world), while yet *it is absurd to speak of a confrontation between belief and reality*. We can be *realists* and '*can insist that knowledge is of an objective world independent of our thought and language*', but no sense attaches to talking about a *scheme–content duality* (a duality between thought and language, on the one hand, and an objective world on the other).[68]

Secondly, Davidson's way out of the coherence problem prompts questions. It rests on the claim that 'coherent belief is in its nature veridical'.[69] But the history of science suggests that this claim is false, and that beyond its being an hypothesis with some utility in getting radical interpretation *started*, it is not an invariably good guide otherwise. For in understanding others, one often has to understand that what they are saying is false, or at least, that they hold certain beliefs true which we take to be false, perhaps for the reason that they are in error, or lying. These two points need to be taken together. The history of science teaches that the truth and the utility – within limits – of our beliefs do not invariably coincide, and historically have often been systematically divergent; and the point about falsehoods suggests that the false beliefs, ignorance, interests, or even malice of others can undermine our confidence in their reliability as truth-tellers, so that the interpretation of their discourse must surely make plenty of room for defeasibility. Taken together, we find that the Principle of Charity is questionable beyond its heuristic applications.

These dissatisfactions over objectivity prompt a direct challenge. Davidson urges the Strawsonian strategy, and commits himself to what we might for convenience call the coherence plus charity view (coherentism saved by the principle of the inherent veridicality of belief). He also says that the world plays a part in causing our beliefs. But then he also says that the world's causal activity with respect to us does not enter into the justification of our beliefs, and is not therefore the source of their objectivity – which, instead, is social. Meanings – reverting to the coherence mode – are functions of mutual interpretation. But the world contributes to the empirical content of our beliefs, and perceptual beliefs are basic to empirical knowledge.

These views do not seem to be consistent. If they are consistent, they have to be so on the grounds of the fine detail of their supporting argument.

Truth and Evaluation

Here is the sketch of an argument to suggest that truth is neither deflatable nor indefinable, but instead consists in a family of cognitively significant notions. Among its side benefits this thesis gives us a diagnosis of why traditional theories of truth are unsatisfactory – but it also shows what is right about them. It shows further that Ramsay is right about truth in a certain respect; namely, that the important task is to state a theory of assertion. But successor conceptions of his redundancy account get no comfort here, for the thesis says that truth is not one insubstantial thing, but many substantial things, none of which is truth as attempts have traditionally been made to conceive it.

First one needs to note something about the way certain expressions function. Consider again the words *thing, do, nice*. 'Thing' does general duty for any noun, 'do' for any or at least many active verbs, 'nice' for any adjective of a generally positive purport. It might be illuminating to call each respectively a 'substitute' or 'dummy' noun/verb/adjective, because each marks places in sentences where more precise expressions go when the utterer is less hurried or lazy. In fact, with a nod towards 'pronouns of laziness' (because although they are not essentially anaphoric, they can have such uses) one might describe these expressions as 'lazy' to give an informative contrast with 'busy expressions' that do more precise and particular work.

Now for these purposes we need to introduce a notion of 'lazy predicates', to be understood as expressions marking a place in sentences for more precise property-denoting expressions. As with the lazy expressions just cited, the lazy predicate tell us something about the range and kind of the busier substitutes it takes: its use implies that whatever they are, use of them in predication implies observance of certain constraints, or at least the aspiration to realise certain desiderata. So the lazy expressions are not mere dummies. There are in fact quite a number of lazy predicates, and they play important roles in the economy of thought. Something more is said about this later. At this point the task is to use the notion of a lazy predicate to state the present thesis about truth, as follows.

The predicate '– is true' is a lazy predicate. It holds a place for more precise predicates, denoting evaluatory properties appropriate to the discourse in which possession of those properties is valued. The properties are explicitly discourse-sensitive properties. As examples one might cite candidates from the history of related debates: verification in the case of discourse about the spatio-temporal realm; constructability in the case of a certain view about mathematics; and, say, universalizability in the case of ethical claims. These are merely examples of more specific properties; well-known debates about these candidates do not make one confident that they are the right ones; and to add to dissatisfaction with at least some of them one might suggest that, anyway, different subdiscourses are themselves likely to vary the evaluations (and associated evaluatory procedures) for which saying '– is true' goes proxy. To see the point one need only think of the difference between talk of Quakers and talk of quarks, both in some sense referents in what we take to be an explanatorily-continuous domain. Indeed the situation is even more complex: how we evaluate perceptual claims, tensed claims, theoretical claims, claims about social objects (and much besides) is a highly various matter; yet in some sense such claims relate to a unified world of temporal and spatio-temporal things, so this is independent of the differences between such evaluations and those applicable to purely formal realms and – differently again – different value realms.

The thesis need not argue for any specific set of values and evaluatory procedures for given discourses. To do so would be for it to engage in the appropriate philosophical enquiry. The concern is more general: to find and state constraints on evaluations which reveal why the same lazy predicate '– is true' collects them all.

So the view is that a theory of truth is (a) globally, a theory of evaluation, and (b) locally, a theory of subject-matter-specific evaluation for a discourse.

Evaluation is an epistemic matter in many cases, but not in all. The aesthetic case and aspects of the moral case are not so – and this observation is important, for the reason that since evaluation is about identifying and measuring value, it might be natural to think that there are fruitful comparisons to be drawn between busy substituends of '– is true' on the one hand, and '– is good' and '– is beautiful' on the other. But the comparisons are not smooth, and this suggests that general constraints on evaluation will have to be understood disjunctively – some evaluations are constrained by one subset of constraints, others by others, and as usual one major interest lies in seeing whether the subsets share any common members.

Constraints on Evaluation

The claim then is that the busy substituends of '– is true' are predicates that denote evaluatory properties of such kinds as, or in appropriate cases better specified than, *verification, constructability, universalizability* (and so on for discourses not mentioned). As just noted, the task is not one of making out some particular local theory of evaluation, but to say something general about evaluation.

We wish to evaluate propositions, claims, beliefs, theories. I shall speak generally of evaluating propositions. What is it to evaluate – to assess the value of – something? Consider a sheepdog. We know what we need it for, and what we need it to be like; and if it answers our needs, and performs as required, we value it – and if it does not, we disvalue it *qua* sheepdog. We need it to herd sheep, not eat them or frighten them; so we require that it be docile and responsive to command, and to have the appropriate temperament. These are among the desiderata it has to satisfy, which can be summarized by saying that *it has to be apt for the job we wish it to do*. Now, as regards propositions we naturally wish them to be true, because then we can rely on them in inference, we can trust them to convey information about how things are, we can use them to test other claims, we can agree on them (at least eventually, as providing the stable points on which we can converge); and because they exercise rational authority over us and therefore provide tests for norms of rationality. Moreover, we are entitled to assert them, and they are typically far more useful than false ones.

Now compare this list of desiderata for truth with what we wish to say about evaluation. If, on the basis of evaluatory procedures appropriate to their domain, we are to attach 'value' (antonym: disvalue) to claims, what we mean is that we at least require them to be:

1. reliable in inference,
2. consistent with other propositions we value,
3. usable in evaluating other propositions,
4. agreement-inviting/promoting,
5. authoritative for us in the domain,
6. such as to entitle us to assert them,
7. such that acceptance of them is a norm for rationality,
8. such that they help us organize the subject-matter they concern more effectively – by appropriate and negotiated standards of effect-iveness – than competitors.

This list has some overlaps with the list for truth, but is more inclusive. Neither list is non-redundant. Some items in both are restatements of one or more others. I list them in this way to bring out aspects of the desiderata. In both it may be that what occurs as 6 in the evaluation list – *viz.*, assertability – is something which the others constitute, as the principal mark and chief point of value – including the case where value is taken to be unanalysed truth.

A valued proposition, by satisfying these desiderata, accordingly has these properties:

(a) Acceptability: it invites acceptance on grounds that involve negotiated ways of maximizing agreement on a triangulation of evidence, aims and context. This is not just 4; it is all of 1–7 in the list of desiderata.
(b) Adequacy: that is, fittingness or appropriateness for the task of meeting needs in that domain of concerns; 1, 5.
(c) Utility: it does the job of providing information, generating predictions, licensing inferences, settling disputes; 1, 3, 5.
(d) Stability: it forms part of a view (for the domain) which is cogent, stable, robust in tests and other demands upon it; 2, 6, 7; it is thus a 'fact' for the domain; 1, 5, 6.

Disvalued propositions are those that fail to have at least (a) and (c) because they fail to satisfy the desiderata (but note that 4 and 8 can – for a time – be failed by novel ideas). Disvalued propositions are rejected. In ordinary parlance we call them 'false' but even when we are using our lazy predicate 'true' it would be more correct to call them 'not true' to mark the fact that there are different ways in which they can fail to be true other than by being false (for example, by being meaningless, inappropriate to the domain, neither true nor false, and so forth).

We allow ourselves to talk of information being conveyed by true propositions. This is allied to the notion of fact, which is what true propositions are said to 'correspond to'. The chief use of this resides in inference: having information enables one to get to further information. (It might also just be satisfying to know it.) On the evaluation theory there is no mention of information or facts; nevertheless we can say, regarding desiderata 1, 5, and 6, that a valued proposition is a fact in the sense that it has the property of standing firm for the domain.

Now the point is that if you take a subdomain of the spatio-temporal case, or a formal case, or an ethical or aesthetic case, the content of evaluations and the procedures involved in them will be specific to the subject-matter in hand. We can evaluate sheep-dogs and we can evaluate grand pianos, but although we can say general things about what we are looking for (not 1–8, for here we are evaluating things, not claims or theories), the specifics will differ. If we thought that there must be one thing that all evaluation consists in or results in, then we would find ourselves testing, say, to see whether Steinways bite sheep. (Although it is surely true of Steinways that they do not bite sheep, this cannot be what we want them for. Saying this is what is meant by denying that truth is a univocal concept.)

To say that '– is true' is a dummy for '– is constructible', '– is verifiable', and so for other cases, is to say that there are, literally, different kinds of truth, individuated by subject-matter. Tarski, as noted, suspected that this might be so. And in line with his hint, this theory is consistent with the view that 'truth' in formal languages should anyway be considered quite separately; the idea being that talk of the *semantics* of a formal language is actually metaphorical, so that what is called 'truth' (or 'constructibility', say) is in fact a metalinguistic description of a syntactic property, such being the only kind of properties formal languages have.

But to say that there are literally different kinds of truth is not to make a relativist remark: the discussion here has nothing to do with such claims as that different points of view upon the same subject-matter can legitimately result in different distributions of truth-value across the propositions expressing it. That suspect claim is the subject of a different debate (see chapter 9).

So much is the merest sketch of a theory, but it offers resistance to the deflationary thought that it is a misconception to think that there is a property denoted by 'truth' with explanatory structure. This theory says that there are a number of such properties, which allow '– is true' to serve lazily for them all because the global desiderata apply to them all in virtue of their epistemic role.

Notes

1   A. Tarski, 'The Concept of Truth in Formalised Languages', in *Logic, Semantics, Metamathematics*, pp. 152–278; and (a very good introduction) Tarski, 'The Semantic Conception of Truth', in Feigl et al. *Readings in Philosophical Analysis*, pp. 52–84. I shall call these 1 and 2 respectively in references to follow.

2   Tarski, 2, p. 52.

3   Ibid., p. 53–4; 1, p. 155.

4   Aristotle, *Metaphysics*, 1011 b 26; a better translation than the one given earlier.

5   Tarski, 2, p. 54; cf. 1, p. 155.

6   Tarski, 1, pp. 157–65; 2, pp. 58–9.

7   Cf. Tarski, 2, p. 59.

8   Tarski, 2, p. 60; 1, pp. 162–5.

9   This informal presentation has closely followed Tarski's own in 2, p. 63.
10 A clear formal account of the notions of satisfaction by sequences and recursion is given by Quine, *Philosophy of Logic*, ch. 3, passim, esp. pp. 35–40, which precedes a discussion of Tarski p. 40 *et seq.*; see also Haack, *Philosophy of Logics*, pp. 106–8. My presentation follows hers.
11 Quine, *Philosophy of Logic*, pp. 40–2; Haack, *Philosophy of Logics*, pp. 108–9. Again I follow Haack.
12 Cf. Tarski, 1, p. 153; 2, p. 54.
13 Tarski, 2, pp. 70–4.
14 'Physicalism' is the thesis that '1. all events are physical events, i.e., have physical descriptions, and 2. under their physical descriptions, all agents are susceptible to total explanation, of the kind paradigmatically afforded by physics, in terms of physical laws'. J. McDowell, 'Physicalism and Denotation in Field on Tarski', in M. Platts, (ed.), *Reference, Truth and Reality*, p. 128.
15 H. Field, 'Tarski's Theory of Truth', *Journal of Philosophy*, lxix, 13, 1972, reprinted in Platts, *Reference, Truth and Reality*, pp. 83–110; cf. esp. Siii, pp. 91–4.
16 Tarski, 1, p. 406.
17 Ibid., and cf. 2, pp. 56–7.
18 Field, 'Tarski's Theory of Truth'. See esp. pp. 84–90, 94–103; and McDowell's reply, 'Physicalism and Denotation in Field on Tarski'.
19 K. Popper, *Conjectures and Refutations*, p. 223. See also Popper's *Objective Knowledge*, p. 320.
20 Tarski, 1, p. 155, 2, pp. 53–4.
21 Popper, *Conjectures and Refutations*, p. 224.
22 S. Haack, 'Is It True What They Say About Tarski?' *Philosophy*, 51, 1976, p. 25.
23 Ibid. See also Haack's *Philosophy of Logics*, p. 113.
24 Ibid.
25 Ibid., pp. 326–7.
26 Tarski, 1, p. 153.
27 Tarski, 2, p. 71. The critic was Gonseth, writing in the *Review Thomiste* xliv, 1938.
28 Ibid.
29 Ibid.
30 D. Davidson, 'On the Very Idea of a Conceptual Scheme', *Proceedings of the American Philosophical Association*, 1974; in *Inquiries into Truth and Interpretation*.
31 Popper, *Objective Knowledge*, p. 45.
32 F. P. Ramsey, 'Facts and Propositions', *Proceedings of the Aristotelian Society*, supp. vol., 1927; reprinted as excerpt in Pitcher, pp. 16–17.

33   Ibid., p. 16.
34   Ibid.
35   Ibid., p. 17.
36   Cf. chapter 4 above.
37   Cf. D. L. Grover, 'Propositional Quantifiers', *Journal of Philosophical Logic*, 1, 1973.
38   Cf. A. N. Prior, *The Objects of Thought*, p. 37f *et seq.*
39   Ibid., p. 37.
40   D. L. Grover, J. Camp and N. D. Belnap, 'A Prosentential Theory of Truth', *Philosophical Studies*, 27, 1973. See D. L. Grover, *A Prosentential Theory of Truth*, esp. pp. 3–45.
41   Haack, *Philosophy of Logics*, p. 133. For other discussions see B. Loar, 'Ramsey's Theory of Belief and Truth', in D. H. Mellor, *Prospects for Pragmatism*, p. 49f *et seq.*
42   Paul Horwich, *Truth*, see esp. Ch. 1.
43   Ibid., p. 3.
44   Ibid., p. 5.
45   Ibid., p. 7.
46   Horwich, 'Theories of Truth' in J. Dancy and E. Sosa, *A Companion to Epistemology*, p. 513.
47   Ibid.
48   Quine, 'Truth' in *Quiddities*, p. 213, and see *The Pursuit of Truth*, passim.
49   Horwich, *Truth*.
50   Ibid., p. 2.
51   D. Davidson, 'The Coherence Theory of Truth and Knowledge' in Le Pore E. (ed.), *Truth and Interpretation*, p. 308.
52   Davidson, 'The Folly of Trying to Define Truth', *Journal of Philosophy*, vol. xciii, 1996, pp. 263–78.
53   Ibid., p. 263.
54   Ibid.
55   Ibid., p. 264.
56   Ibid., pp. 264–5.
57   Ibid.
58   Ibid.
59   Ibid.
60   See below.
61   See Davidson, 'On the Very Idea of a Conceptual Scheme' in *Inquiries into Truth and Interpretation*, and 'The Myth of the Subjective' in M. Kraus (ed.), *Relativism: Interpretation and Confrontation*.
62   But we can break the epistemic circle if we are serious about what transcendental arguments can deliver. Strawson himself does not think they can deliver enough; he accords them at most and at best a role in identifying

orderings, not in giving objectivity or its closest approximation to our scheme. In my view transcendental arguments can indeed give this: see my *Refutation of Scepticism*, and related discussion in chapter 9 below.

63 See Russell in the *Lectures on Logical Atomism*.

64 Russell and Whitehead, *Principia Mathematica*, vol. i, p. 11.

65 See the remarks about truth as 'lazy' for evaluation, below.

66 Davidson, 'On the Very Idea of a Conceptual Scheme' in *Inquiries into Truth and Interpretation*.

67 See Davidson in any of 'Reality without Reference', 'A Coherence Theory of Truth and Knowledge', 'The Content of Truth', 'The Folly of Trying to Define Truth' in *Inquiries into Truth and Interpretation*

68 'A Coherence Theory of Truth and Knowledge' in *Inquiries into Truth and Interpretation*, p. 307, my italics.

69 Ibid., p. 309.

7

Meaning, Reference, Verification and Use

Introduction

This chapter and the one to follow discuss theories of meaning. Elucidating the concept of meaning is the central task in the philosophy of language. Interest in language, as noted more than once earlier, is prompted by the thought that an understanding of language will yield much towards an understanding of thought and the world. Questions of meaning have arisen, in one form or another and in more and less direct ways, in all the preceding chapters, which illustrates how substantial philosophical problems variously assume, turn upon, or arise from views about language and its relation to mind and the world.

It is important to be clear about the nature of *philosophical* interest in language, by discriminating between it and two other kinds of interest in language. One of these is not philosophical at all, although it can give rise to matters of philosophical interest. The other, although certainly philosophical, is philosophical in a sectarian rather than a general sense. The first kind of interest is represented by linguistics, the second by Wittgenstein's view of the nature of philosophy.

First consider linguistics. Language is interesting in its own right, and as a subject for empirical investigation presents numerous and subtle difficulties. The goal of linguistics is to give an account of language structure and functioning. Linguistic theory can be philosophically consequential; the views of Noam Chomsky, for one example (and among other things), provoke reconsideration of a controversy over 'innate ideas' which engaged Locke, Leibniz and the seventeenth century Cambridge Platonists. Chomsky pointed out that children display mastery of the deep structure of language in their early years, and do so upon exposure to fragmentary and degenerate examples of language – so fragmentary and degenerate, indeed, that they could not possibly have inferred the deep structure of language from them. He concluded that linguistic capacity must be innate. Put any infant into any linguistic community and it will rapidly learn the language in question – Chinese, Swahili, Greek, or Swedish – so not only must the infant's linguistic capacity be innate, but all languages must share a common stock of universals arising from that innate capacity.[1] This view, if right, raises a number of important philosophical questions.

Moreover, some philosophers approach semantics specifically from the viewpoint of theoretical linguistics; the joint early work of Katz and Fodor is an example.[2] Other philosophers, although not themselves engaged in semantics of this kind, nonetheless believe it to be the right way to investigate language; Adrienne Lehrer and Keith Lehrer, in another joint work, afford examples.[3]

But philosophical interest in language cannot be satisfied by linguistics. Descriptive treatment of the structure, functioning, and history of language will not by itself answer the metaphysical and epistemological questions raised by investigation of meaning. Philosophers are exercised by the philosophical assumptions and consequences of viewing language in this or that light, and by questions of reference, truth, and *logical* form. They are not concerned with phonetics and morphology, and their interest in syntax and grammar lies beyond syntax and grammar as such.[4] Linguistics and philosophy of language are distinct enterprises.

The second thing that philosophical interest in language is not to be wholly identified with, is a view to the effect that philosophical problems are to be solved – or, as Wittgenstein put it, 'dissolved' – by attention to the currencies of ordinary discourse. Wittgenstein held that philosophical problems arise from misuse of language, from seeing false analogies between different uses of language, or from assimilating different kinds of expressions to one another. We dissolve philosophical problems, on this view, not because we are reforming language, or finding perspicuous paraphrases of it in an ideal philosophical idiom, but simply because we are seeing how language actually and variously works. This is in effect a view about philosophical method, namely, that philosophy is a 'therapy' for disentangling muddled uses of language and showing how these create the illusion that there are philosophical problems. (Wittgenstein's views are canvassed below.)[5]

Looking at the way words are used, with a view to noting where and when misuse of a philosophically treacherous sort arises, is a salutary and pointful exercise. Philosophers from Plato onwards have been aware of its value. But it is contentious to say that it is the whole story. Wittgenstein's claim to this effect does not command widespread assent, not least for the reason that, as noted, there is hope that investigation of language will reveal how we think about the world and therefore – in turn – something of what the world is like. Attention to actual linguistic practice might often prove enlightening; but that would be one of the strategies, not all of the strategies, available to philosophical reflection.

So much for what philosophical interest in language is not. Here and in the following chapter I describe what philosophical interest in language is, adopting the following procedure.

In this chapter I range fairly widely over questions of meaning as these have been treated in 'traditional' theories, together with some contemporary extensions of them. First I consider the denotative theory again, and use it as a point of departure to look at recent discussion of reference. Then I turn to another traditional theory – the 'ideational' theory as some have called it – and follow with discussion of behaviourist views of meaning in both the earlier and the Quine varieties. After that I consider the verificationists' views, and the 'use' theory chiefly associated with Wittgenstein. This provides a survey of all but three principal approaches to meaning, together with some of their developments, and constitutes a background review for the chapters to follow.

The chief reason for discussing some of these theories in their traditional forms is, so to speak, a prophylactic one: it is to note their inadequacies, so that in trying to take more promising approaches to meaning one can be innoculated both against their shortcomings and against the natural-seeming temptations they offer.

In the next chapter I concentrate on two major approaches to meaning, both of which have attracted much recent debate: Gricean views, and truth-conditional semantics. The latter raises further and wider philosophical issues, and these I discuss, both there and in chapter 9.

Meaning

Here is a preliminary view of what we want an account of meaning to explain. Consider the following dicttionary definition:

1. *xyster* n. a surgical bone-scraper,

and contrast it with these sentences:

2. He means to be a millionaire one day.
3. The arrival of the cuckoo means summer is at hand.
4. The French word *plume* means 'pen'.

This is not an exhaustive list of the various ways 'means' enters naturally into our discourse, nor are the senses of 'means' in 2–4 independent of one another. But the sense of 'means' we are principally after is that sense in 4, which we would regard as approximate in some expansion of the dictionary definition in 1, for example ' "xyster" means "a surgical bone-scraper"'. How meaning is to be understood, in this sense of 'meaning', is the problem at hand. Naturally enough one is also concerned with intentions ('means' in 2 has the sense of 'intends') and the nature of signs and their relation to the things they signify ('means' in 3 has the sense of 'is a sign of'); not only for their own sake but also because they have a good deal to do with meaning in the 1 and 4 senses. There are, as noted, a number of other senses of 'means', many of which, like 2 and 3, also contribute to the overall problem. But the 1 and 4 senses provide enough to make a start.

The Denotative Theory of Meaning

This theory has been encountered frequently in earlier chapters. Ryle unlovingly dubbed it 'the "Fido"-Fido' theory in exemplification of its basic tenet. It is, on the face of it, a simple and immediately plausible view, premissed on the paradigm of proper names such as 'Tom', 'Dick' and 'Margaret', which function simply as labels, standing for something in the world. On the one hand there is the name 'Dick', and on the other hand, the man who goes by and answers to that name. From there one moves to the more general view that words mean by denoting things: 'the meaning of a word is the object it denotes'. One recalls that Russell's Theory of Descriptions was invented to show that apparently denoting singular descriptive phrases could be analysed away in order to show that they are 'incomplete', after the fashion of syncategorematic words like 'and', 'if', 'but' and the like, so that we do not have to postulate subsistent entities as the denotations of these phrases in order for them to be meaningful. Russell's choice was to retain the denotative theory and elaborate the Theory of Descriptions as a way of obviating its unpalatable consequences. The unpalatable consequences in question have among them the fact that, on this view, only if an expression such as 'the winged horse' denotes something is it even meaningful to deny of winged horses that they exist. Russell none the less felt that the denotative theory recommended itself too strongly to be abandoned: 'all words have meaning, in the simple sense that they are symbols that stand for something other than themselves'.[6]

Denotative theorists did not, of course, make the trite mistake of thinking that *all* words mean by denoting an object; the syncategorematic words, for example, get meaning 'in context', for obviously there are no ifs and buts in the world (as there are tables and trees) for the words 'if' and 'but' to name.

The idea that the meaning of a word is its referent or denotation is, however, shown to be false by two considerations, already noted in earlier chapters. One is Wittgenstein's point about ostension, the other is Frege's sense–reference distinction.

The first consideration shows that owing to the difficulties which infect ostensive definition, it is problematic at the outset to know how, for most words, even a simple labelling correlation could be established without recourse to more extensive and non-ostensive conventions governing the use of expressions. For, apart from the ambiguity which attaches to ostension (how does the learner of English know that I mean the object rather than its uses, colour, or texture when I point and say 'table'?), there is this problem: 'table' is used, in conjunction with a demonstrative ('that table') or an article ('the table', individuated by context) to pick out some particular table on some particular occasion; but the word itself does not denote this or that particular table, but can be applied indifferently to any member of the class of tables. It is a general term. But what does it mean to say that a general term functions like a proper name? Is there something – a class of things, or a concept, or an 'abstract idea' – it denotes? I return to these questions shortly.

The second consideration is decisive. Frege's distinction between sense and reference shows that two words or phrases might refer to the same thing but have different senses, as 'the morning star' and 'the evening star' exemplify. Accordingly it is out of the question to make a simple identification of the meaning of a word with its referent. This demonstrates that what has been so far characterized is a naïve or crude version of the theory.

One of the most swingeing attacks on the denotative theory in this form occurs in Strawson's discussion of Russell's Theory of Descriptions. In Strawson's view, Russell's belief that the meaning of a term is the object it denotes would, if true, permit one to produce the meaning of the word 'handkerchief' from one's pocket; but this is nonsense, and so too is the idea that the meaning of 'handkerchief' is all the handkerchiefs there are, were, and will be.[7] Because Russell held the denotative theory, he thought that if there were expressions having a uniquely referring use, which are about what they seem and not something else in diguise, their meaning must be the particular object they refer to, and hence the troublesome mythology of the logically proper name. But if someone asks one for the meaning of the expression 'this' – once Russell's favourite candidate for this status – one does not hand him the object just referred to by use of the expression, adding at the same time that the meaning of the word changes every time it is used. Nor does one hand him all the objects it has ever been, or might be, used to refer to.[8] So it is a mistake to conflate the meaning and the denotation of a term.

Defenders of the denotative theory, faced with these criticisms, have however a more sophisticated option to fall back upon. This is to identify the meaning of a term with the *relation* between it and its referent; thus, meaning is the referring or denoting relation between a term and the object it picks out. 'When we ask what constitutes meaning,' Russell later wrote, 'we are asking, not who is the individual meant, but what is the relation of the word to the individual which makes the one mean the other.'[9]

What is this relation? It is first necessary to draw a distinction. One suggestion is that it is not words that refer, but the people who use words. Thus in talking of my pen, it is not the *word* 'pen' that refers to my pen, it is *I* who refers to my pen by use of the word. A possible way out for defenders of the denotative theory is thus to insist on a distinction between referring and denoting, such that it can be left to people to refer, while denoting is reserved to words. On this view, 'pen' *denotes* (some suitable, indicated, described) pen, while *I refer* to my pen by using 'pen'.

This suggests an interesting emphasis in the basic idea. If reference is what occurs when a speaker uses a denoting expression, and if the meaning of the word is to be specified in terms of the relation between it and the relevant object – that relation being denotation – then the theory is specifically a denotative theory of meaning rather than a referential theory of meaning. There is then a way of handling the problem arising from the fact that 'table' is a general term. 'Table' does not, strictly speaking, *refer* to the class of tables, it *denotes* that class; and this says no more than that the class of tables is that class to whose members the word 'table' can be correctly applied.[10] There are other reasons why a reference–denotation distinction is valuable; some of these became apparent in the discussion of Donnellan in chapter 4 above.

But is the move just characterized satisfactory? A 'refers'–'denotes' distinction might seem well-motivated, but it does not solve the problem for defenders of the denotative theory, for we cannot simply say 'a person refers when he uses a denoting expression' without explaining what it is for someone to refer to something by means of a denoting expression, and without giving an account of what the denoting relation is and how it holds between words and things. On both counts there are difficulties: for 'denoting' the familiar questions arise, and for 'referring' as an activity of speakers we need an account, couched perhaps in terms of speakers' intentions, hearers' identifying knowledge, and conventions suitable for words to be so usable as to express the former and invoke the latter in the required way.[11]

There is no need to spell out theories of reference and denotation tailored to salvaging the theory in this form, however, for certain general considerations render it implausible. These are that many classes of terms, like connectives, prepositions, articles, modal auxiliaries and the like, do not have denotations but *functions*, and therefore because they make essential contributions to the meaning of expressions in which they occur, the meaning of such expressions could never be wholly reduced to the denotations of certain of their principle parts. Indeed, because the classes of terms which appear to be paradigmatically denotative contain very many members which do not denote (or at least, do not denote as unequivocally as do concrete nouns like 'table'; leaving aside names of such non-existent objects as 'unicorn', what do abstract nouns like 'hope', 'idea', or 'history' denote?), it is not clear that the meaning of at least many expressions can be explained by appeal to denotation, because none of their parts, principal or otherwise, may denote in a straightforward sense at all.

These thoughts point to an important consideration: that the basic unit of meaning is not the word, as the denotative theory has it, but the sentence. Austin in particular mounted a lively attack on the idea that word-meaning is basic, regarding the phrase 'the meaning of a word' as 'in general . . . a dangerous nonsense-phrase'.[12] I discuss this later.

It is a notable feature of the denotative theory that it leads its adherents into some awkward philosophical places. One is the consequence that if, as the theory demands, every meaningful expression is such in virtue of having a denotation, then whole sentences which are meaningful must have denotations too; and this is not especially intuitive. Whereas it might be natural to describe, and in many cases therefore to identify, something by means of a sentence, it is not natural to think of the sentence as a whole 'picking something out' in the way a designator does. Espousal of the theory, or some of its features, leads however to a demand that this be so; and accordingly one finds talk of 'facts', 'propositions' or 'meanings' as the referents of sentences. Such proposals lead one to think that if the denotative theory is the motivation behind such proposals, it must be mistaken.

Denotation cannot *be* meaning. Nevertheless, the original intuition regarding the way proper names function, and the fact that reference is central to linguistic activity, raises important questions. Manifestly, there are classes of expressions which do, or can be used to, refer to items in the world. How does reference work?

Reference and the Causal Theory

The idea that it is not words but people who refer is one among a number of proposals designed to furnish an account of how certain classes of terms – referring terms – apply or are used to apply to items in the world. In general it has been taken as unexceptionable to view terms which have a referring use as being themselves referring devices, so that investigation of them can proceed in terms which do not involve essential reference to speakers' and audience's intentions and knowledge, leaving treatment of these factors to a more inclusive or an alternative account. In the following sketch, accordingly, I adopt the idiom of referential terms.[13]

A common feature of many theories of meaning, in particular such traditional ones as the denotative theory, is their reliance on a distinction between the intension (sense) and extension (reference) of general terms and names. The idea is that the intension – the concept or meaning – of a term determines the collection of things – the extension – to which the term applies. This distinction was discussed in chapter 2. Traditional theories trade on the idea that names and general terms refer to those things which fit the properties which those names and general terms connote. Consider the different views of Frege and Russell on this point.

Frege regarded the sense of a name as 'the mode of presentation of the thing designated', grasped by anyone with sufficient mastery of the language. Sense 'determines' reference; if two expressions have the same sense, then they refer to the same object (although the converse does not of course hold; which is why the sense–reference distinction solves 'Frege's Puzzle' about how 'Hesperus is Phosphorus' can be a true identity statement while yet being informative). But Frege's account involves a difficulty. It is that the object referred to by a name might be presented to different people differently; one person might attach to the name 'Aristotle' the sense 'Plato's greatest pupil', while another might attach the sense 'the teacher of Alexander'. Frege says these differences have to be accepted in natural language, although they should not be permitted in a perfect language.

Russell, as noted in the discussion of his Theory of Descriptions (chapter 4, above), took it that the only expressions that counted as *logically* proper names, and therefore suitable for service in the subject places of propositions, are such expressions as the demonstratives ('this' and 'that') which are guaranteed a reference every time they are used. All the rest of the apparent referring expressions – common nouns and proper names like 'Napoleon' – are 'usually really descriptions'. Russell's claim in full is that: 'Common words, even proper names, are usually really descriptions. That is to say, the thought in the mind of a person using a proper name correctly can generally only be expressed explicitly if we replace the proper name by a description. Moreover the description required to express the thought will vary for different people, or for the same person at different times. The only thing constant (so long as the name is rightly used) is the object to which the name applies.' Some have taken this to mean that Russell took a name to be *synonymous* with some description or set of descriptions. But the most he seems to be claiming is that a name is *associated* with various descriptions. Given that the various descriptions associated with a name are subjective to the people whose thoughts the descriptions report when they use the name, and given that the name refers to 'something constant', that is, its bearer, a way must be found of avoiding the kind of tension apparent in Frege's views above. A suggestion is that various users of the name must wish their interlocutors to have *some* identifying thought about the bearer of a name they employ, even if it is not the same thought as is in the mind of the user of the name.

These ways of thinking about reference have been challenged in the work of Donnellan, Kripke and Putnam among others.[14] The chief of their views is that names, and by extension certain other terms – in particular, natural kind terms, that is, terms which designate such naturally occurring stuffs as gold and water – have no intension as understood by traditional theorists, and accordingly do not have their references fixed by 'modes of presentation' or by descriptions associated with them; but that reference is effected by a causal chain (or something like it) linking such terms and their referents. This view, which I shall call the 'causal theory' of reference, has some important implications for debates elsewhere in philosophy.

Consider the work which, on the traditional view, an intension–extension distinction does. The intension of a term is given by specifying a list of properties. To use Putnam's example, the meaning of 'lemon' is given by setting out a conjunction of properties $P_1 \ldots P_n$, such that to say 'anything with properties $P_1 \ldots P_n$ is a lemon's is analytic, as is 'lemons have the property P_1'.[15] The idea is then that the conjunction of properties which constitutes the meaning or intension of 'lemon' determines the extension of the term; all and only those things with properties $P_1 \ldots P_n$ are lemons.

Some such view, in one or another variant, has been widely held. The initial task of proposers of the causal theory is to refute it. Donnellan does so by showing, in connection first with proper names, that reference is effected independently of descriptions; which he does by drawing the distinction, discussed in chapter 4 above, between the referential and attributive uses of descriptions.[16]

A recapitulation of that distinction will be useful. Attributive use is made of a description when, it will be recalled, a speaker means to be saying something about whoever or whatever fits the description, even if he has no idea who or what fits it. Suppose, to use the same example as before, Smith has been murdered. We might say 'Smith's murderer is insane', without knowing who Smith's murderer is. Contrasted with this is the referential use. Here the speaker has someone or something definite in mind. Suppose Jones has been indicted for Smith's murder, and has behaved in an unbalanced way during the trial. If we say 'Smith's murderer is insane', referring to Jones, then we have used the description

'Smith's murderer' referentially. If it turns out that Jones is not Smith's murderer, say because Brown confesses, reference has still been effected by the description even though Jones fails to fit it.

This is taken to show that reference can and does occur independently of descriptions. The point is well driven home by consideration of cases like the following. Thales is the philosopher who held that the principle of the universe is water. Now suppose that in fact Thales was a well-digger and not a philosopher at all. Does the fact that he fails to fit the description 'the philosopher who held that the principle of the universe is water' mean that we are not talking about Thales? On the contrary. It only makes sense to say that a description fits or fails to fit someone or something if we can refer independently of descriptions; otherwise we should be obliged to say that if Thales does not fit the descriptions of him, he would not have existed.

Much the same point is made by Kripke.[17] In Kripke's view, names are 'rigid designators', that is, terms which refer to the same individual in every possible world in which that individual exists. Because individuals have different properties in different possible worlds – their being *different* possible worlds will turn in some cases just on the hypothesis that some specified individual answers to different descriptions in those worlds – it cannot be the case that the name of that individual is synonymous with some set of descriptions. (Kripke, in good company, inaccurately attributed what he calls 'the description theory of names' to Frege and Russell.) In other possible dispensations of things Aristotle might have been a hoplite, a physician, or whatever; but his name still rigidly designates him in all the worlds in which he exists. He will only possess in *all* possible worlds such properties as are essential to his being Aristotle.

This allows what is surely true, that we can discover of individuals that certain descriptions fail to fit them. For example, suppose it is confirmed that Bacon did indeed write *Othello, Hamlet*, and the rest; nevertheless the name 'Shakespeare' will not cease to refer because the description 'the author of *Hamlet*' ceases to apply to that individual. For if we irreversibly *identify* whoever is designated by 'Shakespeare' with 'the author of *Hamlet*', it would be impossible to discover that he did not write *Hamlet*.

Rigid designators are to be distinguished from non-rigid designators. The description 'the author of *Hamlet*' is non-rigid because Bacon, or Marlowe, or Beaumont might have written it, or because no such play might have been written – in which case no-one would answer to the description.

This then is the first important feature of the causal theory, that proper names are rigid designators. An interesting consequence relates to identity statements.[18] It might be thought that such identity statements as 'Hesperus is Phosphorus' are contingent, because the fact that the two are one is something that had to be established a posteriori. But Kripke argues that if 'Hesperus is Phosphorus' is true, then since both names are rigid designators and refer to the same entity in all possible worlds in which that entity exists, the identity statement is *necessarily* true. Philosophers had supposed this identity statement to be contingently true merely, because 'Hesperus is Phosphorus' is not analytic; but a failure to distinguish the metaphysical notion of necessity from both the epistemological notion of a prioricity and the semantic notion of analyticity is what causes the muddle here. On Kripke's view, 'necessarily true' means 'true in all possible worlds'; so although 'Hesperus is Phosphorus' is a posteriori, it is necessary – and if this is right, it establishes the existence of necessary a posteriori truths.[19] (See chapter 3 above.)

Another important feature of the causal theory is its implications for our understanding of 'natural kind' terms.[20] These are terms which designate such naturally occurring stuffs as gold and water, as opposed to such artificial categories of things as spinsters, professors, and bicycles. Kripke holds that natural kind terms work like names in being rigid designators, which means that 'gold' always refers to the same stuff whatever its overt phenomenal characteristics might be.[21] Suppose it to be the essence of gold that it is the element of atomic number 79. Then whether or not it is yellow and malleable, if it is the element of atomic number 79 it is gold. Traditionally it had been held that it is a defining characteristic of gold that it is yellow and malleable; but since it is possible to find stuff composed of atomic number 79 which has neither of those characteristics, 'gold is yellow' and 'gold is malleable' cannot be analytic.

This reinforces the point that descriptions commonly associated with a given thing are not decisive in fixing whether a term applies to it or not. Iron pyrites look like gold, but are not gold; here is a case in point, where 'nominal essence' is no guide to 'real essence'. The descriptions might be useful as a general guide to identifying something, but they do not settle what it is for a thing to be a thing of that kind; what settles whether something is or is not gold is its atomic structure. In just the same way, water is water only if it has the right kind of chemical structure, *viz.*, H_2O; something is not water merely in virtue of being a colourless, odourless and tasteless liquid. (Stinking black brackish water is still, after all, water – precisely because it is H_2O.) The point can be put by saying: there is no possible world in which something is H_2O but not water.

The question now arises: if reference does not (to put the matter roughly) go *via* sense, how is it effected? Matters are less clear here. One suggestion is that reference works by a causal chain, historically linking present uses of a term to the occasion on which the referent of the term was fixed. In much the same way as 'Tom' refers to Tom because he was so christened and the name has continued to pick him out ever since, so, on this view, objects were 'baptized' and their names have been handed on from speaker to speaker. So long as later speakers in the chain intend to refer, by means of the name, to what it was originally intended to refer to, the causal chain is of the right kind.

Certain elaborations of this view have been offered; Donnellan talks not of 'causal chains' but of an 'historical explanation theory' which allows that not all links in the chain are causal;[22] while Evans proposes that the causal link is not one between a referent and a current use of a term, but between the referent and the current body of knowledge concerning it.[23] Elaborations of this – in particular Donnellan's – sort are required to deal with terms which fail to refer, like 'Pegasus' and 'unicorn'.[24]

An apparent fault with the causal theory is that it leaves a question-mark over the one respect in which theories relying on a descriptive route for reference succeed in accounting for our intuitions about the use of names. This is that non-accidental success in applying a name would seem to demand that the user of the name has relevant identifying knowledge to the effect that *this* name picks out *that* referent, and that such knowledge is by its nature descriptive. The knowledge in question might be derivative, in the sense that it is not necessary for every user of the name to have a determinate way of identifying the referent so long as someone does;[25] and it may also be that what the user of the name knows is only some or even one contingent fact about the referent. But we would expect a user of a name to have some justification for his claim to be making a genuine use of the name; for if he did not, the comment 'he doesn't know who (or what) he is talking about' would be literally true.

This does not however constitute a serious difficulty for the causal theory. Kripke acknowledges that we may fix the reference of a term by giving descriptions, but that this is not the same thing as giving the meaning. This is to iterate the central point at issue, that names and natural kind terms have references but no senses; to ask for the *meaning* of either kind of term is accordingly misguided. The theory is, in a sense, an updated version of Mill's view that proper names have denotations but no connotations; a name, for Mill, is not bestowed on a variety of individuals 'to indicate any qualities, or anything which belongs to them in common; and cannot be said to be affirmed of them in any *sense* at all'.[26]

There are two related questions which need to be asked about the causal theory, however; what exactly constitutes the reference of a rigid designator? and, what of other referring terms, for example those which pick out non-natural kinds? A rigid designator is defined as a term which designates the same item in every world in which that item exists. But what is the item? It cannot be the extension of the term, because the very idea of a possible world is premised on the fact that extensions can vary across worlds. For example, if there is a possible world in which Aristotle is not a father, the extension of 'father' is different in that world from its extension in a world in which Aristotle has children. It is possible that there are two worlds in which the extensions of a given term are entirely disjoint. Accordingly the extension of a term cannot be what the term designates.

The option is to say that a rigid designator designates the kind or species itself. This is more plausible, but it has the drawback that it confers rigidity on such terms as 'teacher' and 'spinster', designating non-natural kinds, so that 'teacher' would pick out, from world to world, all and only those individuals who (systematically perhaps) instructed others. Putnam takes the view that practically all kind terms are rigid.[27] But the problem is that in the case of non-natural kind terms we do not standardly have a kind of thing in mind; it is rather the case that we employ certain general specifications such that if anything fits a minimum sufficiency of them, we apply the label. We can first name a natural kind and then proceed to find out what it is, as with elements or animals; by contrast, naming a non-natural kind is just saying what it is. A descriptive theory appears therefore to apply here, for non-natural kinds lack biological or atomic essences, and appear to have what Locke called 'nominal' essences only.

If different accounts have to be given of natural and non-natural kind terms respectively, then it will inevitably happen that there will arise disputes as to whether something is a thing of one or the other kind, perhaps in such particularly difficult cases as mental events and sensa- tions.[28] Is a pain, for example, to be differentiated with respect to the essential nature of the system of which it is an expression, or is it arbitrary from nature's viewpoint and differentiated by reason of the classifications we make for our own social convenience?

These last thoughts, touching as they do on the issue of essentialism, draw attention to the fact that if there are problems about the notion of possible worlds, and particularly about the notion of essence which plays a pivotal role in some possible-worlds theories, then these problems are also problems – and significant ones – for the causal theory of reference, which stands or falls by them. Some of the relevant difficulties are sketched in chapter 3 above.[29]

The Ideational Theory of Meaning

Views held in the past about meaning are rarely given an outing, which is at least a pedagogical mistake, because they hold temptations that are worth being inoculated against. (Moreover they tend to come round again, in higher-technology forms; and ought at least to have their rubber-band versions on record.) In this and the next sections I give a brief account of certain such theories.

An historically potent one has it that the meaning of an expression is the idea it stands for. Locke gives the paradigm statement of it: 'The use . . . of words is to be sensible marks of ideas; and the ideas they stand for are their proper and immediate signification'.[30] The theory underlying this view is that language is an instrument for reporting thought, and thought consists of successions of ideas. Ideas are private; only I have access to my thoughts. Therefore to communicate our ideas to each other we need a system of intersubjectively available sounds and marks, so connected to ideas that the proper use of them by one person will arouse the appropriate ideas in another person's mind. Accordingly what a word means is the idea with which it is regularly connected.

The first difficulty with this view is that it seems to make the arguable assumption that thought and language are independent of one another. How could thought above a rudimentary level be possible without language? This is not an easy problem to unravel, but certain observations are pertinent. For one thing, it is somewhat implausible to think that prelinguistic man may have enjoyed a fairly rich thought-life, and invented language to report and communicate it only when the social demand for language became pressing. Philosophical speculation either way on this matter is a priori anthropology at its worst, but it seems clear that anything like systematic thought is possible only with language. A caveman's ability to mull languagelessly over features of his experience in some way which is fruitful of his having theories about it, say, seems incredible, because ex hypothesi he lacks a medium for articulate thought. And the idea that he might have an inner, private, language of some pre-spoken variety is equally incredible; the private language considerations put forward by Wittgenstein in the *Philosophical Investigations*, suggest that any form of language must be a shared public enterprise.[31]

Moreover, it appears that the richer a language, the greater the possibility its users have for thinking discriminatingly about the world. An heuristic set of considerations in support of this thought might go as follows. Consider two men walking in a wood. One of them is a botanist with the name of every tree and shrub at his command. The other man, by contrast, is as ignorant of botany as his companion is knowledgeable, so that his experience of the wood is, on the whole, one of a barely differentiated mass of wood and leaf. Plainly, possession of the botanical language, and all that went into learning it, makes the first man's experience of the wood a great deal more finely differentiated and significant, *qua* experience of the wood as a wood, than is the second man's experience of it. The second man, despite his botanical ignorance, might have aesthetic experiences arising from his walk which leave the first man's more prosaic scientific experience quite in the shade; but the point at issue here is the relevance of their relative commands of the language specific to making their experience of the wood *qua* wood more and less finely discriminative respectively.

This aside, there are more strictly philosophical problems with the ideational theory. What is it for a word to be (in Locke's terminology) a 'mark' of an idea? And what indeed is an 'idea'?

The word 'idea' entered ordinary usage from philosophy in the seventeenth century. There is no consensus as to its meaning in the philosophical tradition. It is what is before the mind in thought or experience, for example, as sense-data, or feelings; as the objects of introspection, memory, and imagination; as the residue or impression on the mind of experiences; as abstractions into generality from particular experiences or reflections; as concepts, rather like definitions, attaching to words; as subjective associations aroused by words (as opposed to their sense – this is Frege's use); as a representation in one's mind of things in the world, that is, an image; and so on. The British Empiricists (Locke, Berkeley, and Hume), classified them into simple and complex ideas of sense and reflection, and specified their relations (for example, a complex idea of sense is composed of simple ideas of sense).

Locke was too sophisticated to construe 'idea' merely as 'image' (that is, a picture in the mind), nor did he hold that the meanings of all words are the ideas they 'signify', for he appreciated that words like 'if' and 'but' have functions rather than meanings – the function being to join words and sentences and to 'signify the connection that the mind gives to ideas or propositions, one with another'.[32] But Locke's use of 'ideas' as the meanings of words is none the less unclear. The most plausible construal is of 'idea' as concept, that is, some kind of specification or definition. On this view my idea of a dog would be the concept of a certain kind of four-footed mammal of a certain general shape, size, behaviour-pattern, and domicile. By this I do not mean that my concept of a dog is some odd image of an indeterminate dog with no specific shape, colour, or size, for, as Berkeley pointed out, any mental image of a dog would be of a dog with particular characteristics. Rather I mean this: suppose the word 'dog' has slipped my mind for a moment, yet I am trying to say something about dogs. I might say, 'You know, those four-legged animals kept as pets, or for herding sheep; they bark, and wag their tails when pleased.' I would be unpacking my concept of 'dog'. But now the problem becomes – what is a 'concept'? Is there any way to define 'idea' in terms of 'concept' such that the definition of 'concept' itself does not covertly rely on our pretheoretical grasp of 'idea'?

It will not do to appeal to 'definition' as in the preceding paragraph, for definitions are not what we would ordinarily classify as ideas or concepts. To begin with, the zoologist's definition of 'dog' will be far more detailed and precise than mine, and mine will be more precise and detailed than a baby's; yet both I and the baby will have ideas about dogs. An example might help. The word 'lexicographer' means (is defined as) 'a writer of dictionaries'. The celebrated Dr Johnson was a lexicographer; and in his dictionary he defined 'lexicographer' as 'a harmless drudge'. Lexicographers may indeed be harmless drudges, but their being so is not of their essence; for all one knows, some might be dangerous firebrands and yet still be lexicographers. Johnson might have conceived of lexicographers as harmless drudges; but his definition of them as such is no more than a joke at his own expense. Thus the distinction, even though it has had to be drawn by circular appeal to the very notions which are up for explanation.

The result of trying to clarify 'idea' in this way is to reveal that it is no more informative a notion than the notion of 'meaning' itself. So to say that the meaning of the word is the idea it signifies is to proceed *obscurum per obscuris.* There are no advances to be made on that front. But suppose, now, that one leaves 'idea' vague, taking it to signify whatever it is before one's mind that one is conscious of thinking about. Is there no way it can be said: words mean by pointing to, or evoking, or in some way being 'translations into public marks' of these things?

To raise the question in this form is to suggest that language encodes thought, that what one is doing in expressing one's ideas is putting them into a code – *viz.,* language – by means of which to transmit them to someone else. But what is the relation between ideas and language in which this encoding procedure might consist?

An analogy with translation from one language into another might help. Translation can proceed by means of a translation-manual that maps words of the foreign tongue into words of the already-understood language; having mastery of a translation-manual explains having mastery of the other language. And it must be possible, in principle at least, to translate one language into another without going via 'meanings'. In this way we know what it is to associate words in two different languages with one another.

But is it clear that we know what it is to associate an idea and a word? For one thing, it seems implausible to say that ideas have representations which mediate between them and words; for if they do have such representations, then we are embroiled in a problem of regress, because the question now arises as to what mediates between the idea and its representation, and between the idea's representation and the word. How an idea and a word can stand in an 'encoding' relation, therefore, is a problem.

An allied consideration is that whereas it appears natural and intelligible to talk of a word or idea 'coming into the mind' or 'occurring to one', to talk of a meaning 'coming into the mind' is not. If ideas are the meanings of words, then we are bound to say that meanings occur to one, or pop into one's mind. This ungainliness suggests that it is mistaken to hold words and meanings apart, and to identify the latter with ideas; there is little sense to the notion of a meaning occurring to one independently of the word whose meaning it is. Ideas or concepts, as constituents of thoughts which, implicitly, have an articulation in language, then come to be seen more appropriately as complexes which, far from being prior to words, are what the use of words manifests.

In this way one abandons the notion that words and ideas (language and thought) are separate, with the latter being presupposed to the former, and there having to be some relation obtaining between them. The problem of a relation of this kind vanishes; on the view of thought and language being substituted here for the transmitter-code notion, language is a vehicle for thought, in the sense that use of a word by an utterer constitutes sufficient grounds for ascribing possession of the concept or idea to the utterer.

On the code conception, by contrast, we must suppose that there can be possession of ideas prior to, or independently of, language. Such a view might seem, at first blush, to do justice to dogs and other intelligent creatures, to whom we frequently ascribe ideas – 'he knows his master is at the door', we say. But, at most, appeal to these facts shows that there can be rudimentary thought without language; on the whole, language-possession is a condition for having thoughts above such a level. A dog cannot be said to have, say, the idea of oneness, because (as Frege pointed out) although it can discriminate between being attacked by one dog and many dogs, it cannot see what is common to being attacked by one dog and chasing one cat. Wittgenstein similarly pointed out that although we can say of a dog that it expects its master home, we cannot say that it expects its master home next week. Here is the difference.

An ideationalist might attempt to preserve something for his theory by pointing out that at least in the case of words closely connected to sensory images (or ideas construed as images), ideas are the meanings of words. But this will not work either. Any image you care to think of could well arise in connection with a number of different words, and conversely a particular word might evoke as many images in people's minds as hear or read it. For an example of the first possibility, I might imagine a cat on the mat before the fire, and the words 'sleep', 'hearth', 'tabby', 'warmth', and a host of, others, could associate themselves. And regarding the second possibility, the word 'gun' might evoke images of pistols, or rifles, or English gentlemen on the moors, or cowboys, or artillery – the associable images are legion. The psychoanalyst's practice of encouraging patients to 'free-associate' is premissed on the sheer variety of image–word nexuses of which we are capable; which fact sharply reduces the credibility of this version of an ideationalist theory.

One feature of the ideational theory worth noting is that, like the denotative theory, it identifies the meaning of a word with an entity: both theories regard meaning as being somehow like labelling. That neither theory convinces in their standard forms perhaps indicates that the covert notion of labelling – what Quine called 'the Museum Myth' of meaning – is misguided.

The Behavioural Theory of Meaning

This theory constitutes an attempt to give an account of meaning based on scientific psychology. On each count in this characterisation, the behavioural theory is highly controversial.

The application of empirical as opposed to speculative techniques in those areas of philosophy concerned with the nature of the physical world gave rise, in the seventeenth century and after, to the natural sciences. The success of natural science prompted practitioners of the social sciences, in particular psychology, to attempt to make their subjects more rigorous by applying quantitative (as opposed to qualitative) techniques to them in imitation. One result has been a schism between – in the case of psychology at any rate – 'experimental' and 'social' branches of the discipline.

This sketch is a little hasty. Because the phenomena studied by natural scientists are repeatable and public, they are in substantial part amenable to quantitative investigation; they can be observed and measured. The phenomena studied by social scientists are often unique and private, as in the case of the sentiments and intentions of individuals; or they are historically parochial, mutable, subtle, and complex, as in the case of social institutions. Some philosophers of social science consequently hold that there is a methodology of social science properly distinct from that of natural science. Dilthey, Weber and others – the hermeneutic theorists – claimed that *Verstehen* theory provides the basis for this methodology.[33] Not all social scientists agree with the *Verstehen* theorists that their disciplines are to be held apart from natural science; these claim that the proper approach is quantitative empirical investigation of public phenomena. Experimental psychologists and behaviourists figure on this influential side of the dispute.

A well-known early example of experimental psychology is furnished by the work of Pavlov, who conditioned dogs so that their salivatory reflexes were prompted by the ringing of a bell. Under the inspiration of work of this kind there arose a school of behaviourist psychology. Exponents of 'behavioural theory' held that the mental life of men and animals is to be explained solely in terms of their overt behaviour, construed on stimulus–response lines, and that appeal to inner, secret, mental goings-on ('intentions') in people's minds is unscientific.[34] Those who hold that there is a ghost-world of mental entities, over and above the firings of cells in a person's central nervous system, are bracketed as 'mentalists' – a derogatory term in the behaviourists' lexicon. One of the founders of behaviourism took the view that thought consists of 'tiny laryngeal spasms' – that is, sub-vocal, self-addressed speech. On a behaviourist view, to say of someone that he is happy is not to attribute to him a certain state of mind, but to say that he is acting, or is disposed to act, in a certain way – smiling, walking with a spring, behaving in a generally sunny and good-humoured manner.[35]

This analysis was extended to the concept of meaning. Since speech and writing – in general, communication – is a developed form of behaviour, the thought was that it can be explained in stimulus–response terms. The behaviourist view went as follows.[36]

In any communicating situation there are, broadly speaking, three elements: the cause of the communication (the utterance or script) whose meaning we are concerned to explain; the context of the communication; and the effect on the audience. This last seemed to the behaviourists the most promising place to look for an account of meaning, especially because the purpose of communication lies in its audience-directedness: we communicate with others in order to inform them, modify their behaviour, prevent or motivate them, and so on.

Accordingly, early forms of the behavioural theory had it that the meaning of an utterance is the response it evokes from its audience in a particular situation. This is best illustrated by recalling Pavlov's dogs: the bell 'meant' food to them, and they responded to a rung bell by salivating. The theory accordingly has it that the constituents of language mean by virtue of the response which people are conditioned to make to them.

This is the simplest version of the theory; as an account of meaning it is woefully inadequate. Suppose I am with two people, one of them an arachnophobe, and the other an arachnophile. Suppose I say, 'there's a spider on the wall'. The responses of the two will be widely different. How can the meaning of what I say consist in the widely divergent effects caused by my utterance? How indeed could my two hearers respond in the way they do unless they first understood the sentence?

Further, suppose my nervous friend dislikes mice as well as spiders. Because his response – anxiety and 'avoiding-action' – will be the same whether I say 'there's a mouse' or 'there's a spider', his response cannot be constitutive of the meanings of these sentences, for his response is the same to both sentences and yet they manifestly differ in meaning. In fact, if the response to an utterance determines its meaning, then any number of such statements, as, for example, 'grass is green', 'yellow is a colour', 'people eat food', 'most dogs have four legs', and so forth – all of which are dull things to assert and would bore one's audience – would have the same 'meaning' – *viz.*, that constituted by the audience's reaction of boredom.

It is more natural and plausible – although perhaps no more clear – to say that part at least of the determinant of an utterance's meaning is indeed an utterance's intended effect on the hearer, but that the effect consists in an evoking of certain concepts in the hearer, the association of which for him will determine his response. But this, in harking back to the ideational theory, reintroduces mentalistic notions; and that is anathema to the behaviourist. But in so far as the behaviourist is right about communication having effects on its audience, some such account – involving appeal to the intentional concepts as it does – seems, even if only prima facie, to do more justice to meaning than the behaviourist theory, in its simple form at least.[37]

A slight sophistication of the behaviourist theory adds, to the audience's response, the context of utterance as a factor in meaning. But this is no great advance. The infinite variety of situations in which a particular term or sentence can be uttered while meaning the same, contains nothing that we could possibly identify as that common contextual element which, together with hearers' responses in all those situations, constitutes the expression's meaning.

There are, however, versions of the behavioural theory a good deal more sophisticated than either of the preceding versions; and these trade on the notions of 'implicit responses' (especially to cover cases where, upon hearing something, an audience does nothing at all but, for example, continues to sit impassively) or, more subtly still, 'dispositions'.

The way these more elaborate construals of the theory work is as follows.[38]

On the 'implicit responses' view, an utterance will evoke in a person certain 'fractional' responses – thus, the word 'telephone' might cause certain of the hearer's muscles to twitch, glands to secrete, and an ear-lobe to engorge minutely with blood; but these responses will constitute only a 'fraction' of the gross overt behavioural responses which would accompany a real telephone call by the hearer. Hence the response is 'implicit'. On the 'dispositions' view, an utterance will not go so far as to issue in these subcutaneous twitchings and secretions, but will dis-pose the hearer's organism in such a way that if certain other conditions were fulfilled, or inhibitions withdrawn, these physiological responses would occur, and, in full and in sum, would cause an actual telephone call.

In all these variants of the behavioural theory, from the crude to the subtle, a basic premiss is that language functions as a system of signs, different only in degree of complexity (to match the far greater neural complexity of humans) from the twittering of birds and foot-thumping of rabbits. Bird-song has, in part, territorial significance; rabbits thump their feet as a danger signal, and self-respecting rabbits disappear down their holes when they hear the signal, as a matter of self-preservatory neural reflex. The question to be asked of more sophisticated versions of the behavioural theory is whether human language is just a more intricate system of signals than the rabbits' danger-signal or the birds' dawn chorus. (It offends human feelings of superiority to think this might be so, but that is no argument against the view. Recall that behavioural techniques in clinical psychology are highly effective; which counts in favour of a behavioural construal of humanity.)

The first element in favour of a negative answer is the fact that the behavioural theory construes language as a system of signs. This is a major difficulty. Only a relatively small proportion of a language's constituent items could, with any plausibility, be construed as such; and for these, something analogous to the problems that beset the denotative theory arise. Secondly, neither the notion of 'implicit responses' nor that of 'dispositions' is helpful. How could one begin to unpack the meaning of 'house', say, in terms of some common set of minute physiological reflexes which all speakers of English over the age of approximately two years display – *per impossibile*, to some super neurosurgeon – upon hearing that word? To put the cavil another way: the entities, *viz.*, the secretions and twitches, which are jointly the meaning of 'house', are incredibly difficult to identify; they do not at all 'distribute' properly to serve as the word's meaning.

If appeal is made instead to 'dispositions' the problem is similar; to specify the meaning of a word in dispositional terms involves us in the infinite task of specifying all the possible modifying conditions which prevent the disposition from realization if it remains unrealized, or all the conditions which are uniquely satisfied for a given hearer in a given context if the disposition successfully wells up through implicit to explicit response.

Quine, Behaviour and Language

There is however a behavioural theory of language-acquisition, advanced by Quine, that merits consideration. Quine is not interested in questions of meaning as such, for the by now familiar reason that he thinks such extensional concepts as reference are more tractable, and hence more fruitful to investigation, than meaning. He early divided semantic notions into two groups, the first consisting in theories of reference (extensional theories turning on such notions as 'designates' and 'satisfies'), and the second consisting in theories of meaning (intensional theories turning on such notions as synonymy). Theories of reference in his view are more philosophically promising, and in 'better shape', than theories of meaning, which are badly infected by obscurities.[39] Nevertheless, an assumption of his views is that making philosophical sense of language is to be achieved by investigating the sources of language-mastery.

Quine shuns mentalism, particularly of the kind given currency by classical empiricism, which turns – as shown earlier – on appeal to 'ideas'. In Quine's view the bankruptcy of the 'way of ideas' is evidenced by the fact that it issued variously in Humean scepticism, Berkeleyan idealism, and a laborious Lockean realism, or cognates of these, none of them tenable.[40] Accordingly standard epistemology is to be rejected and a fresh approach taken. This involves accepting the deliverances of modern science. Taking science for granted, the question to be addressed is, how did we achieve scientific knowledge? Because language is fundamental to the acquisition of such knowledge, and because reference is fundamental to language, the task finally reduces to an enquiry into 'the roots of reference'.[41]

In Quine's view, 'naturalism' (the view that we should accept the deliverances of science and proceed from there in our philosophizing) involves seeing knowledge in terms of the behavioural output which is the response to environmental impingements on human exteriors. There is to be no speculation about inner goings-on in minds; the only evidence is to be utterances of words 'out where we can see and hear them' and thus 'accessible to human science'.[42] Summarily put, language is learned by conditioning; the teacher conditions the child to respond thus-and-so in the appropriate observable situations. Language-learning 'falls within the standard range of animal training', consisting as it does in the bringing about of internal modifications which result in further selective responses to stimuli.

A crucial step in the psychogenetic development from learning simple terms to learning science is the attainment of objective reference, which Quine regards as occurring when the learner has mastered predication by way of quantification. The referential apparatus of natural language is less tidy than that of logic, where it is effected by the quantifiers $(\exists x)$ and (x) and the variables they bind; nevertheless, once the learner has learned predication, he has advanced far enough beyond the primitive level of 'occasion sentences' and 'observation terms' to be properly on the road to science.[43]

The route to predication and reference passes through several stages of prepredicative language use. Observation terms fall into three classes, examples of which are

(1) red, sugar, snow, water, white;
(2) Fido, mama;
(3) dog, buckle, apple, woman.

To begin with, all three classes are alike to the learner, in that it is the recurrence of some recognizable circumstance which prompts utterance of the terms as one-word occasion sentences. But the three classes are significantly different. Items of class 1 can occur in simultaneous scattered chunks, whereas with items of class 2 shape is important; mama is not scattered, she is a body. Nevertheless 1 and 2 terms have a certain semantic simplicity in comparison to 3, for class 3 terms have individuation built into them, which is to say that principles of individuation have to be grasped by the learner in order for him to master terms of that class. Noting this fact constitutes a piece of sophisticated retrospection; so far the learner himself does not distinguish between the classes in this way, for he has not attained to the quantification level. Accordingly these terms are protogeneral and protosingular terms merely, not yet general and singular terms proper.

Class 3 terms come close to being referential because individuation attaches to them; but for the reason that the learner at this stage uses the terms as one-word occasion-sentences, they still involve no predication. This remains so even when the learner develops the ability to formulate 'observation compounds' out of them, as when, from one-word sentences like 'yellow' and 'paper', the learner forms 'yellow paper'. This does not involve predication because assent to 'yellow paper' at this stage still requires the presence of the relevant stimuli, and so is occasion-dependent.

The next step – the transition to predication and reference proper – involves crossing a gulf, Quine says, a gulf bridged by a different mechanism of learning.[44] Whereas observation-sentences are occasion-dependent, 'standing sentences' (Quine sometimes calls them 'eternal sentences') are not so dependent. The step across the gulf to predicative use of language is in Quine's view somewhat mysterious, but he suggests that it involves the following essential feature: there is a 'transfer' from observational stimuli to verbal stimuli, such that, for example, the presence of the word 'snow' will be sufficient to induce assent to the word 'white' irrespective of the presence or absence of snow. The transfer is a transfer of conditioning, a transfer of response from thing to word. Thus the learner learns to respond to eternal sentences like 'snow is white', 'Fido is a dog'.

The picture Quine draws is one in which predication and objective reference belong to eternal sentences, with a gulf lying between these and occasion-sentences. An initial plausibility attaches to this picture; it particularly recommends itself by being dressed in the colours of science. Nevertheless there are good reasons for questioning it.

For one thing, as Quine's account develops from early learning to the more sophisticated conceptual levels where the acquisition of scientific knowledge becomes possible, appeal to physiological mechanisms recedes into the background. Quine simply says: perhaps one day that part of the story will be filled in. But this optimism rests on the expectation that intentional concepts can be analysed in terms of physical concepts, allowing psychology to be reduced to physiology.[45] This thesis is a strong one, arguing more than that the truth-values of statements about mental events are dependent on the truth-values in a reductive class of physical statements; for this latter could be the case without its being true that mental statements can be translated into physical statements without remainder. A strong reductive thesis consists in the claim that just such a translation is possible. If one holds that it is possible that a physiological account can, and one day will, explain language acquisition, one is thereby committing oneself to a strong version of this thesis.

Such theses can be questioned on various grounds suggesting that the required reduction is *in principle*, not merely *empirically*, impossible, for the reason that mental and physical descriptions are incommensurable, which is in part to say that predicates in the two discourses radically fail to match in extension. An example will illustrate this: suppose a physicist and a sociologist are watching a certain event. The physicist describes it in terms of bodies of a certain mass and velocity emitting radiation at certain frequencies. The sociologist describes it as a football match, and explains it in terms of two teams with aims, strategies, and hopes, governed by certain rules. The two descriptions are of the same historical event, but cannot be reduced to one another because there is nothing in the language of physics to take translations of 'team', 'aim', 'strategy', 'penalty', and the like, and nothing in the language of sociology to translate 'mass' and 'velocity'. Accordingly these are irreducibly distinct descriptions of (in some sense) the same events, each being consistent and complete relative to their given theoretical purposes.

The suggestion then is that the language of brain physiology and psychological discourse are mutually irreducible in the same way. Nevertheless, the physicist and sociologist have the means to 'locate' the set of events they are each describing as one and the same set of events; in just the same way, the physiologist and psychologist can agree on certain correlations which establish that at least for some of the time they are both attending to the same phenomena.

One of the first steps in Quine's argument is to make use of the apparently innocuous picture of language being learned in a publicly observable situation. But how does the theorist know what kind of situation counts as a language-learning situation? It makes sense to characterize a situation in this way only if the learner can be credited with a considerable conceptual load. Suppose the learner is in process of mastering the term 'red'. Then he must recognize what is pointed out to him as the feature of the environment which is the correct stimulus for 'red'; and he must also grasp, or antecedently have a grasp of the fact, that what he sees he is seeing as red – and so on. Wittgenstein's comments about the poverty of ostension apply here in full. Similarly, the teacher also has to be credited with a conceptual load – indeed, a greater one; for he is consciously selecting simple sensible qualities instead of, say, function, or origin, or artistic category, as the feature he wishes to name. But then how is one to provide a characterization of learning situations without appeal to intentional concepts in the way just done? Evidently the theorist cannot get going at all without appeal to some sort of mentalistic apparatus.

Strawson challenges Quine on the ordering of primitiveness between the classes of terms 2 and 3, that is, singular and general terms respectively.[46] In Quine's view such singular terms as 'Fido' and 'mama' are more primitive than class 3 terms because the latter require a grasp of principles of individuation for their mastery, and such a grasp consists in being able to make similarity comparisons and the relevant semantic generalizations from them. However, Quine acknowledges that in coming to master 'Fido' as a protosingular term, the learner must rule out a plurality of Fidos, for otherwise 'Fido' would be semantically indistinguishable from 'dog'. Strawson fastens onto this admission, and points out that if Fido is the one-and-only Fido, 'Fido' is more complex than 'dog', because it involves both individuation and uniqueness. Accordingly the ordering of primitiveness between 2 and 3, if it is to be insisted that there is one, has to be reversed.

Strawson then remarks that even if Quine is right in holding that the learner has not acquired the whole quantification apparatus by the time he has mastered terms of classes 1–3 and can use them as occasion-sentences, it does not follow that he has failed to master some of it. For in Strawson's view, even a one-word occasion-sentence has a certain duality which strongly prefigures predication; for such sentences would not be capable of truth-value unless, in addition to the uttered one-word sentence itself, there was an implicit 'here–now' component. Thus when the learner says 'dog' he is in effect saying 'dog here now' – that is, he is effectively expressing an observational judgement about a salience in his perceptual environment, a judgement capable of being assented to or denied by his interlocutors. In this way occasion-sentences have at least a proto-predicative quality, which closes, or goes a long way to closing, the mysterious gulf between Quine's prepredicative and predicative levels of language mastery.

The Verification Theory of Meaning

Views about meaning which involve the notion of 'verification' fall into two categories, one of which merits the label 'the verification theory of meaning' because it purports to specify the nature of meaning, while the other, which sets out to furnish a criterion of meaningfulness for sentences, is better described by the more familiar label, 'the verification principle'. The former view is summed up in Schlick's slogan 'the meaning of a proposition is its method of verification',[47] the latter is summed up in Ayer's dictum, 'a sentence is factually significant to a given person if, and only if, he knows how to verify the proposition which it purports to express'.[48] In both cases 'verification' means checking by observation; which is to say, a proposition is verifiable if and only if there are empirical means by which its truth-value can be determined. It is important to note that if the verification theory of meaning is correct, the verification principle is true; but not vice versa, for even if it is true that a proposition acquires factual significance for me only if I can verify it, it does not follow from this alone that the method of verifying the proposition constitutes its meaning.

The Logical Positivists selected verification as the key concept for a theory of meaning because they wished to have a means of distinguishing genuinely significant propositions from those that are not genuinely significant.[49] Ayer quotes Hume as giving 'an excellent statement of the positivists' position',[50] thus: 'When we run over libraries, persuaded of these principles, what havoc must we make? If we take in our hand any volume; of divinity or school metaphysics, for instance; let us ask, Does it contain an abstract reasoning concerning quantity or number? No. Does it contain any experimental reasoning concerning matter of fact and existence? No. Commit it then to the flames, for it can contain nothing but sophistry and illusion'.[51] On the same grounds the positivists regarded significant propositions as falling into two classes: formal propositions, such as those of logic and pure mathematics, which they regarded as tautological;[52] and factual propositions, which they required to be empirically verifiable.

The verification principle involves a distinction between sentences and propositions, drawn for the reasons discussed in chapter 2. A sentence is said to be 'factually significant' only if the proposition it purports to express is verifiable. A sentence which does not express a verifiable proposition expresses no proposition at all; it is nonsensical in the literal acceptation of this term. Thus the meaning of a sentence, on this view, is the proposition it expresses. Consider the two sentences

(1) God is in his heaven.

and

(2) The dove is in his cote.

Since there are means of verifying whether the dove is in the cote (one can go and look), 2 expresses a proposition, and is therefore meaningful; but there is no way of verifying whether what 1 says is either true or false, so it expresses no proposition, and is therefore meaningless – or, more correctly 'factually insignificant', for the verificationists allowed that 1 might have emotive meaning as expressing a particular non-cognitive attitude to the world. (This applies to all moral, aesthetic, and religious utterances: they are 'factually insignificant' because nothing counts as a method of verification for determining their truth-value; but they have emotive meaning for their utterers.)

So far the verification principle has been given in a restricted form, as stating that a sentence is factually insignificant if for a given person there is no means of verifying what the sentence states. But the principle can be generalized: if what a sentence says cannot be verified by anyone then the sentence is without qualification factually insignificant. In this form the principle itself requires qualification: sentences which are factually insignificant are those for which there is no means of verification *in principle*. If one did not thus qualify the view, a particular sentence might count as meaningless in virtue of the merely contingent fact that no one had so far verified it, but would become meaningful once someone did so. The qualification avoids the difficulty that the pragmatic theory of truth (chapter 5) runs into in one of its variants.

The view is, then, that a sentence is meaningful if and only if what it says is verifiable in principle. There are problems with this view, which proponents of the theory themselves recognized.[53] For one thing, the general laws of science turn out not to be, even in principle, verifiable, if 'verifying' means furnishing proof of their truth. Another victim is history: in what way can the truth of assertions about the past be verified by present or future observations? Yet both science and history are bodies of factually significant sentences. Worse still is the consideration that not even an assertion about some currently observed physical object can be conclusively verified, because the number of observations relevant to its verification might be infinite; and while there remains the possibility of a single future observation refuting what one says about the object, that statement is not and cannot be counted as verified.

The verificationists' response is to suggest a liberalization of the principle, so that it admits of cases where all that is possible is evidence relevant to the truth of a statement. A sentence is on this view factually significant if empirical procedures are relevant to determining its truth-value.[54] This preserves the distinction between 1 and 2 while overcoming the difficulties just sketched. But this merely causes the problem to reappear in another quarter – specifically, to do with the nature of 'relevance'.

One way of illustrating this difficulty is as follows. What is 'relevant' evidence for or against an assertion about empirical matters of fact is, in the sense discussed in connection with Neurath's views in chapter 5 above, to a large extent a matter of policy. What counts as relevant evidence might vary widely according to the conceptual strategy of observers, but only on a relativist view (such as Feyerabend's[55]) would the meaning of terms vary with the relevant verifying context. For example, suppose that in some remote country during a drought it is made to rain. According to the scientists involved, the immediate cause of rain was chemical seeding of clouds from an aeroplane. According to the local community, it was the witch-doctor who prompted the rain by a rain-dance. Each school of thought has different views as to what counts as relevant evidence in verifying what is said by the sentences 'chemical seeding caused the rainfall' and 'the rain-dance caused the rainfall'.

This is an extreme example; but just this sort of dispute over relevance can and does arise within a particular framework. Consider the astrophysical dispute over the question whether quasars are at cosmological distances, or are intergalactic phenomena. If the first, then the redshift they display is Newtonian and is evidence of great speeds and distances; but the energy they discharge is so great that revisions in our present understanding of physics are required to explain it. If the latter, then some account of non-Newtonian redshift is needed, also not available in current theory. The evidence is, to some extent, relevant to both hypotheses, but is not sufficiently strong to license a choice. Both hypotheses are nonetheless factually significant.

More sophisticated attempts to substantiate the verification principle as a criterion of meaningfulness have turned on the idea that a sentence is verifiable if it entails observation statements in certain specified ways. But an objection to such attempts is to claim that the truth of a sentence about some physical state of affairs is consistent with the falsity of any observational report associated with it. Waismann gives this example:[56] suppose someone says 'Jones is on the other side of the street', and I look across the street but fail to see Jones – perhaps because he has just gone into a shop or has been obscured by a passing lorry. My failing to see Jones – that is, the truth of the statement 'I do not see Jones on the other side of the street' – is consistent with the truth of 'Jones is on the other side of the street'. It would be absurd to take it that the failure of the observation cancels the latter statement's truth. If what a sentence says is true and the observation statement it is supposed to entail false, we would have a contradiction on our hands; but there is nothing contradictory implicit in the example.

An objection that opponents of verificationism were quick to make is that the principle itself falls into neither of the categories of significant propositions which it is used to demarcate. It is not a tautology, nor is it empirically verifiable. What status, its critics asked, is it supposed to have? Ayer suggests that the positivists adopted the principle as a convention, in the sense that they were propounding a definition of meaning which accords with the conditions that are in fact satisfied by empirically informative propositions.[57] This, together with their account of the a priori propositions of logic and mathematics, amounted to a description of the classes of significant propositions. They then added a prescriptive element by saying that only statements of these classes should be regarded as having truth-value, and only statements having truth-value should be regarded as literally meaningful.[58]

The difficulty with this is twofold. The prescriptive element can be challenged as merely arbitrary legislation, and the descriptive element as at most showing that the statements of metaphysics, ethics, aesthetics and theology do not fall into the classes of statements preferred by the positivists, from which it does not follow that they lack truth-value or fail to be meaningful. At most, the descriptive element affirms what is already recognized, that an account of the meaning and – if the notion is separately applicable – truth-value of statements, or extremely general statements about the nature of the world or human experience, requires a treatment different both from that which accounts for assertions about observable phenomena, and that which characterizes formal languages. This of itself gives no grounds for excluding metaphysics, or any of the other enquiries, in sole favour of what can be of use to natural science.

If the verification principle as a criterion of meaningfulness encounters difficulties, perhaps the verification theory of meaning constitutes a more promising alternative. The theory – 'the meaning of a proposition is the method of its verification' – has as a virtue the fact that it does not presuppose a view of 'meaning' as some sort of entity. Instead it construes meaning as a method. 'Stating the meaning of a sentence,' Schlick wrote, 'amounts to stating the rules according to which the sentence is to be used, and this is the same as stating the way in which it can be verified (or falsified)'.[59]

This requires explanation, best furnished by considering a rather analogous view, 'operationalism', in the philosophy of science. Consider Bridgman's example of the word 'length'.[60] If we can determine the length of an object, then we know what 'length' means. Determining the length of an object involves the performance of certain physical operations, and it is the set of these operations that can be viewed as constituting the meaning of 'length'. In verificationist terms, this is put by saying that the meaning of 'length' is the method of verifying sentences asserting that 'the length of such-and-such is x units'.

The plausibility of this account does not however extend to other cases. A sentence such as 'the space-shuttle landed in California' does not mean the way we go about checking whether this is true; it means that a space-shuttle landed at an air-base in California. One is tempted to say, surely the business of setting out to verify the statement (that is, determine whether the statement is true or not) would be impossible unless we already knew its meaning.

Schlick believed, against Neurath, that there are protocol sentences which, as observational reports, are directly verified in experience; and that the observational terms occurring in protocol sentences are ostensively defined (see chapter 5 above). He wrote, 'there is no way of understanding any meaning without ultimate reference to ostensive definition, and this means, in an obvious sense, reference to "experience" or possibility of "verification"'.[61] The equation of 'experience' with 'possibility of verification' is interesting; having the experience which protocol sentences report is just to realize the possibility of verification – that is, to make verification actual. It is in this sense that the procedure of looking or testing constitutes the meaning of empirical statements, for the possibility of there being a procedure for ostensively linking terms of protocol sentences to what is observed, is precisely what on this view constitutes the sense of those terms.

Two problems in Schlick's account arise from its dependence on the theory of protocol sentences, attacked by Neurath, and ostension, attacked by Wittgenstein. Reasons were given earlier for thinking that both attacks are successful. Dispensing with the notions of protocol sentences and ostension makes room for a theory of Quine's sort to the effect that observation is theory-laden; the idea here is that our observations are conducted in terms of our antecedent theories, which therefore determine what we observe.[62] Thus recalcitrant observations are as likely to be ignored, or dismissed as aberrant, or put down to observational error, as they are to oblige us to make changes in our web of theory to accommodate them. But if theory is carried to observation, then the 'meaning' of observation terms, and the notion of observational confirmation of theory itself, is established in advance – logically speaking – of observation.

Nevertheless, an important idea is hinted at in Schlick's instrumentalist conception, an idea standardly associated with the later work of Wittgenstein. To say that a word 'means' the method of its verification, where this is construed on operationalist lines, is to say that its meaning is a function of its use; which thought leads one to consider theories based on this insight.

The Use Theory of Meaning: the Later Wittgenstein and Method

The slogan of the use theory is 'don't look for the meaning, look for the use', and Wittgenstein's dictum is 'look at the sentence as an instrument, and at is sense as its employment'.[63] An immediately apparent strength of such a view is that it opposes the thought that meaning is explained by a single feature of language – a view to which Wittgenstein himself fell prey in the *Tractatus* – and focuses instead on the fact that language has a variety of uses, so that meaning is to be understood in the context of the various 'language games', as Wittgenstein called them, of which natural language is constituted.

Some of the theories of meaning considered earlier turn on the thought that meaning consists in what expressions stand for, represent, or evoke. One consequence of such views, if right, would be that 'giving the meaning' of an expression can be done by matching it with some extralinguistic item or event. The use theory denies that expressions have meaning in isolation in this way, by arguing that it is an expression's role in the language that determines its sense; so to 'give the meaning' of an expression is to show how it enters into the language games in which it plays a role.[64] There is therefore no 'giving the meaning' without essential reference to the varied uses to which expressions can be put.

In the opening sections of the *Philosophical Investigations* Wittgenstein attacked the general principle of a denotative model for meaning, and urged instead that we recognize that there is a 'multiplicity of kinds of words and sentences'.[65] Failure to grasp this variety results in our assimilating different kinds of expressions to the denotative model alone, which we are too apt to regard as basic because we think of someone's 'learning the meaning of a word' in situations like this: the learner, already possessed of a large measure of language-mastery, has a word explained to him by means of definition or ostension – the teacher says ——— means . . .' where the second blank is filled by a synonyom or translation of what fills the first blank, or by 'this' together with ostension of an object.[66] But this method of learning depends, in Wittgenstein's view, on the learner's already having a command of stretches of the language, for it constitutes an already developed language game.

The key notions are 'use' and 'language game'. There is nothing sacrosanct about 'use'; Wittgenstein talks variously of the *functions* of words and sentences,[67] of their *aims* and *purposes*[68] and even their *offices*,[69] and of their *roles* and *employments*.[70] Language-mastery consists in being able to employ expressions in different contexts – in stating, describing, asking, commanding, promising, evaluating, denying and so on. Each of these activities constitutes a language game:

> Consider . . . the proceedings which we call 'games'. I mean board-games, cardgames, ball games, Olympic games and so on. What is common to them all? – Don't say: 'there must be something common or they would not be called games', but look and see whether there is anything common to all, – for if you look at them you will not see something that is in common to all, but similarities, relationships, and a whole series of them at that . . . And the result of this examination is: we see a complicated network of similarities overlapping and criss-crossing . . . I can think of no better expression to characterise these similarities than 'family resemblances'; for the various resemblances between members of a family: build,

features, colour of eyes, gait, temperament, etc. etc., overlap and criss-cross in the same way. – And I shall say: 'games' form a family.[71]

To 'give the meaning' of an expression is accordingly to show how it is used in the different but related games of stating, commanding, and so on.

There is something suggestive in the idea that meaning is closely related to use.[72] The notion of use is not entirely clear, but this has not troubled everyone; Quinton wrote, 'the identification of meaning with the way a word is used is vague, but this is inevitable, for words are used in many different ways and have many different sorts of meaning',[73] and in Strawson's view, 'It is not a complaint to say that this central notion is not immediately and wholly clear', for 'the general aim is clear enough: to get us away from our fascination with the dubious relation of naming . . . and to make us look at . . . language as one human activity among others, interacting with others'.[74] Nevertheless it is worth trying to see what is at issue here.[75]

Talk of use is itself various, and not all talk of use will be the required sort for explaining meaning. Consider how one might talk of the uses of objects or stuffs, like hammers or olive oil. One can talk about how the hammer is used ('grasp the handle . . .'), and with what purpose (to drive nails as a paperweight . . . to call meetings to order); one can talk about what olive oil is used *in* (salads, dressings), and *for* (frying).[76] Explanation of the uses of such items – the how, the what in, the what for – explains, or goes a long way to explaining, the nature of the item in question. One can talk of the uses of words in an analogous way; one can explain how a word is used, when its use is appropriate, and what kind of work it can do. But not all explanations of how, when, and what for will be explanations of meaning. For example, 'he used the term frequently/ effectively/insolently' tells one how the speaker used the term, but without any relevance to its meaning.[77] Similarly, saying that it is sometimes appropriate to use 'Help!', 'Let's run!', 'Look!', 'Shoot!', and so on, in the presence of tigers, does not by itself explain what these expressions mean; although, given a longer story, they can exemplify uses of those terms in a way that contributes towards an explanation of their place in the relevant language games. Again, to point out that a word – a swear-word, say – can be used to insult or irritate another, or to relieve one's feelings, does not give the meaning of that word, despite telling us what it can be used to do.

These remarks do not however obscure the point intended by use theorists. When language is taught, what is taught is the relevance and effects of the employment of expressions in given contexts, which is in large part what 'explaining the meaning' comes down to on this view. The thought is that one does not show when, how, and with what purpose an expression is to be used, and then go on to explain the meaning as though it were something *additional*.

For Wittgenstein, in particular, the notion of use as thus construed is essentially linked to behaviour. Language games in his view help constitute a 'form of life'.[78] The uses of expressions are linked to what people do, and accordingly to master a language is to master a scheme of intentions and beliefs and to share a world-view. This explains Wittgenstein's remark that 'If a lion could talk, we could not understand him';[79] the idea is that the lion's world-view is so different from our own that we simply could not comprehend what he meant even if he produced a grammatically well-formed English sentence.[80] Not everyone will agree with the relativism this view entails, but its point is clear: an expression has meaning only as an element of 'language and the actions into which it is woven',[81] 'an expression has meaning only in the stream of life'.[82]

It is helpful to remember, in assessing this theory, that Wittgenstein had a particular view of philosophical method – perhaps it is more accurate to say, a view about the aims of philosophy – which is closely allied to the notion of use. This is that philosophical puzzles arise from *misuse* of language, or from misunderstandings about its nature. If we have an incorrect model of language-functioning we shall be prone to confusions; for example, we shall assimilate the use of one kind of expression to that of a quite different kind, or we shall try to understand an expression in isolation from its normal context, and so fall into error. 'The confusions which occupy us', Wittgenstein wrote, 'arise when language is like an engine idling, not when it is doing work.'[83] 'Philosophical problems arise when language goes on holiday'.[84] To remedy this situation one must look at how language actually works; as Wittgenstein put it, '[Philosophical problems] are, of course, not empirical problems; they are solved, rather, by looking into the working of our language, and that in such a way as to make us recognise those workings: *in despite of* an urge to misunderstand them'.[85]

Philosophical problems will vanish, on this view, when we see that they arise only because we misunderstand the workings of language. Until such a remedy is applied, philosophers are like flies trapped in a bottle;

Wittgenstein remarks. 'What is your aim in philosophy? – To shew the fly the way out of the fly-bottle'.[86] In his view we must therefore grasp the difference between what he called 'surface grammar' and 'depth grammar', for it is concentration solely upon the former which misleads philosophers: 'In the use of words one might distinguish "surface grammar" from "depth grammar" . . . compare the depth grammar, say, of the word "to mean", with what its surface grammar would lead us to suspect. No wonder we find it difficult to know our way about'.[87] Wittgenstein accordingly called his enquiry into the proper workings of language a 'grammatical' enquiry: 'Our investigation is therefore a grammatical one. Such an investigation sheds light on our problem by clearing misunderstandings away'.[88]

Wittgenstein applied his method in the *Philosophical Investigations* to 'dissolving' difficulties not only about meaning but also, for example, the problem about the existence of other minds.[89] Examples of an appeal to use in other philosophers are afforded by, among others, Strawson in his discussion of Russell,[90] and Austin in his discussion of Ayer's phenomenalism.[91] In the latter case – in many respects paradigmatic of the theory in action – Austin sought to show that the problems addressed by Ayer result from misperceptions about language, so that there is no need to discuss the solutions phenomenalists proposed, for they are accordingly otiose. The problems in question arise from misunderstanding the proper workings of such terms as 'illusion', 'seeing', and the like.

A difficulty affecting evaluation of use theories arises from the vagueness of the notion, already remarked. The appeal to use is highly programmatic. Because there are multiplicities of uses to which expressions can be put, no univocal account of meaning is to be expected. Can therefore anything useful be said?

Well, for one thing, it can be argued that it is a mistake to *identify* meaning and use. One can know the meaning of a word without knowing its use, and one can know the use of a word without knowing its meaning. For example, someone may know, because he has been reliably informed, that the meaning of the Latin word *jejunus* is 'hungry', without knowing how to use it in a Latin sentence. Conversely, many people know how to use the expressions 'amen' and 'QED' without knowing what they mean.[92] On certain theories of reference, names have uses without having meanings, and so do prepositions, conjunctions, and the like. Clearly therefore it is wrong to claim generally that meaning *is* use. This is not to deny that in at least many cases there is an important connection between meaning and use, for anyone who knows the meaning of a term will in general and therefore know its use, and vice versa. Rather it is to point out that an appeal to use does not, by itself, explain all there is to meaning.

Use theorists have two possible replies. One is to say that explaining the use of an expression goes far enough towards giving its meaning to count effectively as having done so; the other is to say: one can let questions of meaning fall where they will, what is important is how expressions are used (and misused), and that is what the use theory focuses on.

Considered as a resource for dispelling philosophical problems, attention to use, even so understood, does not appear satisfactory, for it is clear that one can investigate the uses to which certain kinds of philosophically significant expressions are put – consider 'good' and 'mind' – and still find one has philosophical difficulties to resolve. The point can be spelled out by concentrating attention on the idea, integral to the use theory, that a chief factor in giving an account of the use (and hence the meaning) of an expression is to look at what it is used to do. This draws attention to the notion of 'speech-acts'.

Speech-acts

'Stop that!' is standardly used to give an order, 'Where is it?' to ask a question, 'It's on the table' to make a statement, and so on. Ordering, questioning, and stating are speech-acts, and so are promising, appraising, agreeing, denying, criticizing, commending, and the like. Austin drew a distinction in this regard between 'illocutionary' and 'perlocutionary' acts:[93] the former are those in which a speech-act is performed in virtue of the use of an expression – 'I promise' constitutes the act of promising, for example, and 'I do thee wed' constitutes the act of wedding oneself to whomever 'thee' picks out – and the latter are those acts performed by means of, or through, the use of an expression: a command is issued by use of 'Get out', and an appraisal or commendation can be made by use of 'I like it' or 'It's good'. Better examples still are 'He protested against her actions' and 'By protesting against her actions he stopped her'; the former is the illocutionary, the latter the perlocutionary, case.[94]

The idea is that to show how an expression is used to perform certain speech-acts is to state something about the meaning of that expression. Hare, for example, associated the function of the word 'good' with the speech-acts of commending and evaluating; 'the primary function of the word "good" is to commend'.[95] Strawson likewise, in his criticism of Austin on truth, held that the word 'true' has its uses in 'confirming, underwriting, admitting, agreeing with, what somebody has said', and that the problem of truth is the problem of how the word 'true' is used.[96]

This general pattern of analysis has been criticized by Searle among others.[97] The pattern in question has this form: with regard to some word W, it is held that

(1) W is used to perform speech-act A

and

(2) the meaning of W is given or explained by (1).

This seems to suggest that at least part of the meaning of W depends upon the fact that its literal occurrence in the sentence containing it characteristically gives rise to the speaker performing speech-act A by its use. As it stands, this view is easily shown to be false, for one can find readily counter-instances.[98] Suppose W is 'good' and the sentence in which it occurs is 'This is a good car'. Then the speech-act in question will be the act of commending or approving the car. However, one is obviously not commending anything when 'good' occurs in the sentence 'Is this a good car?', despite is occurrence being literal. Here (1) does not hold water, and neither therefore does (2).

Perhaps, however, this is a little quick, for a defender of the analysis will say that something more general is intended; the point is not that 'good' is used in every case to commend, but that its presence in sentences characteristically shows that the relevant speech-act, *viz.*, commendation, is 'in the offing'. For example. 'Is this a good car?' can be viewed as having the force of 'Do you commend this car?', which explains what 'good' is doing (what it means) in 'Is this a good car?'[99]

But this will not do either. Searle offers the following sentences containing literal occurrences of 'good' in which the speech-act of commending is neither performed nor in the offing:

(3) If this is a good electric blanket, then perhaps we ought to buy it.

(4) I wonder if this is a good electric blanket.
(5) I don't know whether it's a good electric blanket.
(6) Let's hope that it's a good electric blanket.

That none of (3)–(6) constitutes commendatory speech-acts, or has them in the offing, can be seen by comparing them with

(3a) If I commend this electric blanket, then perhaps we ought to buy it.
(4a) I wonder if I commend this electric blanket.
(5a) I don't know whether I commend this electric blanket.
(6a) Let's hope I commend this electric blanket.[100]

What the comparison shows is that the speech-act analysis of meaning, in relying upon a similarity of function between 'This is a good electric blanket' and 'I commend this electric blanket', is mistaken because the similarity of function 'is not preserved through the permutations of linguistic context in which each of these expressions can be placed without alteration of the literal meanings of the component words'.[101] Whatever way, therefore, one tries to construe the speech-act analysis of given words, it simply fails to yield an account of their meaning.

The argument here is quite general: no identification of the meaning of a word with a speech-act (other than words which are expressly speech-act words themselves, like 'commend') will do. Consider another example; on Strawson's view, 'p is true' roughly means 'I confirm that p'; but 'if p is true then q is true' does not even roughly mean 'If I confirm that p then I confirm that q'. The pattern of analysis which this exemplifies is accordingly impugned in general. It shows that such philosophically problematic words as 'good' and 'true' cannot be explained by focusing on their connections with such performative verbs as 'commend' and 'confirm', because the sense in which 'good' is used to commend and 'true' is used to confirm differs markedly from the sense in which 'commend' is used to commend and 'confirm' is used to confirm.[102]

It is important to be clear about what work these criticisms do and do not do. One thing that is not being denied is that words are sometimes used to perform speech-acts, or that there are specifiable cases in which explaining the use of a word is to be done by showing what speech-act it can be used to perform. What is being denied is that one gives the meaning of a word W by showing what speech-acts a speaker performs by using W. Schematically, the criticism is this: in terms of the use theory, the meaning of a word is taken to be (or in large part, at least, to be) its use. Accordingly it is thought that questions of the form 'What does W mean?' should be rephrased as 'How is W used?' (This is clear in Strawson's criticism of Austin on truth.) The next step is to ask what acts are performed by the use of W. But the foregoing discussion shows that answers, even correct ones, to questions about what speech-acts are performed by uses of W, are not answers to questions about the meaning of W.[103] A word such as 'good', in other words, makes different contributions in different sentences uttered on different occasions, on some of which the sentences might be used to perform different speech-acts; to select one of these as somehow specifying the meaning of 'good' is a mistake.

Defenders of a use theory might accept this criticism and choose to settle for the view that speech-act analysis does not tell the whole story about use and hence meaning; but they might then go on to say that such analysis plays a part in giving an account of use – and hence meaning. But this simply returns the discussion to its starting-point, where the complaint was that appeal to use is too general; that, in other words, the use theory is so programmatic that it is not even clear how to begin filling in details.

Quinton's and Strawson's defences of the theory's vagueness supports Wittgenstein's own view that it is not possible to construct a systematic theory of meaning. His view, however, is belied by the facts. Anyone able to use a language is *ipso facto* able to understand a potential infinity of sentences; and most of those he hears he has never heard before, and yet understands them. This point is emphasized not only by theoretical linguists but by Wittgenstein himself. But this fact can only be explained by the hypothesis that the speaker has an implicit mastery of rules governing the use of words in the language. But if there are rules they can surely be unearthed and stated. Any success enjoyed by such an enterprise would consist in the formulation of a complete theory of meaning for the language.[104] This plausible thought runs counter to the spirit of the use theory, at least as it stands in its original sources; for there the idea had been that an unsystematic and piecemeal demonstration of the uses of expressions in particular contexts is the right way to settle questions of meaning. This approach is shown by the foregoing considerations to be mistaken. It does not, however, show that questions of use are irrelevant to meaning; far from it.

The notion of a systematic theory of meaning for a language, just suggested, enters into the discussions of the next chapter. Of the theories discussed in this chapter, the verificationist and use theories in particular provide useful materials to carry forward.

Notes

1   Cf. N. Chomsky, *Cartesian Linguistics Language and Mind*.
2   Cf. J. Katz, *The Philosophy of Language*.
3   K. Lehrer and A. Lehrer, *Theory of Meaning*.
4   Some philosophers, like Lehrer and perhaps Bernard Harrison, would disagree with the characterization I am giving here.
5   L. Wittgenstein, *Philosophical Investigations*, 55, 119, 133.
6   B. Russell, *The Principles of Mathematics*, p. 47.
7   P. F. Strawson, 'On Referring', in Feigl et al. p. 40. *New Readings in Philosophical Analysis*, p. 40.
8   Ibid.
9   Russell, *The Analysis of Mind*, p. 191.
10   Cf. Alston, 'Meaning and Use', *Philosophical Quarterly*, 1963, p. 2.
11   Strawson, 'Identifying Reference and Truth-Values', in *Logico-Linguistic Papers*, passim.
12   J. L. Austin, 'The Meaning of a Word', in Feigl et. al., *New Readings in Philosophical Analysis*, p. 232.
13   That is, I take it for the purposes of the following discussion that one can talk of terms referring, even if it is only because they have a referring use (i.e. such that speakers alone refer, but by their use).
14   Cf., e.g., K. Donnellan, 'Reference and Definite Descriptions' and 'Speaking of Nothing' in S. P. Schwartz, *Naming, Necessity and Natural Kinds*, p. 13 *et seq.* and p. 216 *et seq.*; Kripke, 'Identity and Necessity', in Schwartz, p. 66 *et seq.*; H. Putnam, 'Is Semantics Possible?' and 'Meaning and Reference', in Schwartz, p. 102 *et seq.*, and p. 119 *et seq.*
15   Putnam, 'Is Semantics Possible?', p. 103.
16   Donnellan, op. cit., p. 46 *et seq.*
17   Kripke, 'Identity and Necessity', p. 62 *et seq.*, esp. pp. 72–4.
18   Cf. ibid., p. 88 *et seq.*
19   Cf. the discussion in chapter 3 above.
20   Cf. Putnam 'Meaning and Reference', p. 119 *et seq.*, esp. pp. 127–9.
21   Kripke, 'Identity and Necessity'.
22   Donnellan, 'Speaking of Nothing', p. 216 *et seq.*
23   G. Evans, 'The Causal Theory of Names', in Schwartz, *Naming, Necessity and Natural Kinds*, p. 192 *et seq.*

24 Donnellan, 'Speaking of Nothing'.
25 Cf. M. A. E. Dummet, *Frege*, p. 40.
26 J. S. Mill, *A System of Logic*, I. ii. 3.
27 Putnam, 'The Meaning of "Meaning" ', in K. Gunderson, (ed.), *Language, Mind and Knowledge*, pp. 104–5.
28 Cf. Schwartz, 'Introduction' in Schwartz, *Naming, Necessity and Natural Kinds*, pp. 39–40.
29 A good account of reference is to be found in G. McCulloch, *The Game of the Name*.
30 J. Locke, *Essay Concerning Human Understanding*, iii.2.1.
31 Cf. the relevant papers in G. Pitcher (ed.), *Wittgenstein: Critical Essays*.
32 Locke, *Essay*, iii. 7. 1.
33 Cf. P. Winch, *The Idea of a Social Science*.
34 Although not by Pavlov himself; his work only became known outside Russia comparatively late.
35 This view is to be found in the literature – particularly the early literature – of behavioural psychology.
36 Cf. e.g., L. Bloomfield, *Language*.
37 An account of meaning which turns specifically on the utterer's intentions in communicating something to his audience is given by H. P. Grice, 'Utterer's Meaning, Sentence Meaning, and Word Meaning', in J. Searle (ed.), *Philosophy of Language*. See the next chapter. Strawson has defended this approach to meaning too; cf. his *Logico-Linguistic Papers*, and particularly his 'Meaning and Truth', the Inaugural Lecture at Oxford, reprinted in T. Honderich and M. Burnyeat, *Philosophy As It Is*, pp. 519–39.
38 Cf. C. Morris, *Signs, Language and Behaviour*, esp. 1; and C. Osgood, *Method and Theory in Experimental Psychology*, Ch. 16.
39 W. V. O. Quine, *From A Logical Point of View*. Essays ii, iii, and vii.
40 Cf. chapter 8 below.
41 Quine, *The Roots of Reference*; see also *Word and Object*, ch. iii.
42 Cf. *Word and Object*, pp. 3–4; pp. 35–7.
43 Ibid., pp. 37–49; pp. 62–8.
44 Ibid., p. 67 *et seq.*; pt. iii passim.
45 Cf. K. Wilkes, *Physicalism*.
46 P. F. Strawson, *Analysis and Metaphysics*, Oxford University Press, 1992.
47 M. Schlick, 'Meaning and Verification' in Feigl et al., *Readings in Philosophical Analysis*.
48 A. J. Ayer, *Language, Truth and Logic*.
49 Ayer, 'Introduction' in Ayer (ed.), *Logical Positivism*, p. 10.
50 Ibid.
51 D. Hume, *Enquiry Concerning Human Understanding*, § XII, Pt. III.
52 Strictly speaking, Wittgenstein viewed mathematical propositions as iden-

tities, but the view is the same in net.

53   Cf. Ayer, *Language, Truth and Logic*, 'Preface' to the 2nd edn, passim.
54   Ibid.
55   P. Feyerabend, *Against Method*.
56   F. Waismann, 'Verifiability', *Proceedings of the Aristotelian Society*, 1945.
57   Ayer, *Logical Positivism*, p. 15.
58   Ibid.
59   Schlick, 'Meaning and Verification' in Feigl et al. 1949.
60   P. W. Bridgman, *The Logic of Modern Physics*.
61   Schlick, 'Meaning and Verification'.
62   Cf. Quine, 'Two Dogmas' in *From a Logical Point of View*.
63   Wittgenstein, *Philosophical Investigations*, 421.
64   Ibid., 43.
65   Ibid., 23.
66   Ibid, cf. 10, 27, 30, 32.
67   Ibid., cf. e.g., 11, 17, 274, 556, 559.
68   Ibid, e.g., 5, and also 6, 8, 398.
69   Ibid., e.g., 402.
70   Ibid., e.g., (respectively) 103, 108, 421.
71   Ibid., 66ff.
72   Cf. W. P. Alston, 'Meaning and Use', *Philosophical Quarterly*, 1963, reprinted in Feigl et al. *New Readings*, p. 243.
73   A. M. Quinton, 'Contemporary British Philosophy', in D. J. O'Connor, (ed.), *A Critical History of Western Philosophy*, p. 525ff.; reprinted in Pitcher, *Wittgenstein*, pp. 11–12.
74   Strawson, 'Review of the *Philosophical Investigations*', *Mind*, lxiii, 1954; reprinted in Pitcher, *Wittgenstein*.
75   Cf. Alston, 'Meaning and Use' in Feigl et al. 1972. passim; and G. Pitcher, *The Philosophy of Wittgenstein*, Ch. 10, passim.
76   Pitcher, *Philosophy of Wittgenstein*, p. 230.
77   Alston, 'Meaning and Use' in Feigl et al. 1972, p. 245
78   Wittgenstein, *Philosophical Investigations*, 19, 23, p. 226.
79   Ibid., p. 223.
80   Cf. Pitcher, *Philosophy of Wittgenstein*, p. 243.
81   Wittgenstein, *Philosophical Investigations*, 7.
82   Quoted in N. Malcolm, *Wittgenstein: a Memoir*, p. 93.
83   Wittgenstein, *Philosophical Investigations*, 132.
84   Ibid., 38.
85   Ibid., 109.
86   Ibid., 309.
87   Ibid., 664.
88   Ibid., 90.

89 Ibid., 243–315, 350–1, 398–421.
90 Cf. chapter 4 above.
91 J. L. Austin, *Sense and Sensibilia*, passim. Ayer is the main target in this work, but not the only one, Price and Warnock are also in the firing-line.
92 Cf. Pitcher, *The Philosophy of Wittgenstein*, p. 252.
93 J. L. Austin, *How To Do Things With Words*, cf. Lecture viii, passim, p. 94 *et seq.*
94 Ibid., p. 102.
95 R. M. Hare, *The Language of Morals*, p. 27.
96 See above, chapter 6.
97 Cf. J. Searle, e.g., 'Meaning and Speech-Acts', *Philosophical Review*, 71, 1962; reprinted in Lehrer and Lehrer, *Theory of Meanings*, p. 149 *et seq.*
98 Ibid.
99 Ibid., pp. 151–2.
100 Ibid., p. 152. Searle points out that 'commend' is doing duty for many verbs, but that ' "good" is used to commend' means '. . . commend, praise, approve, express satisfaction' and the like. So 'commend' here must be taken as 'commend etc.'
101 Ibid.
102 Ibid., p. 153.
103 Ibid., p. 154.
104 Cf. M. A. E. Dummett, 'Can Analytic Philosophy be Systematic, and Ought It to Be?', *Truth and Other Enigmas*, pp. 450–1.

8

Truth, Meaning, Realism and Anti-realism

Introduction

The last chapter contained informal discussions of some 'traditional' theories of meaning and reference, together with more recent theories dealing with aspects of the same. In this chapter I look at two main recent approaches in the theory of meaning: communication–intention theory, and truth-conditional semantics. Discussion of the latter leads to discussion of the 'anti-realist' criticism of such approaches where truth is understood in an objective, 'realist' sense.

Meaning and Speaker's Meaning

It is a commonplace to say that when in normal circumstances a normally competent speaker utters a sentence, his normally competent hearers understand him. When pressed to explain why we choose to say that his hearers understand *him* rather than the *words* he utters, we might wonder whether we should adjust our claim and say: his hearers understand what he means because they know the meaning of the sentence he utters. And this is partly right. But only partly; for a little reflection shows that, often, a speaker's hearers understand *him* (that is, they understand 'what he is getting at'; they understand the meaning he intends to convey) even though he uses a sentence whose *literal* meaning is different – perhaps even, as in cases of irony or sarcasm, the opposite – of what he intends to convey. What is the relation between speaker's meaning and the meaning of the expressions he uses? Which, if either, is primary?

In saying that the meaning of a speaker's utterance is not, or at least not solely, a matter of what is meant by the words he uses, one is saying that meaning fundamentally depends on the psychological attitudes – namely, the beliefs, desires and intentions – that prompt and inform the speaker's utterances. In most standard cases, hearers grasp a speaker's intentions *via* understanding the meaning of the expressions he uses. He chooses to use them, after all, precisely to fulfil his intention to convey a certain meaning. But because there is a genuine difference between the two kinds of meaning, and therefore a genuine question about their relation, it is useful to distinguish between *speaker meaning* and *semantic meaning*, the latter being the literal meaning of expressions (as one might find them reported in dictionaries).

Many expressions have conventional uses which perspicuously convey the intentions of their utterers. 'What is the time, please?' might be an example; although even here there is room for use of this question to convey other or further speaker-meanings, as when an impatient passenger asks it of a bus-driver as a way of signifying disapproval of a delay. In this case and generally, hearers grasp the speaker's intention by conjoining facts about the circumstances of utterance with their knowledge of word-meaning. The method is not infallible, but usually succeeds.

In the debate about which of speaker's meaning and semantic meaning is primary, two broad families of views about the nature of language are in play. Those who take speaker's meaning to underlie semantic meaning regard language as an elaborate system of signals used by speakers to communicate their intentions; hence the label *communication–intention* theory. Those who take semantic meaning to be independent of speaker's meaning insist on an important feature of (human) natural language which differentiates it from a mere system of signals – such as those of birds and other creatures – *viz.*, its having a *structure* which allows a potential infinity of sentences to be formed from a finite set of elements by application of a finite set of rules. This is natural language's property of *compositionality*. (I turn to views of this kind below).

The chief begetter of recent communication–intention theory is Grice. In a seminal paper published in 1957 he laid the foundations of the theory by sketching a means – since much modified and extended – of showing that speaker's meaning is primary.[1] The key idea is a distinction between 'natural meaning', as when spots 'mean' measles or clouds 'mean' rain – that is, are symptomatic of, portend, or indicate measles or rain respectively – and 'non-natural meaning', abbreviated to meaningNN, in which one person makes a sound or mark with the intention of getting another person ('the audience') to form a belief by recognizing that the issuer of the sound or mark wishes the audience to form that belief. For example: a bus conductor rings his bell three times to inform the driver that the bus is full. He rings the bell three times to bring about this belief in the driver *through the driver's recognition of the conductor's intention so to inform him*. The conductor's ringing thrice accordingly meansNN that the bus is full. If the conductor and driver have a convention that three rings regularly indicate that the bus is full, then the three rings themselves meanNN that the bus is full; they conventionally embody the message – the proposition – that the conductor intends to communicate.

Natural meaning is distinguished from meaningNN by the fact that spots mean measles whether or not anyone believes they do, whereas meaningNN requires that an utterance's audience should recognize the utterer's intention in issuing that utterance, and should attach to the medium he employs to do so – *viz.*, the sentences he utters – conventionally regular understandings of what those sentences can be used to communicate.

This shows that Grice's programme consists in a two-stage analysis. The first stage states the conception of speaker's meaning, the second employs the idea of a conventional regularity; put together they offer a definition of the semantic meaning of a sentence as follows: the semantic meaning of a sentence is the proposition that the sentence is conventionally used to convey. Grice puts matters thus:

> A must intend to induce by x a belief in an audience, and he must also intend that his utterance to be recognised as so intended. But these intentions are not independent; the recognition is intended by A to play its part in inducing the belief, and if it does not do so something will have gone wrong the fulfilment of A's intentions. Moreover, A's intending that the recognition should play this part implies, I think, that he assumes that there is some chance that it will in fact play this part, that he does not regard it as a foregone conclusion that the belief will be induced in the audience whether or not the intention behind the utterance is recognised. Shortly, perhaps, we may say that 'A meantNN something by x' is roughly equivalent to 'A uttered x with the intention of inducing a belief by means of the recognition of this intention.'[2]

Three conditions are here stated to govern A's conveying his meaning to his audience: A utters x intending (1) to get his audience to believe that p, (2) to get his audience to recognize that he intends (1); and (3) that at least part of the reason for his audience's belief that p should be its recognition of (1). There is nothing here that requires that the expressions (or gestures, or any other medium) employed by A in communicating his meaning to his audience should have a literal meaning, or, if it does, that it and the speaker's meaning should coincide. This leaves room for irony and other cases, as we shall see. But the key point is that this analysis does not depend in any way on the semantic meaning of the medium employed by the speaker; and so it is available as a non-circular ground for explaining this latter.

It is clear on inspection that the analysis as first offered by Grice is neither necessary nor sufficient for the intuitive idea of communication. As a result it has since been extensively modified and developed, by Grice himself and others.[3] It is not *necessary* because there are many uses of sentences that do not fall into the category specified by the conditions; in Grice's own examples: giving examination answers, confessing to sins, reminding someone of something, reviewing a set of known facts. Others have offered further examples – Davidson cites false compliments, parodies, tales, charades.[4] Nor is the analysis *sufficient*; it does not specify that the medium used by A to convey his intention should possess some property that would guide his audience to a correct recognition of what he intends; and anyway there are other ways in which people's beliefs can be influenced that are not in any straightforward sense communicative in the sense of the analysis.[5]

An important feature of Grice's proposals is their reliance on a notion of convention. An account of this notion has been offered by David Lewis, who analyses convention as a regularity in action and belief that satisfies the following conditions: everyone conforms to regularity R, and believes that everyone else conforms to it too, which is one of their reasons for so conforming; there is a general preference for *general* conformity to R rather than something less than general conformity; there is at least one satisfactory alternative regularity available; and all the foregoing is common knowledge to observers of R.[6] Combining this notion with Grice's account gives us an analysis of semantic meaning as the joint product of speaker's meaning and convention, thus: a given sentence s means that p in L if and only if there is a convention among L-speakers to use s to communicate that p, where communication is the conveying of speaker's meaning to an audience in the way described above.

In a full statement of this theory, adjustments would be required to account for features such as indexicality and ambiguity. And there would also have to be a weakening either of the notion of speaker's meaning, or of convention, or both, for the reason that as it stands the account just given is too strong. It is plain that expressions can possess semantic meaning independently of whether there is regularity in Lewis's sense, for there are various ways of communicating the same message without having to use a particular given sentence to do so; so the literal meaning of that sentence cannot be a function of its regularly being used to convey that message. For example, there are many ways we can say that music is relaxing other than by using the sentence 'music has charms to soothe a savage breast', so this sentence's meaning cannot be a function of its being regularly used to convey that thought.

Grice himself suggested weakening 'convention' to the idea of some or many speakers of L having a 'procedure in their repertoires' to use a given sentence to communicate that p.[7] The alternative is to qualify the notion of speaker's meaning in such a way that it includes more than the analysis so far allows, perhaps by requiring that A *actively* intends his audience to believe that p, or to get them to believe that *he himself* believes that p, or – most generally of all – to require that there is *some* psychological state that A intends to induce in his audience. This last, under Grice's conditions sketched above, offers a weak notion of speaker's meaning which, combined with the concept of convention, is more promising as a ground for a suitably modified account of semantic meaning.[8]

Conversational Implicature

It was mentioned above, in distinguishing speaker's meaning from semantic meaning, that an expression can be used by a speaker to mean something different from – even the opposite of – its semantic meaning. This aspect of meaning repays investigation. Among other things it draws attention to pragmatic features: the circumstances in which an utterance is made, the tone of voice in which something is said.

Grice was the first to formulate an approach to these matters. To analyse them he introduced as terms of art the verb *implicate* and the correlative nouns *implicature* and *implicatum*, the first denoting an occurrence of implying, the second, the what-is-implied.[9]

Grice was at first prompted by a concern in another area of philosophical debate, the philosophy of perception, where he wished to defend a 'sense-datum' theory.[10] Some writers had tried to formulate a 'sense-datum vocabulary' which refers only to how things appear in experience, independently of how they are in the world. They did this by saying that when one sees, say, a red object, one has to replace talk of it with a more cautious style of talk, namely, talk of appearances in subjective visual experience, which one might have even if there were no red object to cause it. To identify a 'red sense-datum' independently of some external red object, one has to say 'it looks to me as if there were a red object', or some such. This was attacked by Austin on the grounds that the sense-datum theory trades upon illegitimate uses of 'looks' as in 'it looks red to me', for to say this is to imply that it is not red.[11]

Grice argued that 'that looks red to me' can be true even when the object is indeed red. In support he drew a distinction between the *detachability* of what is implied by an utterance, and its *cancellability*. This distinction helps in the analysis of other cases, for example where use of 'and' in ordinary language implies temporal order ('he jumped into the pool and put on his swimming trunks') whereas it does not do so in logic; 'but' which implies a contrast ('he was poor but he was honest'); 'or' which implies ignorance of which disjunct is true ('he is in Paris or Rome'); and so for other cases.[12]

In the case of 'looks' there is no other way of saying what is said by 'it looks red to me' which does not carry the same implication – 'that appears red to me', 'that seems red to me' equally cast doubt on whether the thing in question is red – so the implication is undetachable. But the implication is cancellable: one can consistently say 'it looks red to me, and it is indeed red'. The same applies to 'and' and 'or' and indeed most standard cases of conversational implicature.

The reverse is true of 'but': the implication is detachable but not cancellable, because there is another expression – 'and' – which contributes in the same way as 'but' to the truth-conditions of 'he was poor but he was honest', but does not imply a contrast between poverty and honesty. So the implications of use of 'but' seem to be wholly governed by its conventional meaning, whereas the other expressions seem to lie under the further government of a general conversational principle stated by Grice thus: 'one should not make a weaker statement rather than a stronger statement unless there is good reason to do so'.[13]

Grice extended the analysis later to show that further 'maxims' govern conversational implicature.[14] Those participating in a conversation expect each other to observe a 'Cooperative Principle' which states that one's contributions to conversation should be 'such as is required, at the stage at which it occurs, by the accepted purpose or direction of the talk exchange in which one is engaged'. Grice's maxims state this principle in more detail. First, make your contribution as informative as, but no more informative than, is required for the current purposes of the exchange. Secondly, 'try to make your contribution one that is true' – do not say what you believe to be false, or what you lack sufficient evidence to claim. Thirdly, 'be perspicuous' – avoid obscurity and ambiguity. Fourthly, be succinct and orderly. (The list is not exhaustive.) The general idea of cooperation is not specific to conversation, in Grice's view; it applies to any social or mutual activity. Nor, in the case of language use, are the maxims sufficient by themselves for a hearer to grasp what is implied by some utterance's use, for he must take into account both the literal meaning of the words used, the circumstances of utterance, and any further considerations that help him infer the correct interpretation.

It has been questioned how adequately Grice's theory deals with the two important matters of irony and metaphor. On his view, a hearer detects irony when, to grasp the point of an utterance, he has to understand it as intending the contradictory of the proposition it asserts; and he detects metaphor – as in 'you are the sunshine of my life' – when he sees that the speaker intends the subject referred to ('you') to resemble the mentioned substance ('sunshine'). Both accounts are jejune, and a considerable literature offers improvements or alternatives.[15] Nor does the account deal satisfactorily with the fact that there can be various possible explanations of how the Cooperative Principle is observed in a given utterance – in other words, that implicatures can be indeterminate or open-ended, as Grice himself admits. This is a difficulty because indeterminacy or open-endedness defeats communication, and communication is what is intended; so indeterminacy defeats the speaker's intention.

Again, Grice gives no account of whether, and if so how, the maxims are to be weighted when they conflict. It will often happen, for example, as a result of lack of information, that a speaker prefers to obey the maxim 'do not claim what you have insufficient evidence to claim' in preference to 'make your contribution as informative as it can be for the purposes of the exchange'. Any systematic theory should provide a principled way of weighting maxims to ensure that communication intentions are not thwarted; Grice's view lacks one.[16]

Problems with Grice's account of conversational implicature are less significant, however, than the chief difficulty identified earlier for communication–intention theory as a theory of meaning, namely, that it does not explain the *compositionality* of meaning, that is, the fact that the meanings of sentences depend upon the meanings of their constituent expressions and the way they are put together. The meaning of 'there are four lakes among these mountains' is quite different from the sentence derived by substituting 'towns' for 'lakes'. An account of meaning which proceeds entirely in terms of speakers' intentions, even when understood as conventionally accompanying utterances of sentences, does not address this phenomenon, which is evidently a very important one. To deal with it, a quite different kind of theory seems to be called for; which is what truth-theoretic semantics aspires to provide. A much-discussed version of such a theory owes itself to Davidson, to whose views I now turn.

Truth-theory and Meaning

An idea current since Frege is that the meaning of a sentence can be given by stating the conditions under which it is true. In addition to Frege, this view has been held by, among others, Wittgenstein, Carnap, Quine, and – as its chief recent proponent – Davidson.

It will be recalled from earlier discussion that Frege took names to have both references and senses, and that sentences, as a species of complex names, have as their references either The True or The False. The thought or sense expressed by a sentence is determined by the conditions under which the sentence designates The True; and its sense 'is the sense or thought that these conditions are fulfilled'.[17] Wittgenstein in the *Tractatus* expresses this conception more directly: 'To know the meaning of a sentence is to know what is the case if it is true',[18] and Carnap likewise: 'To know the meaning of a sentence is to know in which of the possible cases it would be true and in which not'.[19] It is this basic idea that Davidson applies in some detail.

A point frequently iterated in earlier chapters is that by investigating language one thereby investigates the world. Davidson puts the point by saying, 'In making manifest the large features of our language, we make manifest the large features of reality'.[20] Accordingly, in his view, 'what we must attend to in language, if we want to bring into relief general features of the world, is what it is in general for a sentence in the language to be true.'[21]

Frege stressed the importance of showing how the semantic constituents of sentences determine their truth-value. He did not think in terms of a general truth-theory for natural language because he took such languages to be defective; and accordingly proposed, and effected, the construction of an improved language, for which he devised a notation whose syntax clearly reflects the interpretation intended for it. He believed this language to have the same expressive power as parts of natural language. But, in part because of his pessimism about natural language, and in part because of the artificiality of certain of his innovations – as, for example, treating sentences as names – Frege's work cannot, in Davidson's view, be applied directly to giving a theory of meaning for natural language.[22]

An essential ingredient in Davidson's theory is provided by Quine; the demonstration, as Davidson views it, of how an holistic approach to the problem of language-understanding furnishes the empirical foundations needed by the theory. 'If metaphysical conclusions are to be drawn from a theory of truth in the way that I propose,' Davidson says, 'the approach to language must be holistic'.[23] Quine did not see holism as having this import, for he did not make truth-theory central either to the question of language's ontological significance, or to the matter of investigating its logical form. Moreover he shared Frege's view that the purpose of devising a regimented language is to improve on natural language, rather than to serve as a tool for its investigation. Accordingly Quine's metaphysics attach to his logic and not to natural language; Davidson, by contrast, sees logic as a device for exploring natural language itself.[24]

The inspiration for Davidson's proposals derives from Tarski's work on truth. The Tarskian theory consists in an enumeration of the semantic properties of the items in a finite vocabulary, together with a recursive characterization of the infinity of sentences which can be generated from that vocabulary; which characterization turns on the 'subtle and powerful concept (satisfaction) which relates both sentences and non-sentential expressions to objects in the world'.[25] The details of Davidson's application of Tarski's theory, together with extensions and modifications of it to account for indexicality and other problematic features of natural language, are described below. What is important for Davidson's purposes is that use of Tarski allows the truth-theory for natural language to reveal and articulate its structure – just what is required for an account of meaning.

Davidson's Proposals

Davidson begins by observing that any adequate theory of meaning must satisfy four conditions:

(i) it must enable us to 'give the meaning' for each sentence of the (natural) language L;[26]

(ii) it must show how the sentences of L are semantically compounded from the finite stock of L's words by means of L's rules;[27]

(iii) it must show that its demonstration of how sentences of L mean is based on the same stock of concepts as L's sentences themselves;[28] and

(iv) it must be empirically testable.[29]

None of these requirements is controversial. The claim is that a theory of truth for L will satisfy them, and will also constitute a theory of L's logical form.

Davidson insists that any theory of meaning must show how the meanings of L's sentences depend on the meaning of their constituents. Unless sentence-meaning is a function of word-meaning it is difficult to see how anyone could learn L. Speakers of L have a creative ability to construct and comprehend sentences never before encountered; which is to say, from L's finite stock of words and rules an (at least potentially) infinite stock of sentences can be produced and understood by L's speakers. To say that a theory of meaning must give an account of this is to say, on Davidson's view, that such a theory must yield all sentences of the form

(1) s means m

where 's' is a description of some sentence that specifies its structure, and 'm' is an expression that denotes its meaning. But appeal to the notion of a sentence's meaning is, says Davidson, unhelpful, as is reformulating (1) as

(2) s means that p

where 'p' is the sentence described by 's'; since 'means that' is no less problematic than the notion of 'the meaning' of a sentence. Accordingly Davidson reformulates (2), using an arbitrary predicate 'T' to replace 'means that' by 'is T iff'. In (2) the idea is that 'p' is a sentence having the same meaning as the sentence described by 's', but, given the obscurity of appeals to meaning, a more perspicuous surrogate is required. If the conditions on 's' and 'p' as just given (namely, that 's' is a structure-specifying description of the sentence 'p') are held in view for use of the arbitrary predicate 'T', then (2) can be reformulated as

(3) s is T if and only if p.

Now, any predicate which satisfies this condition is, Tarski-style, a materially adequate truth predicate; which is exactly what Davidson wants.[30] This comes down to saying that the meaning of a sentence is given by stating its truth-conditions; the difference is that the demand is made with the added muscle of Tarski-style constraints on those truth-conditions.

Although the model for Davidson's approach is Tarski's theory, the approach is not too closely tied to that model. For Davidson's purposes it is sufficient that the adopted truth-theory entails a statement of the conditions under which every sentence of L is true. Take as an example the simplest case, that of an unambiguous declarative sentence free from indexicals and demonstratives (free from references to particular times, places, and utterers, or objects picked out demonstratively by such terms as 'this' and 'that'). Davidson's demand is for a theory that will entail an infinite number of biconditional statements of the form

(4) s is true if and only if p.

Note how this is a reformulation of (3); the arbitrary predicate 'T' has disappeared in favour of 'true', and we have an explicit truth-conditional form. Bear in mind that 's' is a structural description of a sentence, and 'p' – where the object language is contained in the metalanguage in which the description 's' occurs – is that sentence itself. Where the object language and metalanguage differ, 'p' is replaced by a translation of the sentence described by 's'.

It is important for Davidson's purposes that the number of non-logical axioms in a truth theory be finite; if it were not – that is, if we take as axioms every instance of (4) – then requirement (ii) specified above would be violated. This excludes trivial theories with infinite axiom schemata, and restricts attention to Tarski-style truth theory.

It is important to see that 'is true if and only if' is not intended merely as a perspicuous alternative reading of 'means that'. For one thing, 'is true if and only if' and 'means that' are not synonymous. The context following 'is true if and only if' is truth-functional, whereas the context following 'means that' is not. The difference is crucial; if 'means that' were truth-functional, all true sentences would mean the same. Davidson is arguing for the *elimination* of the 'obscure' idiom of meaning, and its replacement by more tractable extensional idioms of truth and truth-conditions.

This echoes Quine's separation of semantic notions into two groups, the first consisting in theories of reference, that is, extensional theories turning on or essentially involving such notions as 'designates', 'satisfies', and 'is true', and the second consisting in theories of meaning, that is, intensional theories turning on or essentially involving such notions as synonymy and analyticity. (Quine's view is that theories of reference are in 'better shape' than intensional theories.[31]) Davidson writes:

> The theory of meaning will have done its work if it provides, for every sentence 's' in the language under study, a matching sentence (to replace 'p' in 's means that p') that, in some way yet to be made clear, 'gives the meaning' of 's'. One obvious candidate for the matching sentence is just 's' itself, if the object language is contained in the metalanguage: otherwise a translation of 's' in the metalanguage. As a final bold step, let us try treating the position occupied by 'p' extensionally; to implement this, sweep away the obscure 'means that', provide the sentence that replaces 'p' with a proper sentential connective, and supply the description that replaces 's' with its own predicate. The plausible result is
>
> (T) s is T iff p
>
> What we require of a theory of meaning for a language L is that without

appeal to any (further) semantical notions, it places enough restrictions on the predicate 'is T' to entail all sentences got from schema (T) when 's' is replaced by a structural description of a sentence and 'p' by that sentence.[32]

The phrase 'sweep away the obscure "means that"' implies revisionism in Davidson's programme reminiscent of Quine's, who insists that 'ascent' from ordinary discourse to the more exact idioms of logic provides better purchase on philosophical problems, despite the fact that ascent does not preserve all that is contained in the former. Davidson is saying that leaving 'means' behind and resorting to truth-theory constitutes an ascent of sorts, which does not merely substitute for talk of meaning but provides a different and more tractable way of handling the issues in question. The 'bold step' of 'treating the position occupied by "p" extensionally' thus constitutes an attempt to overcome the difficulties inherent in Quine's second and unhappy group of intensional concepts by concentrating only on notions in the first, extensional, group.

But what reasons are there for thinking that replacing talk of meaning by talk of truth will yield a satisfactory theory of meaning? Let us retrace a few steps.

The passage quoted from Davidson concludes that a theory of meaning should so constrain the predicate 'is T' as to entail all (T)-sentences. So what is required of a theory of meaning seems to be supplied by Tarski's material adequacy condition. The predicate 'is T' and the truth predicate are coextensive; 'is T' will apply to nothing other than all the true sentences of L. Accordingly, in Davidson's view, 'a theory of meaning for a language L shows 'how the meanings of sentences depend upon the meanings of words' if it contains a (recursive) definition of 'truth-in-L'; we demonstrate how the truth-conditions for sentences are determined by the semantic features of their constituents together with the semantic significance of their structure.[33]

The requirement, recall, is that a theory of meaning must supply pairings between sentences of the object language with sentences of the metalanguage in a way that 'gives the meaning' of the object language sentences. If we ask how to sweep away intensionality and make the context extensional, the obvious answer is to employ the biconditional form, since the aim is to arrive at an appropriate pairing between s and p and the available extensional pairing is biconditionality. We could try 's if and only if p' for this purpose, but this is ill-formed; for 's' is a *name*

– the name of a sentence – so this biconditional says something like 'Roger if and only if snow is white'. The biconditional is a sentential connective; 's' therefore must be turned into a sentence by predicating something of it. Let us take an arbitrary predicate 'X' and attach it to 's'; the biconditional now becomes a well-formed 's is X if and only if p'. And here is where the trick is turned: the metalanguage sentence p is intended somehow to 'give the meaning' of s. If it does so, '. . . is X' and the Tarski truth predicate are at least coextensive; and therefore, because no other reading of '. . . is X' readily suggests itself, it is convenient to interpret it as 'is true'.[34]

But this way of substituting talk of truth for talk of meaning, although plausible on the face of it, is not strictly an argument which settles that the proposal is the right way, or even the best way, to give a theory of meaning. In fact, as it stands, the proposal will not do. To see why, it is necessary to look at an important supplementary element in Davidson's view, concerning the notion of interpretation.

Davidson argues that in interpreting another's discourse, whether his discourse consists in another language or one's own, we require a way of telling when a sentence 'p' of the metalanguage has the meaning possessed by the sentence uttered by the other and described by 's'. An empirical test of whether the Tarski condition is met by, say, '*Schnee ist weiss* is true if and only if snow is white' is to check whether speakers of German hold true '*Schnee ist weiss* if and only if snow is white'. The idea is that one discovers the meaning of a speaker's utterances by invoking a notion of what the speaker holds true; meaning is discovered by holding the speaker's beliefs constant. A 'Principle of Charity' is employed here: in interpreting others we grant that most of their beliefs are true. And it is a corollary that the basic unit of interpretation is the language as a whole; Davidson's views are holistic.

There now seems to be a difficulty. Whereas the notion of translation was available to Tarski in defining a truth predicate (it is a condition on 's is true if and only if p' that p be a translation of s, with homophonic, that is, same-language, translation as the simplest case), it cannot be thus available to a theory of meaning; we are trying to explain meaning, and translation would have to be a consequence, not an assumption, of the theory. Accordingly it seems to be a mistake to think that a Tarski truth predicate does the work required; we do not, at any rate as yet, have a reason for selecting truth as the key concept in such a theory. Why, therefore, truth?

I shall return to this question in a more general way shortly. There are other problems in Davidson's proposal to look at first.

Paradox and Other Problems

Tarski, it will be recalled from chapter 6, was pessimistic about the applicability of his theory to natural languages. Davidson is not. Two features of natural languages troubled Tarski; their semantic closedness, which leads to paradoxes, and their ill-regulated and changeable nature, which makes them inapt for the application of formal techniques. It matters therefore to see what Davidson has to say about these problems.

On the first head – the paradoxes – his reply is that Tarski's point 'deserves a serious answer, and I wish I had one'; nevertheless 'I think we are justified in carrying on without having disinfected this particular source of conceptual anxiety',[35] for these reasons. Paradox arises, Davidson says, because of the over-generous scope of the quantifiers in natural languages; but, for one thing, this fact does not exclude our being able to give an explicit definition of true-in-L for any natural L, and for another thing, attention can anyway be restricted to those fragments of natural languages where the risk of paradox is minimal.[36]

On the second head – formal specifiability – Davidson admits that, if it were true that natural language would have to be refined out of recognition in order to admit the application of formal techniques, that fact would be 'fatal' to his project,[37] for the task of the theory of meaning is not to reform L but to describe it. His response is to waive pessimism –

> Let us look at the positive side. Tarski has shown the way to giving a theory for interpreted formal languages of various kinds; pick one as much like English as possible. Since this new language has been explained in English and contains much English we not only may, but I think must, view it as part of English for those who understand it. For this fragment of English we have, ex hypothesi, a theory of the required sort.[38]

Tarski's doubts centered upon the fact that natural languages are mutable, and contain many features that are difficult to formalize, such as vagueness, indexicality and ambiguity. Davidson thinks that although a certain amount of 'tidying up' will be necessary before Tarski's truth theory can be applied, nevertheless by starting from a tractable fragment and extending outwards, difficulties can be overcome. (He observes, 'it's good to know we shan't run out of work'.)[39]

One of the problems facing Davidson's programme – indexicality – might, for example, be handled as follows. The presence of indexicals in natural language simply requires viewing truth as a predicate of utterances rather than sentences, and relativizing application of the predicate to speakers and times. Then the extended T-schema will require the theory to entail such sentences as:

' "I am tired" (s, t) is true iff s is tired at t'.[40]

For demonstratives ('this', 'that'), the account to be given is:

'this is X' is true iff the object picked out by the speaker's use of 'this' satisfies '. . . is X' at the time of utterance.[41]

And so on for like cases.

Nevertheless, Davidson early admitted the extent of the task facing his proposal: 'But it must be allowed that a staggering list of difficulties and conundrums remain'.[42] On some of the issues listed Davidson claims progress, particularly with respect to propositional attitudes, quotations, adverbs,[43] proper names,[44] imperatives,[45] mass terms, and comparatives.[46] Nevertheless that progress depends upon assuming the validity of the fundamental approach, and although success on these and other items in the 'staggering list' help to vindicate it, the question remains whether taking truth as the key concept will do. To that question I now return.

Why Truth?

One reason truth might serve is that, on the face of it, it makes for an empirically testable theory. This is the fourth requirement, listed above, on a satisfactory theory of meaning. Davidson claims that this is where his own approach does best. The claim merits assessment.

The truth-conditions approach 'has been characterised', says Davidson, 'as issuing in a flood of sentences each giving the truth-conditions of a sentence', so to test the theory 'we need only ask, in selected cases, whether what the theory avers to be the truth-conditions for a sentence really are.[47] The procedure is quite straightforward: all that is required is the ability to recognize as true the T-sentences entailed by the theory. For the simplest cases it is no more difficult to test the theory's empirical adequacy than for a normal speaker of English 'to decide whether " 'snow is white' is true if and only if snow is white" is true'.[48] For Davidson this is analogous to the empirical checks available on a theory of generative grammar; a grammar provides, in potentially infinite numbers, entailments of sentences of the form 's is grammatical', and the chief method of checking the grammar's correctness is to test its deliverances against the 'linguistic intuitions' of speakers.[49] For the semantic theory the homophonic case is straightforward; where metalanguage and object language differ, testing the theory involves determining whether the right and left-hand-sides of the biconditional have the same truth-value. As noted, Davidson's choice of technique for this enterprise is the method of 'radical translation':

> We will try to notice under what conditions the alien speaker assents to or dissents from a variety of his sentences. The relevant conditions will, of course, be what we take to be the truth-conditions of his sentences. We will have to assume that most of his assents are to true, and his dissents from false, sentences – an inevitable assumption since the alternative is unintelligible.[50]

It would indeed seem plausible to think that an empirically testable theory of meaning is best grounded on appeal to assent and dissent patterns, since these appear to carry relatively little theoretical burden;[51] and there is a manifest connection between truth and the notions of assent and dissent. Accordingly, this connection might be argued to count as a good reason for forging links between truth and meaning of the kind suggested.

Is it, though, a good reason? First, one must note that it will be a good reason only if the truth-theory in question is Tarskian. Part of what Davidson maintains is that a truth-theory should issue in an account of logical truth, equivalence, and entailment for the object language. It happens that practically any theory which entails T-sentences for each sentence in a given language will say (in the metalanguage) that the logical truths of the object language are true; but this is trivial, or at least will hardly amount to a theory of the object language's logical form. Tarskian theories, however, show how the truth conditions of sentences depend upon those of their parts, and in doing so entail not just that certain sentences are true, but that every sentence of a given form is true, and that class of sentences can therefore be specified as the object language's logical truths. The merit of Tarskian truth-theories is that they entail generalizations, based on a notion of sentence structure, about true sentences; which is what entitles them to be plausible candidates for theories of logical form. Accordingly Davidson holds that his choice of theory 'entails not only that [given] sentences are true but that they will remain so under all significant rewritings of their non-logical parts'.[52] The connection with testability then goes through: 'It is hard to imagine how a theory of meaning could fail to read a logic into its object language to this degree; and to the extent that it does, our intuitions of logical truth, equivalence, and entailment may be called upon in constructing and testing the theory.'[53]

A question mark is raised, however, by the fact that speakers' intuitions turn out to be the only test for the theory. In the absence of anything else, the theory might as well be reconstrued as a theory about speakers' intuitions, one which sets out to describe and perhaps to explain them; but then it is puzzling to know why such a theory should have the idiosyncratic and restricted form proposed by Davidson, particularly when, on the face of it, a theory of semantic intuition would be better allied to a theory of syntactic intuition – with which a truth-theory of Davidson's preferred kind would be an improbable partner. Certainly, such theory could not propose itself as the simplest or most natural theory of speakers' intuitions; and this is a real problem for Davidson's approach.[54]

Other suggested reasons for thinking that appeal to Tarski-style theory does the required trick are these. Although the claim that 'the meaning of sentences is given by their truth-conditions' is vague, indeed, 'too vague to be of any use as it stands' as one commentator put it,[55] it is not clear that there is any obvious alternative. Tarskian truth theory has the independent merit of precision, particularly in the sense that it shows how the truth-conditions of sentences are determined by structure. What is required, it will be remembered, is that the meaning of sentences should somehow be explained as a function of the meanings of their parts; by substituting talk of Tarskian truth for meaning, this requirement becomes realizable. Moreover if we employ Tarskian notions, system can be added to precision, for the Tarskian device equips us to deal with a potential infinity of sentences in the language under study.

Despite the fact that statements of truth-conditions in the form of T-sentences are individually trivial (Davidson calls them 'snow-bound trivialities'), the Tarskian device provides a way of proving all the near-trivial T-sentences, showing not just what the truth-conditions of a given sentence are but how they are determined.[56] We might accordingly allow ourselves to be encouraged by the thought that an appeal to Tarskian truth will serve well.

These are inclining reasons only.[57] Perhaps the absence of a fully compelling reason results from over-concentration on the notion of truth itself. Perhaps what should be looked for instead is how, in a more general survey of what a theory of meaning should be like, the notion of truth plays a part. Despite early enthusiasm about truth as the key to meaning, it is at least clear that it is not a sufficient condition for a sentence s to 'mean (in L) that p' that 's is true (in L) if and only if p'; something more has to be said.

Truth and a Theory of Linguistic Behaviour

One way that the appeal to truth might be vindicated is to see how it fits into a more general theory. McDowell offers such an approach.[58] The idea is that we begin by locating the place of a theory of meaning in a more inclusive theory of behaviour. A benefit of this tack is that it removes the uncomfortable need, manifest in any theory which starts with truth, to give from the outset a rich enough characterization of truth for it to bear the required load of theory. This is not easy. For one thing, there are no compelling reasons, as we have just seen, why we should start with truth; for another, it would be unsatisfactory to start with an axiomatic definition of truth, or any notion of truth relativized for its intelligibility to a given language, because the threat of circularity reduces the value of using such a notion to explain meaning.[59]

McDowell's proposal is accordingly to start with the idea that pairing sentences of L and its metalanguage must be treated as a component in a theory describing 'what is involved in understanding a language'.[60] That component of a theory of understanding will be a theory of sense, and it will need to be worked out in conjunction with a theory of force,[61] the point of which is to provide us with the means to identify linguistic actions (making assertions, giving commands, asking questions) and therefore the types of propositional acts they consist in (assertion,

command, question); and additionally to correlate an indicative sentence with each imperative, interrogative, and so on, so that their
propositional contents are clear. The theories of sense and force will
then, in combination, and with neither being primary, fit into a wider
picture of speakers' behaviour, both linguistic and non-linguistic, in such
a way that the speakers' behaviour can be rendered intelligible in the light
of their beliefs, desires, and other propositional attitudes. 'Understanding linguistic behaviour, and hence understanding language', McDowell
says, 'involves no more than a special case of understanding what
behaviour, in general, involves'.[62]

The connection between s and p in the incorporated theory of sense
can be seen, then, to play this role: 'p' contributes to an unpacking of the
propositional content of acts performed by use of 's'. Accordingly the
way 's' and 'p' are to be paired invites attention. The theory has to show
how 'p' specifies the propositional content of 's', and evidently what we
require is that the pairing device be such that 'p' says the same thing,
performs the same (or can be used to perform the same) propositional
act, as 's'. Placing 'is true if and only if' between 's' and 'p' acceptably
does the trick.[63] 'That the truth-predicate is insertable is a discovery: the
general ruminations about the role of a theory of meaning within an
explanation of behaviour can be appreciated before the adequacy of the
truth-predicate is realised'.[64] The minimal idea of the truth-predicate as
a disquotation device is all that is required to see that 'truth is what a
theory of sense is a theory of', which is not, note, to say that 'sense is what
a theory of truth is a theory of'.[65]

Why should the truth predicate be invoked here? Is it the only available
way of pairing 's' and 'p'? These questions can be recast as: why 'if and
only if', and why '. . . is true' (rather than some other predicate)? The
reply is that 'if and only if', as an extensional connective, makes the proof
theory unproblematic, for it is after all the right kind of pairing between
's' and 'p' that is being sought, either of sense or (at an earlier stage) of
the propositional acts performed. And '. . . is true' is invoked, according
to Platts, because '(a) this does indeed give us the doctrine that the
meaning of a sentence is given by stating its truth-conditions . . . (b) We
build a bridge with the least theoretically loaded evidential base, and so
ease the route to an empirical theory of meaning. (c) We obtain a
connection with Tarski's work on truth, a connection that replaces
vagueness by precision . . . and . . . provides the essential systematic
structure within a theory of meaning'.[66]

In McDowell's proposals, the question of what should fill the gap in 's . . . p' could be left open by using an unspecified predicate F thus: 's is F if and only if p'; but the requirement that the theory of sense should interact with the theory of force ensures that an acceptable theory of sense will remain acceptable if F is replaced by 'true'.[67] Nevertheless, as McDowell points out, a concept of truth as such does not have to be involved in setting up the theory of sense, and a theory of force need not even be 'sensitive' to the syntactic form of what fills the gap between 's' and 'p'; so the theory of meaning, couched in terms of a general theory of linguistic behaviour, does not turn upon an initial obligation to elucidate truth.[68] Still, the Tarskian truth predicate fits the bill as a replacement for F and brings with it all the benefits listed by Platts. Indeed, because 'true' substitutes acceptably for any F in terms of this theory, it will remain that the theory of sense will specify truth-conditions for sentences, as Frege thought, whether directly or by 'justifiable conversion' of any F into 'true'.[69]

These considerations lend strength to the idea that an appeal to truth is appropriate. But it is not forced; we are not compelled by the foregoing considerations to employ the concept of truth. It is noteworthy that these arguments mix together reasons why the concept can be used with reasons why it should be used. Presumably, part of the argument is this: the fact that the concept of truth *can* be used counts as a reason why it *should* be used in view of the precision and system offered by the well-defined Tarskian notion.

Truth and Realism

In Dummett's view, any theory which has it that the meaning of sentences, in a given class of sentences, is to be specified in terms of truth-conditions, is equivalent to *realism* concerning the subject matter of that class of sentences.[70] Realism is the thesis that the world exists and has its character independently of any knowledge or experience of it, so that sentences about the world are either determinately true or false in virtue of the way things are in the world, whether or not we know or can come to know how things are in the world, and therefore independently of whether or not we can know the truth-value of those sentences. On a realist thesis, the truth-conditions of sentences in a given class of sentences may transcend our capacity to recognize whether or not they obtain.

Dummett objects to the idea that meaning is to be explained in terms of a realist notion of truth precisely because it places many sentences of the language beyond our capacity to know their truth-values. A theory of meaning must tell us is what speakers of a language know when they know (that is, understand) their language; and in telling us what speakers know, the theory must show how that knowledge equips speakers to derive every aspect of the use of sentences from whatever conditions govern their sense. On Dummett's view, a realist theory fails to account for this connection between knowledge and use. Schematically, his argument is as follows (a more detailed account follows shortly).

If a theory of meaning is to tell us what speakers of L know in knowing what its sentences mean, it must consist in a theoretical representation of propositional knowledge implicitly possessed by L's speakers, and it must show how that knowledge enables speakers to use L's sentences. If truth is taken to be the basic concept in the theory of meaning, the theory must explain how knowledge of truth-conditions connects with the practicalities of language use. The demand that this connection be made plain is justified by two requirements on any acceptable theory of meaning: one is that we must be able to tell what counts as a speaker's manifestation of his knowledge of the meanings of L's sentences; and the other is that because language is a tool of communication, sense must be public, and accordingly what it is speakers know in knowing their language must not only be publicly observable in their linguistic behaviour, but also acquirable in public contexts. Dummett's objection to theories of meaning based on a realist (that is, a transcendent) notion of truth is that they fail to satisfy the demand that these requirements be met.

The reason is this: If knowledge of truth-conditions is held to consist in an ability to know when a given sentence is true or false – that is, to recognize whether or not the sentence's truth-conditions obtain – then the connection between knowledge and use is unproblematic, for this is a *practical* ability which connects the conditions of sense for sentences (their truth-conditions, construed as decidable or recognizable) and the use that can be made of them. Because being able to recognize whether or not truth-conditions obtain is a practical mastery of a procedure for settling what truth-value a sentence has, 'understanding a sentence' comes down to having this recognitional capacity; grasp of the sense of a sentence determines and is determined by the uses to which it can be put. So the connection between *knowledge of meaning* and *use* is clear.

But if truth-value is taken to be a possibly recognition-transcendent property of sentences, we cannot associate grasp of their transcendent truth-conditions with possession of an ability to recognize what their truth-values are. For such sentences we therefore have no way of saying how a speaker's knowledge of their truth-conditions could be manifested. But if we cannot say this, the theory does not show how sense and use determine each other.

This is not to say that truth is irrelevant to the theory of meaning. But a different notion of truth is needed; truth is to be thought of as a product of the verification procedures we employ in exercising our capacity to establish truth-value. To construe truth in this way is to reject realism.

Dummett's proposed alternative 'would,' says McDowell, 'require a novel, anti-realist conception of the world: if truth is not independent of our discovering it, we must picture the world either as our own creation or, at least, as springing up in response to our investigations. So verificationist objections to a truth-conditions conception of sense would have far-reaching metaphysical implications'.[71] Dummett's arguments – particularly if they imply the consequences McDowell suggests – accordingly invite fuller treatment.

What is it to Know the Truth-conditions of a Sentence?

Philosophical questions about meaning, says Dummett, 'are best interpreted as questions about understanding: a dictum about what the meaning of an expression consists in must be construed as a thesis about what it is to know its meaning'.[72] So if truth is taken as the key concept, a truth-conditions theory is one which states that to know the meaning of a sentence is to know the condition for it to be true. What is it to know the truth-conditions of a sentence?

Whatever it is to know a sentence's truth-conditions, it has to depend upon understanding the words constituting the sentence and the significance of their arrangement. The problem therefore is: 'what is it that a speaker knows when he knows a language, and what, in particular, does he thereby know about any given sentence of the language?'[73] Any theory offered in reply will constitute a theoretical representation of a *practical* ability, *viz.*, the ability to speak the language. That theory will consist in a set of deductively connected propositions, and will be an explicit setting-out of the speaker's linguistic knowledge. The speaker will not himself be expected to have *explicit* knowledge of these propositions, but it is enough to attribute *implicit* knowledge to anyone who has mastery of a given practice; we should not require that someone knows how to do something – for example, ride a bike or speak a language – only if he can spell out the underlying theory.[74]

If what is being attributed to the speaker is *implicit* knowledge, the theory 'must specify not merely what it is that the speaker must know, but . . . what counts as a *manifestation* of that knowledge'.[75] So at least some individual propositions of the theory must be correlated with specific practical linguistic abilities. (The demand that we do this for every proposition of the theory is too strong.)

A distinction between sense and force is implicit in any such theory. The force of an utterance consists in the linguistic act it effects – asserting, asking, commanding, and so on. Without a sense – force distinction we should not know how to construct a systematic account.[76] In Dummett's view, 'someone who knows, of a given sentence, what condition must obtain for it to be true does not yet know all that he needs to know in order to grasp the significance of an utterance of that sentence'.[77] If we supposed that knowing the truth-condition is enough, we would be smuggling in the idea that speakers understand how a sentence's truth-condition determines its conventional significance; but the point of a theory of meaning is to make explicit the presumed connection between a sentence's truth-conditions and the linguistic act performed by using it. A sentence can be used to perform different acts on different occasions, and it needs to be made clear how the truth-condition relates to the significance of each use; the theory has to offer, in addition to stating how the meaning of a sentence is given by its truth-conditions, a supplementary account of principles required for use of a sentence to be derived from knowledge of its truth-condition.[78]

Accordingly, any theory of meaning taking truth as its basic notion must consist of two parts: (a) a theory about referential relations couched within a theory of sense, and (b) a theory of force giving us an account of the different linguistic acts that can be performed by utterances of the language's sentences. The core of (a), which Dummett calls a 'theory of reference', will be a theory of truth, consisting in an inductive specification of the truth-conditions for sentences of the language. It is better called a theory of reference because, while some of its theorems state the truth-conditions of sentences, its axioms, which govern individual words, assign references to those words. The surrounding theory of sense specifies what a speaker knows in knowing the theory of reference, by correlating the speaker's practical linguistic abilities to certain propositions of the theory.[79]

This characterization shows that knowledge of truth-conditions is not all a speaker has to know; but it is all that a speaker has to know specifically, in connection with any given sentence, because the rest of what he has to know is general in nature, *viz.*, a set of general principles that enable him to derive every aspect of a sentence's use from its truth-conditions. Any theory of meaning having it that there is a single feature of a sentence – in this case, its truth-conditions – such that awareness of it amounts to a grasp of the sentence's meaning, has to conform to this model.[80]

And now the question is 'whether the concept of truth is the right choice for the *central notion* of a theory of meaning . . . or whether we need to employ some other notion in this role'.[81] On Dummett's view, so long as the notion of truth is taken for granted it seems obvious that it is the right one; but the moment we cease taking it for granted its intuitive aptness vanishes.[82]

This becomes apparent when we ask: where, in the process of mastering a language, does a grasp of the notion of truth come in? We cannot think of it as being introduced stipulatively, for so to introduce it we should need mastery of a large fragment of the language already. If we wish to say that learning a language is learning what it is for each sentence of the language to be true, we must be able to state what it is to know that a sentence is true without, on pain of circularity, assuming prior understanding of the sentence.[83] Of course, in many cases the meaning of a sentence can be given by purely verbal means, but here a speaker's knowledge of the sentence's truth-condition is explicit knowledge, and his ability to understand a sentence in this way presupposes antecedent language mastery on his part. It would be circular to say that a speaker's understanding consisted in an ability to specify the meaning of a sentence in other words, that is, by equivalent sentences of the same language; therefore mastery of the lower or more primitive levels of language cannot be explained in this way.[84]

The difficulty at issue is not how to specify what counts as a speaker's recognition that a sentence's truth-condition is satisfied, for – provided that a sentence's truth-condition can be recognized by a speaker to be fulfilled – we can find a way of saying what constitutes his appreciation of that fact. But this restricts us to those relatively few cases where truth-conditions obtain recognizably – that is, for which a speaker has an effective procedure which, in a finite time, will enable him to determine whether a sentence is true or false. Rather, the difficulty is that natural language is full of sentences which are not effectively decidable.[85] Quantifications over infinite or unsurveyable domains are examples of cases where, for the sentences used, there is no effective procedure for determining whether their truth-conditions are satisfied. For any given such sentence we might discover a way of recognizing whether its truth-condition is satisfied; but that is not the point. The point is that for any such sentence 'we cannot equate a capacity to recognise the satisfaction or non-satisfaction of the condition for the sentence to be true with a knowledge of what that condition is,' because

> by hypothesis, either the condition is one which may obtain in some cases in which we are incapable of recognising the fact, or it is one which may fail to obtain in some cases in which we are incapable of recognising that fact, or both: hence a knowledge of what it is for that condition to hold or not to hold, while it may demand an ability to recognise one or another state of affairs whenever we are in a position to do so, cannot be exhaustively explained in terms of that ability. In fact, whenever the condition for the truth of a sentence is one that we have no way of bringing ourselves to recognise as obtaining whenever it obtains, it seems plain that there is no content to an ascription of implicit knowledge of what that condition is, since there is no practical ability by means of which such knowledge may be manifested.[86]

The problem here concerns the theory of sense, conceived as the 'shell' around a theory of reference (a theory of truth) constituting the 'core' theory. It is the task of a theory of sense, as noted, to relate the core theory to the speaker's mastery of his language. What the speaker learns, in learning his language, is a practice; and part of that practice is the acknowledgement of sentences as true or false. What the speaker knows, in knowing his language, must be manifestable in his practice; but 'knowing the condition which has to obtain for a sentence to be true is not anything which [the speaker] does, nor something of which anything he does is the direct manifestation'.[87] So, although in some cases we can ascribe knowledge of truth-conditions to speakers, in crucial cases we cannot; and consequently we 'fail to attain a genuinely explanatory account' of a speaker's language-mastery.[88] This is Dummett's chief point against theories of meaning based on a realist or transcendent notion of truth.

The task in hand, to repeat, is to answer the questions: what is it to know the truth-conditions of a sentence? Is truth the right choice of key concept for the theory of meaning? Dummett suggests that, to make further progress in replying, we need to clarify what is involved in ascribing truth to statements. Doing so involves a detour.

Consider the principle (call it 'principle C'): 'If a statement is true, there must be something in virtue of which it is true'.[89] Principle C underlies the correspondence theory of truth, and it is regulative, in the sense that having chosen our notion of truth for various classes of statements, we conclude from that to the nature of reality (that is, we do not first settle what there is in the world and then settle what, on that basis, makes statements true; but the other way round). In Dummett's view, the force of C is felt when we consider apparent violations of it, as, for example, with counterfactuals alleged to be true despite there being nothing we should accept as grounds for their truth. He cites the example of theological claims about the behaviour of free-willed beings whom God might have created, but chose not to, because He knew how they would behave if created. One might object to such a notion on the grounds that there is nothing that could make the counterfactual true; and what the objection comes down to is a claim that a counterfactual cannot be 'barely true', that is, cannot be true unless there is some other statement, not involving the subjunctive conditional, in virtue of which it is true.[90]

Why should anyone think that a counterfactual might be barely true? Presumably because he thinks it is logically necessary that either it or its negation should be true, without there having to be grounds, of the kind we usually base assertions of counterfactuals upon, for either's truth. Now, it would be mistaken to think that all pairs of counterfactuals are determinately either true or false, but we are disposed to think some pairs are so, because we readily equate the truth of certain ordinary statements with the truth of certain associated subjunctive conditionals. Consider for example the case of ascribing abilities to people. Suppose we say of someone who has never learned any language but his own, 'Michael is good at learning languages'. (Call this statement 'A'.) There are three possible attitudes to the question 'must A be either true or false?': (i) It does not have to be either; (ii) linguistic ability must correlate with or consist in some feature of brain structure, whether or not we know what it is; Michael either does or does not have that feature; therefore A must be either true or false, even if we cannot know which; and (iii) linguistic ability need not depend on brain structure, but people either have or fail to have it none the less, so statement A must be either true or false. Upholders of all of (i)–(iii) agree that the truth-value of A depends upon the truth-value of the associated subjunctive conditional (call it 'B'): 'if Michael were to try learning a language, he would easily succeed', A being true if B is, false if B is false; so the question 'must B be either true or false?' coincides with the question whether the law of bivalence holds for A itself. Upholders of (iii) are committed to believing that B is barely true, if true; upholders of (ii) maintain bivalence for A but, disliking the idea that counterfactuals can be barely true, make A's truth depend on another statement, one which says something about brain structure. Upholders of (i) share with upholders of (iii) the belief that there need be nothing that determines A's truth-value, and with upholders of (ii) they share a dislike of allowing bare truth to counterfactuals; so 'they escape the dilemma by rejecting the law of bivalence'.[91]

Many expressions in our language are introduced by reference to conditionals, including every expression for testable properties and measurable quantities. We regard tests and measurements as revealing how things are in themselves, and proceed therefore to assume that property- or quantity-ascribing sentences are determinately true, independently of whether relevant tests and measurements were or could be carried out. In assuming this, 'we are adopting a realistic attitude to the property or quantity in question', which shows how 'the notion of truth we take as governing our statements determines, via the principle C, how we regard reality as constituted. We may, in fact, characterize realism concerning a given class of statements as the assumption that each statement of that class is determinately either true or false'.[92] Accordingly, theses (ii) and (iii) are different versions of realism about human abilities, and (i) is a rejection of such realism.

Thesis (ii) is a reductionist thesis. Reductionism need not be a strong thesis requiring that statements of one class, call it M, must be translatable into statements of another class, call it R; it need only be the thesis that the truth-value of M statements is related to that of R statements, like this: for any statement A in M, there is a family $\bar{A}$ of sets of statements in R such that, for A to be true, it is necessary and sufficient that some set in the family of statements $\bar{A}$ be true.[93] On such a notion of reducibility, 'bare truth' can be characterized thus: a statement A is barely true if (a) A is true and (b) there is no class of statements, not containing A or trivial variations of it, to which any class containing A can be reduced. While (ii) represents a reductionist realism, (iii) is a naïve realism; 'naïve realism' is a thesis which, for a given class of statements *M, combines realism concerning *M with the notion that the statements in *M are barely true (that is, there is no other class of statements to which statements in *M can be reduced). 'Our view of the constitution of reality – our metaphysical position – depends', says Dummett, 'on which are the classes of statements of which we take a realist view'.[94]

We can now, at last, see what is involved in ascribing to a speaker knowledge of a sentence's truth-conditions. If a sentence s is usable to make statements not capable of bare truth, then any utterance of s is true only if there is a class of statements, R, the members of some appropriate subset of which are true. Grasp of s's truth-conditions will depend on an implicit grasp of how s's truth relates to that subset of R. This relation could be displayed in the truth theory (the theory of reference): if the theory is expressed in a metalanguage which is an extension of the object language, the (T)-sentence for s will be non-trivial (will not have s on the right-hand-side of the biconditional). Alternatively, if there is an obstacle to giving a translation of s in the object-language, the theory of sense (which explains what a speaker's grasp of the truth theory consists in) will have to make the dependence of s on R explicit. Either way, there is nothing problematic about the notion of a grasp of s's truth-conditions here.

However, where s can be used to say something barely true, the associated (T)-sentence will be trivial; so in this case the theory of sense takes the whole burden of explaining a speaker's grasp of s's truth-conditions. The model we use in such cases is the reporting of observations; if someone is able to tell, by looking, that one tree is taller than another, then he knows what it is for one tree to be taller than another, and therefore knows what condition must be satisfied for the truth of 'this tree is taller than that tree'.[95] There are therefore two basic models for explaining what it is to grasp truth-conditions. One model, unproblematically, concerns possession of explicit knowledge, that is, the ability to state the condition for any s's truth; but this model will not serve, for the reasons given earlier, if we wish to base a theory of meaning on the idea of a grasp of truth-conditions. The other model concerns the possession of a capacity to recognize whether or not a sentence is true.

But this does not go far enough, because there are plenty of cases where we cannot settle a sentence's truth-value.[96]

In Dummett's view, we come to think of our mastery of effectively undecidable sentences (for example, counterfactuals, references to inaccessible regions of space–time, and so forth) by means of a sometimes surreptitious, sometimes explicit, appeal to the observational model. That is, we 'try to convince ourselves that our understanding of what it is for undecidable sentences to be true consists in our grasp of what it would be to be able to use such sentences to give direct reports of observation'.[97] We cannot give such reports, of course, but we know what powers a superhuman observer would require in such cases; accordingly we tacitly assume that our understanding of the truth-conditions of undecidable sentences consists in our knowing what powers a superhuman observer would need. This line of thought is associated with another regulative principle, to be set alongside principle C, governing the concept of truth: 'If a statement is true, it must be in principle possible to know that it is true.' (Call this 'principle K'.) C and K are closely related, because if nothing could count as knowledge of the truth of a given statement, how could there be anything that makes it true? Thus 'even the most thorough-going realist must grant that we could hardly be said to grasp what it is for a statement to be true if we had no conception whatever of how it might be known to be true'.[98] So the realist is obliged to extend the observational model (that is, the model for decidable sentences) to cover the case of undecidable sentences.

This account is offered as a 'diagnosis' by Dummett of the motives we have for extending the idea of grasp of truth-conditions at the primitive level, to supposed grasp of truth-conditions at less primitive levels of language. But these motives do not justify that extension; therefore employment of a transcendent concept of truth 'fails to answer the question how we come to be able to assign to our sentences a meaning which is dependent upon a use to which we are unable to put them'.[99] In fact, such an account is indistinguishable from one which has it that 'we treat certain of our sentences as if their use resembled that of other sentences in certain respects in which it in fact does not; that is, that we systematically misunderstand our own language'.[100]

Dummett asked 'whether the concept of truth is the right choice for the central notion of a theory of meaning . . . or whether we need to employ some other notion in this role'. On the basis of the foregoing, the answer is that realistically-conceived truth is the wrong choice An alternative is required; what should it be?

The Anti-realist Alternative

The difficulties identified in the preceding section arose from our assuming a realistic interpretation of all sentences of our language – that is, the difficulty arose from our assuming that all statements, made by use of those sentences, are determinately either true or false, independently of whether we can know them to be so; which makes us 'unable to equate an ability to recognise when a statement has been established as true or false with a knowledge of its truth-condition'.[101]

The solution is to abandon the idea of knowledge-transcendent truth, and to fashion a semantics formulated in other terms.[102] There is, in Dummett's view, a prototype available for such a semantics. It is the intuitionist account of the meaning of mathematical statements, in which the fundamental idea is that an understanding of such statements rests on our being able to recognize, with respect to any mathematical construction, whether or not it constitutes a proof of a given statement. Thus the assertion of a mathematical statement is not to be interpreted as a claim that the statement is true, but as a claim that there is a proof of it. Correlatively, one understands any mathematical expression if one knows how it contributes to determining what counts as a proof of any statement in which it occurs. It is thereby guaranteed that a grasp of any mathematical expression is fully manifestable in the use of mathematical language.[103]

This does not mean that every intelligible statement must be effectively decidable. Understanding a statement consists, not in being able to find, but in being able to recognize, a proof when one is offered; and understanding the negation of a statement similarly consists not in finding, but in being able to recognize, a proof of the negation. Since the intelligibility of statements does not guarantee that we have a decision procedure for them, our understanding of them consists in an ability to recognize proofs when they are found. (It follows that the Law of Excluded Middle is not generally valid for mathematical statements.)[104]

Dummett holds that this theory 'generalises readily to the non-mathematical case. Proof is the sole means which exists in mathematics for establishing a statement as true: the required *general* notion is, therefore, that of *verification*.[105] On such a view, understanding a statement consists in being able to recognize what establishes it as true. This does not mean that we must have, in every case, a way of deciding the truth-value of statements; it means only that we must be able to recognize, when it happens, that the truth of a statement is established. The advantage here is that verification-conditions, unlike realistically-conceived truth-conditions, are such that we have to be credited with an ability to recognize when they obtain; 'hence there is no difficulty in stating what an implicit knowledge of such a condition consists in, for it is directly displayed by our linguistic practice'.[106]

If one is tempted by this verificationist alternative certain points have to be kept in mind. One is that such a theory must take account of holistic considerations. Quine argued against the (positivist) idea that verification of a sentence consists in the occurrence of sense-experiences.[107] This applies only to sentences on the periphery, in Quine's metaphor, of the 'web' of language, where the world impinges on language; in the case of the sentences deeper in the web, inferential procedures will be involved in verification, with mathematical theorems forming a limiting case because they involve only inference. Thus there will be a coherence flavour to the verification of non-peripheral sentences, since the relevant procedures will involve recognizing their connections.[108]

Another point is that the theory generalizes to language from intuitionistically-conceived mathematics, and therefore the differences between language and mathematics must be remarked. One difference is that in mathematics the notion of understanding a statement does not involve both an ability to recognize a proof of it and an ability to recognize a refutation of it, for the theory provides a uniform way of explaining negation. There is no such analogous procedure for language; so the meaning of a sentence has to be regarded as given by the simultaneous provision of means for recognizing both its verification and its falsification, under the constraint that a sentence cannot be both verified and falsified at once. There are other differences, but in general 'all will,' says Dummett, 'remain within the spirit of a verificationist theory of meaning, so long as the meaning of each sentence is given by specifying what is to be taken as conclusively establishing a statement made by means of it, and what conclusively falsifying such a statement, and so long as this is done systematically in terms only of conditions which a speaker is capable of recognising'.[109]

Adopting verificationism does not exclude the concept of truth, which remains important because it is needed to give an account of deductive inference, recognized as valid just in case it is truth-preserving. In any theory of meaning, the dependence of the sense of sentences upon their structure will manifest what we consider to be the most direct way of establishing their truth; but the theory must also take into account not only the fact that many statements are asserted on inconclusive grounds, but also that there are indirect ways of conclusively establishing the truth of statements – the conclusions of deductive inferences exemplify this. The notion of a statement's truth is thus needed to allow the possibility of there being conclusive but indirect procedures for establishing statements; and evidently, such a notion cannot be equated with verification.[110] Dummett concedes that it is not easy to explain what account should be given of truth under verificationism; all we know is that it must be explained in terms of our capacity to recognize statements as true, and not in terms of conditions which transcend human capacities.[111]

Anti-Realism: Some Objections and Defences

One objection to Dummett's anti-realist proposal is that it is revisionary. If we abandon realistically-conceived truth, it seems necessary to frame our semantic theory in a way that involves abandonment of classical logic. Our ordinary practice is to accept classical forms of inference; so a theory that demands the substitution of an alternative logic will not be purely descriptive of our linguistic practice. This would seem to be a weakness in the anti-realist alternative, because it is quite clear that if we have competing but equally viable theories, the conservative theory is the preferable one. However 'we have no ground,' says Dummett, 'to assume in advance that our language is in every way perfectly in order'.[112] Frege held that many features of natural language – vagueness, vacuous singular terms – render it impossible to devise a coherent semantics for it as it stands; Tarski held that the semantic closedness of natural language generates inconsistency. Their apprehensions about natural language suggest that language might require adjustment, which in turn implies the possibility that conventionally recognized principles of inference might need to be reassessed. 'There can be no guarantee,' Dummett says, 'that a complex of linguistic practices which has grown up by a piecemeal historical evolution in response to needs felt in practical communication will conform to any systematic theory'.[113]

The charge of revisionism is thus not so damaging, and in any case, as noted earlier, Davidson's variety of a truth-conditional semantics is itself revisionary, requiring some 'tidying up' of natural language.

Another objection is offered by McGinn,[114] who fastens on an admission by Dummett that a global anti-realism might be impossible. 'There are,' Dummett says:

> a number of reasons for doubting whether global anti-realism is coherent, for instance, behaviourism is one species of anti-realism, namely the rejection of realism concerning mental states and processes; phenomenalism is another species, namely the rejection of realism concerning physical objects and processes; it immediately occurs to us to wonder whether it is possible to consistently maintain an anti-realist position simultaneously in both regards.[115]

McGinn argues that the species of anti-realism mentioned by Dummett are jointly inconsistent; that anti-realism in either case coupled with realism in the other is likewise inconsistent; and that therefore the only alternative is to be a realist in both. His argument is as follows.

Let statements about material objects and statements about mental events be called, respectively, 'M-statements' and 'P-statements'. (This usage recalls Strawson's talk, in *Individuals*, of 'material predicates' and 'person predicates'.) According to McGinn, anti-realism about M- and P-statements is the view that they possess their truth-values 'in virtue of the truth-value of statements drawn from certain other classes of statements not trivially different from the given (statements)'.[116] An anti-realist attitude to M-statements can be characterized as *phenomenalism*, and anti-realism about P-statements, *behaviourism*.[117] Thus M- and P-statements are subject to a reductive thesis, to this effect: a sentence s of a given class K is reducible to (is true in virtue of) some sentence s' of a class R if and only if, necessarily, s is true (or false) just in case s' is true (or false); it is a logically necessary and sufficient condition for a sentence of K to be true that some sentence, or set of sentences, of R be true.[118] The reductive anti-realist theses in question have it that M-statements are true or false according to the truth-value of statements about experiences (call them E-statements), and P-statements likewise according to the truth-value of statements about behaviour (call them B-statements.) E- and B-statements are the 'basal statements' for M- and

P-statements respectively,[119] and therefore are those statements which are *barely true*.[120] The first step in McGinn's argument is then to say that phenomenalism and behaviourism cannot be jointly affirmed; they

> offer competing proposals concerning which statements comprise the basal truths: phenomenalism takes E-statements, a subclass of P-statements, as basic, while behaviourism takes B-statements, a subclass of M-statements, as basic . . . Since a statement that is basal for one anti-realism is derivative for the other, it is plain enough that a vicious regress is generated by the conjunction of the two doctrines; and this, of course, effectively frustrates the reductive ambitions definitive of each anti-realist thesis.[121]

The next step is to see whether an anti-realist attitude towards either class of statements, conjoined with a realist attitude to the other, is feasible.

The answer, according to McGinn, is that neither conjunction is feasible, because of the 'independence thesis'. This is the 'fundamental thesis of realism',[122] and has it that M-facts are not reducible to (that is, are independent of) E-facts, and P-facts are not reducible to B-facts. For realism precisely consists in a commitment to the view that there can be recognition-transcendent facts; therefore, in realist terms, it is possible for M-facts to obtain without there being any experiences of their obtaining, which is to say that it is not necessary for the truth of any M-statement that some E-statement be true. Moreover, since no set of E-statements ever entails the truth of an M-statement, it is also not a sufficient condition for the truth of an M-statement that some related E-statement be true. And similarly for P- and B-statements.[123]

This independence of M- from E-statements, and P- from B-statements, cuts both ways; to say that an E-fact is not necessary for an M-fact is to say that the latter is not sufficient for the former, and to say that the former is not sufficient for the latter is to say that the latter is not necessary for the former. Thus the independence is symmetrical, and 'implies realism as much one way as the other'.[124] 'So,' says McGinn,

> it begins to seem that realism about M- and P-statements implies realism about E- and B-statements, under the independence formulation. But now E- and B-facts are just subclasses of P- and M-facts, respectively; and if we are prepared to admit these in unreduced realist fashion, there can be no objection of general principle to admitting the rest.[125]

The central point in McGinn's argument is his characterization of anti-realism as reductionism. This is a mistake. One does not have to hold to any variety of reductionism to be an anti-realist and since this is so, the apparent difficulty evaporates.[126]

The motive for regarding reductionism as a 'touchstone of whether one adopts or repudiates a realistic interpretation'[127] is that it frequently presages a further move, namely, the observation that there may be no statements of the reducing class which determine that some statement of the given class is either true or false. Realizing this is a motive for rejecting realism; but although this is a familiar way of making the point, it is not the only way. For, accepting a reductive thesis for some class of statements does not inevitably lead to rejection of realism for that class. One has to look at cases. For example, anyone who holds that if a statement ascribing a mental state to someone is true, then it is so in virtue of his neurophysiological states, is likely to place a realist construction on the mental-state-ascribing statement. Conversely, rejecting realism does not require prior commitment to reductionism, for one might hold that a recognition-transcendent concept of truth does not apply to the given class of statements, and that it is irreducible.[128]

In Dummett's view, all four combinations are possible: (1) one may take a realistic view of a class of statements, and yet regard it as subject to reducibility ('sophisticated realism'); or (2) one may construe the class realistically but deny its reducibility ('naïve realism'). Again, (3) one may deny realism of a class of statements because of a reductionist thesis ('reductive anti-realism'); or (4) one may deny realism with respect to the class while holding it to be irreducible ('outright anti-realism').[129]

The term 'reductionism' itself has to be handled with care, for it often means the thesis not just that the truth-values of statements in a given class depend on the truth-values of statements in the reducing class, but that it is at least in principle possible that the former be translatable into the latter without remainder. Now, one may accept some form of reductionism without being a reductionist in this strong sense. For one thing, one may hold some kind of reductive thesis and also hold that statements of the reducing class are unintelligible independently of those in the given class. Or, one might take it that there is no way of settling which statements of the reducing class determine, either way, the truth-value of some statement in the given class. Or again, one might hold either or both of the views that the truth-value of a statement in the given class depends upon those of an infinite set of statements in the reducing class, or, alternatively, involves the truth of only one out of an infinite number of statements in the reducing class – so that, in either case or in both together, translation might be impossible.[130]

These considerations show that it is insufficient to define anti-realism with respect to M- and P-statements as reductive theses without qualification (McGinn says, 'the reductive ambitions definitive of each anti-realist thesis'), since it is open to an anti-realist to advance one or another construal of the reductions, or no construal at all; and either way his doing so will affect the account to be given of the relation between the two classes of statements in question. In any case, there appears to be an allied manoeuvre which undercuts the debate.[131] This is to observe that phenomenalists, for example, have not always construed E-statements as a subclass of P-statements, as in the case of Russell's 'neutral monism', in which sense-data, as the fundamental atoms of the universe, are constituents of both material objects and mental events. Different orderings among statements as to which are basic and which dependent remove the appearance of conflict McGinn identifies; again it depends on cases. Such thoughts suggest that an anti-realist is not without resource as to a global version of his views.

Moreover – a point McGinn admits – scepticism is invited by the 'independence thesis' essential to realism. Scepticism turns on the observation that there at least appears to be a gap between M- and P-statements and the evidence we have for asserting them, such that possession even of the best evidence for the assertion of either is consistent with its falsity. Realism premisses the existence of this gap. On an anti-realist view, by contrast, the sense of M- and P-statements is constituted by their relation to the evidence relevant to asserting them; so the sceptical gap is closed. This seems a very good reason for preferring the anti-realist account.[132]

A final, but very important, point: in early statements of his views Dummett frequently characterized realism about a given class of statements as the thesis that the principle of bivalence holds for that class. He also stated that realism is the thesis that statements in a given class have their truth-values independently of our capacity to recognize what they are. He equated these two theses. Now, it is clear that anyone committed to bivalence will ipso facto be committed to the view that the truth-conditions of some sentences will be recognition-transcendent; but it has been pointed out by McDowell that the converse does not hold.[133] Following Wright, let us call someone who holds the principle of bivalence a 'classical realist', and one who holds that truth value can be recognition-transcendent a 'bare realist'.[134] Then McDowell's view is that the bare realist is not, at least obviously, committed to classical realism, even though the classical realist's position commits him to bare realism as well. In McDowell's view, noting that such a separation can be made between bare and classical realism allows for the possibility that the anti-realist's reservations about bivalence can be conceded, while preserving the workability of a realist conception of sense in which recognition-transcendent truth plays a role.

This is not, however, a problem for the anti-realist position. For one thing, despite the apparent independence of bare from classical realism, it is difficult to see what a bare realist would wish to object to in classical realism, since it is more than merely consistent with his position, but offers a powerful way of unpacking what the bare realist means in talking of recognition-transcendent truth. Nevertheless, what the anti-realist objects to in classical realism is precisely its bare realist core; that is the ultimate target. Dummett's attack lies chiefly there.

The Problem of the Past

A question that sharply points the conflict between realist and anti-realist attitudes to meaning, and which introduces refinements into our understanding of both positions, concerns statements about the past. A realist regards such statements as true or false whether or not we know or can come to know which, and an anti-realist denies this. A consideration of the debate brings features of both positions into focus.

It is clear from the foregoing that Dummett's two main arguments consist in challenges to the realist to explain, first, how a speaker could acquire his language if doing so depends upon forming a conception of what it is for recognition-transcendent states-of-affairs to obtain, and secondly, what counts as a manifestation of the speaker's implicit knowledge of his language if that knowledge involves conceptions of what it transcends his capacities to know. Call the first the 'acquisition challenge', the second the 'manifestation challenge'. This latter is the more fundamental. If anti-realism rested only on the acquisition challenge, then if a realist could show that his view of language-understanding is independently the best on offer, we should have to rest content with the mystery of how such understanding is achieved. The manifestation challenge, however, directly unseats the realist. This is demonstrated by the arguments reported in the last but one section.

Nevertheless the acquisition challenge remains important, especially in tandem with the manifestation challenge, since one way of showing what it is to have (to manifest possession of) a concept is to show what goes into acquiring it. Dummett's arguments for anti-realism about statements about the past rest on this point.

The anti-realist argument about the past goes as follows.[135] We learn the use of past-tense statements by learning what justifies assertion of them. For example, we remember a certain event, and our early training in the use of the past tense includes learning how past-tense statements work as expressions of memories. There can be no leap from what goes into understanding such statements to a notion of what it would be for such statements to be true independently of anything that could now or later justify their assertion. So the only notion of truth for past-tense statements that we could have acquired in learning how to use them, is a notion that coincides with that of conditions for justifiably asserting them. 'What we learn to do,' Dummett says, 'is to accept . . . the occurrence of certain conditions which we have been trained to recognise, as conclusively justifying the assertion of a given statement [about the past, and] certain other conditions as conclusively justifying its denial. In the very nature of the case, we could not possibly have come to understand what it would be for the statement to be true independently of that which we have learned to treat as establishing its truth; there was simply no means by which we could be shown this'.[136]

The thesis Dummett ascribes to the realist is 'truth-value link realism', which has it that a past-tense statement uttered now is true if and only if an appropriate present-tense statement uttered at that past time would have been true at that time. The realist claims that our understanding (our being able to use) past-tense statements rests on our understanding of the truth-value link. The anti-realist – as Dummett grants – has to concede that the notion of a truth-value link is 'a fundamental feature of our understanding of tensed statements', so that denying it, or arguing that it involves an incoherence, would amount to the claim that our use of tensed statements is incoherent.[137] But he resists the temptation to conclude, from the role the truth-value link plays, that past-tense statements, made now, are 'true in virtue of some past fact, if "past fact" means something other than that by means of which we can recognise the statement as true'.[138]

One can see the crux of the dispute in terms of certain models. 'What the realist would like to do', says Dummett, 'is to stand in thought outside the whole temporal process and describe the world from a point which has no temporal position at all'; from this point of privilege the realist wishes to survey time 'in a single glance', regarding different points of time as standing in an order of precedence among themselves, with the privileged point of temporal description having no relation to any of them.[139] The anti-realist, by contrast, 'takes more seriously the fact that we are immersed in time: being so immersed, we cannot frame any description of the world as it would appear to one who is not in time'.[140] It is tempting – but misleading – to characterize the respective positions like this: the anti-realist says the past 'exists only in the traces it has left upon the present', whereas for the realist 'the past still exists as past, just as it was when present'; which is why, in his view, describing things 'as they actually are in themselves' will involve treating all points of time alike, detached from the particular perspective which an observer, immersed in time, is obliged to take.[141] In Dummett's view, the anti-realist considerations are faithful to the fact that we are temporal creatures; the realist thesis, on the other hand, seems inadequate to account for our mastery of tensed statements.

It would seem natural for a realist to respond by defending the notion of truth-value links, taken together with his defining acceptance of the recognition-transcendence of the truth-conditions of statements in the class of statements which are in part understood by means of them. McDowell's reply to Dummett does not however do so. Rather, he rejects the intelligibility of truth-value links as well as anti-realism; and offers instead a middle way as the correct account.[142]

On this view, a 'link-realist', trying to respect the anti-realist view that speakers could only have learned the use of certain statements by having appropriate circumstances available to them in training, accepts that truth-conditions are inaccessible. But he does so by refusing to allow that the circumstances available to trainees are truth-conditions of the utterances they are learning to make. That is, the link-realist distinguishes between assertibility-conditions and truth-conditions; allows that the former, but not the latter, must be available in training; and thus views the obtaining of truth-condition as 'something which, in itself, transcends what is accessible to awareness'.[143] But such link-realism is, McDowell says, 'impotent' to do what its upholders require of it.

To see why, it is first useful to note the similarity between statements about the past and those about other minds. Another's pain, on a link-realist view, is essentially concealed from us behind a screen of behaviour. Others' behaviour might count among the circumstances available to a trainee in learning how to ascribe mental states to them, but it does not constitute the truth-conditions of mental-state ascriptions. Here, as with the past, the truth-conditions are inaccessible.[144] Now, it is precisely the anti-realist's point that inaccessible states-of-affairs cannot enter into an explanation of language mastery. The link-realist replies: 'You can see how a person can have the idea of what it is for someone to be in pain – when the someone in question is himself. So, the sentence "he is in pain" uttered in circumstances which fix a reference for the pronoun "he", is to be understood as saying, of that other person, that he is in the very same state.'[145] And the account of past-tense statements is similar. 'You can see', the link-realist says, 'what it is for rain to be falling. Well, a sentence like "it *was* raining" is understood as saying that that very circumstance obtained at some past time.'[146] In effect, some kind of 'projection' of understanding is effected by means of the truth-value link.

McDowell's objection to link-realism is that, far from solving the problem posed by the anti-realist, it simply ignores it. If someone cannot see how the past obtaining of some circumstance enters into the meaning of a statement, or cannot see how another's unrecognizably being in pain enters into the meaning of some form of words, his doubts will not be settled by the bare claim that past circumstances, or others' mental states, enter into their meaning. Yet this is all that the link-realist offers.

If link-realism and anti-realism were the only competitors, in McDowell's view, anti-realism would win. But there is another option, a species of realism which meets the anti-realist challenge without appeal to truth-value links.[147] This middle-way realism ('M-realism' for short) is as follows.

M-realism differs from link-realism in having it that satisfaction of the truth-conditions of past-tense and other-minds statements is sometimes available to us; and it differs from anti-realism in having it that we understand the possibility that both kinds of statements can be true in virtue of the obtaining of states-of-affairs which are inaccessible to us. (This 'bare realist' commitment to a statement's being true in virtue of recognition-transcendent circumstances is of course what makes M-realism, distinctively, realism; see above.[148]) So McDowell characterizes the M-realist view of other-ascriptions of sensation as follows: 'what warrants the assertion that another is in pain, on one of the relevant occasions, is the detectable obtaining of the circumstance of that person's being in pain: an instance of a kind of circumstance – another person's being in pain – which is available to awareness, in its own right and not merely through behavioural proxies, on some occasions, including this one, although, on other occasions, the obtaining of other instances can be quite beyond detection.[149] Similarly, M-realism about the past is the view that 'what warrants the assertion, on one of the relevant occasions, that, say, some event of a specified kind occurred in the past, is the obtaining of a circumstance which consists simply in such an event's having occurred: an instance of a kind of circumstance which is available to awareness, in its own right and not merely through traces going proxy for it, on some occasions, including this one, although, on other occasions, the obtaining of other instances can be quite outside our reach.[150]

Essential to M-realism, as this shows, is the idea that the generally non-effectively decidable truth-conditions for the kinds of statements in question can on occasion be accessible to us, which thereby permits a genuinely bare-realist conception of what it is for those truth-conditions to be satisfied. The M-realist says: the circumstances which justify the making of assertions are of a kind which are sometimes available to awareness and which are sometimes not available to awareness; 'thus [the M-realist] enables himself to think of [these circumstances] as actually being truth-conditions, realistically conceived'.[151] The link-realist represented truth-conditions as wholly inaccessible; the anti-realist demands that the assertion-justifying circumstances in question must be available to awareness whenever they obtain; the M-realist steers a middle course, satisfying the anti-realist's acquisition challenge while remaining a realist. For he concedes that to learn how to use sentences of the relevant kinds, the trainee must have access to circumstances which justify use of those sentences; but he holds that those circumstances are the truth-conditions of those sentences, and are such that although sometimes accessible, they often are not; and so the notion of recognition-transcendent truth-conditions is retained, and with it a distinctively realist approach to meaning.

Moreover, not only does M-realism meet the acquisition challenge, McDowell claims, it meets the manifestation challenge too. This challenge, to repeat, is that since linguistic competence is a practical capacity, it should be observable in linguistic behaviour. Dummett requires that it be exhaustively so manifestable. On McDowell's view, the challenge is reasonable, so long as the 'exhaustively' is dropped; a conception of the circumstances constituting the truth-conditions of given sentences manifests itself on those occasions when linguistic behaviour is a response to their occurrence when detectable, even though in general such circumstances are not detectable. The conception of 'appropriate circumstances' is that of a kind of circumstance; the M-realist 'claims the right to ascribe [possession of the conception of utterance-justifying circumstances] on the basis of behaviour construable as a response to some instances of the kind, in spite of the admitted fact that other instances, on his view, are incapable of eliciting any response from the possessor of the conception'.[152]

Is McDowell fair to link-realism, and does his M-realism succeed in meeting the anti-realist's acquisition and manifestation challenges? Wright thinks not. In his view McDowell is unfair to link-realism in several ways, the chief of which is his holding that a link-realist cannot without embarrassment acknowledge what the M-realist holds, namely that we can, on occasion, non-inferentially see that certain circumstances obtain. The link-realist invokes truth-value links because he holds that the truth-conditions of the given kinds of statements are inaccessible, and therefore he holds that understanding such statements involves a 'projection' into the past or other minds by means of the link. But even on an M-realist view, in which sometimes-accessible circumstances are admitted, there has to be just such projection; for the trainee has to advance from cases where assertions are justified by detectable circumstances to those where the circumstances are undetectable. Is this not precisely the place for a truth-value link to make such projection intelligible? If it is supposed, on M-realist lines, that observing certain kinds of evidence (say, a grimace together with a bleeding wound) is observing that another is in pain, how does one bridge the gap from such a case to, say, understanding that stoicism is possible?[153]

So it seems a mistake to assume that appeal to truth-value links *presupposes* that the truth-conditions of the kinds of statements in question are always recognition-transcendent. McDowell thinks this, and therefore repudiates link-realism. But the appeal to links presupposes only that there is no essential connection between the realization of those conditions, on the one hand, and on the other hand a speaker's ability to recognize that they are realized. But this presupposition is, as Wright observes, 'exactly the characteristic belief of bare realism'; and accordingly link-realism and M-realism are closer than McDowell supposes. This reduces the advantage McDowell claims for M-realism.[154]

It is important to see how extensive the class of statements is, whose truth-conditions can, in the M-realist view, be available to awareness on some occasions. McDowell talks of circumstances which are available 'in their own right' and not via 'proxies', that is, which are non-inferentially available. Such a view is consistent with a notion of criteria in Wittgenstein's sense; criteria are not symptoms or traces from which some state-of-affairs can be inferred, nor are they truth-conditions, for they are defeasible – in the sense that one can recognize that criteria are present (facial expression, bleeding wound) for the ascription of pain, and yet one can also recognize that there may be no pain present (the person displaying the pain-behaviour might be acting).[155] A notion of criteria has certain advantages over an M-realist notion of 'available truth-conditions', for the claims we make on a criterial basis can be withdrawn consistently with our still holding that the criteria were satisfied. The M-realist, therefore, has to maintain not just that inference via proxies is not always involved when use of a statement is justified, but, more strongly, that those occasions best suited to teaching use of such a statement involve more than mere satisfaction of criteria – they must involve the actual realization of truth-conditions; for if this were not so, experience of the relevant circumstances would be experience of circumstances whose occurrence is consistent with the falsity of the statement whose use is being learned.[156]

This suggests that M-realists are committed to believing that there can be situations in which someone is indefeasibly warranted in claiming something about the past or other minds. But this is implausible; how can an indefeasible warrant ever be claimed for contingent statements, given that we are always open to errors of judgement, perception or understanding? One would be better advised either to give up the M-realist idea that truth-conditions can obtain detectably, or to construct an account of what it is for them to obtain detectably which does not involve our being indefeasibly certain of the statement whose truth-conditions they are.[157]

An account of this latter kind might be modelled on the fact that some classes of statements – for example, effectively decidable mathematical statements – are such that there is a procedure one can follow that, if it is correctly followed, settles the correctness of the statement.[158] But what we arrive at in these cases is not indefeasible certainty; not because we lack access to the truth-value-conferring circumstances, but because it is in general not possible for us to be sure that we have indeed implemented the procedures perfectly – that is, without perceptual, ratiocinative, or other kinds of error infecting it.[159]

At any rate, on this model, the notion of 'detectably obtaining truth-conditions' is the notion that there is a procedure available for deciding the statement whose truth-conditions they are. Now, a clear case of statements for which there cannot be detectably obtaining truth-conditions as thus specified, is the class of *unrestrictedly* generally quantified statements about matters-of-fact. For whatever procedures we carry out here, it is always consistent with our best efforts that we may form an incorrect opinion of their truth-value. And the trouble is that statements about the past and other minds fall into this very category.[160]

Because this is so, the M-realist is faced with a serious difficulty. On his account, learning the use of statements whose truth-conditions in general transcend our capacity to recognize whether they obtain, is meant to be based on occasions when they happen to obtain detectably. But if there is no indefeasible warrant available to the learner on such occasions, not only is it unclear what his grasp of the statement's truth-conditions consists in, but he has still somehow to make a link-realist-like leap of projection to the non-detectable cases.

Other considerations reinforce this point. Replying to the manifestation challenge, McDowell says it is unreasonable to demand that the knowledge underwriting a speaker's practical competence with his language should be exhaustively manifestable; it is, he says, enough that the speaker should manifest his knowledge on occasions when he has the chance to do so. But this says that the M-realist (a) credits speakers with recognitional capacities they may, if it so happens, never get the opportunity to display; and at the same time (b) credits speakers with an understanding of what it is for truth-conditions to obtain undetectably. McDowell's response to the manifestation challenge comes down, in effect, to the equation of (a) and (b). But in Wright's view, McDowell has not made out a case for this equation. On the M-realist arguments presented, the most that can be done is attribution of (a) to speakers; yet what the anti-realist demands by way of the manifestation challenge is a justification for (b).[161] In other words, the problem of the projection from (a) to (b) remains unsolved.

The M-realist response to the acquisition challenge fares no better. It turns, once again, on there being detectable obtainings of truth-conditions; but it is still left unclear how the learner gets from them to undetectable cases. Wright offers this example: suppose you are a language learner. You are confronted with a number of different cases in which another person grimaces, groans and bleeds; and you are told that in each case the person is in pain. But now you are told that other people, who behave quite differently, are or may also be in pain. 'Wouldn't there be a temptation to think you had misunderstood the original examples, that the distinctive behaviour had nothing to do with being [in pain]?,' Wright asks, 'and if you were reassured about that, would you not then be constrained to think that the concept of being [in pain] had a breadth to it which the original examples had not made clear?'[162]

This debate induces much clarity in what is at issue in the stances under discussion. But there is reason to think that while the spotlight remains focused on meaning and understanding, certain considerations of importance remain unexplored. In particular, it might be asked whether it is correct to hold that what is fundamentally at issue in the debate between realists and anti-realists is truth and language-understanding. In the next chapter I offer reasons for thinking that it is not, and that different debates are run together as a result.

Notes

1 H. P. Grice, 'Meaning', *The Philosophical Review*, 1957, reprinted in R. M. Harnish (ed.), *Basic Topics in the Philosophy of Language*, p. 26, and *Studies in the Ways of Words*.

2 Grice, 'Meaning', *op. cit.*

3 Grice, ibid; P. F. Strawson, *Logico-Linguistic Papers*; S. Schiffer, *Meaning*.

4 Grice, ibid., pp. 105–9, D. Davidson, *Inquiries into Truth and Interpretation*, p. 111.

5 Grice, ibid., p. 94; Strawson, ibid.; Schiffer, ibid., pp. 17–18.

6 D. Lewis, 'Languages and Language' in K. Gunderson, (ed.), *Language, Mind and Knowledge*, pp. 164–6.

7 Grice, ibid., p. 127; see also M. Davies, *Meaning, Quantification, Necessity*, Ch. 1; S. Blackburn, *Spreading the Word*, Ch. 4; C. Peacocke, 'Truth Definitions and Actual Languages' in G. Evans, and J. McDowell, (eds), *Truth and Meaning*; Schiffer, *Meaning* Ch. 5.

8 Peacocke, ibid.; Davies, ibid.

9 Grice 'Logic and Conversation' in Harnish (ed.), *Basic Topics*.

10 Grice 'The Causal Theory of Perception' *Proceedings of the Aristotelian Society*, 35, 1961, reprinted in G. Warnock, (ed.), *The Philosophy of Perception*, pp. 85–112.

11   Cf. J. L. Austin, *Sense and Sensibilia*.
12   Cf. P. F. Strawson, *Introduction to Logical Theory*, pp. 80–92
13   Grice, 'The Causal Theory of Perception'.
14   Grice, 'Logic and Conversation' in R. Harnish (ed.), *Basic Topics*, pp. 61–5.
15   See esp. Davidson, *Inquiries*; Searle, 'Metaphor' in A. Ortony (ed.), *Metaphor and Thought*; D. Sperber and D. Wilson, 'Loose Talk', *Proceedings of the Aristotelian Society*, 86, 1986, reprinted in S. Davis (ed.), *Pragmatics: A Reader*.
16   For a different pragmatic approach to semantic theory see A. C. Grayling, 'Perfect Speaker Theory' in J. Hill and P. Kotatko (eds), *Karlovy Vary Studies in Reference and Meaning*, pp. 43–59.
17   G. Frege, *Grundgesetze der Arithmetik*, trans. as *The Basic Laws of Arithmetic*, 1. 32.
18   L. Wittgenstein, *Tractatus Logico-Philosophicus*, 4.024.
19   R. Carnap, *Meaning and Necessity*, p. 10.
20   D. Davidson, 'The Method of Truth in Metaphysics' in P. A. French et al., *Contemporary Perspectives in the Philosophy of Language*, p. 294.
21   Ibid.
22   Ibid.
23   Ibid.
24   Ibid., pp. 296–7.
25   Ibid., p. 297.
26   Davidson, 'Truth and Meaning', *Synthese*, 17, 1967, p. 308; 'Theories of Meaning and Learnable Languages', *Proceedings of the 1964 Congress for Logic, Methodology and Philosophy of Science*, Amsterdam, 1964, p. 387; 'Semantics for Natural Languages', *Linguaggi Nella Societe e Nella Technica*, Milan, 1970, p. 179.
27   Davidson, 'On Saying That', *Synthese* 19, 1968, p. 131, reprinted in Davidson and Hintikka, *Words and Objections*; 'Theories of Meaning and Learnable Languages', *Proceedings of the 1964 Congress*, p. 387; 'Semantics for Natural Languages', *Linguaggi Nella Societe e Nella Technica*, p. 177.
28   Davidson, 'Semantics for Natural Languages', pp. 178–9.
29   Ibid., p. 183; 'Truth and Meaning', *Synthese*, p. 311.
30   Cf. 'Truth and Meaning', p. 309 *et seq.*
31   Quine, *From a Logical Point of View*.
32   Davidson, 'Truth and Meaning', p. 309.
33   Ibid., p. 310.
34   Cf. M. Platts, *Ways of Meaning*, pp. 54–6.
35   Davidson, 'Truth and Meaning', p. 314.
36   Ibid.
37   Ibid.

38   Ibid., pp. 318–20.
39   Cf. ibid.
40   Ibid., p. 319.
41   Ibid., pp. 318–20.
42   Ibid., p. 320.
43   Ibid. and 'The Logical Form of Action Sentences', in N. Rescher, (ed.), *The Logic of Decision and Action*; also Cf. Davidson, 'On Saying That', *Synthese*, 1968.
44   T. Burge, 'Reference and Proper Names', *Journal of Philosophy*, 70, 1973.
45   G. Harman, 'Moral Relativism Defended', *Philosophical Review*, 1975.
46   J. Wallace, 'On the Frame of Reference', *Synthese*, 22, 1970, and 'Positive, Comparative, Superlative', *Journal of Philosophy*, 69, 1972.
47   Davidson, 'Truth and Meaning', *Synthese*, 1967, p. 311.
48   Davidson, 'Semantics for Natural Languages', *Linguaggic Nella Societe e Nella Technica*, 1970, p. 185.
49   Ibid., pp. 185–6.
50   Ibid., p. 184; cf. 'Truth and Meaning', p. 313.
51   In fact, it can be argued (and I shall later show this) that the notions of assent and dissent are more complicated than Quine and Davidson suggest – to an extent, indeed, that generates results contrary to theirs. Cf. below; and Grayling, *The Refutation of Scepticism*, ch. 4.
52   Davidson, 'Truth and Meaning', p. 318.
53   Ibid.
54   S. P. Stich, 'Davidson's Semantic Program', *Canadian Journal of Philosophy*, vol. vi, 2, 1976, § 7.
55   Platts, *Ways of Meaning*, p. 57.
56   Ibid.
57   For more detailed discussion see J. A. Foster, 'Meaning, Truth, Theory'; and B. Loar, 'Two Theories of Meaning', both in G. Evans, and J. McDowell, *Truth and Meaning*.
58   J. McDowell, 'Truth-conditions, Bivalence, and Verificationism' in Evans and McDowell, *Truth and Meaning*, p. 42 *et seq*. For a theory in some respects similar to McDowell's cf. Loar, 'Two Theories of Meaning'.
59   McDowell, 'Truth-conditions', p. 43.
60   Ibid., p. 44.
61   Ibid.
62   Ibid., pp. 44–5.
63   Ibid., p. 46; and cf. Platts, *Ways of Meaning*, p. 61.
64   Platts, *Ways of Meaning*,
65   McDowell, 'Truth-conditions', p. 47; cf. Platts, *Ways of Meaning*.
66   Platts, *Ways of Meaning*, p. 62.
67   McDowell, 'Truth-conditions', p. 46.

68   Ibid., pp. 46–7.
69   Ibid., p. 47.
70   M. A. E. Dummett, see especially 'What is a Theory of Meaning (II)?', in Evans and McDowell, *Truth and Meaning*, and variously in *Truth and Other Enigmas*, (henceforth *TOE*).
71   McDowell, 'Truth-conditions', p. 48.
72   Dummett, 'What is a Theory of Meaning (II)?', p. 69.
73   Ibid.
74   Ibid., pp. 69–70.
75   Ibid., pp. 70–1, my italics.
76   Ibid., pp. 72–3.
77   Ibid., p. 73.
78   Ibid., pp. 73–4.
79   Ibid., p. 74.
80   Ibid., pp. 74–5.
81   Ibid., p. 76, my italics.
82   Ibid., p. 78.
83   Ibid.
84   Ibid., pp. 79–80.
85   Ibid., pp. 80–1.
86   Ibid., pp. 81–2.
87   Ibid., pp. 82–3.
88   Ibid., p. 83.
89   Ibid., p. 89.
90   Ibid., pp. 89–90.
91   Ibid., p. 91.
92   Ibid., p. 93.
93   Ibid., p. 94.
94   Ibid.
95   Ibid., p. 95.
96   Ibid., pp. 96–8.
97   Ibid., p. 94.
98   Ibid., p. 100.
99   Ibid.
100   Ibid., p. 101.
101   Ibid.
102   Ibid., p. 103.
103   Ibid., cf. esp. pp. 103–10, where Dummett sets out an account of intuitionistic semantics for mathematical language; see also 'The Philosophical Basis of Intuitionistic Logic', *TOE*, pp. 216–26 for an exceptionally clear and vigorous account of all these questions.
104   Dummett, 'What is a Theory of Meaning (II)?', p. 110.

105   Ibid., my italics.
106   Ibid., p. 111.
107   Cf. Quine, 'Two Dogmas' in *From a Logical Point of View*.
108   Dummett, 'What is a Theory of Meaning(II)'?
109   Ibid., p. 114.
110   For other reasons why Dummett thinks we need a concept of truth cf. chapter 9 below; and Dummett's 'What Does the Appeal to Use Do for the Theory of Meaning?' in A. Margalit (ed.), *Meaning and Use*, p. 123 *et seq.*
111   Dummett, 'What is a Theory of Meaning (II)?' pp. 115–16. Dummett goes on to consider a theory of meaning with falsification as its central concept (pp. 117–26), and then talks specifically about the notion of force and how the passage from knowledge of meanings to use is forged (pp. 127–37). For his discussions of truth cf. 'Truth' in *TOE* and ch. 13 of *Frege*; also M. Dummett, *The Logical Basis of Metaphysics*.
112   Dummett, *The Logical Basis of Metaphysics*, p. 103.
113   ibid., p. 104.
114   C. McGinn, 'An A Priori Argument for Realism', *Journal of Philosophy*, 1979, p. 113 *et seq.*
115   Dummett, *TOE*, pp. 367–8.
116   McGinn, 'An A Priori Argument for Realism', p. 116.
117   Ibid.
118   Ibid.
119   Ibid.
120   Ibid., p. 118.
121   Ibid., pp. 118–19.
122   Ibid., p. 119.
123   Ibid., pp. 119–20. These observations recall the sense-data debate and the issue of phenomenalism in general.
124   Ibid., pp. 121–2.
125   Ibid., p. 122.
126   The further details are interesting, and spell out the second step in the argument in greater detail.
127   Dummett, 'Common Sense and Metaphysics', in G. Macdonald (ed.), *Perception and Identity*, p. 4. Cf. also *TOE*, pp. 361–2.
128   Dummett, 'Common Sense and Metaphysics', pp. 4–5.
129   Ibid., p. 5.
130   Ibid., pp. 5–6.
131   The following suggestion owes itself to Michael Luntley. Cf. his *Language, Logic and Experience*, ch. 1.
132   Cf. Grayling, *Refutation of Scepticism*, esp. chs 3–5.
133   McDowell, 'Truth-Values, Bivalence, and Verificationism', pp. 54–5.

134   C. Wright, 'Realism, Truth-value Links, Other Minds, and the Past', Ratio, vol. xxii, 2, 1980, pp. 112–32.
135   Dummett, *TOE*, pp. 362–3.
136   Ibid., p. 362.
137   Ibid., p. 364.
138   Ibid., p. 373.
139   Ibid., p. 369.
140   Ibid.
141   Ibid., p. 370.
142   J. McDowell, 'On "The Reality of the Past" ', in P. Pettit and C. Hookway (eds), *Action and Interpretation*.
143   Ibid., p. 132.
144   Ibid.
145   Ibid.
146   Ibid., p. 133.
147   Ibid., p. 135.
148   C. Wright, 'Realism, Truth-value Links, Other Minds and the Past', *Ratio*, 1980, p. 121.
149   McDowell, 'On "The Reality of the Past" ' pp. 135–6.
150   Ibid., p. 136.
151   Ibid., p. 135.
152   Ibid., p. 139.
153   Wright, 'Realism Truth-value Links, Other Minds and the Past', *Ratio*, 1980, p. 139.
154   Ibid.
155   Ibid., p. 123.
156   Ibid.
157   Ibid., pp. 123–4.
158   Ibid., p. 123.
159   Ibid., pp. 122–4.
160   Ibid., pp. 124–5.
161   Ibid., pp. 126–8.
162   Ibid., pp. 129–30.

9

Realism, Anti-realism, Idealism, Relativism

Introduction

The foregoing chapters have aspired to give a largely impartial account of the debates they canvass. This is appropriate for an introductory book. In this chapter I doff neutrality to focus on certain of the topics discussed. Chiefly I offer some comments on the debate about realism, which, raising so many important questions, is central to philosophical logic and therefore to philosophy. I begin with the views of Putnam, and then proceed to argue, in response both to his and to Dummett's views, that what is fundamentally at stake in the debate is a question neither of metaphysics as some think, nor of semantics as others think, but of epistemology.

Putnam and Realism

Putnam identifies a view he calls 'metaphysical realism', and rejects both it and the conception he takes to be its opposite, which he sometimes calls 'positivism/relativism'. To begin with he was prompted to offer a middle course, which came to be called 'internal realism', but subsequently he withdrew from trying to affirm a position, and chose instead a critical stance, a perspective of response to what others in the debate say, both historically and contemporarily. In what follows I sketch Putnam's conception of metaphysical realism, his chief argument against it, and his successively preferred views.

Metaphysical realism is described by Putnam as the thesis that the world consists of mind-independent objects. Indeed he describes the commitment more strongly, as the view that the world consists of a fixed totality of mind-independent objects. And he argues that one who holds this view takes it to follow that there is exactly one true and complete description of the world, and that therefore truth consists in a form of correspondence between that description and the world.[1] Partially under the influence of Dummett's characterization of realism, Putnam puts these points alternatively as the view that metaphysical realism is a set of theses about truth, namely, 'that truth is a matter of Correspondence and that it exhibits Independence (of what humans do or could find out), Bivalence, and Uniqueness (there cannot be more than one true or complete description of Reality)'.[2]

One of Dummett's ways of characterizing realism is to advert to Frege's insistence upon sharply distinguishing the truth of a proposition from the grounds that anyone might have for taking it to be true. Anyone committed to this distinction is a realist. An opponent of this view has to offer an account of truth premissed on the absence of such a distinction. Putnam shares this analysis. In his terminology, the property – 'Independence' – that distinguishes realistically-conceived truth is its 'radically non-epistemic' character; the claim that truths are Independent is the claim that 'the world could be such that the theory we are most justified in accepting would not really be true . . . rational acceptability is one thing, and truth is another'.[3]

Putnam tells us that he had himself begun as a metaphysical realist, holding its 'most tenable current form' which he describes as 'scientific materialism':

> I believed that everything there is can be explained and described by a single theory. Of course we shall never know that theory in detail and even about the general principles we shall always be somewhat in error. But I believed that we can see in present-day science what the general outlines of such a theory must look like. In particular, I believed that the best metaphysics is physics, or, more precisely, that the best metaphysics is what the positivists called 'unified science', science pictured as based on and unified by the application of the laws of fundamental physics. In our time, Bernard Williams has claimed that we have at least a sketch of an 'absolute conception of the world' in present-day physics'.[4]

Putnam rejects metaphysical realism on the grounds that it leads to 'paradox and confusion'.[5] One of his principle arguments against it is celebrated as the 'Brain in a Vat' argument.[6] It goes as follows. Consider an updated version of the Cartesian demon hypothesis, in which one is to suppose that, despite all the evidence of one's experience to the contrary, one's brain has been removed and pickled in a vat of preservative, with electrodes implanted to feed it the experiences of ordinary life. Putnam's argument is that this supposition cannot possibly be true because it is self-refuting. It is self-refuting because if one were a brain in a vat one could not say or think that one is a brain in a vat; and one could not say or think this because to do so one would have to be able to *refer* to brains and vats, but *as* a brain in a vat one cannot refer to the brain one is, or the vat one is in, but only to a brain-as-one-conceives-it from the internal perspective of one's envatment, and a vat-as-one-conceives-it likewise.[7]

The argument, in other words, is that if one were a brain in a vat one's words 'brain' and 'vat' would not refer to one's brain or the vat one is in, but to other things: namely, a brain and a vat occupying the imaginary world of one's brain-in-a-vat experience. The argument has two premisses: that 'magical' theories of reference – as Putnam calls them – are wrong, and that one cannot refer to things unless one stands in the right kind of causal relation to them.[8] A magical theory of reference is any theory which says that words (or more generally, representations) stand in an *intrinsic* relation to their referents, independently of their users, as if 'some occult rays – call them "noetic rays" – connect words and thought-signs to their referents'; but clearly this will not do, for it implausibly has it that 'the Brain in a Vat can think the *words*, "I am a brain in a vat," and when he does the word "vat" corresponds (with the aid of the noetic rays) to real external vats and the word "in" corresponds (with the aid of the noetic rays) to the relation of real spatial containment.'[9] But reference cannot connect representations and their referents in this way. Signs actually employed by their users to refer to given objects do so only 'within the conceptual scheme of those users.'[10]

The second premiss by itself is enough to refute the hypothesis, Putnam thinks; for one can only refer to the real brain one is, and the real vat one is in, if one is in the right kind of causal connection with them – an information-conveying causal connection.[11] But one is not in an information-conveying causal connection with them; therefore the hypothesis cannot be formulated; therefore it is self-defeating.

This argument opposes metaphysical realism by exposing an unresolvable conflict at its centre. Realism takes truth to be 'radically non-epistemic'; it is independent of what we do or can know. So the realist claims that we might all be brains in vats without knowing it. But unless there is some sort of 'noetic ray' to connect our terms with what they are supposed to refer to, an assertion to the effect that we are brains in vats is false. Thus the conflict: 'we might all be brains in vats; but any assertion to the effect that we are, is false.'

There has been much debate about the Brain in a Vat example and what it shows, the aim of some participants being defence of the intelligibility of thinking that we might be brains in a vat. If they are right, they thereby defend the intelligibility of metaphysical realism against at least this line of attack.[12] One argument says that a brain in a vat, in having the ordinary repertoire of thoughts and capacities, has a distinction between its own states of mind and what it takes to be an external world. So it distinguishes between experience of an external world, and hallucinations and other non-standard cases. Therefore it can perfectly well make sense of the hypothesis that it might be brain in a vat.[13] Another line of attack is to say that there are many different ways of characterizing predicaments for minds relative to the knowledge they can acquire or the thoughts they can think; Putnam's example *by hypothesis* makes brains in vats unable to think they are brains in vats; but if we alter the terms of the example – if, say, we allow that the electrodes implanted in them casually transmit information about the extra-vat environment just as normal sense-organs transmit information about the extra-dermal environment – there need be nothing magical about the envatted brains' references to their brains and vats; so the Brain in a Vat hypothesis would be intelligible.[14]

Whatever the merits of these arguments otherwise, the most they do, if right, is to show that Putnam has not established the incoherence of the Brain in a Vat hypothesis. They do not thereby establish the coherence of realism's commitment to a radically non-epistemic account of truth. The discussion below is intended to show that this cannot be done. But one can state an allied objection straight away to Putnam's characterization of realism as 'metaphysical realism'. What this assumes or implies is that realism is a thesis about 'reality', that is, about what exists. Were it such a thesis, it would indeed merit the epithet 'metaphysical'; but questions about what exists, as the argument below shows at some length, is not what is at stake. Realists and their opponents do not disagree about what exists, but about how we are epistemically related to what exists. The realist says that what exists does so *mind-*

independently, that is, *independently of knowledge or experience*; his is a thesis therefore about the extent of our knowledge and its relation to what there is. The anti-realist says that what exists – the same existing things, note – are in some way internally related to knowledge of them (again, see below). Part of the concern is of course to make sense of *another* kind of dependence relation, namely, the way some things are said to exist dependently on other things (chairs on the elementary particles which constitute them, for example); but this too is ultimately a question of how we represent the world to ourselves (a question of our theories), and therefore is an epistemological question.

This point says that it misdescribes realism to take it as a metaphysical thesis. What is further unsatisfactory in Putnam's characterization is a result of this misdescription. One can hold a realist thesis, in the basic sense of holding that the entities in some class exist independently of thought or experience of them, while rejecting or being agnostic about all the other commitments Putnam takes to constitute realism, namely: bivalence, the idea of there being a fixed totality of things, the idea that there is only one correct description of them, and even the idea of truth as correspondence. The only commitment that a realist must make is to the thesis that the entities in some class exist *independently of thought* (or experience, or language, etc.). So in giving arguments to show the incoherence of some or all of these features other than independence, Putnam is wasting ammunition. He acknowledges that the mind-independence thesis is the basic commitment, upon which the others in his characterization lean; we can conclude that, because the other commitments are add-on extras not required by anyone committed to the independence thesis, and only intelligible in the light of a prior acceptance of that thesis, discussion of them is not central.

These last thoughts remove the necessity to say much about another of Putnam's arguments, his 'model theoretic' argument. In brief it goes as follows. There are many different possible models of our language, each satisfying all relevant 'operational and theoretical constaints.' If the entities constituting these models are conceived realistically, that is, as mind-and-discourse-independent entites, then it is 'utterly mysterious' why any one of them should be identified as the uniquely correct model – which is what, Putnam claims, realism distinctively does. A reference relation corresponds to each model, so 'there are infinitely many admissible reference relations'; on what grounds does realism privilege one rather than another?[15] The focus of the argument is the claim, imputed by Putnam to metaphysical realists, that there is only one correct description of the world. As just noted, this commitment leans on the independence thesis, a refutation of which is a refutation of everything depending on it. But even apart from that, it is not clear that anyone committed to the independence thesis is obliged to accept this or any other of the add-on extras, however *natural* they might be as adjuncts of it. For they do not *follow* from the independence thesis, nor, as noted, are they required for it. So the 'model-theoretic' argument applies only to a metaphysical realist who has accepted this richer set of commitments, and need not concern us here.

Internal Realism, Truth, and Criticism

The position first opposed by Putnam to metaphysical realism came to be called 'internal realism'. Put in terms of a conception of truth, internal realism is the thesis that a statement is true if and only if 'fully rationally warranted' use is made of it by a competent speaker who is in a 'sufficiently good epistemic position' to do so.[16] At the time he espoused internal realism Putnam's concern was to connect the notions of truth, language use, rational acceptability and 'sufficiently good' epistemic circumstances, and he still holds this aspect of the view. What he came to reject is internal realism's concession to verificationism – the concession being that truth is never totally recognition-transcendent, which he thought can be rendered consistent with common-sense realism – and its commitment to the idea that the use of words is fixed, as if by a set of algorithms. What he still retains – and this indeed was what anyway distinguished internal realism in its first statement – is the view that 'it makes no sense to think of the world as dividing itself up into "objects" (or "entities") independently of our use of language. It is *we* who divide up "the world" – that is, the events, states of affairs and physical, social, etc., systems that we talk about – into "objects," "properties," and "relations," and we do this in a variety of ways.'[17] A simple example is that we think of the contents of a room, say, either as furniture or as collections of elementary particles, depending on our interests and purposes. A corollary of this view is that different ontologies can be adopted for the same states of affairs, which means that apparently inconsistent pairs of statements can both be true, in the sense of being true 'in the way of speaking to which each belongs' (so the inconsistency is *only* apparent). Putnam calls this 'conceptual relativity'.[18]

In more recent writings, as noted, Putnam's focus is less on stating a position than on criticizing the commitments that give rise to metaphysical realism. In his view the chief current defence of metaphysical realism is 'semantic physicalism', the view that our mental tokens are physicalistically related to the objects they refer to in the external world. The principal component of this view is a causal theory of reference in which 'x refers to y if and only if x is connected to y by a "causal" chain of an appropriate type.'[19] His reason for rejecting this is that the 'appropriate type' of causal chain can only be specified by using 'unreduced semantical notions', which begs the question. Moreover, physicalism wishes to show how semantic facts supervene on physical ones by a bottom-up procedure starting with physiology, or computing science, or behavioural psychology, whereas it can only be done by 'looking from above', that is, by starting with the interests, points of view and circumstances of language-users.[20] In short, the physicalist defence of metaphysical realism tries to dispense with, or to give a reductive account of, intentionality (intentionality is standardly, but *mistakenly* in Putnam's view, characterized as the relation between mind and world); and this Putnam does not believe can or should be done, once one sees how to make sense of intentionality afresh.[21]

One way to see intentionality afresh is to repudiate both metaphysical realism and its equally unattractive (in Putnam's view) opposite, namely, some form of anti-realism—at any rate, a view in which beliefs are not justified by their relation to the world. On certain versions of this latter view, for example Rorty's, the idea of representation loses content; as Rorty puts it, how can we say that statements are made true by things in the world if those things are not independent of our ways of talking about them?[22] Putnam's response is to repudiate the assumptions that underlie the dichotomy itself. The idea of the 'independent existence' of objects from talk about them employs notions of causal or logical independence that are not, Putnam claims, ordinary ones; when we use 'independent' ordinarily ('in the only way I can understand,' he remarks, revealing the Wittgensteinian inspiration of this approach) there is no question but that the blueness of the sky is independent of the way we talk.[23] So we can retain a notion of representation made intelligible by Putnam's own 'conceptual relativism', the view that there are different descriptions of the same states of affairs, that is, different ontologies we can adopt for them. On this conception, we can talk of referring to objects, but not in some metaphysically privileged way, for there is a variety of ways of doing so: 'we can think of our words and thoughts as having determinate reference to objects (when it is clear what sort of "objects" we are talking about and what vocabulary we are using); but there is no one fixed sense of "reference" involved.'[24] This shows that rejection of metaphysical realism does not entail the collapse of the notion of representation, nor does it promote the sense of a certain *confinement* – being trapped inside language or thought – which the idea of internal realism had to some extent helped foster.[25]

Putnam thinks these considerations offer a metaphysically innocent way of taking it that thoughts are about the world, that language represents the world, that our beliefs are justified by how the world is, because they recover the ordinary, 'humble' sense of such words as 'represent', 'justified', 'thought', 'world'. He quotes Wittgenstein with approval: 'if the words "language," "experience," "world" have a use, it must be as humble a one as that of the words "table," "lamp" and "door".'[26]

If one thing is common to Putnam, Davidson and Rorty in these debates, it is their rejection of the mind–world divide as it has manifested itself in so many ways since Descartes. The question of the relation of mental to physical phenomena takes many more forms than its two original manifestations as the traditional mind – body problem and the question of scepticism as conceived in modern (seventeenth century and thereafter) epistemology. With its deepening and nuancing, the debate has come to focus upon truth, reference and representation; upon meaning, and realism. The solution adopted by some (identified by Rorty as Dewey, Heidegger and Wittgenstein[27]) and in various ways followed by others, is to repudiate the divide they see as the source of the problem: the divide between the representing, thinking, referring, perceiving, experiencing, discoursing mind, and what it represents, thinks or discourses about, refers to, experiences or perceives. Realism – 'metaphysical realism' in Putnam's terminology – is taken to be *the* defence of the existence of this divide. But giving up the divide is not – at least in the views of Putnam and Davidson; Rorty might think differently – to opt for a strong form of anti-realism, perhaps of the kind that might be a natural corollary of the metaphysical thesis known as idealism. (Note the care I take here, and which I justify below, to distinguish the *epistemological* thesis of anti-realism from the *metaphysical* thesis of idealism.) But as with the later work of Wittgenstein, it is not quite clear what the non-anti-realistic anti-realism of these writers comes to. They retreat into such claims as that we can help ourselves to philosophically unproblematic, deflated senses of 'truth' and 'reference'; that there are ordinary, 'humble', uses of 'represent,' 'justification' and the like, that only seem philosophically problematic because philosophers wilfully made them so; that everything is all right with our concepts (so claims Wittgenstein, followed by Putnam), just as they seem to be when we are sufficiently unreflective about them.

Stripped of its draperies, this view comes down to saying that philosophical problems prompted by reflection on the relation of thought (etc.) to the world just have no content; and the ground offered for this claim is that thinking otherwise raises too many difficulties. This latter might be a *motive* for refusing to think any longer about problems of truth and representation, but it is not a ground for asserting that they are contentless. Retreat into Wittgenstein-like claims that, because we use 'represent' and 'true' in ordinary speech, they must therefore be philosophically unproblematic, is profoundly unsatisfactory. I propose to take them seriously, and to approach them afresh from a different angle in what follows, by showing that what is at issue turns on the underlying epistemology of truth, meaning, and metaphysics.

Anti-Realism and Metaphysics

McDowell, it will be remembered, said that if we accept a view of sense in terms of verification it would require us to adopt 'a novel, anti-realist conception of the world: if truth is not independent of our discovery of it, we must picture the world as our own creation or, at least, as springing up in response to our investigations. So verificationist objections to a truth-conditions conception of sense would have far-reaching metaphysical implications'.[28] One thing McDowell is wrong about, in saying this, is that the required anti-realist conception of the world would be 'novel'; for neither of the options he specifies is so, having long been familiar in the guise of forms of idealism. But it is questionable whether he is right to claim that anti-realism is a metaphysically consequential thesis. In holding this he is of course following distinguished precedent; Dummett says that 'the whole point of my approach . . . has been to show that the theory of meaning underlies metaphysics'.[29] This, I now argue, is a fundamental mistake.

To begin to see why, it is instructive to quote a statement of a standard realist picture which, unlike the scientific realist picture quoted from Putnam above, is closer to what is unreflectively presupposed to ordinary discourse. There is no better example than that provided by Platts, so I quote it in full. Realism, he says,

> embodies a picture of our language reaching out to, connecting with, the external world in ways that are (at least) beyond our present practical comprehension. It embodies a picture of an independently existing, somewhat recalcitrant world describable by our language in ways that transcend (at least) our present capacities to determine whether those descriptions are true or not. It embodies a picture of our language, and our understanding, grappling with a stubbornly elusive reality. Perhaps, with effort, we can improve our capacities to understand that world, to know that our characterisations of it are true. If we succeed in so doing, we do not bring that world into being, we merely *discover* what was there all along. But that reality will always exceed our capacities: we can struggle to achieve *approximately true* beliefs about that reality, approximately true beliefs about the entities and their characteristics which, independently of us, make up that reality. But we have to rest with the approximate belief, and ultimately to resign ourselves to (non-complacent) ignorance: for the world, austerely characterised by our language, will always outrun our recognitional capacities.
>
> I find this conception of the world profound, sympathetic, and (health-ily) depressing.[30]

This characterization is undoubtedly what underlies our common-sense view of the world. The realist commitments of everyday discourse are readily illustrated; no better way offers of explaining how the world is pictured by the utterer of, say, 'the cups are on the table' than by crediting him with the belief that there are objects whose existence and character is independent of his discourse of them; and like him we take it that it is in virtue of their so existing that language has the sense (that thought has the character) it has. And 'metaphysical realism' in Putnam's sense can be seen as a theoretical elaboration of just these commitments.

But reflection makes it apparent that there is a mystifying gap between what this picture has us believe and the ways we could come to possess and display mastery of it. This, on direct analogy with the language case, is precisely what the 'acquisition' and 'manifestation' challenges are intended to show, as Platts acknowledges: 'the picture, like the realistic truth-based semantics which prompts it, is open to serious challenge [from anti-realism]'.[31] The discussion in the preceding chapter is in part discussion of that challenge; but there it focuses on language-mastery, and accepts a premiss about what is at stake in the realism debate that should, arguably, be rejected. To redraw the picture in the right way one has to begin again at the beginning.

The confusion infecting the realism debate arises from thinking of given realms of entities in two different ways at once, or more precisely, from conflating two ways of thinking. The first is familiar enough, as just noted, in its various guises as a metaphysical commitment, historically expressed as commitment to some notion of substance; but it is difficult to state precisely. It consists in thinking about the entities in a given realm as existing in their own right, independently of other things which cause or, more weakly, sustain them in being. Such entities might be conceived as having the status of Aristotle's 'primary being', or at any rate as substances conceived as those things (or that thing, for monists) which exist, and can only be understood as doing so, in some sense 'in and of themselves'. If anything merited the label 'metaphysical realism', this would be it. I shall refer to it as thesis A. Some of the more heroic moments in the history of philosophy consist in efforts to clarify it, for what is at issue, after all, is no less than the metaphysics of being. But I am not confident that there is clarification ready to hand. The following hints at the difficulties.

Understandings of thesis A fall into at least two broad categories. Such formulations as 'existence in its own right' and 'absolute and ultimate existence' suggest a full Aristotelian concept of primary *ousia*. This is existence which is basic to other, derivative, existence; it at least explains itself, and perhaps indeed – as in theological employments of the notion – causes itself. It is not obvious, without further taxonomy, whether the latter, stronger, notion is coterminous with the notion of necessary being, but apologists at any rate standardly so construe it. A reason for caution is that giving a negative answer to the question 'could there not be a conception of contingently self-caused beings, in the sense that other facts about the universe do not necessitate their existence?' – is not obviously called for by the terms of the question itself. For there might be nothing contradictory in a description of the universe, whether false or not, in which the existence of certain self-caused beings is denied; and the reverse would have to be true if the entities in question were candidates for genuinely necessary existence. But no-one need go out on an ontological limb in this way to get a notion of 'existence in its own right'; there is always an epistemological limb to venture along, which says that it is just a brute fact, to be accepted as primitive, that certain things exist in this basic or primary way. To make it metaphysical *realism* which the thesis thus understood amounts to, a bruteness claim has to be taken as a candidate for literal truth. (The idea of explanatory self-sufficiency is an epistemic notion, note, which shows the close connection between these ideas, as a supposed explanation of epistemic independence, and that thesis itself as discussed below.)

Or thesis A might be taken more weakly to mean that, having been caused, a thing X exists as a genuine individual whose dependence on other things, for example food supplies if X is an animal, is only necessary in the sense of physical law, and hence is metaphysically contingent. It might be a fact that X is in this way dependent on things external to itself; but the point is that any suitable external will do, so there is nothing to which X's dependence is *metaphysically* annexed. Of course it could be argued that X is dependent on a class or classes of things – say, foodstuffs – but this does not alter the descriptive adequacy of treating X as an individuable existent. Consider a pebble: in what sense can it be understood as a dependent individual once its causal history – its having been produced by cooling lava, say – has been discounted? In this guise the thesis aims at asserting the ontological irreducibility of X to its material and efficient causes, and the ontological definability of X in a scheme of things, with its own path through a world, say, or its own separately countable membership of it. This second aspect of the notion is a rich one, for it plays a part in a story whose other themes – individuation, identity, particularity – are familiar indeed. The idea of individual substances has its busiest employment precisely here. The connection between the two aspects is that asserting X's independence in this sense means that X is to be understood as not essentially or internally related to anything else, of which it must therefore be considered part, or along with which it has therefore to be individuated. So it is a true individual.

The question of how, if at all, these two understandings of thesis A are related is a matter of controversy. One can hold some version of either without any entailment to versions of the other. The chief reason is that an ontology can select a range of individuable, persisting and therefore reidentifiable particulars, whose status as such is entirely determined by their relation to a theory or point of view which finds it convenient to treat them as such, without concomitantly holding that these things are in any way ultimate. This is the case with the medium-sized dry goods constituting the ontology of mundane experience. No-one I think would now claim that according them the status of basic particulars in our scheme means that they are the ultimately existing entities *simpliciter*.[32] This would imply, for one thing, a new order of instrumentalism about physics. Given that the basic particulars of a scheme might well be epistemically but not ontically basic, and in acknowledgement of the difficulties attaching to getting to the latter from the former, some – even some contemporary – philosophers hold that the veil of the former is impenetrable, and we are condemned to ignorance about how things really are.[33]

There have however always been more optimistic metaphysicians, whose ambition is to identify what is or has to be basic in the sense of the first understanding of thesis A, and then to explain how whatever seems basic in the second understanding of A is connected to it – perhaps, at the neatest, by being smoothly reducible to it. The denotata of referring terms in folk psychology, for example, are taken by some[34] to be mere dummies, typically misleading ones, for referring terms in a future perfected science which will pick out something ultimate, deeper even than the physiological level at which attempts at explanation currently aim. (There are competing candidates: Leibniz' monads are an historical example. Only those persuaded that physics is metaphysics will think that fluctuations in the quantum field or superstrings – or whatever next – have that sort of ontological status.)

The serious difficulty with A is that there seems to be no precise way of making the notion of 'ultimate existence' or 'existence in its own right' intelligible. It obscures rather than helps to speak, as we have seen, about ultimate things as *uncaused*, or *self-caused*, or *necessary*, or *primary*, or *basic*, or a *brute fact*. The argument of the metaphysicians is that because there is something, there must be something ultimate, in a sense of 'ultimate' vaguely connoted by the foregoing expressions; and they draw this conclusion because they feel that a 'ground' of being is needed for what there is, which either needs no ground itself or is its own ground. (Compare styles of cosmological argument, which employ notions of causality and contingency to just this end.) But talk of grounds keeps us firmly in the realm of metaphor.

Another, allied, symptom of the problem is that efforts to give content to this family of notions – *basic, self-caused, ultimate* and so forth –

quickly slide into appeals to a quite different notion, namely, epistemological independence. I discuss this notion shortly. The slide is revealed by ready allusions to 'explanatory' ultimacy, which at least often substitutes for the purely existential account being sought. But whereas questions of explanation mark out a logical space in a genuine problem, the metaphysical side of the ledger remains insistently blank.

As to the second understanding of thesis A, it seems a commonplace, and an unexceptionable one, that something must serve as the basic nodes of a scheme for a world (a domain), to which reference can be made and by which the domain's historico-geographic contours can be mapped – literally, in the case of the dry goods world. But as we see in the case of this world, such an ontology is determined by the schemers and their needs, and we live familiarly with any number of sometimes only partially commensurable such schemes, and their vocabularies, in our daily lives: for example, the perceptual scheme of medium-sized dry goods, the explanatory schemes afforded by the biological and physical sciences, the folk-psychological scheme of interpersonal interpretation, and the sociological scheme of social explanation. It is a bold thesis which says that any one of these takes, or in a perfected state will take, reductions from any or all the others, or that all are smoothly saved, if we only knew how to recognize it, by a complete description of something else which is ontologically primary. The common-sense belief, of course, is that the dry goods world imposes itself on us, rather than we on it, and our scheme carves it at its independently existing joints, because it has to: but we need only remind ourselves of Russell's remark, 'common sense gives rise to science, and science shows that common sense is false', to recognize that whatever A-type thesis we try to evolve from our epistemic needs, it had better not be precisely that one.

Such remarks are immediately apt to raise the spectre of relativism. It is customary, and indeed appropriate, to find that the first response to calling metaphysical realism into question is the raising of this spectre. Relativism is indisputably a Bad Thing; I show why, below, and also – and more importantly – I show that rejection of realism does not entail it. This point is important: there is a widespread but mistaken view that anti-realist attitudes come to the same thing as relativism, which even some anti-realists believe.

We are not yet done with 'independence', however, nor therefore with the question of what is genuinely at issue in the realism debate; so relativism must wait its turn.

The second sense of 'independence', and the one which I take to be genuinely at issue in the realism debate, is epistemic independence. Someone applies such a notion if he holds that the entities in some realm exist independently of any thought, talk, knowledge or experience of them. Call this thesis B. Often B is expressed in terms of the 'mind-independence' of given entities. When those who discuss realism mistakenly contrast it with idealism, it is clear that they have mind-independence in mind as the chief characteristic of realism. This way of describing realism accords well, however, with more familiar statements of the position in terms of evidence-transcendent truth.

To make out the claim that B is what really matters in the realism debate, and at the same time to locate the issues with respect to more familiar ways of setting them out, the scope of the discussion needs to be widened.

Anti-realism and Epistemology

On Dummett's view, the realism debate is about language, truth and logic. It is a mistake, in his view, to think of it *primarily* as a debate about what exists; we should see it instead as an adjudication of the opposition between the view that to understand a sentence is to grasp its truth conditions, where truth and falsity are understood as epistemically unconstrained properties of what we say or think, and the view that to understand a sentence is to grasp its assertion conditions. So he rejects thesis A as the way to identify and state what is at issue, although he thinks, as we shall see, that thesis A's concerns are settled (automatically, so to speak) by getting the semantic questions straight.

To demonstrate that this way of approaching the problem misses the essentials as much as thesis A does, I use as a foil Dummett's thesis that realism is a theory of meaning crucially based upon an evidence-transcendent conception of truth.

As noted in the preceding chapter, Dummett's view that commitment to bivalence is the mark of realism, and its rejection the mark of anti-realism, came later to be modified. He came to hold that acceptance of bivalence is not sufficient for realism; what is also required is acceptance of a semantic theory setting out the particular classically-based manner in which the truth-values of statements in a given class are determined.[35] Rejection of bivalence remains, however, a mark of anti-realism.

This change results from what are now familiar points about why it is necessary to rethink the connection between realism and bivalence. They show that acceptance of recognition-transcendent truth does not entail acceptance of bivalence, so that if for other reasons one abandons the latter, a notion of recognition-transcendent truth can survive. One can be a realist, in short, whether or not one thinks that there are exactly two jointly exhaustive truth-values. Dummett's earlier linking of realism and bivalence was motivated by the converse relationship, namely the apparent fact that bivalence entails recognition-transcendence; which, whether or not it is right, at least appears plausible. But an implication of the detachability of bivalence and recognition-transcendence is that one's theory of the relation between truth-value and speakers' ability to determine what it is, does not follow automatically from one's choice of semantic principle. This raises questions about the nature of the relationship as Dummett sees it, for in his view choice of semantic principle *determines* the nature of the relationship between the truth-value of a sentence and the capacity of language-users to identify it.

The inspiration for Dummett's view, by his own account, was his coming to think that two quite different debates – between realists and nominalists, and between realists and idealists – share a certain form;[36] and then to have postulated that they share this form with other debates also, for example those which concern the reality of the future and past, mathematical objects, and values.[37] He took the common feature to be that the realist in each of these debates accepts bivalence. Taking this commitment as the mark of realism is, Dummett argues, 'preferable' to treating realism as a thesis in which there is commitment to the existence of certain sorts of entities, because some species of realism, for example those about the future or ethics, 'do not seem readily classifiable as doctrines about a realm of entities'.[38] On this ground Dummett concludes that '*in every case* we may regard a realistic view as consisting in a certain interpretation of statements in some class'.[39]

Dummett describes this interpretation in terms of a classical two-valued semantic theory specifying how the semantic values of statements are determined by the values, and arrangements, of their parts. Any theory of meaning based on such a semantics is 'objectivist' about truth, that is, committed to a sharp distinction between a statement's truth and anyone's being entitled to hold it true. This means that the plausibility of the semantic theory can be tested by assessing the plausibility of the theory of meaning it supports. Again familiarly, Dummett contends – supported by, among other arguments, the 'challenges' over acquisition and manifestation – that an objectivist-truth-conditional theory of meaning will not do.[40]

Essential to this train of reasoning is its identification of classical objectivist truth as the key to realism. This, it seems to me, is where the mistake lies. For the notion of truth in play crucially depends on a pair of prior commitments, one metaphysical and the other epistemological; it is these, and *especially* the latter, which do the work in what Dummett describes as realism. And when one recognizes this, one sees that Dummett has run together quite different things as 'realisms'. His definition thus obscures rather than clarifies what is at stake in different debates.

Dummett himself states that the realist conception of statements in some class turns on the idea that their truth-values are settled by *knowledge-independent* states of affairs. 'The very minimum that realism can be held to involve,' he says, 'is that statements in the given class relate to some reality that exists *independently of our knowledge* of it, in such a way that that reality renders each statement in the class determinately true or false, again *independently of whether we know, or are even able to discover*, its truth-value' (my italics).[41] The immediate interest in this for Dummett is that such a commitment shows – leaving aside problems of vagueness – that the statements in question are bivalent, because they are selected as determinately true or false by an independent reality which settles the matter without reference to any cognizing subject. And this is why he describes realism as a semantic thesis: it is 'a semantic thesis [because it is] a doctrine about the sort of thing that makes our statements true when they are true'. But his unpacking of the expression 'sort of thing' is revealing; the thesis is a semantic thesis, he tells us, by courtesy of something else: 'the fundamental thesis of realism, so regarded, is that we really do succeed in referring to external objects, existing *independently of our knowledge* of them, and that the statements we make about them are rendered true or false by an objective reality the constitution of which is, again, *independent of our knowledge*' (my italics).[42]

This characterization immediately shows that the conception of truth at work cannot be understood otherwise than in terms of the logically antecedent metaphysical and epistemological – and especially epistemological – theses which determine its content. Both theses are simply stated. First, there is a determinately characterized reality. Secondly, truth-values are properties of statements which they possess as a result of standing in certain definite relations – the usual candidate is some sort of 'correspondence' – to that reality, the relations being external ones as required by the independence constraint; which is, thirdly, that both the reality and the truth-values of what is or could be said about it are independent of any knowledge of either. So the semantic theory (the theory of truth and reference) presupposes the existence of a determinately charactered reality (the metaphysical thesis) which is independent of our knowledge, and confers – independently of our means or even our capacity for getting such knowledge – truth or falsity on whatever could be said about it (the epistemological thesis). (Compare Putnam's far stronger characterization of 'metphysical realism', described above.)

The epistemological thesis says that our conception of reality is in no way constrained by our capacities to know anything about it. More precisely, it says that the knowledge relation is external, contingent and limited; it states (a) that the objects of knowledge can and for the most part do transcend our powers of access to them, and (b) that the sense of remarks about the existence and character of these entities or realms is not governed by considerations relating to our epistemic powers. (Note how this summarizes Platt's picture.) In the anti-realist view it is the incoherence of (b) which underlies the incoherence of realism, as we shall see later. Among other things it makes realists construe (a) as saying that the independence of objects of knowledge from *acts of awareness* (or thought, etc.) of them entails the independence of objects of knowledge from thought or knowledge *tout court*. There is no such entailment: which is the starting point for another story.[43]

At this juncture, the claim made by the realist's opponent – that epistemic constraints are ineliminably relevant – can be evaluated while leaving open the question of the constraints' exact nature. All one need say is that they demand that whatever is required for a conception of some object of discourse, it should lie within the ability of discoursers to get it. This can allow that the results of epistemic cooperation, exploiting whatever can be shared and distributed courtesy of language, count among discoursers' resources. Given inherent limitations on individuals' powers of perception, reason and memory – a finitary predicament which imposes narrow boundaries even on what the community of discoursers can cooperatively manage – that demand is an austere enough one. It is what identifies our problem in the theory of knowledge: the problem of trying to understand belief-acquisition and justification, given our strategic need for beliefs whose content often exceeds the empirical grounds we have for holding them.

The realist epistemic thesis has it that we can attribute possession of certain concepts to ourselves without having to provide, or even to possess, grounds for that attribution. It is natural to express this in terms of the meaning of the expressions we use in applying such concepts, not least because the most tractable – often the only – way of specifying the content of a concept lies in inspecting what we say. But what such a thesis turns on is a prior commitment to there being truth-conferring (and so, on this view, meaning-conferring) states-of-affairs whose existence and character is independent of our knowledge of them; which is why a realist holds that language-understanding is not epistemically constrained.

In Dummett's account, acceptance of bivalence and knowledge-independence of truth-value commits one to holding that there is a knowledge-independent reality which confers determinate truth-value on statements. In this ordering – the order of Dummett's exposition – the thesis about truth and its underpinning in classical logic appears to be the decisive factor. But the logical order of dependence among these commitments is, as the foregoing remarks suggest, the reverse of this order of exposition. The fundamental commitment is to there being *knowledge-independent* states-of-affairs, for without this premiss in place for the semantic thesis to presuppose it, that thesis is empty: we have no other way of characterizing the concept of truth required.

If we adhere to Dummett's formulation, in which acceptance of bivalence and knowledge-independence of truth-value commits us to the existence of a knowledge-independent reality, we have indeed thereby identified what that acceptance entails. But there is no converse entailment. It may be natural, but it is not obligatory, for someone to hold the metaphysical and epistemological doctrines in question, and also to hold a recognition-transcendent view of truth. But it is open to someone to hold those same metaphysical and epistemological doctrines and to have different views about truth: for one example, to deny that truth is a property conferred on what we assert by the reality so conceived; or, for another, to deny bivalence. Someone might do this latter even if he accepted that truth is recognition-independent and is so because it is conferred by a knowledge-independent reality.[44] At the same time, it is clear that what a philosophical doctrine of realism seeks to preserve from our ordinary beliefs about the nature of reality is precisely what is conveyed by the metaphysical and epistemological theses which give natural but not inevitable rise to the view of truth in question. Given this, it is hard to resist the view that the metaphysics and especially epistemology of the matter are fundamental.

One motive that some have for thinking otherwise comes from the idea that any adequate conception of truth has to rely on stipulative features. In particular, it might be held that a correspondence principle, for one of the two main senses of 'correspondence' sketched in chapter 6, functions regulatively in our account of truth, prompting commitments about the nature of the corresponding relata. But as that chapter shows, correspondence theories are beset by difficulties; so it has been suggested that to answer our need for a regulative conception of truth we should simply lay it down as a minimum feature of truth that it consist in a correspondence – leaving open the question of what in detail that is – between suitably characterized relata.

There might accordingly be a demand for an independence clause in a specification of truth – that is, one which asserts that 'the facts' exist, and have the character they have, *independently of our investigations* of them – precisely to serve our need for a way of distinguishing true beliefs from those that fail to be true. Given that this matters so much in practice, just that objectivist division is forced, and in the heat of the moment an utterance's failing to be true invites no closer scrutiny as to how it does: we do not stop to ask whether it fails to be true because it is false, or for some other reason (because, say, it is meaningless, or has some third truth-value, or is not a candidate for truth-value at all). The view that falsehood exhausts ways of failing to to be true is doubtless a natural one to have arisen in the history of ordinary uses of language, a fact which might yield a moral for anyone who believes ordinary usage is sacrosanct.

But the need which prompts stipulations about the nature of truth is precisely an epistemic need (all practical needs are such, although the converse is not true). Viewed as a strategic commitment, a correspondence principle entails the allied but further strategic commitment to the independence of truth-conferring states-of-affairs from knowledge of them, because this objectivist attitude alone sustains what is required by the demands of practice – that is, exhaustive classification into 'true' and 'not-true'. Considerations of practice of course lead to the drawing of distinctions among ways beliefs and utterances can fail to be true. But at the outset our view of the character of truth is determined by the controlling influence of our metaphysical and epistemological concerns, namely, those which constitute our commitment to there being a knowledge-independent realm of entities. The power of these concerns is evidenced by the fact that they prompt the very intuitions offended by counterfactual conditionals which not only appear incapable of determinate truth-value, on the grounds that there is nothing 'in virtue of which' they could be either true or false ('if God had created such-and-such beings, they would have done so-and-so' is a familiar example), but that they are not even capable of being either true or not true. Here the lack of something 'in virtue of which' an objective truth-value can be assigned suggests that there is nothing to be committed to *antecedently* which would sustain a notion of truth-value for the cases in question.

These thoughts imply that there is a deep tension in Dummett's account; and it is not far to seek. His reason for characterizing realism as a thesis about truth rather than ontology (still less epistemology), is, as noted, that 'certain kinds of realism, for instance realism about the future or about ethics, do not seem readily classifiable as doctrines about a realm of entities'.[45] Yet he immediately goes on to define realism for any subject matter in expressly ontological and epistemological terms: 'The very minimum that realism can be held to involve is that the statements in the given class relate to some reality that exists *independently of our knowledge* of it' (my italics again).[46] This is inconsistent, so one of these views must give way. It is not hard to say which. If the notion of truth constituting the Dummett hallmark of realism depends for its content on an antecedent commitment to a knowledge-independent reality, and if, as already quoted, 'the fundamental thesis of realism . . . is that we really do succeed in referring to external objects, existing independently of our knowledge of them', it follows that what we should say about those 'realisms' which are not readily classifiable in terms of entities – for example, mathematical 'realism' and ethical 'realism' – is, simply, and on Dummett's own reasoning, that they are not realisms. Disputes concerning them are disputes of a different kind: and insofar as they raise questions about what concept of truth is applicable to them, that concept cannot involve considerations about knowledge-independent entities. And it is accordingly no longer clear whether the concept of truth at stake in these disputes is objectivist. When we find that a theory of meaning rests on a semantics to which that concept of truth is central, commitments of the metaphysical and epistemological kind at issue have therefore already been made.

One point, then, is that whatever else 'realism' might denote, it at least denotes a thesis about a realm of entities. This, although a consequential insight, should hardly be a surprising one; even in traditional debates about universals and the external world this much is a common feature. But as we have just seen, it follows that if ethics and mathematics and talk of other times – especially the future – are not about realms of entities, then controversies over the concepts of truth and knowledge applicable to them are not realism–anti-realism controversies. On this view, although we recognize that, in ethics, the debate is between cognitivists and those who disagree with them, and that in mathematics it is between espousers of different understandings of what makes for the truth of mathematical statements, we also recognize that in neither debate is it just that there is no obligation to talk about the existence of entities (the respective candidates might be 'moral properties' and 'structures'); it is, as Dummett himself suggests, positively misleading. For if, respectively, cognitivist and Platonist theses turn on claims about the existence of certain sorts of moral properties or mathematical structures, the question immediately arises as to how we can reduce the metaphorical character of such claims, given that their sense is imported from the one case (the spatio-temporal world case) which alone has unmetaphorical content.[47] The absence of an answer to this question is precisely Dummett's motive for switching attention to the problem of truth. But as shown, doing so brings too much under one label. The solution is not to find a different reason – one given in terms of truth – for classifying all these controversies together as realism controversies, but instead to recognize that they are controversies of quite different kinds. So we do well to restrict talk of realism to the case where controversy concerns unmetaphorical claims about the knowledge-independent existence of entities or realms of entities – namely, the spatio-temporal case – and to employ more precise denominations for the different debates which arise in other, different, domains.

The most important point to be made about the nature of realism, however, is that what crucially differentiates it is the epistemological thesis that the realms or entities to which ontological commitment is made exist independently of knowledge of them. It is vital to note that existential commitment without this epistemological independence claim is not realism. For it is no-one's view that X is unreal if its existence can only be understood *via* what is involved in detecting X. Obviously enough, an anti-realist metaphysics is a metaphysics of existing entities. What distinguishes such a view from a realist one is that unlike the realist, the anti-realist can make no sense of metaphysical claims without a supporting epistemology that yields grounds for them. If something is asserted to exist, in other words, it is because something counts as validating, supporting or making sense of that claim; in short, something counts as evidence for the claim, grasp of which plays its part in constituting the claim's sense. The anti-realist in this way regards the relations between existing things and the relevant kinds of epistemic access to them as internal ones – from which it does not follow, as in cruder characterizations of anti-realism it is supposed to follow, that the existing things are 'dependent' (perhaps even causally dependent) on cognition of them. This is a hangover from misunderstandings of Berkeley, whose denial of the existence of material substance is too often read as a denial of the existence of the external world.[48] Viewed from this perspective, what is at issue between realists and anti-realists is the epistemological thesis that what exists does or can do so *independently of any thought, talk, knowledge or experience of it.* To make out his case the realist has to show that this claim is intelligible. The chief anti-realist point is that the claim is unintelligible.[49] The arguments against semantic realism discussed in the preceding chapter apply, *mutatis mutandis* but on direct analogy, with the arguments against the realist's epistemological thesis.

Are we helped by recognizing that the realism dispute is primarily an epistemological one? In giving an affirmative answer one must begin by stressing that ordinary discourse is, without question, realist in character. We assume that the entities we refer to exist independently of our cognizing them, and we assume the same about the states of affairs which, we further assume, make true or false our assertions about them. Our realism at the level of ordinary thought and talk, the 'first order' level, is indeed rather promiscuous: we take literally a sense, to be informatively compared with the case of fictional discourse, of there being something we are talking about when we talk. Various ways of cashing this thought suggest themselves, one of which is that it would render explanation of our first order linguistic practice incoherent if we did not or could not attribute to speakers beliefs about the existence, independently of them, of the entities constituting the domain over which their discourse ranges.

The clue lies in the fact that these realist commitments are *commitments* and that they are fundamental to first order practice. We might now – to wax schematic – distinguish between realism, assumed at the first order, and what I shall now baptize as 'transcendentism', the second order thesis that realism is literally true. The label is chosen to reflect the knowlege-transcendent character of the realist's conception of truth. On this way of putting matters, anti-transcendentism is the thesis that it is mistaken to claim that realism is literally true, since nothing can, on the realist view itself, establish that it is either true or false, for the content of realist claims exceeds the possibilities of verification of them. Rather, says the anti-transcendentist, realism is a fundamental assumption of our practice at the first order. It is therefore not true but assumed to be true. The dispute between these positions is accordingly a second order controversy about the correct understanding of our practice and the logical and metaphysical presuppositions of it. Second order commentary might show that there is need to revise a first order practice wherever the commentary reveals the practice to be wrong. A second order thesis like this would constitute an error theory with respect to first order practice, as in the case, say, of Mackie's view about ethics.[50] But it depends on cases, for it can be that second order interpretation of first order practice leaves the latter as it is.

At first blush the difference between the transcendentist and the anti-transcendentist positions looks vanishingly small. But the consequences for a range of issues, including our understanding of truth and knowledge, are great. On the transcendentist view the relations between speakers and what they speak about are external ones, so it is at very least natural to treat truth as a property conferred on our utterances by knowledge-independent circumstances, and our notion of knowledge, in turn, as having it that whatever consequences, if any, our knowing something about the world has for the world, they are contingent ones only. In particular, coming to know things about the world is a process of discovery, one which lies under the austere constraint of our inherent epistemic limitations. (It is in this sense, to use Crispin Wright's phrase, that realism is 'modest'.) Taken together, these theses about truth and knowledge entail commitment to there being a sharp distinction between truth-value and grounds for assigning truth-value. This epistemological commitment is sometimes identified by Dummett as fundamental to Frege's views and – quite rightly, as the argument here has it – as the crux of transcendentism. For the anti-transcendentist, that distinction exists for us only at the first order, as a matter of epistemic strategy.

Either way, therefore, the nub of the matter at the second order concerns the question whether metaphysical commitments at the first order can be regarded as literally true (or false) as transcendentism claims, or, as anti-transcendentism claims, as having an irreducibly strategic character, constituting assumptions of our discourse which we hold true as a framework for organizing experience fruitfully. It is a debate primarily about the role of epistemic constraints in understanding our thought, not a debate about what logical principles our practices should embody, nor a debate about what is taken to exist in our first order scheme of things (or the science by which they are explained and, to the extent possible, manipulated). In this sense the debate leaves everything as it is, and therefore if anti-transcendentism is correct, no revisions to logic, linguistic practice or mundane metaphysics are called for. This marks a sharp contrast with *revisionary* versions of anti-realism, as espoused by Dummett, Tennant and others.[51]

Before leaving the matter of identifying accurately what is at stake in the realism–anti-realism debate – or transcendentist–anti-transcendentist debate, as its second order character suggests – it is worth noting the following.

Earlier it was noted that current orthodoxy defines the debate as primarily about meaning. But despite the fact that, if the foregoing is right, the debate is better understood as primarily about epistemology, and one which moreover applies only where questions about the existence of entities are already settled or assumed, there is nevertheless no suggestion that semantic questions are irrelevant. Far from it. This is because a decision about the role of epistemic constraints one way or the other has immediate results for our view about what sort of theory of meaning we can have; and that in turn tells us where to look for an understanding of truth, reference, and the nature of valid inference.

Dummett is explicit in his opposition to this approach. 'An attack from the top down tries to resolve the metaphysical problem first, and then to derive from the solution to it the correct model of meaning, and the appropriate notion of truth, for the sentences in dispute, and hence to deduce the logic we ought to accept as governing them.'[52] The disadvantage of this approach, he says, is that we have no way of resolving the metaphysical dispute because, despite centuries of debate, we cannot give it a clear content; we cannot reduce the metaphorical character of the terms in which it is posed. Therefore we should proceed bottom-up, starting with the question of the correct model of meaning for statements of the disputed class, 'ignoring,' he says, 'the metaphysical problems at the outset'.[53] When the correct model of meaning has been devised the metaphysical problems will thereby be solved, for there is nothing more to a metaphysics than its being the 'picture of reality' that goes with a particular model of meaning.[54]

The response is to say, first, that metaphysical problems are statable in metaphorical or pictorial terms only if we think they arise in connection with ethics, mathematics, the future, or similar subject matters. One is much inclined to agree with Dummett that no real content can be attributed in such cases; or indeed in any case, for this is just the difficulty noted in connection with thesis A. But as argued above, this too is precisely the reason for saying that disputes in these cases are not realism disputes: they are not candidates for evaluation in terms of transcendentist commitment, that is, commitment to the *knowledge-independent existence of entities*. The only subject matter where this makes non-metaphorical sense is the spatio-temporal case.

But in any event the top-down strategy does not start with the metaphysical problem, not even the unmetaphorical one: it starts with an epistemological one, namely, the question whether epistemic constraints are necessary for the intelligibility of metaphysical claims and indeed for discourse in general. Once that issue is resolved, *ipso facto* one rather than another basis for a model of meaning has been chosen. So much is implicit in Dummett's own characterization of the notion of truth he identifies as the source of realism. The point here is to insist on the dependence of that notion on epistemological considerations, and therefore to urge a redistribution of emphasis in what follows.

In debate about anti-realism two mistakes are standardly made. Anti-realism is either taken to be or to imply idealism; or it is taken to be or to imply relativism. The following section shows that neither is the case.[55]

Anti-realism and Idealism

Anti-realism is not idealism. The former is an epistemological thesis, the latter a metaphysical one. There is no entailment from one to the other.

Idealism is a metaphysical thesis (a family of such theses) about the nature of reality; it states that the universe is mental. Its chief historical opponent is materialism, the thesis that the universe is material (is made of matter – a view that should, strictly, not be confused with physicalism, which claims that the universe consists of what can be described by physics. What can be described by physics is not only not coterminous with matter, but might well entail that there is no such thing as matter.)

Anti-realism is not a metaphysical thesis but an epistemological one; it denies that the relations between thought and its objects, perception and its targets, experience and the realms over which it ranges (these are different, though related, relations) are external or contingent relations. There are realistic forms of idealism (see, for example, Sprigge[56]), and there is no reason in principle why there should not be anti-realistic forms of materialism or – even more plausibly – physicalism. (Quantum theory under the Copenhagen interpretation is one such.)

The claim that the relations between thought and its objects (etc.) are internal is far from the claim that objects of thought are *causally dependent* upon thought (or, more generally, experience, or sentience) for their existence. Certain forms of idealism (for example, Berkeley's) put matters this way, and doubtless this is why some confuse idealism with anti-realism. Rather, it is at most the claim – until more is said; as to which, there can be much variety – that no complete description of either relatum can leave out mention of the other. That is the essence of anti-realism.

It is important to be clear about what this means. Realism is the view that the relation between thought and its objects is contingent or external, in the sense that description of neither relatum essentially involves reference to the other. This is what the independence thesis constitutive of realism comes down to. Much in the foregoing chapter and earlier in this chapter gives reason for showing that this commitment is incoherent. A more direct way of showing this is offered by the idiom of relations. A moment's reflection shows that the claim in question – the claim that the relations between thought and its objects are external – is a mistake at least for the direction object-to-thought, for any account of the content of thoughts about things, and in particular the individuation of thoughts about things, essentially involves reference to the things thought about – this is the force of the least that can be said in favour of notions of broad content. So realism offers us a peculiarly hybrid relation: external in the direction thought-to-things, internal in the direction things-to-thought. It is an easy step for the anti-realist to show that thought about (perception of, theories of) things is always and inescapably present in, and therefore conditions, any full account of the things thought about; the poorly-worded 'Tree Argument' in Berkeley, aimed at showing that one cannot conceive of an unconceived thing, is aimed at making just that elementary point.[57] The best statement of such a view is afforded by the Copenhagen interpretation of quantum theory, in which descriptions of quantum phenomena are taken *essentially* to involve reference to observers and conditions of observation. Such a view does not constitute a claim that the phenomena are caused by observations of them. No more does anti-realism claim this. However, a little thought shows that if this claim – that the relations between thought and things are internal – is correct, then one needs to think again about truth, objectivity, the modalities and knowledge.[58]

One often sees an opposition posed between realism and idealism, as if the labels marked competitors for the same terrain. As the foregoing remarks show, this is a mistake, and a serious one. It is surprisingly common.

Anti-realism and Relativism

Some critics, and some proponents, of anti-realist views take them to imply relativism. The point can be variously argued. If our conceptions of the world are essentially conditioned by how we form them, there is no reason why different people (conceptual communities, perhaps even individuals) might not arrive at different, even incommensurable, such conceptions. Again, the point might be put by saying that if anti-realism consists in the denial of a common co-ordinate reality existing independently of thought about it, and therefore imposing constraints on how many different ways there can successfully be of thinking about it, then there could be many different such ways of thinking.

But relativism is an intellectually unhealthy point of view. It is the extreme form of scepticism – there are various truths, various knowledges, perhaps in direct competition but, even so, incapable of adjudication – and we are familiar with the difficulties it poses for value debates. (Some find these congenial.) I shall not rehearse the sins of relativism at length here, but show that it is anyway false. In doing so I shall demonstrate that no entailments hold between relativism and anti-realism as here understood.

There is a distinction to be drawn between moral or cultural relativism, on the one hand, and cognitive relativism on the other. The former concerns the difference between cultures, or between different historical phases of the same culture, with respect to religious, social, and moral values and practices; that is, with respect to what might be called the 'superstructure' of a culture's conceptual scheme.[59] Cognitive relativism concerns the 'infrastructure', the level of basic beliefs about the world, such as that there are perception-independent, reidentifiable and individually discriminable objects or events, occupying space and time, interacting causally, and bearing properties of various kinds.

On the face of it, cultural relativism presents few philosophical difficulties, because our being able to recognize that another culture, or historical phase in our own culture, differs from our own in certain respects, presupposes our ability to gain access to the other culture and recognize the differences as differences; which means that enough must be common between our own and the other culture to allow access. These points are best made by adopting Davidson's characterization of a conceptual scheme as a language or set of intertranslatable languages, and as access between cultures (schemes) as effected by translation.[60]

It is, however, just this point which is denied by proponents of relativism, who object that the appearance of accessibility is misleading. Far from gaining entry to the alien scheme we have merely reinterpreted it in terms of our own scheme; which is the best we can hope to do, because translation is not possible above an indeterminate level. By failure of translation relativists do not mean the empirically false thesis that no language can be rendered into another, but the philosophical thesis that (in Quine's terminology) synonymy relations cannot be established above the level of stimulus-meanings of sentences, these being native speakers' patterns of assent and dissent to them; and therefore, although we might come to use a term of a foreign language in the correct assent–dissent pattern, we can never be sure which of alternative translations exhaustively captures its sense, for its stimulus-conditions underdetermine the precise construction to be placed on it. Thus 'gavagai' might mean 'rabbit' or 'temporal slices of rabbithood', and so on, without our having means to reduce the indeterminacy.[61]

What underlies Quine's thesis of the indeterminacy of translation, and its such variants as Feyerabend's views on meaning variance,[62] is the problem of the theory-ladenness of observation. If all discourse is theoretical there is no Archimedean point from which subscribers to one scheme can *neutrally* compare an alien scheme. If the problem of translation proves intractable, it follows that relativism is true; and Quine's view, that a difference of language marks a difference of ontology, is substantiated. Accordingly the question of theory-ladenness and its consequences for translation require investigation.

The theory-ladenness thesis is the claim that no difference exists between theoretical and observational terms. The outcome of the

Positivists' debate over whether there can be theory-neutral descriptions of experience was that there can be no such thing because the notion of observationality is itself theoretical;[63] so there is no way out, on either count of whether there can be a neutral observation language into which different theoretical languages can be translated for comparison, or whether certain sets of theoretical statements (for example, about physical objects) can be reduced to observational statements (for example, about sense-data); for the distinction required to license such translations trades upon the possibility of there being formal criteria of synonymy by means of which the translation can proceed. And this Quine denies; he holds that there can be no such formal criteria of synonymy, for they would be constructable only by reference to our knowledge of what things in the world the terms in question apply to, and therefore cannot be independent of our theories about the world.[64] Accordingly, because the synonymy relations will themselves be theory-infected, appeal to them in reduction vitiates the reductive enterprise.

So: the claim that there can be no observation term–theoretical term distinction rests on rejection of synonymy; on which basis it is then denied that the meaning of an expression in some natural language L1 can be stated in another natural language L2; and therefore, because language = conceptual scheme, failure of translation amounts to radical relativism. Feyerabend takes the view further by claiming that because, within a single scheme, all the concepts employed are theoretical, shifts in theory constitute conceptual change and therefore change in meaning; for example, inventing finer ways of calibrating temperature results, in his view, in a change in the meaning of 'temperature'.

These relativist considerations might appear to be a natural corollary of anti-realism in the theory of meaning. Feyerabend's thermometers afford a case in point. If the sense of a term is fixed by its conditions of assertion, evidently changes in these latter – as with finer calibrations of temperature – constitute changes of sense. More generally, if, as Quine's arguments suggest, we never have a determinate grasp of the conditions for assertion of expressions in languages other than our own – and therefore can only grasp the sense of those expressions indeterminately – then relativism is true, and each language is its own conceptual scheme. These arguments also oppose the view that moral or cultural relativism is philosophically unproblematic; we do not, if relativist arguments are right, have access of any genuine kind to other cultures or phases in the history of our own.

We might begin to rebut these views by asking: what explains the idea that, despite our being sealed-off from an alien language or conceptual scheme, we could nevertheless recognize it as such? Surely, in order to recognize an alien language *as a language*, we would need access to it in some way. The idea here is that nothing could count for us as a language unless it were recognizable as such, and that whatever differences there are, in outlook or opinion, between ourselves and speakers of another language, they would, in order to be so recognized, have to occur against a background of shared beliefs and assumptions giving rise to enough mutual comprehensibility. If right, this suggests that relativism is wrong, and indeed furnishes the materials for an argument to show that it is so; for it turns on Davidson's claim that the criterion of languagehood is translatability into our own language. Moreover (but this goes well beyond Davidson) the translatability in question must be better than indeterminate. The argument against relativism proceeds as follows.

Schematically, a language is a conceptual scheme. If we are to recognize a language as such, we must be able to recognize the presence of a certain range of beliefs, specifically empirical beliefs, underlying the speakers' employment of their language. It is fruitful to think of a scheme as 'organizing' the world over which our experience ranges, or, if one prefers, that experience itself.[65] If a scheme organizes the world or experience, then the ontology at issue is puralist.[66] Accordingly the language must contain individuative devices (and thus concepts of individuals) and predicative devices (and thus concepts of properties) as does ours; for otherwise noting failure in coexstensivity of predicates between our own and the other language would be impossible. Accordingly, at least part of the languagehood criterion is that if anything is a language it contains devices for individuation and predication which can be recognized as such. The translatability of the other tongue will indeed rest upon this; for not even recognizing assent and dissent patterns, after the Quine model, would be possible unless we recognized that (taking the simplest cases) what the assent or dissent is relative to is a claim that here or there is something x, or that x is or is not something F. At the base of a model of discourse built on the idea that at its simplest communication rests on pointing out, agreeing upon, or denying such matters as these, is the notion that an x can be marked off from the rest of the perceptual field, and that something can be said about it – that is, that some property can be ascribed to it. Evidently, a wholly uninterpreted discourse would be one just in virtue of our failure to recognize certain strings of sounds or marks as what might on the foregoing be called individuative and predicative claims, for – the reason noted – our failure in this respect would deny us purchase on what is to count as assent or dissent.

It is important to note how taking such a view marks an advance over what might for convenience be called the Quine–Davidson line. Quine allows that for a certain range of sentences, *viz.*, 'observation sentences' falling on to the periphery of the web of language, meanings can be grasped by 'pure ostension'. Mass terms are good examples; 'water' can be learned ostensively by conditioning or induction. In contrast, such terms of divided reference as 'rabbit' cannot be mastered without mastering the principles of individuation governing them, yet these cannot be mastered by ostension; therefore indeterminacy enters the picture, for if one cannot tell, in connection with 'gavagai', where one leaves off and another begins – for example, whether 'gavagai' picks out rabbits, undetached rabbit parts, or rabbit stages – then appeal to reference is of no avail in accounting for however much of the meaning of 'gavagai' we grasp, and in consequence we have to rest content with indeterminate 'stimulus-meaning'.[67] This alone on Quine's view is what enables us to get our translation manual started. (Reference proper, for Quine, is something which only bound variables do, because in order to circumvent the problem of referential opacity, that is, to ensure that reference is successful, it must be restricted to a connection between bound variables in a canonically regimented language and the values which those variables take in the selected domain of discourse.[68]) But this will not do; for all that the stimulus-conditions for 'gavagai' tell us is that 'gavagai' is assertible when current stimulation includes a rabbit, and that native speakers never dissent when 'gavagai' is offered in the presence of one. But this is to know far too little about the assertability-conditions of 'gavagai' to permit translation of the term, for it may be, as some widely different set of circumstances might show, that 'gavagai' means something like 'creature which yields white meat', and may therefore also apply to chickens. Unless the translator had a way of focusing also on what the term contrasts with in native usage, that is, on what it is for something *not* to be gavagai, he could not render the term. Among the complexities known to a speaker about the sentences of his own language are some of the implications which use of them carries; in particular, interpreting a sentence, for example 'this is not red', involves knowing that it implies a certain closed field of options, having the force of 'this is (some other colour)' rather than, say, 'this is liquid' or 'this tastes pleasant'.[69] Unless the translator knew what remained open by a case of dissent to 'gavagai', the expression would be opaque; yet to know the force of such a denial would be to know a principle of individuation for gavagais, for the simple reason that the translator would know, in knowing what was left open by denials, *ipso facto* where a gavagai left off and something else (a non-gavagai) began – and hence, by the same token, where one gavagai left off and another began. Accordingly, for any interpretation to get going, what must be known to the translator is the reference of the relevant terms. And the notion of reference here is not arcane; the reference of a term is just the object which use of the term (if it is a singular term) picks out or individuates, or the objects which the term (if it is a general term) collects.

If it is granted that references must be perspicuous across languages for translation to be possible, it follows that the extension of at least many simple predicates, or, at any rate, the intersection of the extension of such predicates as between the languages, is determinable; for referential scrutability allows the direct enumeration of lists of objects satisfying a predicate in a way that permits correct applications (and withholdings) of a predicate in L1 by a speaker of L2. It follows that for some expressions paired from L1 and L2 there will be a semantic feature of the pairing very like our pretheoretical grasp of intralanguage synonymy; consider 'la plume est rouge' and 'the pen is red'. Evidently, if such a relation obtains between sentences of different languages, it does so in a way both richer and more determinate than is allowable on Quine's view of stimulus-synonymy; and this is as it should be, for the perspicuity of reference and accessibility of predicate-extensions across languages would together be expected to generate a number of matchings of this kind.

This is a point about sentence synonymy within and across languages, holding, for present purposes, to the level of complete sentences of a given class, *viz.*, those expressing perceptual judgements. It will be recalled that in 'Two Dogmas' Quine attacked both the analytic–synthetic distinction and reductionism on the grounds that they are closely linked and mutually supportive, depending as they do on the possibility of extricating factual from semantic considerations and considering their bearing on the truth-conditions of a given statement separately – which, if it were possible, would make reduction a feasible enterprise in that we could display the factual component of truth-conditions independently of the purely semantic features of sentences made true (or false) by them; and we could give an account of analytic statements as constituting a degenerate class wholly dependent for their truth-value on semantic considerations alone.[70] Quine's attack was an attack on Positivist verificationism, to which this 'extricability thesis' is fundamental.[71] Statement synonymy on the Positivist view consists in the fact that because the meaning of a statement is its method of verification, any two statements with identical empirical conditions of confirmation or disconfirmation are synonymous. This demands that unique ranges of sensory events be identifiable for individual statements which, as the case may be, verify or falsify the statements in question. This constitutes the view's reductionism, and this is what Quine finds objectionable. His holism or 'organic' verificationism is opposed precisely to such 'molecular' verificationism.[72]

But it is not clear that what Quine takes to follow from holism does follow, specifically in connection with indeterminacy at the level of observation statements. Here, on his view, the stimulus meanings of observation sentences, construed as the ordered pair of assents and dissents prompted by given stimuli, underdetermine the translation of such sentences from L1 to L2 in the way noted; but for the reason that the range of options left open by dissents must be determinate – again, as noted – this degree of indeterminacy would prevent any translation. Quine's notion of stimulus-meaning as it stands will not therefore do, and the added requirement that the force of dissents be available to the translator is precisely a requirement for determinacy.

This has two results: it entails that sentences indeterminate in L2 will reflect indeterminancy in L1 in the way described by Dummett,[73] – that is, if a sentence of L1 has competing renderings in L2 it will be because speakers of L1 themselves attach competing interpretations to the L1 sentence, and this feature of the sentence's ambiguity or underdetermination will be reflected in L2; and secondly, it entails that the assertability-conditions for unambiguous sentences of L1 will be known to a speaker of L2 if he can translate it, in such a way that for at least some sentences of L1 the speaker of L2 can recognize the assertability-conditions for the sentence to be identical to its translation in L2, and so stand in a relation of statement-synonymy to its L2 translation.[74]

This notion of statement-synonymy trades upon the fact that determinacy of reference and predicate extension must be available to the translator if he is to translate at all. Thus if he knows that a term a in L1 refers to all and only what the term b in L2 refers to, and a predicate F introduces a particular property designated G in L2, then the sentence Fa in L1 is synonymous with the L2 sentence Gb. It is to be borne in mind that, in the most general terms, understanding (knowing how to use) a sentence involves knowing all of (a) what terms correlate with what features of a perceptual environment, (b) how to recognize such features, and (c) in what ways things can go wrong with either (a) or (b), and chiefly the latter. Knowing, at least implicitly, these things is to understand the sentence. To assert as it were across languages, it might seem that what has to be known is extra information under (a), for example, that 'plume' corefers with 'pen', 'voiture' with 'motor-car', and so on; but matters are tighter than this, for knowing (a) is *ipso facto* to know all of (a)–(c); displaying mastery of a term presupposes mastery of all three conditions. Because understanding a sentence of L1 involves the same as understanding a sentence of L2, knowing extra information about terms (or rather, just knowing more terms) which apply to certain features in perceptual environments is to know how things must be for their use to be licensed. This strengthens the requirement of option-closure connected with negation. For it is a corollary of these conditions that one has failed to grasp the sense of an expression if one does not know what alternatives are left open by dissent to it, for all one would know in such a case is that use of the term is inappropriate, not why or how, and this violates the conditions for mastery.

This is not to say, however, that unique ranges of sensory evidence have to be available for the confirmation or disconfirmation of a sentence in order for it to be assertable, although they would be available on each occasion of an undefeatedly licensed use of such a sentence. What the speaker has to know is what circumstances would license use of the sentence. The conditions for understanding a sentence do not require that for every understood sentence there is an occasion on which a speaker is actually licensed in its use.

A difficulty may appear to arise here: it follows, most clearly in connection with option-closure, that understanding a sentence involves understanding other sentences, or more generally a portion at least of a language. This would seem to require of a translator that he knows other sentences of L1 before he can understand whatever sentence of L1 is in question. Not so; in so far as he is a translator, he knows L2, and the sentence of L1 at issue can be placed in the context of what can be said in L2 on the topic in hand. This affords an alternative means of marking the sense in which, for a language, to be recognizable as a language, it must be accessible, that is, translatable into a familiar idiom.

The foregoing arguments show that relativism is false, for if languages = schemes, and any language, to be recognizable as such, is translatable into one's own, then there is only one conceptual scheme. So much was the terminus of Davidson's argument; the adaptation of it here goes further in claiming that translation has to be determinate for at least some classes of expressions, which strengthens the claim that the conception of alternative schemes, other than in the reducible cultural sense, is incoherent.

Nothing in these arguments speaks to the question of what kind of relations obtain between thoughts and their objects (and the other relations in the family), and in particular does not entail the claim that only a realist view of such relations is consistent with rejection of relativism. For that reason alone, there is no entailment in either direction between anti-realism and relativism. But there is a stronger point to be made. If either of the two '-isms' under discussion is more naturally consistent with relativism, it turns out to be realism; for realism promotes the idea that *there can be* things we do not and perhaps cannot know (or think about, etc.), and so the idea that there might be schemes, or kinds of experience, sealed off from the possibility of our grasping what they are like, is entirely consistent with that view. In its semantic guise, anti-realism is a repudiation of the idea that such possibilities make sense.

Notes

1 H. Putnam, 'A Defence of Internal Realism', APA Address 1982, in J. Conant (ed.), *Realism With a Human Face*, p. 30.
2 H. Putnam, *Representation and Reality*, p. 107.
3 Putnam, 'Model Theory and the Factuality of Semantics', in *Words and Life*, ed. J. Conant.
4 Putnam, *Renewing Philosophy*, p. 2.
5 Putnam, 'Simon Blackburn on Internal Realism', in P. Clark and B. Hale (eds), *Reading Putnam*, p. 253.
6 Putnam, *Reason, Truth and History*, pp. 5–6.
7 Ibid., pp. 7–8.
8 Ibid., pp. 16–17.

9   Ibid., p. 51.

10   Ibid., p. 52.

11   Putnam, 'Reply to David Anderson', *Philosophical Topics*, 20 (1992) n. 27, p. 404.

12   Cf. e.g. M. Sacks, *The World We Found*; C. Wright, 'On Putnam's Proof That We Are Not Brains in a Vat', in Clark and Hale (eds), *Reading Putnam*.

13   Sacks, *The World We Found*, pp. 66–75.

14   A similar point is made by Wright, 'On Putnam's Proof', pp. 238–240.

15   Putnam, 'Beyond Historicism' in *Realism and Reason*, p. 295; see also his 'Model Theory and the Factuality of Semantics', *Words and Life*, ed. J. Conant, Harvard 1994.

16   Putnam, 'Replies' in Clark and Hale (eds), *Reading Putnam*, p. 242.

17   Ibid., p. 243.

18   Ibid., p. 244.

19   Putnam, *Words and Life*, in J. Conant (ed.), p. 492.

20   Ibid., p. 78.

21   Ibid., p. 307.

22   Rorty, R., 'Putnam on Truth', *Philosophy and Phenomenological Research* 52 (1992), p. 416.

23   Putnam, *Words and Life*, pp. 300–2.

24   Ibid., p. 309.

25   Cf. Conant's remarks, ibid., p. xxvi.

26   Putnam is quoting Wittgenstein's *Philosophical Investigations* sect. 97 in 'The Question of Realism', *Words and Life*, op. cit.; and see Conant ibid., p. xxvii.

27   R. Rorty, *Philosophy and the Mirror of Nature*, 1980.

28   McDowell, 'Truth-Values, Bivalence, and Verificationism', in Evans and McDowell (eds), *Truth and Meaning*, p. 48.

29   Dummett, *TOE*, p. xi. It is interesting to remark, in passing, a curious irony here. It is that, as a consequence of Logical Positivism, the term 'metaphysics' was for a time pejorative. If one places the stronger of the two possible constructions on McDowell's remarks, it turns out that verificationism, once wielded by its votaries as a weapon for deflating metaphysical pretensions, has become a target for that charge itself. Contemporary anti-realism differs from its forebear, but there are continuities too.

30   Platts, *Ways of Meaning*, pp. 237–8.

31   Ibid., p. 238.

32   Cf. P. F. Strawson, *Individuals*, Part I.

33   Cf. McGinn, 'Can We Solve the Mind–Body Problem?', *Mind*, 98 (1989) and Nagel, *The View from Nowhere*, are examples.

34   Cf. P. Churchland, *Matter and Consciousness*.

35 M. A. E. Dummett, 'Realism', *Synthese*, 52 (1982), pp. 56–7 (references to this paper henceforth *RS*); *The Logical Basis of Metaphysics* (henceforth *LBM*), pp. 9–10, 325–6.

36 Dummett, 'Realism', *Truth and Other Enigmas*, p. 45. References to this paper henceforth *RT*.

37 Ibid., and *RS* p. 55, *LBM*, ch. 1 passim.

38 *RS*, p. 55

39 Ibid., my emphasis.

40 Dummett, 'What is a Theory of Meaning (II)?', in Evans and McDowell (eds), *Truth and Meaning*. Also see, for example, C. Wright, *Realism, Meaning and Truth*, p. 13 *et seq.*

41 *RS*, p. 55, my italics.

42 Ibid., p. 104, my italics. See also *LBM*, p. 9, p. 345.

43 See A. C. Grayling, *The Question of Realism*, forthcoming, passim esp. ch. 2.

44 See e.g. J. McDowell, 'Truth-Values, Bivalence and Verification', in Evans and McDowell (eds), *Truth and Meaning*, and C. Wright, 'Realism, Truth-Value Links, Other Minds and the Past', *Ratio* xxii (1980), p. 112 *et seq.*

45 *RS*, p. 55.

46 Ibid., my italics.

47 The beginnings of the difference would be marked by the response of the man on the Clapham omnibus to attempts at running them together in a putatively univocal way: 'tables and numbers exist' instead of 'tables exist' and 'numbers exist'.

48 See A. C. Grayling, *Berkeley*, passim.

49 It is to Colin McGinn's credit that he has recognized this obligation and tried – heroically but unsuccessfully – to meet it; see McGinn, *The Subjective View*, for one attempt, and 'Can We Solve The Mind–Body Problem?', *Mind*, 1989 for another, premissed on an abandonment of the first; and my respective replies in *Berkeley*, ch. 4 and *The Question of Realism*, ch. 3.

50 J. L. Mackie, *Ethics*, Ch. 1 passim.

51 Dummett, *The Logical Basis of Metaphysics* and Tennant *Anti-Realism and Logic*, p. 12. See also C. Wright, 'Anti-realism and Revisionism' in *Realism Truth and Meaning*, p. 317 and S. Rasmussen and J. Ravnkilde, 'Realism and Logic', *Synthese*, 52 (1982), pp. 379–80.

52 Dummett, *The Logical Basis of Metaphysics*, p. 12.

53 Ibid.

54 Ibid., p. 15.

55 I have elsewhere discussed the following issues in greater detail; cf. Grayling, *The Question of Realism*, forthcoming, chs 3–5, passim, esp. chs 4 and 5.

56 T. L. S. Sprigge, *The Vindication of Absolute Idealism*.

57   Berkeley, *Principles*, sect. 23, Grayling, *Berkeley*, pp. 113–17.

58   See Grayling, *The Question of Realism*, forthcoming, for a full discussion of these matters.

59   For 'conceptual scheme', cf. ibid., ch. 4, esp. pp. 144–96.

60   Cf. Davidson, 'On the Very Idea of a Conceptual Scheme,' *Proceedings of the American Philosophical Society*, 1974, passim, and Grayling, ibid., p. 171 *et seq.*

61   Cf. W. V. Quine, *Word and Object*, ch. 2, passim.

62   P. Feyerabend, *Against Method.*

63   Cf. the discussion of Neurath and Positivism in chs 5 and 7 above

64   Cf. the discussion of Quine on synonymy in chapter 3 above.

65   For 'organizes' cf. Grayling, *The Question of Realism*, ch. 4, passim, esp. p. 190 *et seq.*

66   That is, the language (scheme) ranges over an ontology of more than one different and discriminable item.

67   Cf. Quine, *Ontological Relativity and Other Essays*, p. 31 *et seq.*

68   Cf. ibid., p. 124.

69   Cf. B. Harrison, *Introduction to the Philosophy of Language*, pp. 116–17.

70   Quine, 'Two Dogmas of Empiricism', in *From a Logical Point of View*, passim.

71   Dummett calls Quine's rejection of this thesis 'the inextricability thesis'; thus the coining here. Cf. Dummett, 'The Significance of Quine's Indeterminacy Thesis', *TOE*, p. 375f *et seq.*

72   Dummett's coinings, ibid., p. 379.

73   Ibid., p. 4 *et seq.*

74   It is an unavoidable complication that, however demarcated, sentences in a language have different degrees of theoreticity. For more rather than less theoretical sentences, underdetermination and therefore same-language indeterminacy will be greater than for more rather than less observational sentences. The first entailment speaks to the former more than to the latter, and vice versa for the second entailment. Observational or perceptual statements are what chiefly concern me here, however, and my remarks centre upon them unless qualified.

Bibliography

Alston, W. P. 'Meaning and Use'. *Philosophical Quarterly*, 1963.

Aristotle, *Analytica Posteriora, De Interpretatione, Categories, Metaphysics*. Oxford: Clarendon Press, 1928.

Armstrong, D. M. 'Meaning and Communication'. *Philosophical Review*, 1971.

——. *Universals and Scientific Realism* (2 vols). Cambridge: Cambridge University Press, 1978.

Aune, B. 'Statements and Propositions'. *Nous*, 1967.

——. 'On an Analytic–Synthetic Distinction'. *American Philosophical Quarterly*, 1972.

——. *Metaphysics: The Elements*. Oxford: Basil Blackwell, 1985.

Austin, J. L. *Sense and Sensibilia*. Oxford: Clarendon Press, 1962.

——. 'Performative–Constative' in Caton 1963.

——. 'Truth' in Pitcher 1964.

——. 'The Meaning of a Word' in Feigl et al. 1972.

——. *How To Do Things With Words* (2nd edn). Oxford: Clarendon Press, 1975.

Ayer, A. J. *Language, Truth and Logic* (2nd edn). London: Gollancz, 1946.

——. *Philosophical Essays*. London: Macmillan, 1954.

——. (ed.) *Logical Positivism*. London: Macmillan, 1959.

——. *The Concept of a Person*. London, 1963.

Bach, K. *Thought and Reference*. Oxford: Clarendon Press, 1987.

Beaney, M. *Frege: Making Sense*. London: Duckworth, 1996.

Bertolet, R. 'The Semantic Significance of Donnellan's Distinction'. *Philosophical Studies*, 1980.

Biro, J. and Kotatko, P. *Frege: Sense and Reference*. Dordrecht: Kluwer, 1995.

Black, M. 'The Semantic Definition of Truth'. *Analysis*, 1948.

Blackburn, S. (ed.) *Meaning, Reference, Necessity: New Studies in Semantics*. Cambridge: Cambridge University Press, 1973.

——. 'Truth, Realism and the Regulation of Theory' in French et al. 1980.

———. *Spreading the Word*. Oxford: Clarendon Press, 1984.

Blanshard, B. *The Nature of Thought*. London, 1939.

Bloomfield, L. *Language*. London, 1935.

Boorse, C. 'The Origins of the Indeterminacy Thesis'. *Journal of Philosophy*, 1975.

Bradley, F. H. *Essays on Truth and Reality*. Oxford, 1914.

Bradley, R. and Schwartz, N. *Possible Worlds*. Oxford: Basil Blackwell, 1979.

Bridgman, P. W. *The Logic of Modern Physics*. New York, 1960.

Burge, T. 'Reference and Proper Names' *Journal of Philosophy*, 70, 1973.

———. 'Truth and Singular Terms'. *Nous*, 1974.

———. 'Belief De Re'. *Journal of Philosophy*, 1977.

Butler, R. J. (ed.) *Analytical Philosophy*. Oxford: Basil Blackwell, 1965.

Carnap, R. *Introduction to Semantics and the Formalization of Logic*. Cambridge, Mass.: Harvard University Press, 1942.

———. *The Unity of Science*. London, 1934.

———. *Meaning and Necessity*. Chicago: University of Chicago Press, 1947.

———. *The Logical Structure of the World*. London: Routledge and Kegan Paul, 1967.

Carruthers, P. 'Frege's Regress'. *Proceedings of the Aristotelian Society*, 1981.

Cartwright, R. L. 'Some Remarks on Essentialism'. *Journal of Philosophy*, 1968.

Caton, C. E. (ed.) *Philosophy and Ordinary Language*. Urbana: University of Illinois Press, 1963.

Chisholm, R. (ed.) *Realism and the Background of Phenomenology*. Glencoe, Ill.: Free Press, 1960.

Chomsky, N. *Cartesian Linguistics*. New York: Harper and Row, 1966.

Church, A. 'Propositions'. *Encyclopaedia Britannica*, 14th edition Chicago, 1958.

Churchland P. *Matter and Consciousness* (revised edn). Cambridge, Mass.: Harvard University Press, 1988.

Clark, P. and Hale, B. *Reading Putnam*. Oxford: Basil Blackwell, 1994.

Copi, I. M. and Gould, J. A. *Readings in Logic*. New York, 1964.

Craig, E. J. 'The Problem of Necessary Truth' in Blackburn 1975.

Currie, G. *Frege: An Introduction to his Philosophy*. Brighton: Harvester Press, 1982.

Dancy, J. and Sosa, E. *A Companion to Epistemology*. Oxford: Basil Blackwell, 1992.

Davidson, D. 'On the Very Idea of a Conceptual Scheme'. *Proceedings of the American Philosophical Society*, 1974.

———. *Essays on Actions and Events*. Oxford: Clarendon Press, 1980.

———. *Inquiries into Truth and Interpretation*. Oxford: Clarendon Press, 1984.

———. 'The Myth of the Subjective' in Kraus 1989.

———. 'The Folly of Trying to Define Truth'. *The Journal of Philosophy*, 93, 1996.

—— and Harman, G. (eds) *Semantics of Natural Language*. Dordrecht: D. Reidel, 1972.

—— and Harman, G. (eds) *The Logic of Grammar*. Encino, Calif.: Dickinson, 1975.

—— and Hintikka, J. (eds) *Words and Objections: Essays on the Work of W.V. Quine*. Dordrecht: D. Reidel, 1969.

Davies, M. *Meaning, Quantification, Necessity*. London, 1981.

Davies S. (ed.) *Pragmatics: A Reader*. Oxford: Oxford University Press, 1991.

Descartes, R. *Meditations*.

Devitt, M. *Realism and Truth*. Oxford: Basil Blackwell, 1984.

—— and Sterelney, K. *Language and Reality*. Oxford: Basil Blackwell, 1987.

Dewey, J. *Experience and Nature*. London: Dover, 1958.

Donnellan, K. 'Reference and Definite Descriptions'. *Philosophical Review*, 1966, reprinted in *Schwartz* 1977.

——. 'Proper Names and Identifying Descriptions' in Davidson and Harman 1972.

——. 'Speaking of Nothing'. *Philosophical Review*, 1974.

——. 'Kripke and Shoemaker on Natural Kind Terms' in Ginet and Shoemaker 1983.

Dummett, M. A. E. *Frege: Philosophy of Language*. London: Duckworth, 1973 (2nd edn 1981).

——. 'What is a Theory of Meaning (I)?' in Guttenplan 1975.

——. 'What is a Theory of Meaning (II)?' in Evans and McDowell 1976.

——. *Elements of Intuitionism*. Oxford: Clarendon Press, 1977.

——. *Truth and Other Enigmas*. London: Duckworth, 1978.

——. 'What Does the Appeal to Use Do for the Theory of Meaning?' in Margalit 1979.

——. 'Common Sense and Metaphysics' in Macdonald 1979.

——. *The Interpretation of Frege's Philosophy*. London: Duckworth, 1982.

——. 'Realism'. *Synthese*, 52, 1982.

——. *The Seas of Language*. Oxford: Clarendon Press, 1993.

Edgington, D. 'Meaning, Bivalence and Realism'. *Proceedings of the Aristotelian Society*, 1980.

Enc, B. 'Necessary Properties and Linnaean Essentialism'. *Canadian Journal of Philosophy*, 1975.

Engel, P. *The Norm of Truth*. London: Harvester Press, 1991.

Erwin, E. et al. 'The Historical Theory of Reference'. *Australasian Journal of Philosophy*, 1976.

Ewing A. C. *Idealism: A Critical Survey*. London, 1934.

Evans, G. *The Varieties of Reference*. Oxford: Clarendon Press, 1982.

——. *Collected Papers*. Oxford: Clarendon Press, 1985.

—— and McDowell, J. *Truth and Meaning*. Oxford: Clarendon Press, 1976.

Feigl, H. et al. *Readings in Philosophical Analysis*. New York: Appleton-Century-Crofts, 1949.

———. *New Readings in Philosophical Analysis*. New York: Appleton-Century-Crofts, 1972.

Feyerabend, P. *Against Method*. London, 1975.

Field, H. 'Tarski's Theory of Truth'. *Journal of Philosophy*, 69:13, 1972.

Fodor, J. A. and Lepore, E. *Holism: A Shopper's Guide*. Oxford: Basil Blackwell, 1992.

Forbes, G. *The Metaphysics of Modality*. Oxford, 1985.

Foster, J. A. 'Meaning, Truth, Theory' in Evans and McDowell 1976.

Frege, G. *Translations from the Philosophical Writings of Gottlob Frege*. Black, M. and Geach, P. (eds) Oxford: Basil Blackwell, 1960.

Frege, G. 'The Thought' in Strawson 1967.

———. 'Sense and Reference' in Black and Geach 1960.

French, P. et al. (eds) *Contemporary Perspectives in the Philosophy of Language*. Midwest Studies in Philosophy, Minneapolis: University of Minnesota Press, 1977.

——— (eds) *Studies in Epistemology*. Minneapolis: University of Minnesota Press, 1980.

——— (eds) *Realism and Antirealism*. Midwest Studies in Philosophy XII, Minneapolis: Minnesota University Press, 1988.

——— (eds) *Contemporary Perspectives in the Philosophy of Language II*. Midwest Studies in Philosophy XIV, Minneapolis: University of Minnesota Press, 1989.

Fricker, E. 'Semantic Structure and Speaker's Understanding'. *Proceedings of the Aristotelian Society*, 1982.

Geach, P. *Reference and Generality*. Ithaca: Cornell University Press, 1962.

George, A. (ed.) *Reflections on Chomsky*. Blackwell, 1989.

Ginet, C. and Shoemaker, S. (eds) *Knowledge and Mind: Philosophical Essays*. Oxford: Oxford University Press, 1983.

Grayling, A. C. 'Internal Structure and Essence'. *Analysis*, 1982.

———. *The Refutation of Scepticism*. London: Duckworth, 1985.

———. *Wittgenstein*. Oxford: Oxford University Press, 1988.

———. 'Mind, Meaning and Method' in *Wittgenstein: Centenary Essays*. Cambridge: Cambridge University Press, 1990.

———. *Philosophy: A Guide Through the Subject*. Oxford: Oxford University Press, 1995.

———. 'Perfect Speaker Theory' in Hill and Kotatko, 1995.

———. *Russell*. Oxford: Oxford University Press, 1996.

Grice, H. P. 'Meaning'. *Philosophical Review*, 1957.

———. 'Utterer's Meaning, Sentence Meaning and Word Meaning'. *Foundations of Language*, 1968.

——. *Studies in the Ways of Words*. Cambridge, Mass.: Harvard University Press, 1989.

—— and Strawson, P. F. 'In Defense of a Dogma'. *Philosophical Review*, 1956.

Grover, D. L. 'Propositional Quantifiers'. *Journal of Philosophical Logic*, 1973.

——. et al. 'A Prosentential Theory of Truth'. *Philosophical Studies*, 1973.

——. *A Prosentential Theory of Truth*. Princeton: Princeton University Press 1992.

Gunderson, K. (ed.) *Language, Mind and Knowledge*. Minneapolis: University of Minnesota Press, 1975.

Guttenplan, S. *Mind and Language*. Oxford: Clarendon Press, 1975.

Haack, S. *Philosophy of Logics*. Cambridge 1975.

——. 'Is It True What They Say About Tarski?' *Philosophy*, 1976.

——. 'The Pragmatist Theory of Truth'. *British Journal for the Philosophy of Science*, 1976.

——. 'Lewis's Ontological Slum'. *Review of Metaphysics*, 1977.

Hacking, I. *Why Does Language Matter to Philosophy?* Cambridge, 1975.

Hanfling, O. (ed.) *Essential Readings in Logical Positivism*. Oxford: Basil Blackwell, 1981.

Hare, R. M. *The Language of Morals*. Oxford: Clarendon Press, 1952.

Harman, G. 'Three Levels of Meaning'. *Journal of Philosophy*, 1968.

——. *Thought*. Princeton: Princeton University Press, 1973.

——. 'Moral Relativism Defended'. *Philosophical Review*, 1975.

Harnish, R. M. (ed.) *Basic Topics in the Philosophy of Language*. London: Harvester Press, 1994.

Harrison, B. *Introduction to The Philosophy of Language*. London, 1979.

Hartshorne, C. *Collected Papers*. Cambridge, Mass.: Harvard University Press, 1930–58.

Hempel, G. C. 'On the Logical Positivists' Theory of Truth'. *Analysis*, 1935.

Hill, J. and Kotatko, P. *Karlovy Vary Studies in Reference and Meaning*. Prague: Philosophia Publications, 1995.

Honderich, T. and Burnyeat, M. *Philosophy As It Is*. London: Penguin, 1979.

Hook, S. (ed.) *Language and Philosophy: A Symposium*. New York: New York University Press, 1969.

Horwich, P. 'Three Forms of Realism'. *Synthese*, 1982.

——. *Truth*. Oxford: Basil Blackwell, 1990.

Hughes, G. and Cresswell. M. *An Introduction to Modal Logic*. London 1968.

Hume, D. *A Treatise of Human Nature* (ed. Selby-Bigge). Oxford: Clarendon Press 1978.

——. *An Enquiry Concerning Human Understanding* (ed. Selby-Bigge). Oxford: Clarendon Press, 1975.

James, W. 'The Will to Believe' in *Selected Papers in Philosophy*. London 1917.

——. *Pragmatism*. New York, 1970.

Joachim, H. H. *Logical Studies.* Oxford, 1948.

Johnson, P. 'Origin and Necessity'. *Philosophical Studies,* 1977.

Kant, I. *Critique of Pure Reason* (trans. Norman Kemp Smith). London, 1933.

Katz, J. *The Philosophy of Language.* New York: Harper and Row, 1966.

Kenny, A. *Wittgenstein.* London: Allen Lane, 1973.

——. *Frege.* London: Penguin, 1995.

Kirkham, R. L. *Theories of Truth.* Cambridge, Mass.: MIT Press, 1992.

Kitch, P. 'Apriority and Necessity'. *Australasian Journal of Philosophy,* 1980.

Klemke, E. D. (ed.) *Essays on Frege.* Urbana: University of Illinois Press, 1968.

—— (ed.) *Essays on Russell.* Urbana: University of Illinois Press 1971.

Kornblith, H. 'Referring to Artefacts'. *Philosophical Review,* 1980.

Kraus M. (ed.) *Relativism: Interpretation and Confrontation.* Notre Dame, 1989.

Kripke, S. 'Identity and Necessity' in Munitz 1971 and Schwartz 1977.

——. 'Speaker's Reference and Semantic Reference' in French et al. 1977.

——. *Naming and Necessity.* Oxford: Basil Blackwell, 1980.

——. *Wittgenstein on Rules and Private Language.* Oxford: Basil Blackwell, 1982.

Kroon, F. W. 'The Problem of "Jonah": How *Not* To Argue For the Causal Theory of Reference'. *Philosophical Studies,* 1982.

Kung, G. *Ontology and the Logistik Analysis of Language.* Dordrecht: D. Reidel, 1967.

Lehrer, K. and Lehrer, A. *Theory of Meaning.* Englewood Cliffs: Prentice-Hall, 1970.

Leibniz, G. *The Monadology* (trans. Latta). Oxford: Oxford University Press, 1898.

——. *New Essays Concerning Human Understanding* (trans. Loughley). Chicago: Chicago University Press, 1916.

——. *Philosophical Writings* (ed. Parkinson). London: J. M. Dent, 1973.

Leonardi, P. and Santambrogio, M. (eds) *On Quine.* Cambridge: Cambridge University Press, 1995.

Lepore, E. *Truth and Interpretation.* Oxford: Basil Blackwell, 1986.

Lewis, C. I. and Langford, C. *Symbolic Logic* (2nd edn). New York: Century, 1951.

Lewis, D. *Counterfactuals.* Harvard: Harvard University Press, 1975.

——. 'Languages and Language' in Gunderson 1975.

——. *Philosophical Papers.* Oxford: Clarendon Press, 1983.

——. *On the Plurality of Worlds.* Oxford: Basil Blackwell, 1986.

Lewy, C. *Meaning and Modality.* Cambridge: Cambridge University Press, 1976.

Linsky, L. *Reference and Modality.* Oxford: Oxford University Press, 1971.

Lipton, M. R. 'Review of Orenstein'. *Philosophical Review,* 1980.

Loar, B. 'The Semantics of Singular Terms'. *Philosophical Studies*, 1976.
———. 'Two Theories of Meaning' in Evans and McDowell 1976.
———. 'Ramsay's Theory of Belief and Truth' in Mellor 1980.
———. *Mind and Meaning*. Cambridge: Cambridge University Press, 1981.
Locke, J. *Essay Concerning Human Understanding* (ed. Nidditch). Oxford: Oxford University Press.
Loux, M. J. (ed.) *The Possible and the Actual*. Ithaca: Cornell University Press, 1979.
Lovibond, S. and Williams, S. G. *Identity, Truth and Value: Essays for David Wiggins*. Aristotelian Society Monographs, 1996.
Luntley, M. *Language, Logic and Experience*. London: Duckworth, 1988.
Lycan, W. G. 'The Trouble with Possible Worlds' in Loux 1979.
Macdonald, G. (ed.) *Perception and Identity*. London: Macmillan, 1979.
——— and Wright, C. (eds) *Fact, Science and Morality*. Oxford: Basil Blackwell, 1986.
Mackie, J. L. *Truth, Probability and Paradox*. Oxford: Clarendon Press, 1973.
———. *Ethics*. London, 1977.
Malcolm, N. *Wittgenstein: A Memoir*. Oxford: Oxford University Press, 1958.
Margalit, A. (ed.) *Meaning and Use*. Dordrecht: D. Reidel, 1979.
Martin, R. L. *Recent Essays on Truth and the Liar Paradox*. Oxford: Clarendon Press, 1984.
Mates, B. 'Analytic Sentences'. *Philosophical Review*, 1951.
———. *The Philosophy of Leibniz*. Oxford: Clarendon Press, 1986.
McCulloch, G. *The Game of the Name*. Oxford: Clarendon Press, 1989.
McDowell, J. 'Truth-Conditions, Bivalence, and Verificationism' in Evans and McDowell 1976.
———. 'On the Sense and Reference of a Proper Name'. *Mind*, 1977.
———. 'On The Reality of the Past' in Pettit and Hookway 1978.
———. 'Physicalism and Denotation in Field on Tarski', in Platts 1980.
———. *Mind and World*. Cambridge, Mass.: Harvard University Press, 1996.
McFetridge, I. G. *Logical Necessity*. Aristotelian Society Monographs, 1990.
McGinn, C. 'On the Necessity of Origin'. *Journal of Philosophy*, 1976.
———. 'An A Priori Argument for Realism'. *Journal of Philosophy*, 1979.
———. 'Truth and Use' in Platts 1980.
———. 'Can We Solve the Mind–Body Problem?' *Mind*, 98, 1989; reprinted in *The Problem of Consciousness* (Oxford: Oxford University Press, 1991).
Meinong, A. 'The Theory of Objects' in Chisholm 1960.
Mellor, D. H. 'Natural Kinds'. *British Journal for the Philosophy of Science* 1977.
———. (ed.) *Prospects for Pragmatism*. Cambridge: Cambridge University Press, 1980.
Mill, J. S. *A System of Logic*. London: Longmans, 1979.
Millikan, R. *Language, Thought and Other Biological Categories: New Founda-*

tions for Realism. Cambridge, Mass., 1984.

Mondadori, F. and Morton, A. 'Modal Realism: The Poisoned Pawn' in Loux 1979.

Moore, G. E. 'Professor James' 'Pragmatism'. *Proceedings of the Aristotelian Society*, 1908.

——. 'Is Existence Never a Predicate?' *Proceedings of the Aristotelian Society*, supp. vol., 1936.

——. *Some Main Problems of Philosophy*. London: Allen and Unwin, 1953.

Morris, C. *Signs, Language and Behaviour*. New Jersey, 1946.

Munitz, M. K. (ed.) *Identity and Individuation*. New York: New York University Press, 1971.

——. (ed.) *Existence and Logic*. New York: New York University Press, 1974.

——. (ed.) *Logic and Ontology*. New York: New York University Press, 1975.

Nagel, T. The *View from Nowhere*. Oxford: Oxford University Press, 1986.

Neale, S. *Descriptions*. Cambridge, Mass., 1990.

Nerlich, G. 'Presupposition and Classical Logical Relations'. *Analysis*, 1967.

——. 'Presupposition and Entailment'. *American Philosophical Quarterly*, 1969.

Neurath, O. 'Protocol Sentences' (trans. M. Schlick) in Ayer 1959.

Orenstein, A. 'On Explicating Existence in Terms of Quantification' in Munitz 1975.

——. *Existence and the Particular Quantifier*. Philadelphia, 1978.

Ortony, A. (ed.) *Metaphor and Thought*. Cambridge: Cambridge University Press, 1979.

Osgood, C. *Method and Theory in Experimental Psychology*. New York, 1953.

Passmore, J. *Philosophical Reasoning*. London: Duckworth, 1961.

——. *A Hundred Years of Philosophy*. London: Duckworth, 1966.

——. *Recent Philosophers*. London: Duckworth, 1985.

Peacocke, C. A. B. 'Proper Names, Reference and Rigid Designation' in Blackburn 1973.

—— (ed.) *Understanding and Sense* (2 vols). Brookfield: Dartmouth, 1993.

Pears, D. F. 'Is Existence a Predicate?' in Strawson 1967.

——. *The False Prison* (2 vols). Oxford: Clarendon Press, 1989.

Peirce, C. S. 'How To Make Our Ideas Clear' in Hartshorne 1930–58.

Pettit, P. and Hookway, C. (eds), *Action and Interpretation*. Cambridge, 1978.

—— and McDowell, J. (eds) *Subject, Thought and Context*. Oxford, 1986.

Pitcher, G. (ed.) *Truth*. New Jersey, 1964.

——. (ed.) *Wittgenstein: Critical Essays*. London, 1966.

Plantinga, A. 'World and Essence'. *Philosophical Review*, 1970.

——. *The Nature of Necessity*. Oxford: Clarendon Press, 1971.

——. 'Actualism and Possible Worlds' in Loux 1979.

Plato, *Republic, Phaedrus*. Oxford: Clarendon Press.

Platts, M. *The Ways of Meaning.* London: Routledge and Kegan Paul, 1979.
——. *Reference, Truth and Reality.* London: Routledge and Kegan Paul, 1980.
Popper, K. *Conjectures and Refutations.* London: Routledge and Kegan Paul, 1960.
——. *The Logic of Scientific Discovery* (3rd edn). London: Hutchinson, 1972.
——. *Objective Knowledge.* London, 1973.
Prawitz, D. 'Meaning and Proof'. *Theoria*, 1977.
Prior, A. N. *The Objects of Thought.* Oxford: Clarendon Press, 1971.
Putnam, H. *Mind, Language and Reality.* Cambridge: Cambridge University Press, 1975.
——. 'Meaning and Reference' in Schwartz 1977.
——. *Meaning and the Moral Sciences.* London: Routledge and Kegan Paul, 1978.
——. *Reason, Truth and History.* Cambridge: Cambridge University Press, 1981.
——. *Representation and Reality.* Cambridge, Mass.: MIT Press, 1988.
——. 'Model Theory and the Factuality of Semantics' in George 1989.
——. *Renewing Philosophy.* Cambridge, Mass.: Harvard University Press, 1992.
——. 'Reply to David Anderson'. *Philosophical Topics*, 20, 1992.
——. *Words and Life.* Cambridge, Mass.: Harvard University Press, 1994.
——. 'Simon Blackburn on Internal Realism' in Clark and Hale 1994.
Quine, W. V. O. *From A Logical Point of View.* Cambridge, Mass.: Harvard University Press, 1953.
——. 'Two Dogmas of Empiricism' in 1953.
——. *Word and Object.* Cambridge, Mass.: MIT Press, 1960.
——. *Ontological Relativity and Other Essays.* New York, 1961.
——. *The Ways of Paradox.* New York: Random House, 1966.
——. 'Epistemology Naturalized' in 1969.
——. *Philosophy of Logic.* Englewood Cliffs: Prentice-Hall, 1970.
——. 'Ontology and Ideology' in Feigl et al. 1972.
——. *The Roots of Reference.* La Salle, Illinois: Open Court, 1974.
——. 'Designation and Existence' in Feigl et al. 1979.
——. *Quiddities.* Cambridge, Mass., 1987.
——. *The Pursuit of Truth.* Cambridge, Mass., 1990.
Quinton, A. M. 'The A Priori and the Analytic'. *Proceedings of the Aristotelian Society*, 1964; reprinted in Strawson 1967.
Ramsay, F. P. 'Facts and Propositions'. *Proceedings of the Aristotelian Society*, supp. vol., 1927.
——. *The Foundations of Mathematics.* London: Kegan Paul, Trench, Trubner, 1931.
Rasmussen S. and Ravnkilde J. 'Realism and Logic'. *Synthese*, 52, 1982.
Read, S. *Thinking About Logic.* Oxford: Oxford University Press, 1994.

Rescher, N. (ed.) *The Logic of Decision and Action*. Pittsburgh, 1968.

——. (ed.) *Studies in Logical Theory*. Oxford: Basil Blackwell, 1968.

——. *The Coherence Theory of Truth*. Oxford, 1973.

——. 'The Ontology of the Possible' in Loux 1979.

Richards, T. 'The Worlds of David Lewis'. *Australasian Journal of Philosophy*, 1975.

Rorty, R. *Philosophy and the Mirror of Nature*. Oxford: Basil Blackwell, 1979.

——. 'Putnam on Truth'. *Philosophy and Phenomenological Research*, 52, 1992.

Rosenberg, J. F. and Travis. C. (eds) *Readings in the Philosophy of Language*. Englewood Cliffs: Prentice-Hall, 1971.

Rundle, B. *Wittgenstein and Contemporary Philosophy of Language*. Oxford: Basil Blackwell, 1990.

Russell, B. *The Principles of Mathematics*. London: Allen and Unwin, 1903.

——. 'James' Conception of Truth' in *Philosophical Essays*, London, 1910.

——. *The Problems of Philosophy*. Oxford: Oxford University Press, 1912.

——. *Our Knowledge of the External World*. London: Allen and Unwin, 1914.

——. *Mysticism and Logic*. London: Allen and Unwin, 1917.

——. 'Knowledge by Acquaintance and Knowledge by Description' in 1917.

——. *Introduction to Mathematical Philosophy*. London: Allen and Unwin, 1919.

——. *The Analysis of Mind*. London: Allen and Unwin, 1921.

——. *An Inquiry into Meaning and Truth*. London: Allen and Unwin, 1940.

——. *Logic and Knowledge* (ed. Marsh). London: Allen and Unwin, 1956.

——. 'On Denoting' in 1956.

——. 'The Philosophy of Logical Atomism' in 1956.

——. *My Philosophical Development*. London: Allen and Unwin, 1959.

—— and Whitehead, A. *Principa Mathematica*. Cambridge: Cambridge University Press, 1910–12.

Ryle, G. *Dilemmas*. Cambridge: Cambridge University Press, 1960.

——. 'The Theory of Meaning' in Caton 1963.

——. *On Thinking*. Oxford: Basil Blackwell, 1979.

Sacks, M. *The World We Found*. London: Duckworth, 1989.

Sainsbury, R. M. *Russell*. London, 1979.

——. *Logical Forms*. Oxford: Basil Blackwell, 1991.

——. 'Philosophical Logic' in Grayling 1995.

Scheffler, I. *Science and Subjectivity*. New York, 1967.

Schiffer, S. *Meaning*. Oxford: Oxford University Press, 1972.

Schlick, M. 'Meaning and Verification' in Feigl et al. 1949.

——. 'The Foundations of Knowledge' in Ayer 1959.

Schwartz, S. P. *Naming Necessity and Natural Kinds*. Ithaca: Cornell University Press, 1977.

Searle, J. R. *Speech Acts*. Cambridge: Cambridge University Press, 1969.

———. (ed.) *The Philosophy of Language*. Oxford: Oxford University Press, 1971.

———. 'Metaphor' in Ortony 1979.

Slote, M. *Metaphysics and Essence*. Oxford, 1974.

Sluga, H. *Gottlob Frege*. London: Routledge and Kegan Paul, 1980.

Sommers, F. *The Logic of Natural Language*. Oxford: Clarendon Press, 1982.

Sosa, E. *Causation and Conditionals*. Oxford: Oxford University Press, 1975.

Sperber, D. and Wilson, D. 'Loose Talk'. *Proceedings of the Aristotelian Society*, 86, 1986.

Sprigge, T. L. S. 'Internal and External Properties'. *Mind*, 1962.

———. *The Vindication of Absolute Idealism*. Edinburgh, 1983.

Stalnaker, R. C. 'A Theory of Conditionals' in Rescher 1968.

———. 'Possible Worlds' in Loux 1979.

Stich, S. P. 'What Every Speaker Knows'. *Philosophical Review*, 1971.

———. 'Davidson's Semantic Programme'. *Canadian Journal of Philosophy*, 1978.

Straaten, Z. van (ed.) *Philosophical Subjects*. Oxford: Clarendon Press, 1980.

Strawson, P. F. *Introduction to Logical Theory*. London: Methuen 1952.

———. 'Review of the *Philosophical Investigations*'. *Mind*, 1954, reprinted in Pitcher 1966.

———. *Individuals*. London: Methuen, 1959.

———. 'Truth' in Pitcher 1964.

———. *The Bounds of Sense*. London: Methuen, 1966.

———. (ed.) *Philosophical Logic*. Oxford: Oxford University Press, 1967.

———. *Logico-Linguistic Papers*. London: Methuen, 1971.

———. 'On Referring' in 1971.

———. 'Intention and Convention in Speech Acts' in 1971.

———. 'Meaning and Truth' in 1971.

———. 'A Reply to Mr Sellars' in Feigl et al. 1972.

———. *Freedom and Resentment*. London: Methuen, 1974.

———. 'Scruton and Wright on Anti-Realism'. *Proceedings of the Aristotelian Society*, 1976.

Swinburne, R. G. 'Analyticity, Necessity and Apriority'. *Mind*, 1975.

Tarski, A. 'The Semantic Conception of Truth' in Feigl et al. 1949.

———. *Logic, Semantics, Metamathematics*. Oxford: Clarendon Press, 1956.

———. 'The Concept of Truth in a Formalised Language' in 1956.

Taylor, B. 'On the Need for a Meaning Theory in a Theory of Meaning'. *Mind*, 1982.

———. *Michael Dummett*. Dordrecht: M. Nijhoff, 1987.

Tennant, N. *Anti-Realism and Logic*. Oxford: Clarendon Press, 1987.

Thomson, J. 'Is Existence a Predicate?' in Strawson 1967.

———. 'Truth-Bearers and the Trouble About Propositions'. *Journal of Philosophy*, 1969.

Unger, P. 'The Causal Theory of Reference'. *Philosophical Studies*, 1983.

Waismann, F. 'Verifiability'. *Proceedings of the Aristotelian Society*, 1945.

Walker, R. C. S., *The Coherence Theory of Truth: Realism, Anti-Realism, Idealism*. London, 1989.

Wallace, J. 'On the Frame of Reference'. *Synthese*, 22, 1970.

——. 'Positive, Comparative, Superlative'. *Journal of Philosophy*, 69, 1972.

Warnock G. 'A Problem about Truth' in Pitcher 1964.

——. (ed.) *The Philosophy of Perception*. Oxford: Oxford University Press, 1967.

Wettstein, H. 'Demonstrative Reference and Definite Descriptions'. *Philosophical Studies*, 1981.

White, A. R. *Truth*. London, 1970.

Wiggins, D. *Sameness and Substance*. Oxford, 1980.

Wilkes, K. *Physicalism*. London, 1978.

Williams, C. J. F. *What Is Truth?* Cambridge: Cambridge University Press, 1976.

Williams, M. J. 'Do We (Epistemologists) Need a Theory of Truth?' *Philosophical Topics*, 1986.

Winch, P. *The Idea of a Social Science*. London: Routledge and Kegan Paul, 1958.

Wittgenstein, L. *Philosophical Investigations*. Oxford: Basil Blackwell, 1953.

——. *Remarks on the Foundations of Mathematics*. Oxford: Basil Blackwell, 1956.

——. *Tractatus Logico-Philosophicus*. London: Routledge and Kegan Paul, 1961.

——. *Blue and Brown Books*. Oxford: Basil Blackwell, 1964.

——. *On Certainty*. Oxford: Basil Blackwell, 1969.

Wolfram, S. *Philosophical Logic: An Introduction*. London: Routledge and Kegan Paul, 1989.

Woodfield, A. (ed.) *Thought and Object*. Oxford: Clarendon Press, 1982.

Wright, C. 'Strawson on Anti-realism'. *Synthese*, 1978.

——. *Wittgenstein on the Foundations of Mathematics*. London: Duckworth, 1980.

——. 'Realism, Truth-Value Links, Other Minds and the Past'. *Ratio*, 22, 1980.

——. (ed.) *Frege: Tradition and Influence*. Oxford: Basil Blackwell, 1984.

——. *Realism, Meaning and Truth*. Oxford: Basil Blackwell, 1987.

——. 'On Putnam's Proof That We Are Not Brains in a Vat' in Clark and Hale 1994.

Zemach, E. 'Putnam's Theory of the Reference of Substance Terms'. *Journal of Philosophy*, 1976.

Ziff, P. 'On H. P. Grice's Account of Meaning'. *Analysis*, 1967.

Index

irenically p 45
otiosity p 47